This book offers insights into the complex and various ways in which international frontiers influence cultural identities. The ten anthropological case studies collected here describe specific international borders in Europe, Asia, Africa, the Middle East and North America, and bring out the importance of border politics and the diverse forms that it may take. The border itself may be of great symbolic significance, like the Berlin Wall; in other cases the symbolism lies rather in the disappearance of the traditional border, as in the European Union today. A border may be a barrier against immigration or the front line between hostile armies. It may reinforce distinctive identities on each side of it, or it may be disputed because it cuts across national identities. Drawing on anthropological perspectives, the book explores how cultural landscapes intersect with political boundaries, and discusses ways in which state power informs cultural identity.

Border identities

Border identities

Nation and state at international frontiers

Edited by

Thomas M. Wilson and Hastings Donnan
The Queen's University of Belfast

CAMBRIDGE
UNIVERSITY PRESS

PUBLISHED BY THE PRESS SYNDICATE OF THE UNIVERSITY OF CAMBRIDGE
The Pitt Building, Trumpington Street, Cambridge CB2 1RP, United Kingdom

CAMBRIDGE UNIVERSITY PRESS
The Edinburgh Building, Cambridge CB2 2RU, United Kingdom
40 West 20th Street, New York, NY 10011–4211, USA
10 Stamford Road, Oakleigh, Melbourne 3166, Australia

First published 1998

Printed in the United Kingdom at the University Press, Cambridge

Typeset in Plantin 10/12 pt. [CE]

A catalogue record for this book is available from the British Library

Library of Congress cataloguing in publication data
Border identities: nation and state at international frontiers / edited by Thomas
M. Wilson and Hastings Donnan.
    p.   cm.
ISBN 0 521 58315 2 (hc: alk. paper). – ISBN 0 521 58745 X (pbk.: alk. paper)
1. Boundaries – Case studies.
2. Ethnicity – Case studies.
3. Nationalism – Case studies.
I. Wilson, Thomas M.   II. Donnan, Hastings.
JC323.B645   1998
306.2–dc 21   97–13181   CIP

ISBN 0 521 58315 2 hardback
ISBN 0 521 58745 X paperback

Contents

Maps

Contributors

ILDIKÓ BELLÉR-HANN currently teaches social anthropology at the University of Kent, Canterbury. She has written several articles on marketing, smuggling and prostitution in north-eastern Turkey.

JOHN BORNEMAN is the author of *After the Wall: East meets West in the new Berlin* and of *Belonging in the two Berlins: kin, state, nation.* He is Associate Professor of Anthropology at Cornell University.

JANET CARSTEN is Senior Lecturer in Social Anthropology at the University of Edinburgh. She co-edited *About the house: Levi-Strauss and beyond* with Stephen Hugh-Jones and is the author of a monograph on Langkawi which is currently in press.

ANGELA CHEATER is the author of *Idioms of accumulation, The politics of factory organisation: a case study from independent Zimbabwe,* and *Social anthropology: an alternative introduction.* She is Professor of Anthropology at the University of Waikato in New Zealand.

HASTINGS DONNAN is Professor of Social Anthropology at The Queen's University of Belfast. He is the author of *Marriage among Muslims* and co-editor of a number of books including, most recently, *Irish urban cultures* and *Islam, globalization and postmodernity.* He was the editor of *Man: The Journal of the Royal Anthropological Institute* from 1993 to 1995.

WILLIAM A. DOUGLASS has written several books based on his research in Spain and Italy including *Death in Murelaga: funerary rites in a Spanish Basque village, Echalar and Murelaga: opportunity and rural depopulation in two Spanish Basque villages,* and *Emigration in a south Italian town: an anthropological history.* His most recent book (with Joseba Zulaika) is *Terror and taboo: the follies, faces, and fables of terrorism.* He is Professor of Anthropology and Director of the Basque Studies Program at the University of Nevada, Reno.

HENK DRIESSEN is Associate Professor in the Institute of Social and Cultural Anthropology at the Catholic University of Nijmegen. He is the author of *On the Spanish–Moroccan frontier: a study in ritual, power, and ethnicity* and editor of *The politics of ethnographic reading and writing.*

CHRIS HANN is Professor of Anthropology at the University of Kent, Canterbury. He has carried out research in Hungary, Turkey, Poland and China and is the author of *Tázlár: a village in Hungary* and editor of *Socialism: ideals, ideologies and local practice* and of *When history accelerates: essays on rapid social change, complexity and creativity.*

MICHAEL KEARNEY is Professor of Anthropology at the University of California, Riverside. His most recent book is entitled *Reconceptualizing the peasantry.*

DAN RABINOWITZ teaches anthropology at the Hebrew University of Jerusalem. He is the author of many articles and chapters, and of *Overlooking Nazareth: the ethnography of exclusion in Galilee.*

PETER SAHLINS is Associate Professor in the Department of History, University of California at Berkeley. He has written extensively on the Spanish–French border and is the author of *Boundaries: the making of France and Spain in the Pyrenees.*

MARTIN STOKES is the author of *The Arabesk debate: music and musicians in modern Turkey* and editor of *Ethnicity, identity and music: the musical construction of place.* He was until recently Lecturer in Social Anthropology and Ethnomusicology at The Queen's University of Belfast and is now Associate Professor in the Department of Music at the University of Chicago.

THOMAS M. WILSON is Lecturer in European Studies, The Queen's University of Belfast and is co-editor of *Cultural change and the new Europe* and of *Ireland from below,* as well as of several other books on Ireland and Europe. He is the editor of the series on national identities for State University of New York Press.

Acknowledgements

The editors wish to express their thanks to the publishers concerned for permission to reproduce here in modified form material which first appeared as follows: to the University of Chicago Press for permission to reprint an article by Peter Sahlins originally published in the *Journal of Modern History* 60: 234–63, 1988 (© 1988, The University of Chicago); to the University of California Press for permission to use maps 1 and 2 from Peter Sahlins, *Boundaries: the making of France and Spain in the Pyrenees* (1989); and to Blackwell Publishers Limited for permission to reprint an article by Michael Kearney which first appeared as 'Borders and boundaries of state and self at the end of Empire' in the *Journal of Historical Sociology* 4: 52–74, 1991. They are also grateful to Barbara Watson Andaya and Leonard Y. Andaya for permission to reproduce the map of Peninsular Malaysia from their book *A history of Malaysia* (Basingstoke: Macmillan 1982). The index was prepared by Michael Donnelly of University College Galway.

1　Nation, state and identity at international borders

Thomas M. Wilson and Hastings Donnan

According to some scholars, we are living in a world where state borders are increasingly obsolete. This view holds that international borders are becoming so porous that they no longer fulfil their historical role as barriers to the movement of goods, ideas and people, and as markers of the extent and power of the state. This withering away of the strength and importance of international borders is linked to the predicted demise of the nation-state as the pre-eminent political structure of modernity. The threatened passing of the state, in turn, heralds the weakening of most of the world's existing political, social and cultural structures and associations. As a result, the role of individuals in these structures is called into question, especially in terms of their loyalties and identities. In line with this fall-off in the determinative power of traditional political statuses is the rise of the new politics of identity, in which the definitions of citizenship, nation and state vie with identities which have acquired a new political significance, such as gender, sexuality, ethnicity and race, among others, for control of the popular and scholarly political imaginations of the contemporary world. Moreover, these processes are supposedly accelerating, continually shifting the ground upon which nation-states once stood, changing the framework of national and international politics, creating new and important categories of transnationalism, and increasing the significance and proliferation of images and a host of other messages about the relevance of 'other' world cultures in the everyday lives of us all.

It is the goal of this book to return to the seemingly self-evident proposition that the deterritorialised nature of post-modernity is only one interpretative slant on politics and power in the contemporary world. On its own, the study of the new politics of space and place, identity and transnationalism is incomplete. The balance must be supplied by a reconfiguring of the perspectives of modernists and traditionalists, many of whom are historians and political scientists, whose work continues to point out the necessity of complementing the seductive discourse of the new politics of person and identity with a renewed commitment to the recognisable and concrete manifestations of government and politics, at local levels and at the level of the state. We hold that definitions of 'political' which privilege notions of self, gender, sexuality, ethnicity, profession, occupation, class and nation within discussions of sign, symbol, contestation and representation risk underestimating the role the state continues to play in the everyday lives of its own and other citizens. Post-modern political analyses often fail to query the degree to which the state sustains its historically dominant role as an arbiter of control, violence, order and organisation for those whose identities are being transformed by world forces.

While the organs and personnel of the nation and the state have been excluded from, or minimised in, much recent political anthropology, the nation-state has been rather more successful in weathering the storms of post-socialism, post-colonialism and globalisation than some anthropologists have credited. Paradoxically, the world of expanding deterritorialised identity politics is a world of many more and, in some cases, stronger states. Lost in the crush of much contemporary social science is one simple fact – the new politics of identity is in large part determined by the old structure of the state. In fact, the new politics of representation, redefinition and resistance would be nowhere without the state as its principal contextual opponent. It is then, in our view, not a question in anthropology of positioning symbolic politics, or the politics of culture, against 'real' politics, but one of returning to the proposition that all politics is by definition about the use of authority and power to direct the behaviour of others, thereby achieving an individual or group's public goals. Both perspectives are necessary for political anthropology precisely because the physical structures of territory, government and state have not withered away in the face of the perception that people are now more free or more forced to slip the constraints of territorially based politics.

This book constitutes a tentative step in furthering the development of an anthropology of international borders, one which specifically concerns itself with the confluence of symbolic and politico-jural boundaries between nations and states. It is an explicit attempt to integrate seemingly divergent trends in the study of power and culture, trends which cursory examination might place at loggerheads. We suggest that their integration in an anthropology of borders resides in the focus on the place and space of visible and literal borders between states, and the symbolic boundaries of identity and culture which make nations and states two very different entities.

The study of the politics of identity which uses the metaphors of borders and borderlands to clarify the deterritorialised aspects of post-modern life is not our concern here, until and unless these identities are linked in concrete ways to the experiences of living at or crossing state borderlines, and of managing the myriad structures of the state which establish microborders throughout the state's domain, such as in airports, floating customs and immigration checks, post and passport offices, armed service installations, and internal revenue institutions.[1] While the use of 'borderland' as an image for the study of connections between cultures wherever these connections are found has opened up new ground in social and cultural theory (see, for example, Rosaldo 1988, Gupta and Ferguson 1992, and Alvarez and Collier 1994), it has often done so at the expense of underplaying changes in political economy. To address questions of how dual but unequal state power operates at borders, and of how cultural relations develop historically in frontier zones, we must return to a localised, particularistic and territorially focused notion of borders (cf. Heyman 1994: 46). As one of our contributors has written elsewhere:

local experience of the state and resistance to it cannot be limited to the imaginative experience of representations: attention must also be paid to the very concrete material consequences of the actions of states for local populations. (Hann 1995: 136)

This volume offers a number of perspectives on borders, nations and states as a way of demonstrating the possibilities inherent in an integration of a variety of anthropological approaches to power and culture.

The anthropology of borders

The growing interest of social scientists in the structure and function of international borders, and in the lives of border peoples and communities, has increasingly demonstrated the dialectical relationships between borders and their states – relationships in which border regions often have a critical impact on the formation of nations and states. These relationships are like many between the state and its regions, and they remain one of the most important and least understood in the general scholarship of nations and states, which too often takes a top-down view in which all power flows from the 'centre'. Perhaps more so than colleagues in other disciplines, anthropologists are well placed to view borders from both local and national perspectives, from the distance of capital cities to the villages of border areas (or, indeed, in those metropolitan centres – such as Jerusalem and Nicosia – which are themselves divided by international borders).

An anthropology of borders is distinctive in a number of ways

(Donnan and Wilson 1994). Anthropological theories and methods enable ethnographers to focus on local communities at international borders in order to examine the material and symbolic processes of culture. This focus on everyday life, and on the cultural constructions which give meaning to the boundaries between communities and between nations, is often absent in the wider perspectives of the other social sciences. The anthropology of borders is one perspective in political anthropology which reminds social scientists outside the discipline, and some within it, that nations and states, and their institutions, are composed of people who cannot or should not be reduced to the images which are constructed by the state, the media or of any other groups who wish to represent them. The anthropological study of the everyday lives of border communities is simultaneously the study of the daily life of the state, whose agents there must take an active role in the implementation of policy and the intrusion of the state's structures into its people's lives. When ethnographers study border peoples, they do so with the intention of narrating the experiences of people who often are comfortable with the notion that they are tied culturally to many other people in neighbouring states. An anthropology of borders simultaneously explores the cultural permeability of borders, the adaptability of border peoples in their attempts ideologically to construct political divides, and the rigidity of some states in their efforts to control the cultural fields which transcend their borders. Anthropologists thus study the social and economic forces which demand that a variety of political and cultural boundaries be constructed and crossed in the everyday lives of border people.

   The anthropology of borders has a long but not very deep history, which began in many ways with Barth's (1969) paradigmatic ideas on ethnic boundaries, but which owes just as much to work that, although not specifically focused on culture, nation and state at international borders, nevertheless showed the value of localised studies for the understanding of how cultural landscapes are superimposed across social and political divides (see, for example, Cohen 1965 and Frankenberg 1989 [1957]). Historical and ethnological studies (as collected, for example, in Bohannan and Plog 1967) also helped to develop this interest, though it was only in the 1970s as anthropologists began to address issues of nationalism, political economy, class, migration and the political disintegration of nations and states that a distinctive body of anthropological work on international borders emerged.

   Following the ground-breaking research in the Italian Tyrol by Cole and Wolf (1974) on the durability of cultural frontiers long after the

political borders of state and empire had shifted, anthropologists began
to use their field research at international or interstate borders as a
means of widening perspectives in political anthropology to encompass
the formal and informal ties between local communities and the larger
polities of which they are a part (in ways so clearly solicited by many of
the most influential anthropologists of their time, such as Wolf (1966)
and Boissevain (1975)). They have accomplished this in a variety of
ways: some have looked at how international borders have influenced
local culture (Douglass 1977, Heyman 1991, Kavanagh 1994) or have
created the conditions which have shaped new rural and urban communities (Alvarez 1991, Price 1973 and 1974); others have examined
nation- and state-building (Aronoff 1974, Kopytoff 1987, Pettigrew
1994); and yet others have focused on people who choose or are forced
to move across borders (Alvarez 1994, Alvarez and Collier 1994, Hann
and Hann 1992, Hansen 1994, Malkki 1992). Recent studies have
concentrated on the symbols and meanings which encode border life
(see, for example, Lask 1994, Lavie 1990, Shanks 1994, Stokes 1994).
Regardless of theoretical orientation or locale, however, most of these
studies have focused on how social relations, defined in part by the
state, transcend the physical limits of the state and, in so doing,
transform the structure of the state at home and its relations with its
neighbours.

Anthropological attention to the ways in which local developments
have an impact on national centres of power and hegemony has been
influenced in part by historical analyses of localities and the construction of national identities (see, for example, Sahlins 1989). These
analyses are indicative of the need to view the anthropology of borders
as historical anthropology. Borders are spatial and temporal records of
relationships between local communities and between states. Ethnographic explorations of the relationship between symbolic and political
or juridical boundaries are salient beyond anthropology because of what
they may tell us of the history of cultural practices as well as the role of
border cultures and communities in policy-making and diplomacy. For
example, Driessen's study (1992) of the Spanish enclave in Morocco, at
the interface of two states and two continents, provides a history of the
creation and maintenance of a variety of identities in an urban border
zone, but also suggests how local forces have influenced the Spanish
state. Borneman's analysis (1991, 1992a) of kin and state in Berlin
before and after the dramatic changes of a few years ago problematises
the divergent 'national' traditions of law and social policy in East and
West Germany in terms of generational adaptations to the new, 'unified'

state. These books are perhaps the best recent examples of the growing importance of a border perspective in political anthropology, in which the dialectical relations between border areas and their nations and states take precedence over local culture viewed with the state as a backdrop.

All these studies are valuable components of an anthropology of international borders, even though some seem to minimise the roles of the state and the nation, and even the border, in their efforts to delimit their 'community' study. Early ethnographic research at the United States–Mexico border – the one border to have generated a systematic and sustained body of work – was subject to the same limitations, and while many of the studies carried out there in the 1950s and 1960s used the border to frame their focus, the border itself was rarely a variable in the analysis. Only more recently have the wider political and economic contexts of international borders featured in analyses of the United States–Mexico border, where the issues of underdevelopment, trans-nationalism and the globalisation of power and capital, among other aspects of culture, increasingly occupy the growing number of histori-cally informed and wide-ranging ethnographic accounts (see Alvarez 1995). Much of this research focuses on the implications of the economic asymmetry between the United States and Mexico in which wage differentials both draw labour migrants northwards and ensure the profitability of locating unskilled occupations on the Mexican side. Migration across and increasing urbanisation along this border have both been major topics of study, particularly within applied anthro-pology, and have generated research on a broad range of related issues such as local labour markets, health, pollution and the environment (Alvarez 1995: 454–6, Herzog 1990: 9–12). Nevertheless, discussion of the region frequently lapses into straightforward description of the area and how it might develop, with researchers being 'constantly pulled toward the specific, the unique (sometimes the folkloric), and the problematic' (Fagen 1984: 271), thereby eschewing comparison for a focus on more local and immediate concerns (Alvarez 1995: 463). Recent efforts to move beyond this to something more general, by elaborating classificatory schema for different types of border (Martinez 1994: 5–10) or by suggesting that border areas be seen as a particular kind of local, politically organised ecology (Heyman 1994: 51–9), have largely not been taken up. Only the idea of the border as an image for cultural juxtaposition has entered wider anthropological discourse, and this, as we noted above, underplays the material consequences of state action on local populations.

Nations, states and their borders

Despite the large and growing literature on the anthropology of borders, there has been little comparative research and little in the way of anthropological theories of border regions. This parallels the situation in other social sciences, as summarised by Prescott (1987: 8):

> Attempts to produce a set of reliable theories about international boundaries have failed. Attempts to devise a set of procedures by which boundaries can be studied have been successful.

This is due in part to a misconception about what it is that might be theorised. The theoretical importance of an anthropology of borders lies primarily in what it might reveal about the interplay between nation and state, and about the role of the border in the past, present and future of nation and state. As such, an anthropology of borders sits squarely within the wider anthropology of nationalism (for a review of the relationship between the concepts of nation and state, in anthropology and in other disciplines, see Grillo 1980). It is our view that the more anthropologists objectify border cultures and communities in ethnographic study, the less able they will be to trace the relationships among culture, power and the state, thereby missing a valuable opportunity to contribute to the wider social science of nationalism.

Given the long tradition of anthropological analysis of the evolution of the state, in archaeology as well as in social and cultural anthropology, it is surprising how few anthropological studies of borders focus principally on the modern nation-state and nationalism. Here anthropologists' reticence to problematise 'nation' and 'state' as the terms of reference for local studies of society and culture plays a part (cf. Alonso 1994). 'Nation' and 'state' are concepts which do not readily fit classic anthropological notions about cultures, because all three concepts are seen by many people to share the same properties of integrity, unity, linearity of time and space, and discreteness. Nevertheless, anthropologists have made many important and lasting contributions to the comparative study of culture and power among nations and states. Among the most influential have been studies of the origins of nationalism (Gellner 1983); nationalist ideologies (Verdery 1991; Fox 1990); nation- and state-building (Wolf 1959; Löfgren 1995); states and empires (Mintz 1972; Wolf 1982); and post-colonial states (Geertz 1973). Over the last generation political anthropology has increasingly turned to the analysis of the roles of state institutions at local levels, the impact of policies on localities, and the symbolic constructions of ethnicity and nation which are often treated as aspects of 'identity'. But difficulties in problematising nation and state remain for many anthropologists. As Handler points out with reference to Québécois identity, the nation may be perceived as bounded, continuous and homogeneous, but the current content of national identity is continuously contested and negotiated (1988: 32; see also Handler 1994). In this view, a 'culture' is simultaneously objectified, an entity associated with a place and owned by a people, and subjectified, a context for relations which seek the realisation of the idealised goals intrinsic to the objectified culture.

We recognise that the state is also simultaneously a form of objectified and subjectified culture. While the subjective and constructed notions of culture have become for many anthropologists the principal means of understanding national identities, we must not forget that the institutions and the agents of the state, as well as the representatives of national and international capital, see themselves as objective entities with concrete, bounded and unilinear goals. Simply put, the state is an object whose reality will be denied if we focus exclusively on deconstructed representations of it, and nowhere is this more apparent than at borders, where the powers of the state are monumentally inscribed. Nations and their individuated members may be in a perpetual condition of becoming, but this is only partially true of the state. The state exists. Its institutions and representatives make and enforce the laws which regiment most daily activities of its citizens and residents, in direct relations of cause and effect. Border peoples, because of their histories, and objectified and subjectified cultures, not only have to deal with the institutions of their own state, but with those institutions of the state or states across the border, entities of equal and sovereign power which overshadow all border relations. An anthropology of borders is simultaneously one of a nation's history and of a state's frontiers.

In our assessment of the theoretical and disciplinary implications of an anthropology of international borders in the contemporary world, it may be worth recalling how such borders differ from those in stateless societies. Considering Turner's frontier thesis in relation to Africa, Kopytoff (1987) suggests that the term 'border' must include the notion of shifting margins if it is to accommodate the particularities of a situation where it is people and not land that are seen as relatively scarce. Much like the traditional Southeast Asian state (see Carsten, this volume), social formations and their frontiers in West Africa arguably developed in response to a need to bring ever greater numbers of people within their domain. Governance of people rather than place thus characterised large parts of pre-colonial Africa. But as the government of people gave way to the government of territory, so the need for clearly bounded divisions of ownership and control correspondingly increased, and land came to be seen as something potentially valuable and of limited availability. These new borders still operated as part of 'a relation between people and space, but where the space is finite, and the centre can control a more or less continuous boundary, such relationships change, and the border becomes a state weapon' (Tonkin 1994: 27). Territoriality thus became one of the first conditions of the state's existence, and the *sine qua non* of its borders.

It may also be worth recalling, then, just what these state borders are supposed to be and what they are supposed to do. States establish borders to secure territories which are valuable to them because of their human or natural resources, or because these places have strategic or symbolic importance to the state. These borders are signs of the eminent domain of that state, and are markers of the secure relations it has with its neighbours, or are reminders of the hostility that exists between states. Borders are the political membranes through which people, goods, wealth and information must pass in order to be deemed acceptable or unacceptable by the state. Thus borders are agents of a state's security and sovereignty, and a physical record of a state's past and present relations with its neighbours. In our view, borders have three elements: the legal borderline which simultaneously separates and joins states; the physical structures of the state which exist to demarcate and protect the borderline, composed of people and institutions which often penetrate deeply into the territory of the state; and frontiers, territorial zones of varying width which stretch across and away from borders, within which people negotiate a variety of behaviours and meanings associated with their membership in nations and states (cf. Martinez 1994: 5; Prescott 1987; Herzog 1990: 16). Historically frontier areas have been associated with a variety of political forms, such as city-states, kingdoms and empires. These frontiers, which are territorial in nature, are political and social features of the borders of all modern nation-states, and should be distinguished from the metaphorical frontiers of identity which have become so useful in describing aspects of post-modern society.

Territory is only one of the necessary conditions of the nation-state. Since the birth of the modern age states have either attempted to forge a homogeneous nation from the disparate cultural and regional groupings within its domain, or ethnic groups have sought political autonomy in order to establish themselves as independent actors on the world stage. These processes of nation-building and state-building are twin tracks in the creation of the nation-state, on the model of the original French, American and British versions. But all nation-states sit uneasily on the bases of nationalist activity, principally because there is no precise fit between nation and state. As one consequence, a state's borders never function precisely according to the model outlined above: if the 'principal fiction of the nation-state is ethnic, racial, linguistic and cultural homogeneity, then borders always give the lie to this construct' (Horsman and Marshall 1995: 45).

We suggest that the relationships of power and identity at borders and between the borders and their respective states are problematic precisely because the state cannot always control the political structures which it establishes at its extremities (and which one day may topple the state or empire which has given rise to them, as Ibn Khaldun, Wittfogel and Lattimore, among others, have shown). Local forces of politics and culture, possibly influenced by international forces from other states, give borders specific political configurations which may make their relations with their governments extremely problematic. States, on the other hand, may seek to leave only a nominal presence at borders, and may wish their borderlines to be relatively porous, as with the internal borders of the members of the European Union. Both processes are evident in the contributions which follow.

Borders and their states are separate but related political structures, each somewhat dependent on the other for their power and strength. In this regard we follow the Weberian definition of the state as an institution which holds the legitimate use of force in a territory. Borders are always domains of contested power, in which local, national and international groups negotiate relations of subordination and control. Although an international border is a structure of the state, this does not mean that states can guarantee their borders' security from foreign influence. In many cases the central state is unable to control its border regions, as Serbia and Russia have recently discovered in Bosnia and Chechnya. Other states must devolve power to their border areas or run the risk of destabilising the state itself. This is the dilemma before the United Kingdom regarding Northern Ireland and Scotland, a situation averted in Spain by the devolution of power to the provinces.

States need to control their borders because they are their first lines of defence, institutions of social coercion, and symbols of a variety of state powers. But the people of a border's frontiers are often members of political institutions and informal networks which compete with the state. Many of the activities in which they engage may not seem, at first glance, to be political, or a threat to the state. However, many of them, such as smuggling, are certainly illegal, and may concern the state very much. Our point here is that many states with strong structures of control at their borders are also faced with cultural frontiers which are just as strong, and which may one day pose a threat to the state's power at its borders or at its core. For example, the British state is one of the most centralised in Europe, and it has attempted to create strong structures of social and political control at its land border with Ireland, but a long history of shared culture and power in Ireland has created fluid frontier relations of smuggling and ethnonationalist struggle which compete with the state. Events in Ireland are far removed from the everyday experiences of London, except when Irish republicans use the bomb to remind the English of their existence, and they may never destroy the United Kingdom, but it seems likely that they will result in a reconfiguration of the British state and its relationship with its borders in Ireland.

Frontiers of culture are regimes which may compete with the state's borders. They may subvert or bolster those borders, depending on the relative strength of the state and the cultural ties which bind and divide peoples at international borders. We are reminded of Braudel's insistence that civilisations are inescapably linked to their territories because of their civilisation's cultural imprint; men may betray their civilisations by physically leaving them, but their cultures would live on, resistant to the influences of incomers. 'That is why there are cultural frontiers and cultural zones of amazing permanence: all the cross-fertilisation in the world will not alter them' (Braudel 1976: 770). We recognise that this is true of both nation-states and the frontiers which we have defined as zones of cultural relations. But we also recognise that cross-fertilisation in the borders of the world has resulted in strong relationships of culture and territory which often fly in the face of the received wisdom of hegemonic national cultures. Anthropology reminds scholars of the state that these cultural frontiers are as old, as important, and as strong as any state, and that to walk away from international borders with the notion that they are just extensions of the state is to betray the many cultures and nations rooted in those borders. Mindful of Prescott's comment cited above, we suggest that anthropological practices should be directed towards international borders in order to generalise and theorise the issues of culture and the state. Among the principal focuses of such an anthropology are national, ethnic and gender identities.

Border identities

When organising this book, we invited contributors to consider how and why and whether the border is or was significant in the lives of those with whom they had carried out their research, and to document this as far as possible with specific ethnographic examples drawn from Turkey, Spain, France, Germany, Israel, Zimbabwe, Malaysia, the United States and Mexico.[2] Our aim was not to be geographically comprehensive, nor was it to provide a compendium of the globe's border hot-spots of which, of course, there are currently many. Rather, we sought out anthropologists with a long and close experience of particular borders, whose work addressed the kinds of issues outlined above. This often meant omitting consideration of borders only now coming into being, and for which, unfortunately, detailed ethnographic research does not yet exist as far as we are aware. But we hope that what this may sacrifice in breadth of coverage is outweighed by the depth and intimacy of the chapters that follow, a level of understanding we have sought to further by including more than one chapter on both the Spanish–French and Turkish borders.

Nevertheless, we have been able to include consideration of a range of borders: those of long historical standing as well as those newly created or dissolved; those which seem to be stable as well as those which are not; those characterised by conflict and those which are not; and those associated with strong and weak states. We have also included discussion of borders both within and beyond Europe, from traditions in which borders are very differently conceptualised. In this respect, Carsten's discussion of the Malaysian *negeri* and its borders (chapter 9) serves as an important reminder that we should not be too quick to export European experiences of the border to other regions of the globe, such as Southeast Asia, where indigenous understandings and meanings may be quite different.

Taken together, the book's contributors not surprisingly reveal borders as complex and multi-dimensional cultural phenomena, variously articulated and interpreted across space and time. This suggests that *a priori* assumptions about the nature of 'the border' are likely to founder when confronted with empirical data; far from being a self-evident, analytical given which can be applied regardless of context, the 'border' must be interrogated for its subtle and sometimes not so subtle shifts in meaning and form according to setting. Our contributors use a range of analytical strategies to explore such variation. At the same time, they share a focus on a number of common themes and identify certain similarities in the processes through which borders can emerge and to which they give rise. We consider these in relation to three key concerns which occupy the chapters that follow.

Borders and ethnicity

Almost all our contributors focus on identity, particularly on how social identities are shaped by the state and may emerge as a result of, or in response to, the state's attempts to define or redefine its outer limits. Because of their liminal and frequently contested nature, borders tend to be characterised by identities which are shifting and multiple, in ways which are framed by the specific state configurations which encompass them and within which people must attribute meaning to their experience of border life. As many of the chapters show, this is true not only of national identity, but also of other identities such as ethnicity, class, gender and sexuality, identities often constructed at borders in ways which are different from, and shed light on, how these identities are constructed elsewhere in the state.

The anthropological concern with ethnic groups and their boundaries which has motivated much of the political anthropology of ethnicity in the modern world has sometimes obscured the interplay of national and ethnic identity. At the very least, a focus on borders does not allow us to forget that national identity is a politicised ethnicity. In our view many national identities come about when ethnicity is politicised in the course of pursuing self-determination. Sometimes this process of national self-determination excludes those who do not share the dominant nation's view of state-building. These minority populations are often labelled as ethnic or religious groups, whereas they might see themselves as nations, or as part of nations who have their homeland there or elsewhere.

One of the most obvious, and perhaps most problematic, situations in which people's national identity must be negotiated is where a border is drawn with little reference to the ties of blood and/or culture which in some cases bind those across its reaches. Several of the borders described in this book are of this type: those between East and West Germany, those between Turkey and Syria and Turkey and Georgia, between Israel and its Arab neighbours, and between Spain and France in the Pyrenees. As Borneman, Stokes, Hann and Bellér-Hann, Rabinowitz and Douglass respectively describe, those living in these border areas must evolve a *modus vivendi* which incorporates contradictory identities. Citizenship, state nationalism, and various other social ties draw border people away from the border, inward, to the centres of power and culture within the state. Borderlanders are often simultaneously pulled across the border by similar ties of ethnic and national unity. This may give rise to nationalist struggles of the kind described by Douglass (chapter 3), as well as to the kind of heterotopic reality outlined by Stokes for the Hatay region of Turkey, where local life is a complex mix of different cultural traces drawn from both sides of the border (chapter 11). These contributions suggest that choice of national identity must thus be understood in terms as much of local as of supra-local interests (cf. Vermeulen 1978, cited in Grillo 1980; Herzfeld 1985: xiv).

But not all border communities have the same characteristics, since not all are dissected by the border in the same way. In terms of their ethnic identities, at least three main types of border population can be identified: (i) those who share ethnic ties across the border *as well as* with those residing at their own state's geographical core; (ii) those who are *differentiated* by cross-border ethnic bonds from other residents of their state; and (iii) those who are members of the national majority in their state, and have no ethnic ties across the state's borders. All three types of community may be found at one border, but they need not be. Examples of the first type are the borderlanders of the Republic of Ireland who share ethnic ties both across and within the state boundary with Northern Ireland, and Hungarian borderlanders who share ethnic ties with those across the state's borders in Slovenia, Romania and Slovakia. The Basque borderlanders described by Douglass provide an example of an ethnic minority within two states – Spain and France – but who define themselves as a nation tied to a homeland dissected by those two states. One might anticipate these different configurations to have varying consequences for the expression of identity within the state concerned such that, for instance, borderlander identity is more anomalous in the latter than the former. Moreover, it is more likely to be subversive, coming into conflict as it does with the state's projected image of itself, as indeed the Basque case in Spain bears out. In contrast, the expression of an Irish identity at the border of the Irish Republic is broadly consistent with that state's wider national project, although the situation clearly differs across the border in Northern Ireland, where one section of the population, the Nationalists, share ethnic ties with the majority in the Republic of Ireland, while Unionist borderlanders' ethnic connections in Northern Ireland extend inward to Belfast, and perhaps as far as Edinburgh and London. It is in this sense, then, that frontiers intrude more deeply into Spanish territory than is the case in the Republic of Ireland, since, as Douglass points out, those sympathetic to Basque nationalism will be borderlanders in a political sense, irrespective of where they live in Spain, and though they may be geographically distant from the border's other realities.

There are fewer examples of the third type of ethnic identity at borders, principally because there are very few homogeneous nation-states whose members do not share ethnicity with neighbouring peoples across international state boundaries. The French and the Spanish cases provide good textbook examples of the idealised model of the correlation between nation and state, but, as Sahlins and Douglass consider in this collection, even they are complicated by the presence of Catalans and Basques where their two states meet. The Turkish–Syrian border described by Stokes offers yet another variant on this theme. Like Spain, with its minority Basque population, the Turks of the Hatay live alongside a minority population of Arabs who share cultural ties across the border with Syria. But unlike the Spanish Basqueland, this border is characterised less by regularly activated cross-border ethnic ties than by an anxiety among the Arabs on the Turkish side that Syrian expansionism will ultimately incorporate them, an anxiety generated by a fear of what they believe to be a 'backward' and totalitarian regime. Turkish identity in this region is also characterised by ambivalence, shaped as it is by the contradictory pull of a Turkish nationalism which requires antipathy to Arabs and the realities of an everyday existence necessarily dependant on some degree of compromise and accommodation with them. The result is a weakening or dilution of Turkish national identity which is in striking contrast to the situation in north-east Turkey outlined by Hann and Bellér-Hann (chapter 10).

Like so many international borders, that between north-eastern Turkey and the former Soviet Union was created with little regard to local cultural and linguistic continuities across it, which parallel processes of closure under Stalin and Atatürk, and strict control of cross-border movement, did their best to play down or undermine. In the Kemalist state there was no category of 'national minority', and even the mere mention of the existence of such groups was likely to result in accusations of seeking to fragment the state. For over fifty years complete closure of this border thus effectively precluded any possibility of cross-border ethnic ties subverting the project of the state, and allowed the process of nation-building to continue unhindered on the Turkish side. Surprisingly, however, given what we know of the aspirations of so many cross-border ethnic minorities elsewhere in the globe, the border's reopening in 1988 has done little to disturb the effects of this process. Cross-border ethnic ties have been reactivated to facilitate trade, but they have not stimulated an ethnic or regional consciousness, nor posed a threat to Turkish national identity. On the contrary, national identity has been strengthened as a result and offers a marked contrast to the fragmentary and hybrid identities of the Hatay where, as we saw, an identity as 'Turk' is at best ambivalent.

One possible explanation for this striking difference in orientation towards national identity at different borders of the same state would seem to be religion. Inhabitants of north-eastern Turkey are distinguished from their co-ethnics across the border by their faith in Islam, which simultaneously binds them to their fellow Turks. In contrast, Turks in the Hatay share their Muslim faith with Syrians, albeit belonging to a different sect, thereby rendering a crucial element in Turkish national identity largely ineffective as a distinguishing feature. Thus where in one case religious difference underpins the border and ethnicity transcends it, in the other case the force of these variables is inverted, with marked consequences for the strength with which national identity is experienced and expressed.

Two points might be drawn out from this comparison. The first concerns the way in which attempts to construct a unitary national culture are inevitably mediated by the specific configuration of circumstances at state borders (see also Sahlins, this volume). The varying strengths with which people subscribe to a particular national identity, and its uneven spread across a state's domain, may thus be illuminated by a knowledge of border dynamics. And secondly, border studies can help to reveal the relative strength of national and ethnic identities, the gap between which may become particularly visible where closed borders reopen and vice versa. Among the many things potentially influenced by the changing economic and political configuration of international borders is the expression of local ethnicity and even the national project itself, which may be strengthened not just in spite of, but because of cross-border ties. In a world where state attempts to construct a unitary national culture seem ubiquitously compromised by rising ethnicities, this may be a salutary reminder.

This theme is taken up and developed by Rabinowitz (chapter 6), whose analysis demonstrates that the cultural problems and political contradictions of life on the border can be as much a reality for the majority population as for the minority one. In his discussion of Natzerat Illit, a new town in Galilee, Rabinowitz provides a useful counterpoint to the prevailing emphasis in the literature on border minorities (see, for example, Lavie 1992; Ghosh 1989) by drawing attention to the practices of exclusion adopted by the dominant majority towards the potentially dissenting and subversive others in their midst. Founded initially as a Jewish 'settler town' to exclude Palestinians from their ancestral agricultural land, Natzerat Illit has ironically attracted a substantial number of middle-class Palestinian inhabitants who, viewed with suspicion by their Jewish neighbours, find themselves 'trapped' between the state in which they live – Israel – and the dispersed nation of Palestinians of which they feel a part. As Rabinowitz shows, the town is much more than a physical structure accommodating a Jewish presence on one of Israel's contested frontiers; it has become a discursive object created by Israelis as a way of turning Galilee into a

particular socio-political space in which Palestinians, though not actually physically kept out, are largely excluded. This is particularly evident
in state provision for nursery education. Though not segregated like the
rest of the educational system in Israel, the pedagogic environment of
nursery schooling in Natzerat Illit is permeated by the power of the
Israeli state. Not only must Palestinian pupils learn Hebrew, they must
also participate alongside their Jewish class-mates in centrally organised
public ceremonies celebrating Jewish feasts and national events. These
events, which are predicated on a putative common descent and ties of
belonging based on Jewish blood, embody the exclusionary nature of
Israeliness. Rather than accepting that Palestinians have an identity
legitimately incongruent with that of the state, and allowing them the
discursive space in which to express it, Rabinowitz thus demonstrates
how 'the system attempted to reform them by subjecting them to loaded
occasions with strong nationalistic overtones'.

Rabinowitz's case clearly shows how living near a frontier can push
liberalism to its limits, exposing the contradictions of a majority population who, while proclaiming equal treatment for all citizens regardless of
ethnicity, tries to hold on to power. The result is a deepening rift
between Israelis and Palestinians and a clash of ethnicities which is a far
cry from the hybridisation of border identities so widely reported in the
literature (see, for instance, Anzaldua 1987). Identities may indeed be
ambivalent at borders but, as Rabinowitz reminds us and as Heyman
(1994: 47) has cautioned, we should not allow 'a facile idea – at the
border, two sides equal one hybrid' – to replace analysis and so
minimise the very real power which the dominant majority can exert in
its efforts to further the project of the state.

Borders, sexuality and gender

Borders may mark the extremities of state power, but this need not
entail its weakening there, as Rabinowitz's example so compellingly
illustrates. While not everywhere the case, it is often precisely at borders
that state power is most keenly marked and felt, in ways that ethnographic research can be particularly effective at uncovering. For instance, underlying the evident success with which the dominant
majority inculcates its political vision on the Israeli frontier is the fact
that nursery education is delivered by women, who in Israel are still very
much associated with the private sphere and stereotyped as keepers of
tradition and stability. According to Rabinowitz, this both masks and
marginalises the political dimension of nursery schooling, effectively
defusing the threat of what is the only officially recognised context

within which Palestinians and Israelis meet. This sensitivity to gender in the construction and maintenance of national identity at borders, and the part which gender plays in the politics of the state, is taken up and developed elsewhere in the volume. Like Rabinowitz, Borneman and Cheater both show that the discursive space in which borderlanders articulate their identities inevitably depends on the outcome of a tension between state control and the possibility of its evasion, a tension which, in the cases they describe, is played out in the language of sexual and gendered identities.

The extended narrative in chapter 7, which describes the experiences of Heidi, a middle-aged woman, and her family in pre- and post-unified Germany, is used by Borneman to explore how Cold War oppositions transformed and exacerbated the dynamic interplay between what he presents as a tripartite system of difference – sex, gender and nation. Contrary to popular Western misperceptions, which commonly represented socialist countries as deliberately inhibiting cultural change, neither men nor women in East Germany were left the same as a result of their experience of a divided Germany. Once the Berlin Wall was erected, new gendered identities at the East German border began to be forged in the dialectic between 'security' and 'liberty'; a security which offered a lifetime of employment and welfare guaranteed by the East German state, and the equally desirable liberty to experience what lay beyond the borders of the state. Prewar notions of German masculinity and sexuality underwritten by a pervasive association between 'the father' and the state ceased to apply when the Wall was built, compelling East German men to search for positive alternatives. They were rarely successful, with the men in Borneman's account stumbling forward ineffectually, only reluctantly revising their notions of gender and remaining sexually inhibited. Heidi, in contrast, had always sought openness and a lack of boundaries in her life. Even before the demolition of the Wall she had planned to cross to the West, and in her personal life was prepared to experiment sexually and to form relationships which violated the usual gender norms. Unlike her two husbands, whose fecklessness in the face of change suggests that not all masculinities are powerful and dominant – a point also developed by Stokes for Turkey's southern border – Heidi's 'openness' enabled her to construct a resilient femininity which both anticipated and survived the great changes to come. This tension between security and liberty, between control and escape, was thus an element of the oppositional nation-building processes during the Cold War which provided what Borneman refers to as a 'meta-framework in which social identities unfolded'.

The local identities of the female entrepreneurs described by Cheater (chapter 8) at the Zimbabwean border have similarly unfolded against a background of state efforts to define citizenship and national identity in the wake of the creation of a new border, in this case at independence. Like the GDR, the Zimbabwean state is dominated by a male elite, but unlike the GDR it has not encouraged a reconsideration of the rights of women within the state. In fact, officially recognised membership of the Zimbabwean state has become more exclusive since independence, with membership defined by descent through the patriline, an interpretation clearly at odds with the trend in other nation-states and which, in Zimbabwe, precludes exogamously married women from transmitting membership. The women described by Cheater must work within the interstices of a state definition of nationality which seeks to limit and control the flow of goods and personnel across its borders. In the process of plying their cross-border trade in consumer goods, these women must 'transcend' the state, constructing 'borderline' identities without reference to ethnicity or nationality in ways which challenge the received male definitions of citizenship. By traversing the borders unaccompanied, they flout Zimbabwean conventions of female dependency on men – much like the female 'traders' who cross the border into north-east Turkey as we consider later – creating an anomalous gendered identity which the state has sought to bring under symbolic control by branding them as 'dangerous citizens'. Symbolic control of gendered identities thus here becomes synonymous with control of political order at the edges of the state, in a manner analogous to that which Borneman describes for the GDR.

Where state power is not so keenly felt, the expression and negotiation of border identities may be permitted more discursive space than is the case in Israel, GDR or Zimbabwe, though it is still possible to discern comparable processes at work. According to Stokes, local relations between Arab and Turk are worked out through a form of cultural performance known as Arabesk, a popular musical genre which both articulates and helps to explain some of the feelings of ambiguity and submissiveness which minority and majority borderlanders experience in the Hatay. Turkish gendered nationalist historiography constructs the country's borders as an act of paternity on the part of Atatürk, the 'father Turk', whose decisive and effective action built the modern Turkish nation-state on the remains of the Ottoman empire. The exception is the Hatay, at which border, Stokes argues, Turkey's virile national masculinity is compromised in the popular imagination, because it was left out of Atatürk's scheme and because of the state's continued ineffectual involvement there. This imagery of depleted masculinity is in turn reflected in the sexual ambiguity of many of the best known Arabesk performers and in a corresponding hyper-machismo on the part of their following in the Hatay. Many of the former are openly gay or transsexual, ambivalent and 'unproductive' sexual identities which mirror the anomalous gendered representation of the border as an impotent product of the state.

Similarly, where borders and the state's role in maintaining them are differently conceptualised, we might expect the identities of borderlanders and their interrelationships to take a different form. This is indeed so in the Malaysian case described by Carsten (chapter 9). In contrast to the closure characteristic of the classic European nation-state, the borders of the Malaysian *negeri* were shifting and permeable; power was concentrated at the centre and state sovereignty weakened and became more diffuse as one approached the edges. This greatly facilitated the ease with which new members of the state could be incorporated or old ones abandoned as the power at the centre expanded or contracted. According to Carsten, the effervescence of political identities historically characteristic of the Malaysian state has left its traces on the peninsula and today is paralleled in the everyday lives of villagers on the island of Langkawi, whose familial identities easily absorb newcomers through fostering and marriage, while forgetting ties to kin who have moved away or otherwise become irrelevant to the daily round. State boundaries and those between kin are thus similarly permeable and incorporative, only incompletely encompassing those whose lives they situationally circumscribe. Though not specifically concerned with gender or sexuality, Carsten's analysis offers a useful counterpoint to the proprietary and exclusionary notions associated with the impermeable borders described above, and once again highlights how a border, and its openness or closure, has a bearing on the most intimate aspects of people's lives.

It is worth adding here that these links between the border, sexuality, gender and the state are not relationships readily referred to by other scholars of the state, but are the kinds of association which anthropology's twin focus on identity and locality is especially good at revealing. Such associations of structure and belonging not only offer a perspective on the ambiguities of border life experienced by those who live there, but also provide an insight into the manner in which a state manages and maintains extension of its power on a daily basis. In other words, such associations provide an insight into the ideological workings of the state itself, and into how the meanings it attaches to the border are negotiated both by people at the border, and by those throughout the state.

Negotiating borders

The negotiation of borders includes both the practical negotiations involved in cross-border transfers of people and goods, as well as the more abstract negotiations over meaning to which these activities, among others, give rise. The border may be viewed in very different ways by those to whom it has relevance, and of concern to many of our contributors is how these meanings are expressed and collide. As Stokes remarks in relation to the Hatay, borderlanders are often 'very much absorbed by the question of the ways in which movement (imaginary and otherwise) is constrained and permitted'.

Such negotiations simultaneously support and subvert the classic and commonsense understanding of international borders as politico-legal constructions negotiated and delineated at the highest level of state authority and imposed as the result of top-down decision-making by an administration attempting to forge and define the bounds of a national culture. In fact, borders themselves have been marginalised by theories of nation-building which too often have seen them as the end result of policies emanating from a political centre intent on nurturing a sense of national identity. Sahlins (chapter 2; and 1989) turns this notion on its head by drawing attention to the ways in which notions of nationhood can be as much the result of a reverse process in which local level negotiations construct the nation from the outside in. Borders may thus emerge, as Sahlins shows for the French–Spanish border in the Pyrenees, as the product of activity at peripheral localities, or in the interaction between local rivalries and national ones. Even where borderlines are already established and relatively stable, the borders themselves, and the identities of those who live there, may be characterised by continual change and negotiation; the boundary line itself may not shift, but the relations across it as well as within it – between a border people and their political core – may be subject to repeated redefinition. In such cases, as Douglass (this volume) succinctly puts it, '*how*, as opposed to *where* . . . [two nations meet] . . . is subject to constant negotiation', and may not be the same for the entirety of a particular border's reach. Such insights advocate a radical reorientation of how we view nation-building and the construction and emergence of national boundaries by refocusing attention on activities in border regions which can have a bearing on these processes.

As we pointed out earlier, many of these activities may not be overtly political, but may nevertheless be of interest to the state which endeavours to control them. Smuggling, migration, cross-border shopping and other kinds of trans-border movement occurring within or outside the limits of the law may challenge and even undermine state efforts to define the identities of those who live at the border, a point touched upon by almost all our contributors. Such activities certainly offer an opportunity for exploring the strength or fragility with which state structures impose their definitions and exert their influence, for it is in the ease or difficulty with which exit and entry are exercised that state regulations are frequently made most apparent. We have already mentioned how the activities of the female shoppers described by Cheater challenge the Zimbabwean state's definition of citizenship and national identity, but other contributors similarly consider how a variety of cross-border economic pursuits play a part in the process of national construction. In this regard the anthropological study of borders is as much about the exploration of economic barriers and opportunities as it is about the examination of moral and social systems, or the successful achievement of nationalist self-determination.

It is self-evident that borders can create the reasons to cross them, and may act both as barriers and opportunities, often simultaneously. Thus Kearney (chapter 5) describes how Mixtecs from the state of Oaxaca in Mexico are drawn northwards across the border with the United States, lured by the promise of a higher standard of living, and risking life and liberty when crossing illegally. As Kearney argues, the consequences are contradictory for both the states involved, whose inability to define the legal and cultural identities of their border populations is exposed by the movements of these migrants. Thus the United States has been compelled to accept large numbers of undocumented 'aliens' in its midst – a liminal population which is *in* but not *of* the United States – since its West Coast economy depends to a great extent upon this pool of cheap, unskilled labour. Mexico's oversaturated labour market compels it too to accept the movements of these migrants, but again not without cost; a porous border may facilitate the flow of these workers and the much-needed remittances they return, but the assault on the integrity of the border which their passage represents constitutes a threat to Mexico as a modern nation-state by blurring the edges of its sovereignty.

A broadly similar situation characterises the Mediterranean shores of Spain described by Driessen in chapter 4 where, like Kearney, the focus is again on illegal migrants who traverse a frontier at which the West and Third World meet. According to Driessen, Spain's historical record of the non-assimilation of minorities has made especially problematic the lives of the North African workers who clandestinely seek an often hazardous passage from Tangier to Tarifa across the Strait of Gibraltar, only to encounter imprisonment, exclusion or a life in which any possibility of citizenship is denied. Driessen focuses particularly on the competing and contested images of this frontier generated by the different kinds of border crossings which occur there. Viewed from Europe, Tarifa has long been seen as a gateway to the Orient, to the exotic and the primitive, and has been sold as such to the many day-trippers and shoppers who regularly make their way across the Strait, and whose encounters with the 'other' there confirm their own identity as Europeans. Viewed in the opposite direction, from the beaches of Morocco, the vision of an imaginary European paradise soon gives way to the realities of a life of squalid boarding houses, menial jobs and harassment from the public and state authorities alike. This chapter clearly shows us, then, how efforts to control borders operate not only at the politico-jural level of regulating population flows but also at the level of meaning construction, where the relatively benign interpretations of the border promulgated by the state are continually subverted by the experiences and understandings of subaltern groups who seek entry, understandings which, in turn, confront, if not yet transform, localised and historically sedimented conceptions of what it means to be Spanish.

By drawing attention to competing conceptions of border life – in image and in reality – Driessen's analysis hints at the moral dimension which sometimes accompanies economic exchanges at borders, a point also briefly considered by Douglass and Borneman but developed at length by Hann and Bellér-Hann in their account of Turkey's north-eastern border with Georgia. Here too, as in North Africa and Mexico, border traffic is economically motivated. Since the collapse of the Soviet Union, and facilitated by cross-border ethnic ties reactivated at the end of the Cold War, former Soviet citizens have streamed across the border as traders to ply their wares at roadside stalls or urban markets in an 'informal economy' largely unregulated by the Turkish state. For the most part, even if not actually welcomed, these traders have enjoyed the sympathy and the commercial patronage of most sections of the popula-tion on the Turkish side who appreciate the selection of goods and the cheaper prices. However, they unequivocally condemn one aspect of this recent influx – prostitution; moral outrage at this has coloured perceptions not just of the Georgian traders but of all foreigners, resulting in a heightened awareness of a more significant, more alien 'other' and leading to a renewed emphasis on a Turkish identity which transcends local cultural and linguistic boundaries. Like Heidi and Zimbabwe's female traders, these prostitutes challenge the border's official masculinity by seeking to cross it on their own terms, thereby creating a breach through which, if unchecked, subversive femininities and other moral seepages may contaminate the body politic.

These chapters do more than just remind us of the kinds of reasons periodically reported in the literature for why people cross borders. They suggest that the border, far from being the same phenomenon for all for whom it is significant, is a focus for many different and often competing meanings. In Spain, for instance, the seductive and inviting images of the picture postcards and tour guides for sale in Tarifa are belied by the harsh realities boldly stated in the political graffiti on the town's walls. Similarly, in northern Turkey the potential advantages of the new commercial exchange with traders from Georgia are tempered by posters and banners warning of the sexually transmitted diseases these merchants allegedly carry. Elsewhere attempts to construct the meaning of the border and those who cross it are more obviously written on the landscape, most visibly and most powerfully by the physical structures of control which the state erects there. The 'fence' separating the United States from Mexico clearly operates at the practical level of keeping people out, but it simultaneously functions as a powerful symbol of state power as Kearney notes, constructing the border as a virtually impenetrable barrier which protects the national integrity of all who live within it. Similarly, 'the Wall' dividing the two Berlins, once a pervasive symbol marking East from West, continues to symbolise the many differences between the city's recently reunified inhabitants even though the physical structure itself has been removed (see also Borneman 1992b). Identity cards, watch towers, the colours of the border-guards' jackets, the rubber customs stamp all exert their influence on borderlanders, irrespective of on which side of the border they live, visibly substantiating the local imaginings of state limits and condensing a number of ideas about identity and belonging (Thornton 1994: 10). Thus for residents of the Hatay, the border with Syria evokes ambiguous and sometimes conflicting notions about the nature of Turkish and Arab identity, the present and the past, and the nation-state and Islam. How the state ideologically constructs itself at borders through symbol and image, and the way in which this is confirmed or resisted in the imaginings of those who live there (cf. Lavie 1992), is an undercurrent in many of the contributions, and suggests the aesthetics of borders and the symbolic encoding of space and place as potentially productive lines for further inquiry.

Not surprisingly, then, the institutions of the state at borders are not the only elements which define borders as structures of power. Whether borders are old or new, their frontiers are volatile social and cultural spaces. As Douglass indicates, static borderlines may be surrounded by dynamic frontiers. New and changing borderlines, on the other hand, may be accompanied by static social relations, that is, by long-standing and only slowly changing patterns of behaviour within and across the various communities who live at and traverse the border. In fact, as our contributors demonstrate, mobility and fixity in place are aspects of border society which have a bearing on the identities of those who live there, and which help to define the strengths and weaknesses of communities, nations and states at their juncture in the borders. Nations and states construct borders as places of economic and political opportunity, giving rise to frontier zones of a variety of moral and social orders. Why, how and where people cross borders encode these frontiers with multiple meanings, and demonstrate the diversity with which institutional and non-institutional organs of power in local and national society are negotiated.

Conclusion

A number of points emerge from this discussion of international state borders which are directly relevant to research in political anthropology: (i) borders are not homogeneous (although this may be self-evident, the risk is that this very self-evidentness may arrest analysis of how and why borders differ through time and space); (ii) anthropologists, by focusing on borders, can theorise changing definitions of peripheries and their relationships to their centres; (iii) frontiers are territorially and tempo-rally defined zones linked to borders, and have heuristic utility beyond the metaphorical; (iv) borders are physical, literal structures of the state, which also structure a range of meanings and belongings associated with a variety of identities; (v) borders help us to understand the imprecise fit between nations and states; and (vi) the study of territorial borders is part of a wider ensemble of studies of border-crossings and frontiers of identity. In all these respects we have maintained that the study of borders adds to our understanding of national, ethnic, gender and sexual identities, among others, because borders inflect these identities in ways not found elsewhere in the state.

There are those who have recently claimed rather more for border studies. Alvarez, for instance, suggests that the 'borderlands genre is a basis upon which to redraw our conceptual frameworks of community and culture area' (1995: 447) and is thus one way to challenge the canon of anthropology. This may be so, but we maintain that such challenges should be rooted in comparative and empirical approaches to nationalism and identity. A comparative anthropology of borders could take a number of forms which have distinct research possibilities and problems: the historical analysis of one border within a state; the comparison of both sides of an inter-state border; the comparison of different borders in the same state; and the comparison of the borders of different states.

Borders are contradictory zones of culture and power, where the twin processes of state centralisation and national homogenisation are disrupted, precisely because most borders are areas of such cultural diversity. Part of political anthropology's task is to understand how structures of power are created, reproduced and experienced. This book explores borders as a place for researching the structures and agencies of the state and the ways in which national and other identities provide meaning and order to the forces of the state. In so doing it suggests that borders are research sites which also may serve as frontiers of scholarship among the social sciences.

Notes

We are grateful to Scott Dixon, Graham McFarlane, Kay Milton, Martin Stokes and three anonymous referees for their very helpful comments on an earlier version of this introduction.

1. As metaphors for referring to the meeting of cultures in metropolitan centres 'border' and 'borderland' clearly have an appropriateness, since they emphasise many of the issues which also characterise a country's territorial and political limits: marginality, interstitiality, the juxtaposition of cultures. Nevertheless, there are dangers inherent in appropriating the image of the 'border' as a way of studying the relationships between cultures everywhere, not least that authors may be carried away by their own post-modern rhetoric, reifying a set of linguistic contrasts between, for instance, legal and illegal/rich and poor, which mystify the border (Heyman 1994).

2. The editors recognise that the Irish border, near which we both live, influences our perceptions of borders elsewhere and has played a part in our interest in the comparative anthropology of international borders. As with other borders mentioned earlier, the Irish border has not been the focus of anthropological research to a degree which matches its relative importance in local, national and state affairs, particularly in relation to the twenty-seven-year conflict which has raged across it, and in which the border has played a significant political and ideological role. In fact, since the return of open hostilities to Northern Ireland in 1969, the border has barely featured in work by anthropologists, despite its evident centrality to those who live there (exceptions include Harris 1972; Vincent 1989, 1991; Wilson 1993, 1994; Kelleher 1994).

References

Alonso, A. M. 1994. 'The politics of space, time and substance: state formation, nationalism, and ethnicity', *Annual Review of Anthropology* 23: 379–405.

Alvarez, R. R. 1991. *Familia: migration and adaptation in Baja and Alta California, 1800–1975*. Berkeley: University of California Press.
1994. 'Changing ideology in a transnational market: chiles and chileros in Mexico and the US', *Human Organization* 53 (3): 255–62.
1995. 'The Mexican–US border: the making of an anthropology of borderlands', *Annual Review of Anthropology* 24: 447–70.
Alvarez, R. R. and G. A. Collier 1994. 'The long haul in Mexican trucking: traversing the borderlands of the north and the south', *American Ethnologist* 21 (3): 606–27.
Anzaldua, G. 1987. *Borderlands/La Frontera: the new Mestiza*. San Francisco: Spinsters/Aunt Lute.
Aronoff, M. 1974. *Frontiertown: the politics of community building in Israel*. Manchester: Manchester University Press.
Barth, F. 1969. 'Introduction', in F. Barth (ed.), *Ethnic groups and boundaries: the social organization of cultural difference*. Boston: Little Brown.
Bohannan, P. and F. Plog (eds.) 1967. *Beyond the frontier: social process and cultural change*. Garden City, NY: The Natural History Press.
Boissevain, J. 1975. 'Introduction: Towards a social anthropology of Europe', in J. Boissevain and J. Friedl (eds.), *Beyond the community: social process in Europe*. The Hague: Department of Educational Science of the Netherlands.
Borneman, J. 1991. *After the Wall: East meets West in the new Berlin*. New York: Basic Books.
1992a. *Belonging in the two Berlins: kin, state, nation*. Cambridge: University Press.
1992b. 'State, territory, and identity formation in the postwar Berlins, 1945–1989', *Cultural Anthropology* 7 (1): 45–62.
Braudel, F. 1976. *The Mediterranean and the Mediterranean world in the age of Philip II*, vol. 2. Glasgow: Fontana/Collins.
Cohen, A. 1965. *Arab border-villages in Israel: a study of continuity and change in social organization*. Manchester: Manchester University Press.
Cole, J. W. and E. R. Wolf 1974. *The hidden frontier: ecology and ethnicity in an alpine valley*. New York: Academic Press.
Donnan, H. and T. M. Wilson 1994. 'An anthropology of frontiers', in H. Donnan and T. M. Wilson (eds.), *Border approaches: anthropological perspectives on frontiers*. Lanham, MD: University Press of America.
Douglass, W. A. 1977. 'Borderland influences in a Navarrese village', in W. A. Douglass, R. W. Etulain and W. H. Jacobsen, Jr. (eds.), *Anglo-American contributions to Basque studies: essays in honor of Jon Bilbao*. Reno (Nevada): Desert Research Institute.
Driessen, H. 1992. *On the Spanish–Moroccan frontier: a study in ritual, power and ethnicity*. Oxford: Berg.
Fagen, R. R. 1984. 'How should we think about the borderlands?: An afterword', *New Scholar* 9 (1–2): 271–3.
Fox, R. G. (ed.), 1990. *Nationalist ideologies and the production of national culture*. Monograph Series No. 2. Washington, DC: American Anthropological Association.

Frankenberg, R. 1989 [1957]. *Village on the border*. Prospect Heights, IL: Waveland Press.

Geertz, C. 1973. 'After the revolution: the fate of nationalism in the new states', in C. Geertz (ed.), *The interpretation of cultures*. New York: Basic Books.

Gellner, E. 1983. *Nations and nationalism*. Oxford: Blackwell.

Ghosh, A. 1989. *The shadow lines*. New York: Viking.

Grillo, R. D. 1980. 'Introduction', in R. D. Grillo (ed.), *'Nation' and 'state' in Europe: anthropological perspectives*. London: Academic Press.

Gupta, A. and J. Ferguson 1992. 'Beyond "culture": space, identity, and the politics of difference', *Cultural Anthropology* 7 (1): 6–23.

Handler, R. 1988. *Nationalism and the politics of culture in Quebec*. Madison: University of Wisconsin Press.

    1994. 'Is "identity" a useful cross-cultural concept?', in J. R. Gillis (ed.) *Commemorations: the politics of national identity*. Princeton: Princeton University Press.

Hann, C. 1995. 'Subverting strong states: the dialectics of social engineering in Hungary and Turkey', *Daedalus* 124 (2): 133–53.

Hann, C. and I. Hann 1992. 'Samovars and sex on Turkey's Russian markets', *Anthropology Today* 8(4): 3–6.

Hansen, A. 1994. 'The illusion of local sustainability and self-sufficiency: famine in a border area of Northwestern Zambia', *Human Organization* 53 (1): 11–20.

Harris, R. 1972. *Prejudice and tolerance in Ulster: a study of neighbours and 'strangers' in a border community*. Manchester: Manchester University Press.

Herzfeld, M. 1985. *The poetics of manhood: contest and identity in a Cretan mountain village*. Princeton: Princeton University Press.

Herzog, L. A. 1990. *Where North meets South: cities, space, and politics on the US–Mexico border*. Austin: University of Texas.

Heyman, J. 1991. *Land, labor, and capital at the Mexican border*. Flagstaff: University of Arizona Press.

    1994. 'The Mexico–United States border in anthropology: a critique and reformulation', *Journal of Political Ecology* 1: 43–65.

Horsman, M. and A. Marshall 1994. *After the nation-state: citizens, tribalism and the new world disorder*. London: HarperCollins.

Kavanagh, W. 1994. 'Symbolic boundaries and "real" borders on the Portuguese–Spanish frontier', in H. Donnan and T. M. Wilson (eds.), *Border approaches: anthropological perspectives on frontiers*. Lanham, MD: University Press of America.

Kelleher, W. 1994. 'Ambivalence, modernity and the state of terror in Northern Ireland', *PoLAR: Political and Legal Anthropology Review* 17 (1): 31–9.

Kopytoff, I. 1987. 'The internal African frontier: the making of African political culture', in I. Kopytoff (ed.), *The African frontier*. Bloomington: Indiana University Press.

Lask, T. 1994. ' "Baguette heads" and "spiked helmets": children's constructions of nationality at the German–French border', in H. Donnan and T. M. Wilson (eds.), *Border approaches: anthropological perspectives on frontiers*. Lanham, MD: University Press of America.

Lavie, S. 1990. *The poetics of military occupation: allegories of Bedouin identity under Israeli and Egyptian rule.* Berkeley: University of California Press.

1992. 'Blow-ups in the borderzones: Third World Israeli authors' gropings for home', *New Formations* 18: 84–106.

Löfgren, O. 1995. 'Being a good Swede: national identity as a cultural battleground', in J. Schneider and R. Rapp (eds.), *Articulating hidden histories: exploring the influence of Eric R. Wolf.* Berkeley: University of California Press.

Malkki, L. 1992. 'National Geographic: the rooting of peoples and the territorialization of national identity among scholars and refugees', *Cultural Anthropology* 7 (1): 24–44.

Martinez, O. J. 1994. *Border people: life and society in the US–Mexico Borderlands.* Tucson: The University of Arizona Press.

Mintz, S. 1972. *Caribbean transformations.* Chicago: Aldine.

Pettigrew, J. 1994. 'Reflections on the place of the border in contemporary Sikh affairs', in H. Donnan and T. M. Wilson (eds.), *Border approaches: anthropological perspectives on frontiers.* Lanham, MD: University Press of America.

Prescott, J. R. V. 1987. *Political frontiers and boundaries.* London: Unwin Hyman.

Price, J. A. 1973. 'Tecate: an industrial city on the Mexican border', *Urban Anthropology* 2 (1): 35–47.

1974. *Tijuana: urbanization in a border culture.* Notre Dame/London: University of Notre Dame Press.

Rosaldo, R. 1988. 'Ideology, place, and people without culture', *Cultural Anthropology* 3: 77–87.

Sahlins, P. 1989. *Boundaries: the making of France and Spain in the Pyrenees.* Berkeley: University of California Press.

Shanks, A. 1994. 'Cultural divergence and durability: the border, symbolic boundaries and the Irish gentry', in H. Donnan and T. M. Wilson (eds.), *Border approaches: anthropological perspectives on frontiers.* Lanham, MD: University Press of America.

Stokes, M. 1994. 'Local Arabesk, the Hatay and the Turkish–Syrian border', in H. Donnan and T. M. Wilson (eds.), *Border approaches: anthropological perspectives on frontiers.* Lanham, MD: University Press of America.

Thornton, R. 1994. 'South Africa: countries, boundaries, enemies and friends', *Anthropology Today* 10 (6): 7–15.

Tonkin, E. 1994. 'Borderline questions: people and space in West Africa', in H. Donnan and T. M. Wilson (eds.), *Border approaches: anthropological perspectives on frontiers.* Lanham, MD: University Press of America.

Verdery, K. 1991. *National ideology under socialism: identity and cultural politics in Ceausescu's Romania.* Berkeley: University of California Press.

Vermeulen, C. J. J. 1978. 'Ethnicity, nationalism and social class: the case of the Orthodox population of Macedonia (1870–1913)', paper presented to SSRC 'European Seminar' [cited in Grillo 1980].

Vincent, J. 1989. 'Local knowledge and political violence in County Fermanagh', in C. Curtin and T. M. Wilson (eds.), *Ireland from below: social change and local communities.* Galway: Galway University Press.

1991. 'Irish border violence and the question of sovereignty', in M. D.

Zamora, B. B. Erring and A. Laruffa (eds.), *The anthropology of war and peace*. Nueva Vizcaya: Saint Mary's College of Bayombong.

Wilson, T. M. 1993. 'Frontiers go but boundaries remain: the Irish border as a cultural divide', in T. M. Wilson and M. E. Smith (eds.), *Cultural change and the New Europe: perspectives on the European Community*. Boulder and Oxford: Westview Press.

1994. 'Symbolic dimensions to the Irish border', in H. Donnan and T. M. Wilson (eds.), *Border approaches: anthropological perspectives on frontiers*. Lanham, MD: University Press of America.

Wolf, E. R. 1959. *Sons of the shaking earth*. Chicago: University of Chicago Press.

1966. 'Kinship, friendship, and patron-client relations in complex societies', in M. Banton (ed.), *The social anthropology of complex societies*. London: Tavistock.

1982. *Europe and the people without history*. Berkeley: University of California Press.

2 State formation and national identity in the Catalan borderlands during the eighteenth and nineteenth centuries

Peter Sahlins

'The history of the world can be best observed from the frontier', wrote Pierre Vilar (1985: 23), the noted French historian of modern Catalonia and Spain. Vilar's claim is not without exaggeration, yet it underscores the critical if too-frequently ignored role of borderlands as both sites and metaphors in the political and cultural constructions of a modern world of nation-states. Indeed, the perspective from the periphery challenges much of the received wisdom common to both histories and anthropologies of contemporary national states.

According to an old but still vital historical paradigm, modern nations, especially those of the older, contiguous states of Western Europe, are frequently depicted as being built from political centres outward and imposed upon marginal groups and peripheral regions in a process of institutional integration and cultural assimilation (see, for example, Deutsch 1953, 1963; Macartney 1934; Bendix 1964). National identity, from this perspective, is the simultaneous expression of a cultural unity and a national consciousness which is the political *oeuvre* of the centralised state. France, in this view, is the paradigm of state and nation building, although in the past 100 years, succeeding generations of scholars have hotly contested the question of which was the formative period in the creation of French unity. Once Saint Louis was considered to have presided over the birth of the nation France, then it was Louis XIV, then the French Revolution. More recent scholarship suggests that France only became a unified nation at a surprisingly late date, for only during the early Third Republic (1870–1914) did the French state create the road and railway networks, policies of compulsory primary education, and the universal military conscription by which peasants became Frenchmen (Martin 1951; Kohn 1967; Weber 1976; Tilly 1979; Margadant 1979). Eugen Weber, writing of this belated transformation of the French countryside, has stressed the extent to which the state had to impose a unitary national culture on the peasantry. Peasants responded, in his view, by accepting

31

this formal means of national integration and willingly abandoning their local identities and loyalties. In a related manner, Agulhon's (1982) study of the Var department suggested that the early nineteenth century saw the gradual formation of national identities and loyalties which the Second Republic (1848–51) at once affirmed and reinforced. Agulhon and others since (for example, McPhee 1976, 1978; Bezucha 1975; Berenson 1985) have argued that the diffusion of Republican party politics represented the critical means of becoming French, although they have stressed more than Weber the lag between the adoption of 'modern' national/political identities and the abandonment of 'traditional' local/folkloric ones.

The historiography of nation-building in France has thus emphasised the extent to which the nation was imposed from the top down and from the centre outward, requiring the loss of local identities and loyalties in the process, and denying the role of borderland peoples in the construction of their own identities. Across the Pyrenees in Spain, the development of peripheral nationalisms in Catalonia and the Basque countries beginning in the late nineteenth century has led historians and anthropologists to greatly de-emphasise the expression of a Spanish national identity emanating from Madrid (Payne 1981). Yet in Spain, as in France, the role of borderland peoples in the construction of national identities has largely been ignored.

Older paradigms of state-building and nation-formation have not gone unchallenged. Since the late 1960s, the scholarship of nationalism and national identity has undergone an important renovation, especially in the English-speaking world. The seminal work of Benedict Anderson, for example, has described nations as 'imagined communities' in the sense that they are created and invented, as opposed to fabricated and dissimulated,

because the members of even the smallest nations will never know most of their fellow-members, meet them, or even hear of them, yet in the minds of each lives the image of their communion. (1983: 15)

Such definitions are useful in their focus on the symbolic construction of national and political identities through the invention of national languages and literatures, in contrast to earlier studies which looked more exclusively at the material and economic conditions of national community and communication. But approaches like Anderson's still fail to focus on the specific ways in which individuals and communities construct symbolically, in their own communities, the means of linking themselves to the wider worlds of the nation. Moreover, historians have not yet consistently followed the lead of anthropologists who link the development and expression of ethnic, gender, class or national identities to the process of distinction and differentiation – of drawing boundaries between a collective self and an Other. In the French–Spanish borderland, it was this sense of difference – between 'us' and 'them' – which was so critical in defining an identity (on the cultural and symbolic dimensions of the nation 'imagined' see, for instance, Beaune 1986; Hunt 1984; Agulhon 1979; on the oppositional character of identities see Grillo 1980; Wallman 1978; Cohen 1986; Armstrong 1982).

Drawing on this literature, this chapter examines the process of state-building and the articulation of national identities in one valley in the Catalan Pyrenees. The history of the Cerdanya valley, divided between France and Spain by the Peace of the Pyrenees in 1659–60, is marked by a notable intersection of state, nation and ethnicity in a neatly delineated region; as such, it is a privileged site for rethinking these common assumptions about the formation of national states and national identities in the eighteenth and nineteenth centuries (see maps 2.1 and 2.2).

Its experience suggests that 'traditional' peasant communities did not disintegrate and decline while becoming part of 'modern' societies; that abstract national loyalties and identities did not necessarily displace a local sense of place; and that the process of nation-formation was not simply, as is suggested by the French models, the imposition of politics, institutions or culture from the top down and the centre outward. The Cerdanya is a case where the nation appeared on the periphery before it was built by the centre, and its example may illuminate a rarely examined side of the general process of nation-building in Europe.

Peasants, artisans and notables on both sides of the political boundary shared a common language and ethnicity other than either French or Spanish: they were Catalans. This unity of language and custom did not disappear in the two centuries following the Treaty of the Pyrenees. Nor did the formation of a national boundary line break the continuity of social relations across the frontier. The division of the Cerdanya, rather, created a paradoxical unity of the two Cerdanyas: members of the local communities became more closely linked across the boundary by marriage, property ownership and economic interests. Yet this inter-twining of the Cerdans hardly assured the homogeneity of local society and culture. United in their social and economic relations, as well as by their inherited language and ethnicity, the village communities of the Cerdanya nevertheless became divided by their adopted nationalities as Frenchmen and Spaniards.

The construction of French and Spanish citizenship in the borderland

Map 2.1   France, Spain, Catalonia (Source: Sahlins 1989)

was intimately linked to the emergence of the national territorial boundary and territorial sovereignty after the seventeenth century. In 1660, the French and Spanish monarchies divided the jurisdiction over the valley between them. That the Cerdans came to identify themselves as Frenchmen or Spaniards was an unanticipated result of the division of the valley. Article 42 of the Treaty of the Pyrenees stated that 'the Pyrenees Mountains, which anciently divided the Gauls from the

Map 2.2   The Cerdanya (Source: Sahlins 1989)

Spains, shall also make henceforth the division of the two kingdoms'.[1]
Unlike most seventeenth-century treaties, the text invoked at once a
historical and a natural frontier and bade commissioners to judge what
parts of the Cerdanya and its neighbouring district, the Conflent, lay on
the distinct sides of the mountain range.[2] Over the following year, the
commissioners debated the geographical distribution of pre-Roman
'nations' and the administrative divisions of their Roman and Visigothic
conquerors. But they were unable to harmonise their distinctive visions
of where the Pyrenees mountains lay – although both sides continued to
believe in the 'natural frontier' of the Pyrenees as something more than
the mask of military interests.[3] By the Llívia accord of November 1660,
French and Spanish plenipotentiaries agreed to cede thirty-three villages
of the Cerdanya to France, not including the town of Llívia, which those
villages completely surrounded (Sahlins 1989: 49–53).

A memoir prepared for Don Miguel de Salvà, the Spanish commis-
sioner in 1660, read that 'the line of this division, which has to be almost
mathematical, has necessarily to occupy a very narrow width' (Arxiu
Històric de la Ciutat de Barcelona MS B 184, fol. 2). But while the
diplomats and commissioners spoke of the 'delineation' and 'demarcation' of the frontier, they did not think in terms of the modern notion of
a linear boundary separating distinct national territories. Instead, they
posed the problem in jurisdictional terms. 'The division of France and
Spain will be understood as a division between the [village] jurisdictions'
ceded to France and those that remained part of Spain, read the Treaty
of Llívia. Sovereignty was also jurisdictional in that each polity had a
number of distinct frontiers in the borderland, one for each of the
different 'provinces' of government, including the administration of
justice, the collection of taxes and customs dues, and the policing of
religious affairs. Since each province had its own spatial dimensions of
competency, the jurisdictional boundaries failed to coincide in a neatly
determined line (Brette 1907; Girard d'Albissin 1969; Alliès 1980).

The boundary line itself appeared only in 1868 when the final Treaty
of Bayonne laid down the official boundary stones that separated the
national territorial states of France and Spain. The act of delimiting the
boundary, according to modern jurists and students of international law,
is the formal juridical definition of territorial sovereignty specific to the
modern state. Lapradelle (1928: 14–15) discusses the act of delimitation, which he sees as creating a 'zonal' frontier, 'an area of contact and
relations of contiguity between states' where governments have 'good
neighbourly relations (*relations de bon voisinage*)' (see also Pop 1968;
Visscher 1957). Since the eighteenth century, European polities have
either delimited their own frontiers or have had linear boundaries

imposed on them. Political geographers see the act of delimitation as the completion of an evolution from 'frontier' or 'boundary', from a broad, sterile and empty zone to a simple, non-substantial line of demarcation (Brunhes and Vallaux 1921; Dion 1945; Truyol y Serra 1957; Guichonnet and Raffestin 1974). The formation of a national boundary of France and Spain between 1659 and 1868 involved the more specific historical movement from a jurisdictional to a territorial polity – the 'territorialization' of the state. Over the course of two centuries, the tendency was for the separating jurisdictional frontiers to collapse into a linear border line separating contiguous national territories.

The French and Spanish states did not simply impress this linear boundary upon the valley nor did they impose the national identities that emerged on either side. Rather, the village communities in the borderland constructed the national boundaries of territory and identity on the basis of, but without ever abandoning, their inherited local boundaries.

The valley of the Cerdanya

'Beautiful, fertile, and well populated, this land can be compared with any other.' So wrote an anonymous early seventeenth-century native of the 'Land and County of the Cerdanya' (Biblioteca de Catalunya Ms 184, fol. 7). The valley was 'in the form of a ship', he continued, seven leagues long and 'much less wide with high mountains that appear as the sides of the galley'. At the centre of the valley lay the town of Puigcerdà, the capital of the county and the administrative, commercial, and religious seat of the district (Biblioteca de Catalunya Ms 184, fol. 1v; Biblioteca de Catalunya Ms 184, fols. 22–35v; Galceran i Vigué 1978). In the early seventeenth century, the General Council of Syndics still met regularly in Puigcerdà. Elected from the four 'quarters' of the valley, the council acted 'like the ancient tribunals of Rome, watching over the public good'.[4]

The Cerdanya was one of the most unified cantons (*comarques*) of early seventeenth-century Catalonia. The internal political unity of the Cerdanya and its relations with wider polities bear a striking resemblance to the neighbouring valleys of Andorra. Both 'valley communities' had developed traditions of local autonomy, and both experienced a form of dual sovereignty. But the dualism of political sovereignty in the Cerdanya represented the obverse of Andorra's. In Andorra since the thirteenth century, the bishops of Urgell and the counts of Foix (later the kings of France) were co-sovereigns over an undivided territory; in the Cerdanya, the division of sovereignty was to become territorial. Writing about the unity of the *comarca* more generally in seventeenth-century Spain – a unity of 'production, language and culture' – Kamen suggests that 'beyond the canton, loyalties began to fade as other identities, notably the emphasis on 'provinces', took priority' (1981: 5). Not only did the comarca only come into being in the seventeenth century, as Pau Vila (1979) noted, but I argue in this chapter that loyalties to and identification with the encompassing polities of France and Spain after 1659 did not necessarily displace or eliminate local and cantonal loyalties. Nevertheless, with the division of the Cerdanya between France and Spain in 1659, its institutional unity was dissolved; but its constituent parts – the eighty or so village communities – continued to thrive in the eighteenth and nineteenth centuries.

These village communities resembled tens of thousands of others across Europe at the end of the Old Regime. The Cerdanya villages were neither as small nor as homogeneous as the 'Iberian structural type' described by Freeman (1968), since they were socially differentiated and included hierarchical distributions of property that were pronounced and growing more severe. Despite an evident maldistribution of wealth, the Cerdanya village communities were closed corporate groups that collectively exploited common pasture lands and forests, regulated the grazing of stubble on meadows within village boundaries, and enforced an institutionalised moral presence on the constituent households. (For a fuller discussion of Cerdanya village communities and their hierarchies of property ownership, see Sahlins 1989: 144–59; Sorre 1913; Gavignaud 1980; Assier-Andrieu 1981; Font i Ruis 1985.) Membership in the community – village citizenship – was a highly regulated affair defining access to ecological resources held by the community or by its members (Assier-Andrieu 1987: 147–68).[5] Basic subsistence activities – grazing on pasture land or recently harvested meadows, irrigating fields and meadows, passing through arable land, collecting firewood – were the privilege and prerogative of 'neighbours' (*veïns*). 'Foreigners' (*forasters*) – a category that included landowners living elsewhere and inhabitants of other villages – were excluded from full access to resources, and increasingly so during the eighteenth century (cf. Gutton 1979).

As highland villages seen in the contexts of both the Mediterranean world and the Pyrenees, the communities in the Cerdanya enjoyed a certain 'mountain liberty', resisting the heavy tutelage of 'that lowland, urban civilization [that] penetrated to the highland world very imperfectly and at a very slow rate' (Braudel 1966, vol. 1: 38). Politically represented by their 'councils', the communities of the eighteenth and nineteenth centuries defended their own local 'liberties'. Composed of elected syndics and sometimes the 'principal inhabitants of the village', these councils upheld the collective rights and privileges of the village community against encroachments by the crown and seigneurial powers. (On political organisation in Pyrenean villages see Zink 1969: 214–28; Soulet 1974: 45–53; on village councils in the valleys see Poumarede 1984; Lefebvre 1963: 117–85.) The community enforced its moral presence through local ordinances. Renewed almost every generation in the Cerdanya, these *crides* established the rules for exploiting common resources and the penalties and fines designed to limit the collective exploitation of pastures, waters, firewood and grazing rights to members of the community itself (Archives du département des Pyrénées-Orientales Bnc 439).

The collective identity of the village community had a specific, if contested, territorial basis in the seventeenth and eighteenth centuries. It was contested, in part, because the idea of a village territory was not yet completely formed in the seventeenth century. In fact, the emergence of the community as a 'moral person' against the seigneurie, in 'collaboration' with the monarchical powers in the later medieval period, did not necessarily imply the notion of village territory as a contiguous and enclosed space (cf. Bloch 1966; Gutton 1979; Font i Ruis 1985; Timbal 1984). The sense of an enclosed territory, encompassing individually held parcels of arable land and meadows, and collectively owned pastures and mountains which formed a contiguous and delimited space, was modified by the notion and practice of usufruct rights (*empriu* in Catalan). The villages and valleys of the Catalan Pyrenees were entwined within elaborate 'webs of usufruct' that had spatial and territorial extensions beyond the contiguous space surrounding each nucleated village. Communities of inhabitants had collective rights of *empriu* to the pastures and forests in the possession of seigneurs and the crown, a right affirmed by the 'stratae statute' of Catalan customary law. In addition to collective rights over communal property, *empriu* also included the exercise, by a neighbour, of rights to cross parcels of arable land and to pasture herds on meadows after the first grass (on the changing legal interpretation of *empriu* in French Catalonia since the seventeenth century, see Assier-Andrieu 1987: 91ff.). Moreover, these collective usufruct rights had specific territorial boundaries. In 1674, an accord between the town of Puigcerdà and the College of Priests of Santa Maria, seigneurs of Bolquera, named definite boundaries and border stones demarcating those areas where the peasants of Bolquera could pasture their herds; the limits named were distinct from the boundaries of Bolquera's territory itself (Arxiu Històric de Puigcerdà Protocols 1674). And in 1705, the communities of Guils and La Tor de Carol signed an accord that named the boundaries of their reciprocal grazing rights but not the boundaries of their territories (Archivo Histórico Nacional Estado Libro 673d, fols. 96ff.; Archives du département des Pyrénées-Orientales C 1083–4). The notion of an enclosed territory was only emerging slowly.

That the 'territorialisation' of the village community was beginning to take shape in the early modern period is evidenced by the increasing attention paid by village communities and by the state to their local boundaries. Royal privileges and court decisions reveal growing disputes among communities themselves over the extent of their respective rights of usufruct and the extension of their local territories. Angostrina and Llívia had disputed the priority access to a shared irrigation canal as early as 1307 – a contention revived in 1410 and again in 1754. But questions concerning the extension of their territories were raised only in 1540, when Llívia erected boundary markers in the terrain of 'El Nirvol' and Angostrina protested to the courts of the Royal Patrimony. Llívia lost, but after appealing directly to Charles V it received a set of royal 'letters of maintenance' that established the boundaries in its favour. The same territory and boundary markers were contested in 1659 and periodically until the later nineteenth century.[6]

Official documents and court decisions included descriptions of communal territories that defined community boundaries as 'straight lines' traced between distinct markers. The border markers included piles of rocks called 'oratories', stones 'engraved with crosses', pierced with holes, or implanted with an iron cross (Archives du département des Pyrénées-Orientales C 2046). In practice, however, as the French Intendant wrote to the Foreign Minister Choiseul in 1761, 'The territories of Llívia and Angostrina are not in truth separated and distinguished by boundary markers; the arable land and pastures that belong to one or the other have always served as a guide to and proof of the boundaries' (Archives du Ministère des Relations Extérieures Limites 459, no. 87). But these customary boundaries were contested by neighbouring communities as claims about village territory came to overlap. They overlapped as well with parish and seigneurial jurisdictions. Local seigneurs were not much interested in defining the boundaries of their jurisdictions, content as they were to collect their revenues and rents from individual parcels of lands.[7] But occasional disputes among seigneurs reveal the existence of boundary stones distinct from those defining the village territories of their vassals; thus, for example, the jurisdictional dispute between the College of Priests of Puigcerdà and the Royal Jesuit College of Perpignan in 1751, during which was found such 'a great confusion' of communal boundaries and seigneurial jurisdictions that it was impossible to 'verify and collate the signals and marks of the division with the titles respectively produced' (Archives du département des Pyrénées-Orientales C 2084).

Disputes among communities over questions of boundaries and usufruct rights did not always involve overt conflict since village representatives could settle local differences amicably according to customary and unwritten procedures. A mid-nineteenth-century description of a boundary stone offers a rare glimpse of the rituals of dispute settlement:

In the meadow situated next to the wall which follows the stream, there is a large rock, covered with brambles, on which five holes had been made. It was used for the reunions of the mayors of Guils, Saneja, Meranges, and La Tor de Carol. The middle hole, larger than the others, was a neutral place. In each of the other holes, the mayors placed their staffs of office while they discussed the difficulties which had arisen among themselves.[8]

Yet such amicable settlements were consistently overridden by a marked propensity of village communities to involve themselves in lengthy and costly lawsuits in defence of their rights, privileges and growing territorial integrity.

These lawsuits were invariably started by contested seizures (*penyores*) of cattle. The 'customary' or 'extra judicial' right of seizing cattle was a ritual and juridical defence of the community's territorial identity, recognised and bureaucratically registered by the state. It involved sequestering an animal belonging to a 'foreigner' who failed to comply with a community's ordinances. Seizures were most frequent during the annual transhumant cycles when herds crossed village territories. If a fine was paid, the animal was released; if the seizure was contested, the result was often a lawsuit which might drag on for years.[9]

Village communities throughout the Cerdanya had disputed their rights and boundaries before the Treaty of the Pyrenees, but such struggles increased in number, scope and intensity during the eighteenth and nineteenth centuries. The increase occurred among communities throughout the valley, on both sides, regardless of the political division. There were two reasons – the first ecological, the second political. The population of the Cerdanya more than doubled between the early eighteenth and the mid-nineteenth centuries, passing from about 10,000 inhabitants around 1720 to over 22,000 in 1860 (see Sahlins 1989: appendix B). Such a dramatic increase strained local resources, especially as pasture was more frequently being turned into arable land. The perceptible shift away from pastoralism is documented in the declining percentage of meadows as a proportion of all arable land, which for the French Cerdagne went from 29 per cent in 1700 to 23 per cent in 1775, and in the changing ratios of bovine and ovine species (see Sahlins 1989: appendix B; Pastor 1933; Vila 1929: 140–1). Cries of 'usurpation' of communal lands by neighbouring villages were widespread in the nineteenth century, as were lawsuits; and the development of additional irrigation canals beginning in the 1820s – the first signs of an 'agricultural revolution' – created new disputes over water rights.

Another reason behind the intensified competition among village communities was the distinctive but parallel transformation of the state in Spain and France. Village communities increasingly defended their boundaries as both the weight of taxation increased and the territorial character of direct taxation took shape. The territorialisation of the community occurred in the context of, even if it preceded, the territorialisation of the state itself.

As long as the crown organised its sovereignty by jurisdictions, it taxed lands on the basis not of their spatial location but of the identity of their owners. Jurisdictional sovereignty was above all a relation between king and subject, not between king and territory. At opposite ends of the eighteenth century, Spain and France each began to raise a property tax based on the territorial location of lands rather than the nationality or residence of owners. The Spanish Bourbons introduced the *catastro*, a land cadastre, in Catalonia in 1717 and undertook a land survey in 1732, thus showing themselves decidedly in advance of their French cousins, despite their relative failure in state-building during the nineteenth century (on the reorganisation of direct taxes in Catalonia as part of the Bourbon reforms known as *Nueva Planta*, see Mercader i Riba 1968: 149–94; Artola 1982: 232–49). Under the Old Regime, France relied quite heavily on a 'personal' tax – the *capitation* – which was replaced by the revolutionary tax rolls of 1791. The 'Napoleonic' cadastration and survey of the late 1820s completed the territorialisation of land taxes in France (see Konvitz 1987: 41–62). As each state defined, through its land surveys, the precise territorial boundaries of the communities, the village communities themselves sought to defend their maximum territorial dimensions. The more visible and intrusive the state, the more likely the community was to identify and defend its own boundaries against neighbouring communities.

The emergence of national differences in the borderland

On the first Sunday in July 1825, hundreds of peasants from the villages of the French and Spanish sides of the Cerdanya valley gathered in

Puigcerdà to celebrate the Feast of the Rosary. It was the major local festival of the Spanish town and of the eastern Pyrenean valley as a whole. As a group of young male musicians from the French village of La Tor de Carol began to perform in the town square, the festive atmosphere quickly turned sour. The town's gates closed, and a crowd swelling to several hundred began to stone and beat the French peasants, shouting (in Catalan): 'Kill the *gavatx*, they have ruled Spain for too long.'

Gavatx, 'the most offensive vituperative of the Spaniard against the Frenchman' according to the English traveller Richard Ford (1970 [1846]: 26), was used customarily in the Cerdanya to designate French men and women – mainly Occitans and Gascons from north and west of the Cerdanya, many of whom were actually in the valley during July 1825 to work the harvest. But the townsmen and peasants of the Spanish Cerdaña also stoned and mistreated their Catalan counterparts from the French side of the valley, just across the boundary, singling out in particular the peasants from the neighbouring village of La Tor de Carol. A century and a half after the French monarchy had annexed the County of Roussillon and part of the Cerdanya by the Treaty of the Pyrenees and its addenda (1659–60), the political and administrative division of the valley had become an organising structure of national identity: at the Feast of the Rosary in 1825, the Cerdans expressed – in Catalan – their distinctive nationalities as French people and Spaniards.

Behind the outbreak of nationalist sentiment during the 1825 Feast of the Rosary lay a world of local struggles and sentiments. Competition and animosity among villages, in the Cerdanya as elsewhere, involved the sense of attachment to village or parish and a corresponding hostility towards neighbouring settlements. Describing village conflicts in the Roussillon at the end of the Old Regime and during the Revolutionary decades, Brunet (1986: 50–68) emphasises the local character of such 'municipal patriotisms', adding that they often 'wore the mask' of national differences. Expressing such a *sociocentrismo* was often the prerogative of young unmarried men who defined and enforced the social and territorial boundaries of the corporate community. Unmarried men could ritually initiate 'outsiders' who married into the community, punish agricultural abuses, enforce restrictions on common lands, or maintain road networks of the parish. Carnival and feast days brought the festive and ritual prerogatives of the youth groups that performed the rites of 'rough music', which sanctioned and enforced social norms, especially concerning mismatched marriages (Le Goff and Schmitt 1981; Davis 1975: 97–123; Van Gennep 1937–45, vol. 1: 196–226; Sahlins 1994). Fairs often brought youth groups from neighbouring villages to blows in confrontations that might be related directly to struggles over pastures or waters. The fight between youths of Angostrina and Dorres at a fair in 1844, in which one young man was killed, formed part of the ongoing struggles over usufruct rights on the Carlit mountain (Archives du département des Pyrénées-Orientales Mnc 1883/1).

The Spanish town of Puigcerdà and the French communes La Tor de Carol and Enveig were also engaged in a long-standing competition. Puigcerdà had been fighting for several centuries, but especially since the outbreak of the French Revolution, to guarantee its privileged usage of an irrigation canal. The canal, born of the Aravó river in France, crossed the communal territories of La Tor de Carol and Enveig and supplied Puigcerdà with its only water; the two French communes had been 'usurping' the water to irrigate their fields and meadows. Recent storms had filled the canal with debris, and during the hot summer of 1825 water was scarce. Already in May, the youths of La Tor de Carol and Puigcerdà had skirmished over the rights of the latter to dance at the former's village feast. Six weeks later, at the Feast of the Rosary in Puigcerdà, the French youths were 'serenaded' by their Spanish counterparts (Archives du département des Pyrénées-Orientales Mnc 1824/1). The 'serenade' was a ritual involving a symbolic payment of coin to the host musicians. According to subsequent testimony, it was this 'local custom bespeaking confraternity and friendship' which had been subverted.

The events that followed might have been simply another case of unruly youths expressing a local rivalry. The Spanish authorities who investigated the July incidents concluded as much. But the prying French inquiry, held over the following year, produced more disquieting evidence. The event, it seems, had been at least in part the premeditated 'conspiracy' of some Puigcerdà notables. Peasants from the Spanish Cerdaña had arrived that day with clubs, and the *émotions* – to use a word of the time – had gone far beyond those of a traditional rivalry. 'National hatred, above all, ruled this ugly scene', claimed a seasoned Brigadier. Those who saw only a communal struggle were 'recent arrivals, people who do not know the district well'. Testifying at the official inquiry, 'a great number of local people' shared the belief that 'national hatred' was involved; some of the French Cerdans, such as the outspoken mayor of La Tor de Carol, even denied the local and ecological basis of the 'massacre'.

The nationalism displayed at this Feast of the Rosary arose from the intersection of a local dispute over a canal and the international political crisis of the early 1820s which brought national struggles and party politics to the French–Spanish borderland. According to the young liberal journalist Adolph Thiers, 'the eyes of France and all of Europe' were focused on the Cerdanya in November and December of 1822 (Thiers 1823). In the Catalan Pyrenees, the Royalist Regency at the Seu d'Urgell led a guerrilla war of the Armies of the Faith against the Constitutional forces of General Espoz y Mina. Spain's first liberal experiment – the Constitutional Triennium of 1820–3 – was threatened in Catalonia by a resurgent strain of popular royalism combined with economic downturn (see Comellas García-Llera 1963; Torras 1976, 1977). To prevent these struggles and the dual plague of cholera and liberal ideas from spreading into French territory, the reactionary French government constructed a *cordon sanitaire* across the Pyrenees and through the Cerdanya (Thiers 1823; Hoffman 1964: 27–49; Archives Nationales F(7) 9692; Archives du département des Pyrénées-Orientales Mnc 2100/1–3).

The French built the barracks of their 'sanitary cordon' along a line that, according to the Spanish communities in the Cerdaña, usurped a portion of their territories and, by extension, of the national territory. Such usurpations, as well as the arbitrary executions of peasants working in their fields in the contested zone, led to the 'dishonour of the Spanish nation', as the mayor of Guils wrote in 1822 (Archivo Histórico Nacional Estado libro 673, fols. 263–4). Most of all, the town of Llívia – left by the Treaty of the Pyrenees completely surrounded by French territory – was outspoken in defence of 'the property rights of its fellow citizens and . . . the integrity of Spanish territory'. A militaristic nationalism dominated the petitions of Llívia:

The Spanish government should announce that its Nation will not let itself be subjugated by any other one, and that it seriously protects its rights. Does not the French Nation recall that the Spaniards are valiant warriors, and that the Spaniards beat back the wings of the eagle? [i.e., Napoleon] . . . Has it forgotten that the Spaniards created the most powerful army of warriors, that the Nation is now resplendent, and that the Spanish Nation has always triumphed despite [France's] treachery? (Arxiu Municipal de Llívia vii.5; Archivo Histórico Nacional Estado libro 672, fols. 303, 331, and libro 673, fol. 229; for French accounts of disputes during these years, see Archives du département des Pyrénées-Orientales Mnc 1722/3)

A year later, the *cordon* was officially disbanded, but French troops remained along the frontier. After the Royalist Congress of Verona in 1822, '100,000 Sons of Saint Louis' marched into Spain in the spring of 1823, restored the absolute monarchy, and briefly occupied the Spanish Cerdaña (Sanchez Mantero 1981; Hugo 1824–5). It is no wonder that in July 1825 Spanish townsmen and peasants cried 'Kill the *gavatx*, they have ruled Spain for too long.'

The immediate political context transformed an essentially local ecological conflict between neighbouring settlements into a national revolt pitting French and Spanish Cerdans against each other. Such was the obvious source of the 'national hatred' and 'party spirit' so widely noted during the Feast of the Rosary. Yet there was a more enduring logic structuring the appearance of national identity in the borderland, one that made local struggles among communities divided by the boundary distinct in nature and intensity from those among villages of the same side. If the political context of the 1820s produced a vitupera- tive nationalism on the periphery, national identity in the Cerdanya more generally emerged from the repeated appeals of the village communities to their respective states, using the evolving language of the nation.

Beginning in the third decade of the eighteenth century, border communities petitioned and engaged the provincial and national autho- rities of the French and Spanish states. As the territorialisation of the local communities took shape, the villages and their representatives increasingly defended their territorial claims, seeking to mobilise the monarchy in defence of their local boundaries and rights. What began as a dispute among the French villagers of La Tor de Carol and the Spanish ones of Guils over a 'measly pasture', for example, ended up as a problem of state for the French and Spanish courts. A generation after the communities had agreed to the territorial extension of their usufruct rights in 1705, the syndics of La Tor de Carol sought to define the actual boundaries of their local territory. In 1740, they claimed that 'the Spaniards, more enterprising than the petitioners, have invaded a portion of the territory and are attempting to keep this usurpation' (Archives du département des Pyrénées-Orientales C 2084; Archives du Ministère des Relations Extérieures Limites 436, no. 36).

The village communities of the Cerdanya traditionally distinguished 'foreigners' and 'neighbours'. But during the 1730s and 1740s, they began to distinguish those who were foreign to the kingdom (*gavatxos* and *espanyols*) from those who were simply foreign to the community. The La Tor de Carol peasants did not yet call themselves 'French', other than identifying themselves as subjects of the French king, as *regnicoles*. Rather, it was their enemies across the political boundary whom they defined by a distinctive nationality, as 'Spaniards'.[10] National identity was contextual and oppositional: a statement about the 'otherness' of their neighbours across the boundary appeared in the context of communal struggles.

National identity was founded on segmentation and structural rela- tivity. Individual villages of the French Cerdagne opposed each other as 'enemies', particularly during their struggle over usufruct rights on the Carlit mountain. But concerning the adjoining pastures of the Royal Pasquiers, the French Cerdans joined together in a petition to the crown. In July 1777, a General Council of the French Cerdagne requested that

all preference be given to the inhabitants of the French Cerdagne, to the exclusion of the Spaniards, to use and make use of the pastures of the Royal Pasquiers in the Cerdagne and Capcir . . . [the inhabitants] offer His Majesty the same dues that are paid annually by Spanish herds. It is natural that *regnicoles* have precedence over foreigners to the fruits which the territory offers. (Archives du département des Pyrénées-Orientales C 2049)

Through such continuous appeals to their separate administrations, villagers moved from naming the 'other' by nationality to identifying themselves as members of what Anderson (1983: 15) has called the 'imagined communities' of nations. And they did so without abandoning their sense of place or their identities as members of local communities. By the early nineteenth century – in part as a result of their experiences during the French Revolution – the communities gave meaning to their own nationalities while consistently demanding that the two states define their boundary line (on the experience of the French Cerdagne during the Revolution, see Sahlins 1990b).

The rhetoric of appeals to the French and Spanish nations served to distinguish struggles among communities divided by the political boundary from other conflicts between villages on either side. But appeals amounted to more than mere rhetoric. There were practical consequences to casting one's interests and identities in national terms. Communities manipulated the structure of an ill-defined boundary and used the absence of a unified jurisdictional and administrative authority in the borderland to pursue their local claims. The General Director of Customs described this process in a letter to the Finance Minister in 1827:

Contiguous communes often have interests to debate. When they do not come under the same higher authority which could contain their rivalries, stop the infringements of territory, arrest the usurpations of pasturing rights and so forth, their petitions are not heeded, and they call upon armed force. (Archives du Ministère des Relations Extérieures Limites 461, no. 31)

The communities were the first to recognise the proliferation of such struggles, and they were also the first to propose a solution. Beginning in the early eighteenth century, both French and Spanish communities consistently petitioned for the official and definitive territorial delimitation of the boundary as the means of ending their local disputes.

The emergence of a national boundary

Bourbon kings sat on the Spanish and French thrones during the eighteenth century, and the dynastic alliance was solidified in the Family Compacts, which affirmed their unity against Great Britain and settled the respective rights of their subjects in both the Old World and the New (Palacio Atard 1921; Renaut 1922). The Bourbon courts also signed accords by which lesser authorities would cooperate in the policing of contraband trade and military desertion along their contiguous frontier (Defourneaux 1971: 147–63). But until the later eighteenth century, the two monarchies were fundamentally unconcerned with their exact territorial boundaries and were unmoved by local demands to delimit their border line.

It is true that the two provincial Intendancies of Roussillon and Catalonia sought to put an end to the local struggles in the borderland as early as 1736, when they signed an accord defining the boundary between Guils and La Tor de Carol. But the central governments in Paris and Madrid rejected the convention, claiming that only kings (and their ministers) could define the territorial limits of sovereignty (Archives du département des Pyrénées-Orientales C 2083; Archivo Histórico Nacional Estado libro 673, fols. 67–117) – yet they remained uninterested in doing so and directed the communities to come to 'extra-legal' conventions arranging their rights and limits. The Spanish town of Puigcerdà thus signed accords with the French villages of La Tor de Carol and Enveig in 1731 and 1732, and Angostrina and Llívia, fighting not only over their limits but also over an irrigation canal that they shared, signed an agreement in 1754. These accords – and others like them – failed to quell local disputes.

During the second half of the eighteenth century, both the French and Spanish governments, struggling for their possessions in the New World, simultaneously began to concern themselves with repressing local quarrels all along the Pyrenees. The term 'territorial violation' makes its first consistent appearance in administrative correspondence of the later eighteenth century.[11] And just as the idea of a community's territory found expression at its boundaries, so too did the idea of a state territory become articulated on the frontier. Provincial administrations sought to protect their territories from both the 'violations' of foreign guards and soldiers and from the 'usurpations' of local communities across the boundary.

In the later eighteenth century, the French Foreign Ministry organised its archives and created numerous 'border commissions' (*commissions de limites*) with the intention of formally delimiting France's territorial boundaries. Though stricken by political crises, a succession of French governments actually ratified twenty-two separate delimitation treaties with neighbouring states between 1770 and 1789 (Noël 1966; Lapradelle 1928: 46–50, appendix 3; Archives du Ministère des Relations Extérieures Limites 7). France and Spain began a formal delimitation of the Pyrenean frontier in 1784, starting with the western end of the chain; while the 'international commission' was interrupted by the Revolution, the deeper cause of its failure was the insistence of both governments on the concept of 'natural frontiers' (Archives du Ministère des Relations Extérieures Limites 459, nos. 91–2; Archives du Ministère des Relations Extérieures Limites 463; Ministère de la Guerre, Archives de l'Armée de la Terre MR 1084, no. 75; Sermet 1983).

The Revolution abolished the multiple jurisdictions that had formed the basis of sovereignty and replaced them with a 'direct relationship between power and territory' in the form of the *départements* (Alliès 1980: 176–84; Ozouf-Mangnier 1989). The revolutionary governments thus realised a project of territorial administration that, in substance, had been proposed several times during the final decades of the Old Regime.[12] But neither the French revolutionary government nor Spain, in its reaction to the news and events of the French Revolution, actually moved to have their frontier delimited. The peace treaties of Basel (1795) and Paris (1814) explicitly ordered the governments to negotiate a 'treaty of limits', but nothing was accomplished. Instead, each state devoted greater efforts to policing and preventing 'territorial violations' of opposing customs guards and of local communities (Sahlins 1989: 168–76).

Governmental concerns of preventing territorial violations thus intersected with the interests of the village communities in maintaining their own territorial integrity. Such an intersection is especially evident in the transformation of the customary forms of village competition – the *penyores* – into a structure of international conflict and an official form of rivalry. Customs agents and soldiers defending a national territory joined local villagers defending their communal boundaries. 'Seizures' of supposed contraband goods by national customs guards often set communities against each other, as happened between Angostrina and Llívia in 1826. A veritable 'border war' erupted between Guils and La Tor de Carol in August 1848, with customs guards and soldiers of each side taking part in the seizures and counterseizures of herds of hundreds of sheep (Archivo del Ministerio de Relaciones Exteriores TN 221–2). Government officials claimed that the problem of territorial violations lay in a badly demarcated boundary, which 'no inhabitant can flatter himself in saying that he knows well', according to the French Customs Director in 1826 (Archives du Ministère des Relations Extérieures Limites 461, no. 14). But the problem seemed to lie in locally contested visions of where the boundary ought to be. On 29 March 1826, the mayor of Angostrina reported that

> one of the stones serving as the boundary of the territories of the two kingdoms of France and Spain had changed places; . . . the said stone had been pierced in a way to prove that attempts had been made to destroy it, which evidently proves the bad faith of our Spanish neighbours . . . About 500 metres into French territory [there was] a large stone with a newly engraved cross on it, the customary way in which limits are marked . . . This new boundary takes away a considerable part of French territory.

The mayor of Llívia replied that the stone involved was not a boundary marker and that the local French officials had 'violated Spanish territory' while attempting to verify that the boundary had been altered. The boundary stone had become a symbol of the dispute itself, which was never settled to the satisfaction of the two communities.[13]

During the 1825 Feast of the Rosary, local and national rivalries had neatly intersected both structurally and temporally. The disputes between Angostrina and Llívia a year later suggest that such was not always the case. Although both the states and the local communities were moving in the direction of territorialisation, they were doing so at different rates and in different ways. The village communities insisted on their separate national identities and on the need to defend their national territorial boundaries well before the two governments' officials defined what these boundaries were. By evoking national identities and engaging the two states in defence of communal limits, local society remained one step ahead of either state, creating dissonance and conflict between France and Spain. In order to eliminate this source of conflict, increasingly an 'embarrassment' in times of peace and alliance, the two governments agreed to the delimitation of their boundary in the second half of the nineteenth century.

'Villages of foreign nations and of different mores'

The local communities of the Cerdanya had been demanding the delimitation of the international boundary since the early eighteenth century, but when France and Spain achieved a settlement in 1866, the communities rejected it due to its incomplete character. The municipality of La Tor de Carol, for example, refused to accept the continued existence of a shared pasture land on its frontier with Guils, just as Angostrina protested against the persistence of terrain to be held jointly with the Spanish enclave of Llívia. The mayor of La Tor de Carol insisted on 'a dividing line that will forever separate two villages of foreign nations and of different mores' (Archives du Ministère des Relations Extérieures CDP10, fol. 298).

The villagers' perception of differences did not necessarily imply the cultural differentiation of the two Cerdanyas (cf. Wallman 1978: 203). In fact, it is difficult to verify whether neighbouring villages of France and Spain had 'different mores' or any distinct cultural characteristics in 1866 – other than the minutiae of linguistic, sartorial and architectural differences occurring among European village communities more generally. After all, the town council of Puigcerdà had supported the reannexation of the French Cerdagne to Spain in 1814 by underlining the identity of the two sides of the valley.

The peasants follow the same agricultural methods; the families of the two sides are intertwined; the landowners of one Cerdanya harvest the fruits of their lands in the other, and vice versa; they speak a single language; they wear the same costumes; so that seeing together two individuals from the Cerdanya, one Spanish and the other French, it is impossible to distinguish which is which without knowing them already. (Archivo Histórico Nacional Estado libro 674, fols. 58–64)

A half century later, the same could have been said; at the time of the delimitation, the two Cerdanyas were hardly distinguishable by their 'mores' or costumes or language. Language, especially, was unaffected by the political division. Although many inhabitants of both Cerdanyas were bi- and even tri-lingual, the Catalan language itself remained the lingua franca of rural society on both sides of the boundary. At the elite level, things were different: by the later nineteenth century, elites in Roussillon had abandoned the Catalan language in favour of French, while in Catalonia elites had revived the Catalan language as a vehicle of political nationalism.[14] But among peasants in the French and Spanish Cerdanyas there were few differences, if any, in the spoken language of everyday life. Modern linguistic surveys reveal only minor phonetic variations and lexical 'gallicisms' introduced by the political boundary (see Costa i Costa 1983: 207–13; Guiter 1966).

The political boundary, in fact, produced a *greater* social and demographic unity of the Cerdanya; in the mid-nineteenth century, the two Cerdanyas were more closely integrated than they had been two centuries earlier. In 1868, families on both sides of the boundary were intertwined as kin and godparents; demographically, the two Cerdanyas were linked by the large-scale movement of Spanish Cerdans and Catalans into the French Cerdagne. The movement of Spanish Catalans into the French Cerdagne was such that by 1866, over 16 per cent of the population of the French Cerdagne was Spanish either by birth or by descent of one generation, while only 2.2 per cent of the population of the Spanish Cerdaña was French by these criteria. The expressions of national identity despite social continuity across the boundary recall Barth's reflections on ethnic boundaries: 'categorical ethnic distinctions do not depend on an absence of mobility, contact, and information, but do entail social processes of exclusion and incorporation whereby discrete categories are maintained *despite* changing participation and membership in the course of individual life histories' (1969: 10, emphasis in original). The origins of this movement lay in both the political strife that pushed and the economic opportunity that pulled the Catalans from Spain into France (see Sanchez Mantero 1975; Rubio 1974: 64–114). The demographic and social permeability of the frontier increased during the eighteenth and nineteenth centuries not because the Cerdans ignored the emerging territorial boundary line but because the differences introduced by the boundary created new reasons to cross it. During the eighteenth century, royal edicts permitting the enclosure of meadows in the French Cerdagne (Assier-Andrieu 1987: 115–46) and the exemption of Spanish landowners from paying personal taxes for their lands in France (Sahlins 1984, vol. 1: 411–18) created economic differences between the two Cerdanyas. Under the Old Regime, these were opportunities that reshaped social relations, but the local economy and landscape were not structurally differentiated. Only after the mid-nineteenth century did the economy of the French Cerdagne 'take off' relative to the increasing 'underdevelopment' of the Spanish side of the valley (Tulla 1977). The timing of this transformation was in large part a function of the dates at which paved roads reached the valley. The French side experienced its *désenclavement* in 1854, when the paved road reached from Perpignan to Bourg-Madame across the Perxa pass; twelve years later the Puigmorens pass was conquered. It was not until 1914 that the public paved roads from Vic and the Seu d'Urgell to Puigcerdà were opened to wheeled vehicles (Pastor 1933: 191; Gomez-Ibáñez 1975: 56–94; Sermet 1962).

Victor Dujardin, a 'man from the north' who travelled through the valley in the 1880s, was astonished by the material and economic contrasts of the two Cerdanyas:

From the last French village to the first one in Spain, the contrast is striking: on this side, in France, usable paths, superb roads, a comfortable population, well-constructed, clean and comfortable houses, excellent schools, magnificent fountains and drinking troughs; on the other side, in Spain, awful, muddy ruts of goat trails, fallen down and dirty farms, and misery everywhere. (Dujardin 1891)

Although he exaggerated, economic differentiation was plainly visible, as it was to the Cerdans themselves. Even before the delimitation of the boundary, the Cerdans were aware of the infrastructural and technological differences emerging in the borderland. Indeed, they often glossed such differences in cultural terms, as the mayor of La Tor de Carol had done, referring to 'foreign nations' and 'different mores'.

The perception of national differences, however, long antedated the structural differentiation of economy and landscape, as in the 1740s when the villagers of Guils and La Tor de Carol opposed each other as foreign nationals. With a certain periodicity – the 1740s, the 1820s, the 1860s – the villagers of the two Cerdanyas highlighted their identities as French people and Spaniards. These periods appear in the wake of important moments of state-building and political consolidation in France and Spain. International political events left residues: they were contexts that transformed, each time with greater intensity, general claims about national identity into extreme strains of nationalism.

At no time was such nationalism more obvious than during the conferences leading to the Bayonne Treaties of Delimitation of 1866 and 1868. For sixteen years, French and Spanish commissioners met in Bayonne and completed the delimitation of the Pyrenean frontier (Sermet 1983; Sahlins 1989: 238–66). The expressed purpose of their lengthy negotiations was to resolve and uproot the local quarrels that had proved so distracting to the practice of territorial sovereignty. The commissioners cast themselves as judges and historians, researching and debating the historical boundaries of village territories. In the words of the French General Callier, their aim was to 'resolve definitively the secular litigation . . . precisely by taking into account the habits, customs, and claims of the inhabitants, and by reconciling them . . . with the law resulting from authentic documents which have escaped the ravages of time' (Archives du Ministère des Relations Extérieures CDP 10, fol. 208).

Yet while the French and Spanish commissioners were eventually able to come to terms with each other concerning the validity of specific claims, the local communities were rarely content with official decisions. The French villages of La Tor de Carol and Enveig opposed the provisions of the 1866 Treaty giving Puigcerdà a full property right to the canal, and in a petition they wrote:

When the Treaty of 1660 had reunited [sic] the communes of La Tor de Carol and Enveig to France, national rivalries gave birth to frequent struggles between the water users of the two different countries. These struggles gave way to private accords of which tradition alone is the witness; the accords gave the town of Puigcerdà permission to use the canal while imposing upon it . . . the obligation to recognize the right of the young men of La Tor de Carol to use the town square of Puigcerdà during the dances of the Feast of Puigcerdà.

The petition linked the juridical right of the Spanish town to use the canal with the festive rite of French villagers to dance in Puigcerdà; further, the petitioners remembered the Feast of the Rosary half a century earlier when the townspeople of Puigcerdà took the rights of the French community and 'drowned them one day in the blood of the young men of La Tor de Carol' (Archives du Ministère des Relations Extérieures CDP 11).

Nearby, the mutual animosity of the French village of Palau and the Spanish hamlet of Aja was such that it provoked Fivaller, a Spanish deputy to the Cortes who had lived in Palau, to remark:

I come from the district. I know the feelings of the inhabitants of Palau. If we [Spaniards] had the misfortune of incorporating one more inhabitant or one more house [from France into Spain], the other inhabitants of Palau would burn his house down so that he would not have to become Spanish (quoted in Brousse 1899: 68).

Despite its exaggeration, Fivaller's statement nevertheless evokes the depth of local oppositions that found a national expression in the border-land. The sense of national identity owed much to the political construction of the territorial basis of sovereignty, though it went beyond the intentions of the two states: predating the territorialisation of the state, national identity drew strength from the territorialisation of the village community and from the enduring expressions of local identity. The stubborn nationalism put forth during the delimitation conferences was based on minute territorial cessions that the states had been willing to make but that the communities forcefully resented. Yet by the mid-nineteenth century the evocation of national identities was not confined to those communities that had fought over their frontiers. The boundary of Aja and Palau, for example, had not been at issue before the 1860s. The two communities had even cooperated to prevent a third village in France from extending its irrigation canal in 1847 (Archives du département des Pyrénées-Orientales xiv S 108). During the delimitation conferences themselves, Aja and Palau were less interested in defending their own communal territories than in defending the national territories that lay at the foundation of their distinctive nationalities.

Locality and nationality

'The evils of Spain', wrote John Stuart Mill (1846, bk. 6: ch. 10, sec. 5), liberal theorist of the nation-state, 'flow as much from the absence of nationality among the Spaniards themselves as from the presence of it in their relations with foreigners.' What Mill saw as a defect of Spanish national character was a more general 'weakness' of national identity in the nineteenth century – even in that paradigm of nation-building, France. National identity was not a condition or a sentiment that could be imposed on local society; nor, as historians have been wont to argue, were peasants forced to abandon their local identities as members of a community or even, in our case, as Catalans. The adoption of national identities was part of a contextual and oppositional process of self-differentiation. Peasants became either French or Spanish because they were not the other, but not because they were no longer Catalans, Cerdans or peasants.

If Mill had bothered to visit the frontier of Spain, like his intrepid contemporary Richard Ford, he might have observed the 'evils of nationality' in both countries:

The [Spaniard's] hatred of the Frenchman . . . seems to increase in intensity in proportion to vicinity, for as they touch, so they fret and rub each other: here is the antipathy of an antithesis; the incompatibility of the saturnine and slow, with the mercurial and rapid; of the proud, enduring, and ascetic, against the vain, the fickle, and the sensual; of the enemy of innovation and change, to the lover of variety and novelty; and however tyrants and tricksters may assert in the gilded galleries of Versailles that *Il n'y a plus de Pyrénées*, this party wall of Alps, this barrier of snow and hurricane, does and will exist forever. (Ford 1970 [1846]: 29–30)

Revealing more about the enduring stereotypes of national character than about the people of the Pyrenees themselves, Ford nonetheless noted a significant feature of life in the borderland – the importance of differences *perceived* among villagers in proximity to each other. The importance of a sense of difference is especially striking in the Cerdanya, where there *were* no Pyrenees – where the border had been drawn through the centre of the plain – and where the inhabitants remained ethnically Catalans, even when they became French and Spanish citizens.

The French and Spanish identities of the communities in the borderland had their origins within a set of local conflicts; yet national identity among the Cerdans was more than the rhetorical expression – and gloss – of local differences. The claims of French and Spanish identities put forth by the village communities gave significance to the political and administrative division of the valley. The arbitrary division had become a historical reality: not the states but the communities had defined the international boundary line. And in constructing the national boundary of France and Spain, they had created for themselves new identities as French people and Spaniards.

Notes

The Catalan spelling of Cerdanya is used when the entire valley is referred to; otherwise, French Cerdagne and Spanish Cerdaña are used. All other place names, except Roussillon and Perpignan, are given in modern Catalan.

1. The political and diplomatic background of the Treaty of the Pyrenees, along with a discussion of the negotiations before and after the treaty itself, are treated in Sanabre (1956: 577–604; 1961). The French text of Article 42 may be found in Vast (1894: 115–16). The Spanish text differed slightly in wording, a difference which the commissioners were to make substantial in their subsequent debates (Sahlins 1989: 44–9).

2. On the terminology of boundaries and frontiers in the seventeenth century, see Febvre (1973). See also Clark (1961: 140–52) and Sahlins (1990a).

3. See Torreilles (1900), Regla Campistol (1951). The French position is put forth in Bibliothèque Nationale FR 8021, fols. 249–67, and Archives du Ministère des Relations Extérieures CP Espagne vol. 433; the Spanish position can be found in Arxiu Històric de la Ciutat de Barcelona Ms B 184.

4. Biblioteca de Catalunya Ms 184, fol. 3v; see also Galceran i Vigué (1973). The four districts (*quarters*) of the canton (*comarca*) each sent militia levies, taxes or provisions as requested by the royal administration in Puigcerdà, or by the 'General Council', which had the privilege of raising its own tax, the *tall de la terra*.

5. On Pyrenean customary law regulating village membership during the medieval period, see Ourliac (1958) and Toulgouat (1981). On membership in the Spanish *pueblo*, see Pitt-Rivers (1954: 1–13) and Freeman (1970: 27–63).

6. These court decisions and royal privileges were discussed and reproduced verbatim in a series of memoirs which resulted from the revival of the rivalry in 1760-1 (see Archives du département des Pyrénées-Orientales C 2050-51) and again in the debates among the Bayonne commissioners: for France, see especially Archives du Ministère des Relations Extérieures Callier 16; for Spain, Archivo del Ministerio de Relaciones Exteriores Tratados y Negociaciones 221–2.

7. Periodic *capbreus* beginning in the fourteenth century (comparable to the French *livres terriers*) contain lists of declarations of specific dues and rents paid on specific parcels of land but do not describe the boundaries of seigneurial jurisdiction or a village territory itself. Examples of such *capbreus* may be found in Arxiu de la Corona d'Aragó Real Patrimoni, Batlle General de Catalunya and in the Arxiu Històric de Puigcerdà.

8. Archives du département des Pyrénées-Orientales Mnc 1924/1. Dion (1945: 24–32) lists similar meetings among representatives of rural communities (or valley communities) at a common point. Note the parallels with heads of states, examples of which are given in Lapradelle (1928: 18–20).

9. The *prenda* or *penyora* was a rural and pastoral version of a wider legal institution – the 'ordinary means of fulfilling obligations born of contracts

or infractions' (Hinojosa 1915: 81). For Spain, see Hinojosa (1915: 79–106); for France, see Timbal (1958, vol 2: 110–38).

10. In the Catalan language spoken in Roussillon and French Cerdagne today, the term *espanyol* is generally reserved for Spanish Catalans; other Spaniards are more often described by their provincial origins: Castilians, Andalusians, etc. (see Bernardo and Rieu 1973: 323, n. 44).

11. The growing concern with 'territorial violations' in the eighteenth century received its philosophical expression in the works of the Swiss jurist Emmerich de Vattel (1757, bk. 7: sec. 2): 'Since the slightest usurpation of another's territory is an injustice, to avoid this, and to abolish all subjects of discord and occasions for quarrels, one must mark clearly and with precision the boundaries of territories.'

12. Eighteenth-century precedents for the creation of administrative–territorial divisions include plans by Turgot in the 1760s, the geographer Letrosne in 1779, and the Assembly of Notables in 1787 (Berlet 1913: 39–43).

13. Archives Nationales F(2) I 447; Archives du Ministère des Relations Extérieures Limites 461, no. 32; Archivo Histórico Nacional Estado libro 673, fols. 303–13. This was not the only instance of a wandering border stone, see also Archives du département des Pyrénées-Orientales AC La Tor 2 and Archivo del Ministerio de Relaciones Exteriores TN 221–2 (1850). For some reflections on boundary stones as symbols of conflict, see Fernandez (1990).

14. Henri Baudrillart (1893, vol. 3: 333) wrote of the Roussillon that 'landowners are forced to use Catalan, it is imposed on them by the peasants'. On the nineteenth-century gallicisation of elites in the Pyrenees-Orientales, see McPhee (1977).

References

Agulhon, M. 1979. *Marianne au combat*. Paris.
   1982 [1970]. *The Republic in the village: the people of the Var from the French Revolution to the Second Republic*. Cambridge.
Alliès, P. 1980. *L'invention du territoire*. Grenoble.
Anderson, B. 1983. *Imagined communities: reflections on the origins and spread of nationalism*. London: Verso.
Armstrong, J. 1982. *Nations before nationalism*. Chapel Hill, NC: University of North Carolina Press.
Artola, M. 1982. *La hacienda del antiguo régimen*. Madrid.
Assier-Andrieu, L. 1981. *Coutume et rapports sociales: étude anthropologique des communautés paysannes du Capcir*. Paris.
   1987. *Le peuple et la loi: anthropologie historique des droits paysans en Catalogne française*. Paris.
Barth, F. 1969. 'Introduction', in F. Barth (ed.), *Ethnic groups and boundaries: the social organization of cultural difference*. Boston: Little Brown.
Baudrillart, H. 1893. *Populations agricoles de la France*. 4 vols. Paris.
Beaune, C. 1986. *Naissance de la nation France*. Paris.
Bendix, R. 1964. *Nation-building and citizenship*. New York.

Berenson, E. 1985. *Populist religion and left-wing politics in France, 1830–1852.* Princeton: Princeton University Press.

Berlet, C. 1913. *Les tendances unitaires et provincialistes en France à la fin du XVIIIe siècle.* Nancy.

Bernardo, D. and B. Rieu 1973. 'Conflit linguistique et revendications culturelles en Catalogne-Nord', in *Les temps modernes* (Minorités nationales en France), nos. 324–6.

Bezucha, R. 1975. 'Mask of revolution: a study of popular culture during the Second French Republic', in R. Price (ed.), *Revolution and reaction: 1848 and the Second French Republic.* London.

Bloch, M. 1966. *French rural history: an essay on its basic characteristics.* Trans. J. Sondenheimer. Berkeley: University of California Press.

Braudel, F. 1966. *The Mediterranean and the Mediterranean world in the age of Philip II.* 2 vols. New York.

Brette, A. 1907. *Les limites et les divisions territoriales de la France en 1789.* Paris.

Brousse, E. 1899. *La Cerdagne française.* Perpignan.

Brunet, M. 1986. *Le Roussillon: une société contre l'Etat, 1780–1820.* Toulouse.

Brunhes, J. and C. Vallaux 1921. *La géographie de l'histoire.* Paris.

Clark, G. 1961. *The seventeenth century.* New York.

Cohen, A. P. 1986. *Symbolizing boundaries: identity and diversity in British cultures.* Manchester: Manchester University Press.

Comellas Garcia-Llera, J. 1963. *El Trienio Constitucional.* Madrid.

Costa i Costa, J. 1983. 'Aproximació lingüística al català de Cerdanya', in *Primer congrés internacional: Institut d'Estudis Ceretans.* Puigcerdà.

Davis, N. Z. 1975. *Society and culture in early modern France.* Stanford: Stanford University Press.

Defourneaux M. 1971. *Les relations franco-hispaniques: actes du 94e congrès national des sociétés savantes.* Paris.

Deutsch, K. 1953. *Nationalism and social communication: an inquiry into the foundations of nationality.* Cambridge, MA.

1963. 'Some problems in the study of nation-building', in K. Deutsch and W. Foltz (eds.), *Nation-building.* New York.

Dion, R. 1945. *Les frontières de la France.* Paris.

Dujardin, V. 1891. *Souvenirs du Midi par un homme du Nord.* Perpignan.

Febvre, L. 1973. '*Frontière*, the word and the concept', in P. Burke (ed.), *A new kind of history: from the writings of Lucien Febvre.* London.

Fernandez, J. 1990. 'Enclosures: boundary maintenance and its representations over time in Asturian mountain villages (Spain)', in E. Ohnuki-Tierney (ed.), *Culture through time: anthropological approaches.* Stanford: Stanford University Press.

Font i Rius, J. M. 1985. *Estudis sobre els drets i instituciós locals en la Catalunya medieval.* Barcelona.

Ford, R. 1970 [1846]. *Gatherings from Spain.* London.

Freeman, S. T. 1968. 'Corporate village organisation in the Sierra Ministra: an Iberian structural type', in *Man* 3: 477–84.

1970. *Neighbors: the social contract in a Castilian hamlet.* Chicago: University of Chicago Press.

Galceran i Vigué, S. 1973. *L'antic sindicat de Cerdanya: estudi socio-econòmic basat en la historia inedita dels segles XIV al XVII, inclusius.* Gerona.
1978. *La indústria i el comerç a Cerdanya.* Barcelona.
Gavignaud, G. 1980. 'L'organisation économique traditionnelle communautaire dans les hauts pays catalans', in *Conflent, Vallespir, et Montagnes Catalanes.* Montpellier.
Girard d'Albissin, N. 1969. 'Propos sur la frontière', *Revue historique du droit français et étranger* 47: 290–407.
Gomez-Ibáñez, D. A. 1975. *The western Pyrenees: differential evolution of the French and Spanish borderland.* Oxford.
Grillo, R. D. 1980. 'Introduction', in R. D. Grillo (ed.), *'Nation' and 'state' in Europe: anthropological perspectives.* London: Academic Press.
Guichonnet P. and C. Raffestin 1974. *Géographie des frontières.* Paris.
Guiter, H. 1966. *Atlas linguistique des Pyrénées-Orientales.* Paris.
Gutton, J. P. 1979. *La sociabilité villageoise dans l'ancienne France: solidarités et voisinages du XVIe au XVIIIe siècle.* Paris.
Hinojosa, E. de 1915. *El elemento germánico en el Derecho español.* Madrid.
Hoffman, J. F. 1964. *La peste à Barcelone.* Paris and Princeton, NJ.
Hugo, A. 1824–5. *Histoire de la campagne d'Espagne en1823.* 2 vols. Paris.
Hunt, L. 1984. *Politics, culture, and class in the French Revolution.* Berkeley: University of California Press.
Kamen, H. 1981. *Spain in the later seventeenth century.* London and New York.
Kohn, H. 1967. *Prelude to nation-states: the French and German experience, 1789–1815.* Princeton: Princeton University Press.
Konvitz, J. 1987. *Cartography in France, 1660–1848: science, engineeering, and statecraft.* Chicago.
Lapradelle, P. de 1928. *La frontière: etude de droit international.* Paris.
Lefebvre, H. 1963. *La vallée de Campan.* Paris.
Le Goff, J. and J.-C. Schmitt (eds.) 1981. *Le charivari.* Paris.
Macartney, C. A. 1934. *National states and national minorities.* Oxford.
Margadant, T. W. 1979. 'French rural society in the nineteenth century: a review essay', *Agricultural History* 53: 644–51.
Martin, M. M. 1951. *The making of France: the origins and development of national unity.* London.
McPhee, P. 1977. The seed-time of the Republic: society and politics in the Pyrénées-Orientales. University of Melbourne, PhD thesis.
1978. 'Popular culture, symbolism, and rural radicalism in nineteenth-century France', *Journal of Peasant Studies* 5: 235–53.
Mercader i Riba, J. 1968. *Felip V i Catalunya.* Barcelona.
Mill, J. S. 1846. *System of logic.* London.
Noël, J. F. 1966. 'Les problèmes de frontières entre la France et l'Empire dans la seconde moitié du XVIIIe siècle', *Revue Historique* 235: 333–46.
Ourliac, P. 1958. 'La condition des étrangers dans la région Toulousain au moyen âge', in *L'étranger. Recueils de la société Jean Bodin pour l'histoire comparative des institutions,* 10: 101–8.
Ozouf-Mangnier, M. V. 1989. *La formation des départements: le représentation du territoire français à la fin du XVIIIe siècle.* Paris.

Palacio Atard, V. 1921. *El tercer pacto de familia*. Madrid.

Pastor, F. de 1933. La Cerdagne française. *Bulletin de la société languedocienne de géographie* 3: 170–5.

Payne, Stanley G. 1971. 'Catalan and Basque nationalism', *Journal of Contemporary History* 6 (1): 15–51.

Pitt-Rivers, J. 1954. *People of the Sierra*. London.

Pop, I. 1968. *Voisinage et bon voisinage en droit international*. Paris.

Poumarede, J. 1984. 'Les syndicats de vallée dans les Pyrénées françaises', in J. Blum (ed.), *Les communautés rurales*, pp. 385–409.

Regla Campistol, J. 1951. 'El tratado de los Pirineos de 1659', *Hispania* 11: 101–66.

Renaut, F. P. 1922. *Le pacte de famille et l'amérique: la politique coloniale franco-espagnole de 1760 à 1792*. Paris.

Rubio, J. 1974. *La emigración española a Francia*. Barcelona.

Sahlins, P. 1984. 'Nationality, residence, and the 'capitation' tax in the eighteenth-century French Cerdagne', in *Primer congrés d'història moderna de Catalunya*. (2 vols.) 1: 411–18. Barcelona.

 1989. *Boundaries: the making of France and Spain in the Pyrenees*. Berkeley: University of California Press.

 1990a. 'Natural frontiers revisited: France's boundaries since the seventeenth century', *American Historical Review* 95: 1423–51.

 1990b. 'The use and abuse of the nation', *Critique of Anthropology* 10: 73–96 (special issue on 'Family, class and nation in Catalonia').

 1994. *Forest rites: the War of the Demoiselles in nineteenth-century France*. Cambridge: Harvard University Press.

Sanabre, J. 1956. *La acción de Francia en Cataluña en la pugna por la hegemonía de Europa*. Barcelona.

 1961. *El Tractat dels Pirineus i la mutilació de Catalunya*. Barcelona.

Sanchez Mantero, R. 1975. *Liberales en exilio: la emigración política en Francia en la crisis del antiguo régimen*. Madrid.

 1981. *Los cien mil hijos de San Luis y las relaciones franco-españoles*. Sevilla.

Sermet, J. 1962. 'Les communications pyrénéennes et transpyrénéennes', in *Actes du 2e congrès international d'études pyrénéennes*. (7 vols.) 7: 59–193. Toulouse.

 1983. *La frontière des Pyrénées*. Lourdes.

Smith, A. E. 1986. *The ethnic origins of nations*. London.

Sorre, M. 1913. *Les Pyrénées méditerranéennes*. Paris.

Soulet, J. F. 1974. *La vie quotidienne dans les Pyrénées sous l'Ancien Régime*. Paris.

Thiers, A. 1823. *Les Pyrénées et le midi de la France pendant les mois de novembre et décembre, 1822*. Paris.

Tilly, C. 1979. 'Did the cake of custom break?', in J. Merriman (ed.), *Consciousness and class experience in nineteenth century Europe*. New York.

Timbal, P. C. 1958. 'Les lettres de marque dans le droit de la France médiévale', in *L'étranger. Recueils de la société Jean Bodin pour l'histoire comparative des institutions* 11: 110–38. Brussels.

 1984. 'De la communauté médiévale à la commune moderne en France', in *Les communautés rurales. Recueils de la société Jean Bodin pour l'histoire comparative des institutions* 43: 337–48. Paris.

Torras, J. 1976. *Liberalismo y rebeldía campesina, 1820–23*. Barcelona. [First chapter translated as 'Peasant counterrevolution?', in *Journal of Peasant Studies* 5: 66–78, 1977.]

Torreilles, P. 1900. 'La délimitation de la frontière en 1660', *Revue historique et archéologique de Roussillon* 1: 21–32.

Toulgouat, P. 1981. *Voisinage et solidarité dans l'Europe du Moyen Age*. Paris.

Truyol y Serra, A. 1957. 'Las fronteras y las marcas', *Revista española de derecho internacional* 10: 107.

Tulla, A. F. 1977. 'Les deux Cerdagnes: example de transformations économiques asymétriques de part et d'autre de la frontière des Pyrénées', *Revue géographique des Pyrénées et du Sud-Ouest* 48: 409–24.

van Gennep, A. 1937-45. *Manuel de folklore français*, 3 vols. Paris.

Vast, H. 1894. *Les grandes traités de Louis XIV*. Paris.

Vattel, Emmerich de 1757. *Droit des gens*. Paris.

Vila, P. 1929. *La Cerdanya*. Barcelona.

Vila, Pau 1979. *La divisió territorial de Catalunya*. Barcelona.

Vilar, Pierre 1985. *L'Avenç*, no. 101.

Visscher, C. de 1957. *Theory and reality in public international law*. Princeton: Princeton University Press.

Wallman, S. 1978. 'The boundaries of "race": processes of ethnicity in England', *Man* 13: 200–17.

Weber, E. 1976. *Peasants into Frenchmen: the modernization of rural France, 1870–1914*. Stanford: Stanford University Press.

Zink, A. 1969. *Azereix, la vie d'une communauté rurale à la fin du XVIIIe siècle*. Paris.

3 A western perspective on an eastern interpretation of where north meets south: Pyrenean borderland cultures

William A. Douglass

In *Boundaries: the making of France and Spain in the Pyrenees* Peter Sahlins argues that French and Spanish national awareness evolved as an autochthonous process within the borderland area itself, rather than as an imposition from the outside (Sahlins 1989). He bases his conclusion upon historical developments in the Cerdanya Valley of the eastern Pyrenees.

The work has fascinating, counter-intuitive implications for historians and political scientists, since their usual assumption is that international borders crystallise where the limits of the hegemony of two political epicentres (in this case Paris and Madrid) meet and become stalemated.[1] Establishment of the border is therefore a reciprocal measure for consolidating and delineating the defence of their respective national sovereignties. In this view the border is truly the proverbial 'line in the sand', with the implication that the inhabitants of the borderlands are more or less passive and incidental agents of wider national purposes. Sahlins's argument that the inhabitants of the Cerdanya, although ethnically Catalan, precociously infused local disputes and competition for scarce resources with French versus Spanish connotations, well before the full maturing of the national distinctions between the two emerging nation-states, is therefore quite radical. At a stroke it turns the borderlanders into the architects of their own destiny, as well as catalysts in the nation-building process of both France and Spain.

From an anthropological viewpoint the argument also has some intriguing implications. The notion that the inhabitants of a valley could become faction-riven is scarcely news to anthropologists, well accustomed as they are to conflict and division even within households, let alone neighbourhoods, communities and valleys. The popular Spanish saying *pueblo pequeño, infierno grande* ('small town, large hell') comes to mind. However, that such factionalism can configure wider political arrangements is thought-provoking; that it can configure international borders is nothing short of startling.

Sahlins's treatment, therefore, possesses an uncanny ability to challenge conventional wisdom. To what extent can its findings be generalised to other borderland contexts? This is an empirical question that should stimulate considerable (and, I suspect, revisionist) research elsewhere. My concern here is whether Sahlins's argument is valid throughout the Pyrenean region? In my view the answer must be qualified, for I find the evidence and his analysis of it convincing when dealing with the historical realities of the Cerdanya. However, it must be noted that the east–west international dividing line running through the Cerdanya does not terminate at *its* boundaries. Rather, the French–Spanish border runs for the entire length of the Pyrenees – from the Mediterranean to the Cantabrian Sea. How applicable, then, is Sahlins's argument in the western Pyrenees, i.e. the Basque Country?[2]

To broach the question properly it is important to examine both the remote and recent history of the two areas. For all practical purposes Sahlins's historical baseline is the Treaty of the Pyrenees, signed between Spain and France in 1659, which essentially delineated the modern French–Spanish border (1989: 25–60). In his view, it was the actions and attitudes of the borderlanders that quickly gave the hypothetical division real meaning. His primary analytical time-frame embraces the subsequent two centuries, or until the mid-1800s. Sahlins does, however, give cursory treatment to the period preceding the treaty while providing an epilogue that considers 'States and Nations since 1868', which in actuality provides recent historical and almost ethnographic treatment of Catalan nationalism, as well as its local expression in the Cerdanya.

Historical configuring of the Pyrenean borderlands

How, then, can we characterise the remote and recent contrasts between the eastern and the western Pyrenees (see maps 3.1 and 3.2)? The question must be asked against the backdrop of *both* the contested hegemony of the Pyrenees by Spain and France *and* the fate of a Pyrenean tradition of foral law. Regarding the latter, the elaboration of a series of charters or *fueros*, codifying and preserving local custom, was so evident and ubiquitous from the Basque Country in the west to Catalunya in the east as to prompt the famed jurist Joaquín Costa to speak of a Pyrenean community characterised by a common system of primitive law (Costa et al., 1902). Over time there were clear differences in the historical fate of the eastern and western Pyrenees with respect to Spanish or French hegemony and the foral regime.

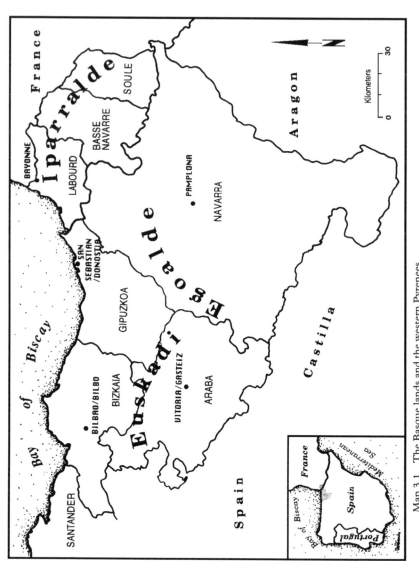

Map 3.1   The Basque lands and the western Pyrenees

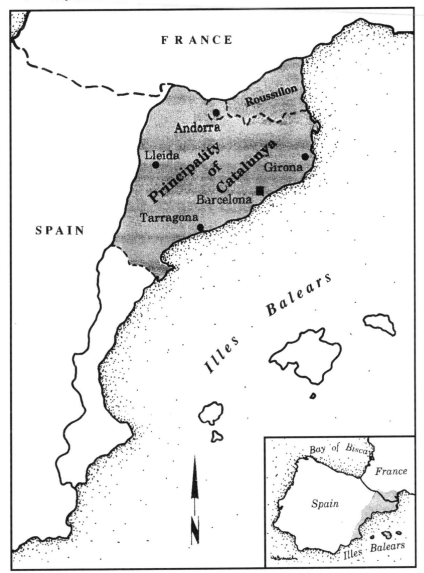

Map 3.2   Catalunya and the eastern Pyrenees

In the east, during the late fifteenth century, the Cerdanya and the wider Roussillon area passed from the control of Aragón (and an emerging modern Spain) to France and then back again, leaving a legacy which favoured some factions over others within local contexts as the pendulum swung (Payne 1973: vol. 1, 166–7; Sahlins 1989: 18–19). In 1542, 1543 and 1597 the French invaded the Roussillon, but were unable to hold it against counterattacks (Capdeferro 1967: 174, 178). However, when, in 1641, the Catalans placed their principality under French protection as a part of their revolt against Spain, Roussillon and the Cerdanya were lost to the Spanish crown, a loss that was formalised in the drawing up of the permanent border some eighteen years later under the Treaty of the Pyrenees (Payne 1973: vol. 1, 313–14). Indeed, Sahlins's book in large measure may be viewed as minute historical documentation of the consequences in the Cerdanya of this fluid political legacy.

The crystallising frontier in the west proved more durable and stable (though far from pacific) during the pre-treaty period, or throughout the sixteenth and early seventeenth centuries. The situation was further complicated by the shifting political fortunes of the kingdom of Navarra, which, since the thirteenth century, maintained a series of dynastic ties with the French crown, and then was absorbed by Aragón and subsequently invaded by Castilla in the early sixteenth century (Bard 1982: 59–97).

In the broadest sense the term *fueros* refers to local charters which guarantee the precedence of specified rights of a determined population over external legal codes and political claims. The scope and scale of a particular charter could vary considerably. Thus, Spanish jurists tend to view foralism as a part of the royal strategy for Christian resettlement of transitional zones during the reconquest of Iberia from the Moors (Bleiberg 1979: vol. 2, 142–4). In Castilla the earliest *fueros* were royal concessions to municipalities at the expanding margin of Castilian hegemony. In the thirteenth century King Alphonse X launched an only partially successful attempt to promulgate a *Fuero Real*, standardising Castilla's municipal charters. At the same time the Basque regions of Bizkaia, Gipuzkoa and Araba,[3] while incorporated into Castilla, had provincial *fueros* in addition to the municipal ones obtaining in some of their urban centres. In the fourteenth century Navarra had its overarching *Fuero General*, in addition to the particular ones of certain of its municipalities. León was another kingdom with both a general *fuero* and a number of more local ones (Bleiberg 1979: vol. 2, 142–8).

In the north-east we can speak of the *fueros* (plural) of Aragón encompassing the *cartes de població*, or municipal charters, and customary laws, or *constitucions* of Catalunya, after the twelfth century, or when Catalunya became a principality within the Aragonese kingdom. Neither the kingdom nor its principality had an overarching general *fuero*, but Catalunya, in particular, had a plethora of municipal ones (Rovira i Virgili 1977: vol. 4, 262–8).

Thus, the term *fuero* embraces a wide range of arrangements and purposes. As a rule of thumb it may be stated that the municipal ones tended to be short and concise, clearly constituting concession from monarchs to municipalities of certain autonomy regarding local affairs. These privileges operated within a narrow and predictable range since the language of former concessions was frequently adopted in later ones (with some local variation). The provincial *fueros* and those embracing entire kingdoms (e.g. Navarra's) tended to be extensive and wide-ranging documents which, through their hundreds of clauses, specified in surprisingly minute detail the customary bases of everyday life. Whether or not they were 'concessions' by monarchs, and hence rescindable 'privileges' held at their pleasure, or were codification of inviolable ancient customs which the monarchs were sworn to respect in perpetuity is at the core of a centuries' long power struggle between the Basques (including the Navarrese), on the one hand, and Spanish central authority on the other – a contest which continues at present.

Regarding the structure and fate of their respective foral regimes there is clear and considerable difference between the eastern and western Pyrenees. *Grosso modo* it may be stated that foralism demonstrated less staying power in the east than in the west. In the former it was championed by Aragón's baronial oligarchy as a counterweight to royal authority. Prior to the thirteenth century Aragón and Catalunya were classic feudal societies with a powerful landed nobility jealous of its prerogatives. Indeed, according to Shneidman, Aragonese nobles were so powerful that they were capable of ignoring their feudal obligation to heed their monarch's call to battle (1970: vol. 1, 220). When, in the mid-thirteenth century, King Jaime attempted to divide the realm between his sons, he was opposed by the nobles and forced to sign a humiliating document which severely impaired his authority (Shneidman 1970: vol. 1, 221). Shortly thereafter there surfaced documents called the *Fueros de Sobrarbe*, supposedly dating from the ninth century, but which many historians consider to be a fabrication. They gave rise to the famous oath whereby the Aragonese pledged their fealty to their monarch while retaining their independence. The key phrase, supposedly contained in the *Fueros of Sobrarbe*, was,

We, who are worth as much as you, make you our King and Lord provided that you guard for us our fueros and liberties, and if not, not. (Giesey 1968: 6)

Despite the dubious genealogy, Shneidman argues that the *Fueros of Sobrarbe* must be placed in historical context,

Although the *laws* representing the ancient traditions to which the nobility appealed were fabricated in the late thirteenth century, they accurately reflected the *tradition* of both Visigothic Spain and Merovingian France, where powerful monarchs were unknown. The spurious fueros represented what should have been set down in writing but wasn't: the system under which the kingdom had been governed since the hill-warriors freed themselves of foreign invaders (1970: vol. 1, 226).

Meanwhile, by the second half of the thirteenth century an increasingly powerful Catalan merchant class, oriented towards international trade, was becoming disenchanted with the nobility's prerogatives under the feudal charters or *usatges*. They employed their political influence in the *Corts*, or Catalan parliament, to substitute Roman Law for the outmoded feudal system. In the aftermath of a series of defeats at the hands of the Aragonese nobility the kings of Aragón made common cause with the Catalan merchant class (Shneidman 1970: vol. 1, 222–3). The Catalan nobility, far weaker than its Aragonese counterpart, had little choice but to join in a political coalition with the merchants (Shneidman 1970: vol. 1, 231).

The union of Castilla and Aragón in the late fifteenth century and the political ascendancy of the former over the latter (Payne 1973: vol. 1, 178), coupled with the revolt and defeat of the Catalans, had already begun to assail local privilege in the eastern Pyrenees. In the wake of the Revolt of the *Comuneros* in Castilla in 1520, when Castilian municipalities rose up in protest of increasingly intrusive and onerous royal administration of local affairs and in defence of their local privileges (Haliczer 1981: 143–4) and were defeated, foralism within the Castilian orbit was further undermined (Payne 1973: vol. 1, 182–3). Phillip II's invasion of Aragón in 1591 led to additional restrictions upon the Aragonese *fueros* (Capdeferro 1967: 178). During the seventeenth century the Portuguese and Catalans rebelled against Spanish rule, resentful of the greater tax demands and stricter administrative control of an over-extended state and empire (Elliott 1963). The Portuguese successfully seceded from Spain, while in 1653 the Catalans attained formal recognition of their political liberties with corresponding strict limits upon royal authority (Pi-Sunyer 1983: 18). However, in 1716 the Aragonese and Catalonian foral regimes were effectively abolished as charters structuring civic life by the *Nueva Planta* decree issued by the Bourbon victors in the aftermath of the War of Succession (Payne 1973: vol. I, 255–6).

In the west the Basque provinces of Bizkaia and Gipuzkoa, and, to a lesser degree, Araba, while firmly within the Castilian political orbit prior to the union of the crowns of Castilla and Aragón, made common cause in a largely successful defence of their *fueros*. Navarra, even after its setbacks in the early sixteenth century, remained a kingdom within a kingdom (Bard 1982: 104–48; Payne 1971: 32) until suffering a series of defeats (with consequent erosion of autonomy) in the Carlist Wars of the nineteenth century. The collective success of the Basque provinces in the western Pyrenees in defending their *fueros* is perhaps best epitomised by the fact that the Spanish customs houses were removed from the Ebro River, or the southern border of the Basque Country and Navarra, to the French–Spanish border in the Pyrenees quite recently, i.e. in 1841. It was only in 1876 that Basques for the first time became subject to conscription for Spanish military service outside their home area.

A critical distinction between the eastern and western Pyrenees regards the significance in the latter of the general (as opposed to municipal) *fueros* (those of Gipuzkoa, Bizkaia, Araba and the Kingdom of Navarra). In their language and spirit they rather echo the fabled *Fueros of Sobrarbe*. However, if in Aragón the intent was to defend noble privilege against royal encroachment, in the Basque region the result was to extend protection to the general populace, given the Basques' claim to collective noble status. The notion that all Basques were of pure and noble blood, stemming from the fact that they had never been under Moorish domination, was both formalised in legal codes and enshrined in Basque self-identity (Greenwood 1977). Indeed, the concept of collective nobility was frequently cited in the seemingly interminable (and, until the nineteenth century, largely successful) defence of foralism by both the Basques and Navarrese against the periodic attempts by the Spanish state to extend a uniform legal code and tax structure to the entire country.

It should be noted as well that in the western Pyrenees, or particularly in the case of Labourd, Basse Navarre and Soule, which constitute the French Basque area or Iparralde, as well as Béarn, there was a northern slope's equivalent of the Iberian foral regime with local charters (*fors*), an arrangement largely lacking in the east. It was only with the triumph of Jacobin centralism in the French Revolution that western Pyrenean local charters were abolished in France (Goyheneche 1979: 119–48; Jacob 1994: 3–6).

Finally, there is the consideration that the actual configuration of the frontier by the Treaty of the Pyrenees in the west more or less followed the crests of the mountains (Bard 1982: 129) while, as Sahlins deftly notes, in the case of the Cerdanya it provided an east–west division across a valley floor that was itself an ancient corridor for north–south trans-Pyrenean communication and movements (Sahlins 1989: 16–20). Consequently, in the west the frontier was established between discrete local physical and legal domains; in the east it was a more arbitrary division within physical and political continua.

Sahlins sums up the situation in the Cerdanya as follows:

> Living on the boundary, the Cerdans conceptualised the differences of French and Spanish territory and nationality long before these differences became apparent in the two states. Through their local struggles and disputes, the landowners, peasants, and municipalities of the two Cerdanyas gave meaning to these distinctions, bringing the nation into the village and the village into the nation. The struggles of propertied elites during the eighteenth century to win tax exemptions for their properties in the French Cerdagne led them to identify themselves as Spaniards; communities, in their opposition to these exemptions, saw themselves as French. The disputes of village communities across the boundary over limited ecological resources led them to adopt new national identities while never abandoning their local ones; and the communities' exclusion of 'outsiders' from their midst amounted to an assertion of their own nationality. The Cerdans came to identify themselves as French or Spanish, localizing a national difference and nationalizing local ones, long before such differences were imposed from above. (1989:286)

If in the Cerdanya valley local transnational relations tended to be confrontational and conflictive much the opposite obtained in the western Pyrenees. Writers like Lefebvre (1933), Descheemaeker (1950) and Gómez-Ibáñez (1975) emphasise the transnational agreements between adjacent border communities to introduce livestock onto one another's mountain pastures. These local agreements, *facerías* in Spanish and *faceries* in French, were tantamount to international treaties and were negotiated, signed and reaffirmed periodically with considerable ritual fanfare.

Such arrangements were not entirely lacking in the eastern Pyrenees. In Catalunya they were called *patzeries*. According to Rovira i Virgili, it was their purpose to resolve the frequent conflicts and disputes over the intervening mountain pasturage between valleys on opposite slopes of the Pyrenees (1977: vol. 5, 518).[4] A conflict-resolution interpretation of the *facerías*, as well, is not altogether lacking (Fairén Guillén 1946); however, according to Gómez-Ibáñez,

> The pastoral agreements, in replacing bloodshed with compromise, also became commercial and political instruments. To further trade within the mountains the treaties also protected the free circulation of persons and goods. They enjoined the inhabitants of each valley to come to their neighbours' aid in case of emergency. The treaties were also treaties of peace. The valleys concluded them

independently of the central powers. After the fifteenth century, despite
continued French and Spanish wars, many treaties pledged their valleys to
eternal peace, whatever the quarrels of their titular sovereigns. Villages even
promised to warn their neighbours of approaching soldiery, and there were
instances in which citizens of these valleys refused to bear arms in the service of
Spain or France, citing their obligations to the medieval *facerías*. During the War
of Spanish Succession (1701–13) both the Spanish and French armies were
frequently thwarted in the Pyrenees by the inhabitants' refusal to fight or even
contribute to the military effort. Even during Napoleon's Peninsular Campaign
(1812) both sides resisted participation and collaborated to keep their
mountains peaceful. For three centuries the frequent wars between France and
Spain rarely troubled the trans-Pyrenean harmony. (1975: 45)

The contrast between Sahlins's description of the contentious and
fissiparous transnational relations in the eastern Pyrenees and Gómez-
Ibáñez's depiction of the cooperation and local sense of common
purpose in the west could scarcely be starker.

Modern echoes of ancient sounds

If we find marked contrasts between the eastern and western Pyrenees
in the remote historical transnational relations of their respective
borderlanders, what of the recent and contemporary periods? To frame
the question properly we must first consider the modern Basque and
Catalan ethnonationalist movements in terms of both their similarities
and differences. Ultimately, I will argue that such considerations help to
explain the differing quality of transnational relations in the two regions.
Of related interest are the ways in which both Iberian and wider
European developments have reconfigured internal divisions within the
Basque and Catalan regions of Spain.

   Given the labyrinthine nature of modern Basque and Catalan history
I will, of necessity, restrict my treatment to salient points of a general
nature. I would, however, begin with the caveat that much of what
follows should be regarded as matters of degree rather than of kind, for
I would argue that Basque and Catalan nationalism share common
elements and differ only in terms of their weighting. Above all I wish to
avoid an essentialist argument, since it is becoming increasingly
common in the literature to equate Basque ethnonationalism with ETA
violence in contrast to moderate, pacific Catalan nationalism, thereby
explaining the difference in 'ethnic' terms[5] rather than as a reflection of
differing historical and structural features.

   Both Basque and Catalan modern ethnonationalism began as nineteenth-century expressions of the wider flirtation with nationalism by
Europe's 'peoples without history', i.e. those lacking an ethnically

configured nation-state. In Catalunya the first stirrings of ethnonation-alist sentiment are discernible by the late 1830s, first reflected in a robust Catalan literary movement. Its very sobriquet, the *Renaixçença*, invokes its restorative nature, according to Payne:

The first book about the 'Catalan problem' – the development and representa-tion of Catalan political and economic interests – appeared in 1855 (in Castilian), but was couched in moderate terms, accepting the framework of an essentially integrated Spain. (1971: 18)

It was Valentí Almirall, arguably the father of Catalan ethnonation-alism, who, by 1875, despaired of achieving Catalan goals within a Spanish federalist framework. In 1882 the *Centre Català*, a coalition of several cultural associations, was formed to promote regionalism. In 1886 Almirall published his book *Lo Catalanisme*, 'the first categorical expression of political Catalanism' (Payne 1971: 19). In 1891 Catalan regionalists formed the *Unió Catalanista*. The Unió produced the ideologue Enric Prat de la Riba who, in 1906, published *La Nationalitat Catalana*, the political bible of Catalan ethnonationalism. According to Payne,

Prat defined Spain as the political state and Catalonia as the true fatherland of Catalans, who were said to constitute a distinct and fully developed nationality; hence their state must be altered to conform to their nationality. Catalan nationalism was not separatist but demanded a regional parliament and government and a fully autonomous regional administrative system, which would develop the economy, society, and culture of Catalonia while preserving its traditions. Catalanism was to be the vehicle of middle-class modernisation, promoting social harmony and well-being. (Payne 1971: 22)

The emergence of Catalan ethnonationalism paralleled rapid indus-trialisation of the Catalan economy with attendant radical labour politics in Catalunya accompanied by anarchist violence (Payne 1971: 22). Thus, Catalunya provided a classic context for the struggle between class and ethnicity – divided loyalties which at any given time threatened to undermine patriotism on the one hand and class solidarity on the other.

Consequently, the history of Catalan ethnonationalism is extraordina-rily complex as factions established their own political parties and formed coalitions of convenience with one another and even, at times, with non-Catalanist ones. However, in broad terms it might be stated that Catalanism: 1) wished to recapture the greater political autonomy of Catalunya's former golden age, 2) aspired to economic development by wresting control of Catalan affairs from an inefficient and corrupt Spanish state apparatus, and 3) sought to defuse the threat of a growing socialist challenge from an expanding and increasingly militant industrial work force that was itself becoming less Catalan in its makeup due to massive in-migration from other parts of Spain. This ultimate concern underscores the elitist, bourgeois and ultimately conservative dimension that is one of the several faces of Catalan ethnonationalism, although in fact throughout its history the movement has a history of 'pacting' across class lines. Thus, it might be argued that Catalan ethnonationalism is, at its core, founded upon compromise between cultural and class concerns, although the coalition is intrinsically fragile and subject to schism (Pi-Sunyer 1985: 110–11, 114–16).

In terms of political successes, it might be argued that the greatest triumph to date of Catalan ethnonationalism was the Statute of Autonomy achieved under the Spanish Republic (1930–9) which empowered a Catalan *Generalitat* with its own parliament and presidency. Franco's victory and the execution of Catalan President Luis Companys in 1940 drove the movement underground for the many long years of the Franco dictatorship. Despite a laundry list of repressive measures (prohibition of Catalan political expression, suppression of the language, etc.), *Catalanisme*, which in a broad sense includes both exclusively Catalanist parties and the PSC or *Partido Socialiste Catalane* (with its dual leftist and ethnonationalist political agenda) has emerged as the major political force in Catalunya during the post-Franco era.

Between 1882 and 1888 a young Basque, Sabino de Arana y Goiri (1865–1903), son of a Bilbao industrialist, attended university in Barcelona where he experienced first hand the emerging Catalan ethnonationalist movement. He returned to Bizkaia and, in 1895, founded the PNV (*Partido Nacionalista Vasco*) or Basque Nationalist Party (Clark 1979: 41–3).

I have noted that modern Catalan ethnonationalism, at least in part, may be depicted as a response to the danger posed to Catalan culture by the arrival of other Spaniards in search of employment in a rapidly industrialising Catalunya. It can also be characterised as a middle-class alternative to working-class radical politics. In this regard there is little to distinguish the Basque and Catalan movements, since the Basque region, and particularly Bizkaia, was Spain's other emerging industrial centre and competed with Catalunya as a destination for migrant labourers from throughout the country. Arana was explicit in viewing this migration as the potential death-knell of Basque culture. His handful of followers were clearly middle-class persons who espoused the nascent movement as an antidote or alternative to Bilbao's emerging radical working-class politics.

Like Catalanism, Basque ethnonationalism enjoyed political successes during the Spanish Republic. However, the relationship between the

Basques and the Republican government in Madrid were strained by the former's strong emphasis upon Catholicism and their suspicion of an increasingly secular, and even anti-clerical, Spanish state (Payne 1971: 43). At the time of Franco's uprising the Basque Statute of Autonomy was still languishing in political limbo, unapproved by the Spanish parliament. The need to keep Gipuzkoa and Bizkaia in the Republican camp (Araba and Navarra were a part of the insurgency) prompted its expedient wartime passage – empowering the Basques to create a parliament and presidency. However, Basque resistance collapsed after only nine months and the Basque government became an underground force within Spain with many of its members living abroad as political exiles.

Unlike Catalanism, during the repressive Franco years there was a schism within the Basque ethnonationalist movement between the supporters of a moderate Basque Nationalist Party, advocating patience and passive resistance, and a more radical and youthful ETA (*Euzkadi eta Azkatasuna* or Basque Country and Freedom) faction disposed to answer Franquist oppression with violence. The resulting cycle of action and reaction has produced western Europe's second bloodiest confrontation (after that in Northern Ireland) over the past three decades. In the aftermath of the Franco years Basque ethnonationalist political parties have constituted an electoral majority, if not a working coalition, within Basque politics (excepting Navarra).

From the outset there were certain salient differences between the historical backgrounds and contemporary settings of Catalan and Basque nationalism. Catalunya had its tradition of *pactisme* or pact-making, legacy of the medieval political compromising between the nobility and the emerging bourgeoisie that was considered earlier.[6] In terms of both territory and population Catalunya constituted a greater 'critical mass' within Spain,[7] and hence was arguably capable of absorbing considerable migration without losing its character. Furthermore, the Catalan language was alive and well (Bratt Paulston 1987: 49), although languishing as the popular vernacular within a diglossic relationship with Castilian, which had become Catalunya's more esteemed cultural and administrative medium (Payne 1971: 18). Finally, Catalunya, both culturally and linguistically, was a part of a wider Latin world which embraced most of the Iberian peninsula as well. Thus, migrants to Catalunya were able to assimilate with relative ease. Indeed, Woolard underscores Catalunya's long-standing tradition as a *terra de pas*. She notes,

This phrase has no neat translation in English. Literally, 'step-land' or 'land of passage', it refers to Catalonia's geographical position, which makes it a frontier zone where population movements occurred during the social and political formation of Europe and trade routes were articulated under the Catalan domination of the Mediterranean. Romans, Visigoths, Occitans, French, Castilians, Italians and Jews are just some of the cultural groups that have left their mark on Catalonia. For this reason most commentators discount any claim of Catalan racial purity. (1986: 59, 69)

In contrast, it might be argued that at the advent of its ethnonationalist movement the Basque Country was both more alienated from, while integrated into, Spain than was Catalunya. Basque alienation stemmed from chagrin over the recent defeat in the last Carlist War (1873–6), which had resulted in the formal abolition of the *fueros* by the victors which was unaccepted by the vanquished (Payne 1971: 35). Remember that the Catalans had lost their juridical autonomy more than a century and a half earlier. Integration was a function of the Basque area's relative small size in terms of both population and territory, as well as its history of involvement in wider Spanish affairs. Thus, while Catalunya, with its Mediterranean orientation, remained apart and aloof from both the Spanish national and imperial enterprises until the eighteenth century (Pi-Sunyer 1983: 24–8), the Basques, from the outset, were the handmaidens of empire, providing it with many of its mariners, missionaries, mercenaries and merchants (Douglass and Bilbao 1975).[8] Within the Basque Country itself there had been steady erosion and marginalisation of the Basque language. By Arana's time it had all but disappeared from Araba and Navarra (except for a few northern mountain villages) and was essentially confined to the rural districts of Bizkaia and Gipuzkoa. Its very survival was in serious doubt, exacerbated by the fact that the language had practically no written literary tradition and its speakers were divided among a bewildering variety of dialects and subdialects. Conversely, Catalan had both a rich literature and common literary standard (Bratt Paulston 1987: 47). Thus, Basque, in its many guises, was the vernacular of a few hundred thousand speakers, while standard Catalan was used by several millions. Furthermore, Basque is a non-Indo-European language that is difficult for a Romance-language speaker to learn, a factor which inhibited the assimilation of non-Basque migrants resident in the Basque area.

It may therefore be argued that Basque culture was considerably more threatened than was its Catalan counterpart by the in-migration of Spanish workers. The bitter defeat and subsequent loss of the foral regime were a living memory for Basques. Given the disparity in size of territory and autochthonous population between the Basque Country and Catalunya, the impact of the same number of Spanish immigrants upon local life was considerably greater for the Basques than for the

Catalans. In Catalunya there was incentive for the migrants to learn Catalan, which remained a widely used vernacular even in the urban centres, whereas in the Basque Country there was neither incentive nor a need to learn Basque, particularly since it was scarcely heard in any Basque city. Furthermore, in Catalunya newcomers were actively encouraged to assimilate. They, or certainly their children, were readily accepted as 'Catalans' given the heterogeneous biological makeup of the Catalan population. Conversely, 'Basqueness' was defined much more in racial terms, harking back to the medieval notion of a Basque racial purity unsullied by the infidel as justification of the concept of Basque collective nobility and attendant privilege. In short, *vis-à-vis* outsiders Catalan ethnicity tends to be *inclusive* whereas Basque ethnicity is more *exclusive*.[9]

To my mind, the above factors help to 'explain' why Basque ethnonationalism strikes a less compromising pose than its Catalan counterpart, whether assuming the guise of Arana's denigration of non-Basque Spaniards as racially inferior 'maketos' who should be repatriated, or ETA's violence. That is, late nineteenth- and subsequent twentieth-century developments, both locally and within the wider Spanish context, were far more ominous threats to the persistence of Basque than of Catalan culture. The sheer magnitude of Catalan territory, population and economic clout translated more readily into influence and staying power, making it more feasible for Catalans to pursue a more processual rather than confrontational political agenda.

And what of the Roussillon and Iparralde during the modern era? Both are tiny in terms of population and territory[10] within the broader context of the French hexagon, as well as with respect to their corresponding Catalan and Basque areas of Spain. Agriculture and, in recent times, tourism dominate the economies of both the Roussillon and Iparralde.

Given the evident economic differences for about the last century and a half between a developed France and a less developed Spain, the Catalan and Basque borderlands pose a modern anomaly. To wit, both the Roussillon and Iparralde constitute economic backwaters within the stronger French economy whereas Catalunya and Egoalde (the Spanish Basque Country including Navarra) are the twin industrial pillars of the weaker Spanish one. Both Sahlins (1989: 280–6) and Gómez-Ibáñez (1975: 56–133) agree that this disparity between the two nation-state economies has configured transnational relations in both the eastern and western Pyrenees since at least the mid-nineteenth century and continues to do so at present.

While the statement holds true at a general level, again the details differ between the two areas. It is with regards to state infrastructure, defined broadly to include, for example, schools, roads and medical care, that there is the greatest similarity between the eastern and western French Pyrenean borderlands. The quality of services improved much earlier in France than in Spain, with evident gains in the 'quality of life' in the Roussillon and Iparralde. Arguably, then, they were subjected to greater assimilative forces within their wider state settings than were Catalunya and Egoalde. As tiny tiles within the French mosaic, the Roussillon and Iparralde were clearly quite vulnerable to assimilative forces of external origin, which is not to say that the outcome was identical in the two areas.

Eugen Weber's classic text argues that it was only during the nineteenth century that French peasants were transformed into Frenchmen and, by extension, that French regional cultures were integrated into a wider national economy and polity (1976). However, there is evidence that the process was more pronounced in the Roussillon than in Iparralde. Indeed, in the wake of the French Revolution, when French Basques lost their foral status, Iparralde was one of the more recalcitrant regions of the new France in accepting central authority. Initially, it was imposed upon the region militarily (Goyheneche 1961: 59–64) and received only grudging acceptance throughout the nineteenth century. Called to service in the French army, young French Basques regularly slipped across the frontier and entered the robust stream of Basque emigration to both North and South America (Douglass and Bilbao 1975: 123–4). Arguably, it was only during and since World War I that Iparralde began to manifest genuine support for French national purposes (Jacob 1994: 55–7).

It is fair to say that both the Roussillon and Iparralde have been marginalised with regard to the respective Catalan and Basque ethnonationalist movements. However, this is more the case regarding the former than the latter. Catalanism in the Roussillon is limited to a nascent concern with preserving the Catalan language. At the same time, within Spain's Catalan ethnonationalist movement the notion of a 'greater Catalunya' encompassing the Roussillon is but a minor concern for even the most ardent nationalists.[11]

Conversely, Iparralde has served as a refuge for Basque political exiles – whether escaping the defeat of the Carlist forces in the nineteenth century or Franco's victory in the twentieth. During the Franco years the 'moderate' Basque National Party and Basque Government-in-exile used Iparralde (as well as various centres of the Basque emigrant diaspora) as a haven from which to engage in anti-Franco political propaganda, while a more 'radical' ETA staged its *ekintzak*, or actions, across the frontier.

As a result of their differing histories and roles within contemporary structures and struggles, there are evident differences between the Roussillon and Iparralde in the ethnonationalist sentiment of their inhabitants. In the Roussillon the Catalanist movement remains largely literary and cultural (Gras and Gras 1982: 144; Guiter 1973: 300–2; Salvi 1973: 205; Sérant 1965: 225). The attempts to form a leftist-oriented ethnonationalist movement in the early 1970s managed to garner only 2 per cent of the popular vote (Beer 1980: 24). Arguably, even this was more a reflection of the political discontent in the aftermath of the events in France of 1968 than a deep-rooted ethnona-tionalist challenge to French authority. It is more difficult to dismiss ethnonationalism in Iparralde, since there its proponents, while always a tiny minority, were active prior to the French political crisis of the late 1960s. Indeed, some were punished for collaborating with the German occupational forces during World War II in the hope of furthering their Basque ethnonationalist agenda. Furthermore, Basque ethnonational-ists have managed to win electoral support in the 8 per cent range in the 1991 election (Jacob 1994: 381), and the French Basque ethnonation-alist movement includes factions willing to resort to violence (Jacob 1994: 366–78). Thus, while ethnonationalism is not a driving force or mass movement in either the Roussillon or Iparralde, it is clearly more important in the latter than in the former.

If politics provide the most evident contrast between the Roussillon and Iparralde, there is also a salient economic consideration that has configured certain differences in the transnational relations between the respective borderland populations of the eastern and western Pyrenees. In the eastern Pyrenees Spanish customs were established at the French–Spanish border in the seventeenth century, whereas in the western Pyrenees (as we have seen) Spanish customs houses were removed from the Ebro region to the French border as recently as 1841. As a consequence, the transnational exchange of goods and services in the eastern Pyrenees has long been organised along official lines. The ethnically Catalan political enclave of Andorra services the demand for 'bargain-hunting' created by the disparities between the French and Spanish economies. Conversely, in the western Pyrenees, since the mid-nineteenth century, contraband-running has emerged as a ubiquitous cottage industry – particularly in border communities.[12] Indeed, smuggling became so institutionalised within Basque culture that priests did not regard it as a matter for the confessional and the smuggler figure provides one of the most pervasive Basque ethnic stereotypes[13] during the modern era.

Pyrenean borderlands and the new Spain

With the implementation of democracy and a new constitution in the post-Franco era, at a stroke Spain went from being one of the world's most centralised states to Europe's most federalist one. Any region within the country was accorded the right to constitute itself as an autonomous community – the Basque Provinces, Galicia and Catalunya were given even greater latitude in recognition of their status as unique 'historical territories', i.e. those which were accorded a Statute of Autonomy under the Republican government in recognition of their linguistic and ethnic uniqueness.

In response to the restored opportunity both the Catalans and Basques entered into often protracted and bitter negotiations with Madrid. In 1978, under what is called the Moncloa Accord, moderate Catalan and Basque ethnonationalists settled for a modicum of regional autonomy which permitted restoration of the Generalitat and Euskadi (a name for the Basque Country coined by Arana and adopted by Bizkaia and Gipuzkoa during their brief period of relative independence during the Spanish Civil War). The former embraced all four traditional Catalan provinces, whereas the latter included only the three provinces of Araba, Bizkaia and Gipuzkoa. Within both Catalunya and Euskadi the Moncloa agreement has divided moderate from hard-line ethnonationalists. The former espouse gradualism as the efficacious path to true autonomy while the latter brand the accord a sell-out of Catalan and Basque interests by opportunistic careerists.

To the north of the French/Spanish border there has been an echo, if not an emulation, of this process. Mitterand's socialist government proposed devolution of authority to, and empowerment of, the regions of France, though in fact it delivered far less than it promised. The Basque area was to be allowed to constitute its own department and thereby extricate itself from the Bearnais-dominated *Département des Pyrénées-Atlantiques* centred in Pau (Jacob 1994: 334). There was no such proposal for political realignment in the eastern Pyrenees – providing additional evidence that Iparralde is more politicised in ethnonationalist terms than is the Roussillon.

On the Spanish side of the frontier there are interesting contrasts between Catalunya and Euskadi with regard to the consequences of their respective new Statutes of Autonomy. To my knowledge Catalunya has experienced little difficulty in encompassing its four traditional provinces – Girona, Barcelona, Lleida and Tarragona – into a single and rather seamless autonomous region. Nor was there any serious attempt to include the closely related, Catalan-speaking areas of Valencia and the Balearic Islands into a greater Catalunya. Rather, each has consti-tuted its separate autonomous region within the Spanish state.

The political realignment of the western Pyrenees has been config-ured through delicate (at times unsuccessful) negotiation and compro-mise. Arana was Bizkaian, and his original treatise regarding Basque nationalism was entitled, revealingly, *Bizcaya por su independencia* (1892). While, by the time of his death, Arana's vision had expanded to incorporate all seven traditional Basque areas on both sides of the frontier, it is safe to say that one meta-theme throughout the history of modern Basque ethnonationalist discourse is the other regions' con-cerns of being dominated by the industrial and demographic Bizkaian behemoth. Within Egoalde Navarra and Araba were always viewed as the weakest links. Both were, until quite recently, essentially agricul-tural. In Navarra the use of the Basque language was restricted to a small part of the northern extremity of the province while in Araba it was limited to a handful of villages. Then, too, Navarra has its legacy of having remained an independent kingdom well after the time when the three Basque provinces had been incorporated into the Castilian political orbit. During the nineteenth century Navarra constituted the core of the Carlist movement, a political sentiment which has subse-quently contested political turf with the modern Basque nationalist movement since the latter's inception.

In the late 1970s the Basque Nationalist Party (PNV) was the primary Basque political force in the Moncloa negotiations. Meanwhile, an earlier debate that raged within the ranks of ETA had resulted in a schism between ETA-m (military ETA), dedicated to an uncompro-mising military struggle, and ETA-pm (political-military ETA), which was prepared to negotiate while retaining the option of continued political violence. Political hardliners who were at least sympathetic to ETA-m formed the HB party or *Herri Batasuna* (People United), while a much smaller minority constituted EE or *Euzkadiko Eskerra* (Basque Country Left). HB contested and won elections but, following Sinn Féin's lead in Northern Ireland, refused to occupy its parliamentary seats (it did seize and exercise control of some town councils). Conse-quently, the political configuration of Euskadi was pretty much left up to the PNV.

To oversimplify, the initial objective was to incorporate all four Basque regions of Egoalde into a unified Euskadi. During the Second Republic, in 1932, there had been a serious, but failed, attempt to encompass Navarra within the Basque Statute of Autonomy process. During the subsequent Civil War Bizkaia and Gipuzkoa, on the one hand, and Navarra and Araba, on the other, had actually ended up as battlefield adversaries. This legacy notwithstanding, in the late 1970s there was a serious attempt to woo Navarra into the future Euskadi's fold. The PNV had but a small minority of the electorate in Navarra, and it is scarcely coincidental that the party's proposed candidates for Euskadi's first president, minister of education, and rector of the university system were all Navarrese. Despite such obvious inducement the effort failed, and Navarra constituted itself as an autonomous region. The relations between the two regions, while not hostile, are certainly wary. If politics may be regarded as human activity replete with irony, then Basque politics are no exception. The aborted attempt to incorporate Navarra into Euskadi under the Spanish regional auto-nomic process arguably gave more meaning and substance to a new internal boundary within the western Pyrenees than was evident in the Franco era.

And what of Araba? Clearly the stepsister and the least 'Basque' of all, at the outset of the process it was by no means certain that Araba would join Euskadi. The southern portion of the province was highly hispanicised and, as part of the Riojan wine-growing region of the Ebro, was as oriented towards an accessible Logroño as to its own capital city of Vitoria, travel to which entailed crossing a mountain range. Soria's decision to constitute the autonomous region of La Rioja, coupled with Euskadi's attempts to conduct Basque cultural missionary work in southern Araba, have converted the Arabese Rioja into a borderland of contested loyalties (Hendry 1991: 339–61; Parrish 1985: 242–4).

The evident and successful way of securing Araba as a whole for Euskadi was to name Vitoria-Gasteiz its capital. In this fashion Araba was proferred an enormous economic windfall in the form of both jobs and expenditure on infrastructure. The decision not only ensured Araba's participation,[14] it also avoided a potentially fatal struggle between Bizkaia and Gipuzkoa over political hegemony and economic advantage.

Earlier I claimed that Basque ethnonationalism has greater transna-tional significance and expression than does its Catalan counterpart. Thus, there have been several attempts by Euskadi to reach out to Iparralde, although I would not wish to overstate their importance. Indeed, most have taken the form of well-intentioned, benign, regional economic and cultural commissions that occasionally encompass Navarra, the Acquitaine or even 'the Pyrenees'. There are several political reasons for this. Mention might be made of the French government's sensitivity to anything that smacks of intrusion in French affairs. Both the Basque government-in-exile and ETA needed and cherished their haven in Iparralde during the Franco years and were therefore leery of antagonising French officials. However, the notion of haven is quite relative since GAL or *Grupos Antiterroristas de Liberación* (Anti-terrorist Liberation Groups), a shadowy coalition of Spanish nationalists with alleged ties to the military (Clark 1990: 66–8), has killed several ETA members resident in Iparralde. In recent years, with a socialist government in both Paris and Madrid, a number of ETA operatives exiled in France has been ordered to reside outside of Iparralde as a condition of remaining in the country. Others have been deported to Africa and Latin America or extradited to Spain to face charges. This, in turn, has produced mass demonstrations in Egoalde, with a boycott against French products and a backlash against French nationals. At times, vehicles with French plates have been vandalised. In short, during the post-Franco era there has been considerable basis for transnational political tension in the western Pyrenees, none of which is echoed in the eastern Pyrenean borderlands.

In light of such political volatility the transnational attempt to integrate a greater Euskadi has assumed cultural guise. During the late Franco era *Euskaltzaindia* (the Basque Language Academy) undertook the daunting task of producing a unified Basque language (*Euskera Batua*). Given the paucity of a Basque literary tradition, the fragmentation of spoken Basque into several dialects, and the imperative of developing a standard that could be taught in the emerging *ikastolak* (Basque language schools) and employed in the mass media, its proponents argued that the very survival of Basque as a modern vernacular was at stake. The two largest speech communities were the Bizkaian and Gipuzkoan ones. Within Egoalde, Gipuzkoan had traditionally served as the literary standard. At the same time, the entire exercise met with considerable indifference in Iparralde. Furthermore, the French Basque dialects posed the added problem that, orthographically, they incorporated a silent letter h (e.g. *harri* versus *arri* for 'stone') which was quite foreign to the Basque speakers of Egoalde. The compromise which emerged was that *Euskera Batua* is substantively closer to Gipuzkoan than any other dialect while incorporating the silent h. The ploy was designed to both defuse, at least somewhat, the Bizkaia–Gipuzkoa rivalry that always lurks in the background, while creating a strong incentive for Iparralde to join in. Indeed, a couple of decades into the experiment it seems fair to say that the strategy has worked, since an initial die-hard defence of the Bizkaian dialect has largely dissipated, Iparralde is increasingly on board and there is an emerging generation of young Basque speakers, as well as adult graduates of night school classes, who are fluent only in *Euskera Batua*.

Given all of the foregoing, there is an event held periodically since

1980 in the western Pyrenees which would be inconceivable in Catalunya. Reference is to *Korrika*, or a marathon, in which the 'witness' (a hollowed-out, baton-like object crafted by sculptor Remigio Mendiburu) is carried throughout the Basque Country (Del Valle 1993). Thousands participate in the 'happening,' which lasts for several days. The ostensible purpose is to raise money for Basque language instruction, so each kilometre is sold to sponsoring individuals and groups who then designate their runner for that portion of *Korrika*. The symbolism is blatant in that the route is carefully selected to cross, and thereby erase, the internal political divisions of Basque territory. Iparralde and Navarra are inevitably included. In the cartographics advertising each *Korrika's* route provincial boundaries and the French–Spanish frontier are omitted. Rather *Euskalerria*, or the greater Basque Country, is displayed as a seamless whole.

However, at another level *Korrika* manifests the profound divisions within the ranks of Basque ethnonationalists – a new kind of internal frontier that creates conceptual borderlands that are far less permeable than the French–Spanish one that Ramuntcho used to cross with such ease. For *Korrika* is designed to raise money for *Alfabetatze Euskalduntze Koordinakundea* (AEK), an extra-governmental organisation dedicated to Basque instruction and largely denied financial support by the Basque government (which has its own competing language instruction division). AEK is supported by the radical Basque left. Emotions reach fever pitch when the witness crosses the French–Spanish frontier or when it is carried by a family member of a slain or imprisoned ETA-operative. The Basque government remains icily aloof throughout the celebration of *Korrika*, and it is a rare moderate politician who volunteers to carry the witness. Thus, while *Korrika* seeks to transcend symbolically the internal boundaries within the Basque Country, ironically it underscores and enhances divisions within Basque society. In short, borders can be as much mental as physical with resulting 'borderlands' that are philosophical rather than geographical realms.

Pyrenean borderlands and the new Europe

Finally, we must consider that all of the foregoing is played out within a rapidly evolving western Europe 'without frontiers'. Since Franco's death Spain has joined both NATO and the EU. While the collapse of the Soviet empire and German reunification have complicated the western European political, economic and social agenda, frontiers continue to be erased rather than erected.

In December of 1992 French and Spanish officials met at Dantxarinea in the western Pyrenees for a brief ceremony celebrating the abolition of their border posts as a contribution to Europe's political and economic integration (*Deia*, 7 December 1992: 12). After the ceremony the French simply raised the barrier bar on their side of the border and walked away. The Spaniards were somewhat less certain about what to do, so they continued to staff their border post but ceased challenging travellers. The ceremony itself focused upon French and Spanish national agendas and the future of Europe.

While it was therefore easy to identify the 'winners' of this laudable exercise in international camaraderie, there was little attention given to the possible 'losers'. For it might be argued that those most affected by the abolition of the border, at least over the short term, are the inhabitants of the borderlands. Within their local context winning and losing are likely to assume quite different guises. My following remarks will be limited to developments and portents in the western Pyrenees, since I am much less knowledgeable about the evolving contemporary situation in Catalunya and the Roussillon.

Without purporting to be exhaustive, I would underscore six ways in which the new order created by the abolition of the border may force reconfiguration of the economic and political realities of the Basque borderland:

1. In the struggle of Basque nationalists for greater autonomy or even independence the frontier served as a strategic factor which created a sanctuary and staging area in the French Basque area for nationalists in Egoalde.[15] This was particularly true during the Franco era. More recently, the willingness of the French authorities to curtail Basque nationalist activities on French soil and to extradite alleged ETA members to Spain has diminished the strategic value of the frontier, but its abolition configures a new arena in which Basque nationalism will play out its destiny.

   The implications are not altogether clear. An argument can be made that, stripped of its northern sanctuary, virulent and violent Basque nationalism will be considerably weakened in Egoalde. Conversely, it might be argued that Iparralde is now less 'sanitised' or 'protected' from the influences of Basque nationalism. In this view Basque nationalism may well expand and strengthen there, particularly since the nationalist dream of unification of Euskadi and Iparralde (Navarra is another matter) is considerably more plausible once the French–Spanish border running through the Basque Country is removed or at least trivialised.

   There also remains the question of the viability of a Basque political identity once its foes are removed or their power reduced.

One unintended consequence of the obliteration of the French–
Spanish frontier may well be to depoliticise the significance of
Spanishness, Frenchness and Basqueness within a larger European
configuration. That is, if removal of borders weakens the premises of
nation-states, then what becomes of the aspirations of some Basque
nationalists to create their own?

2. The future of labour relations in the Basque borderland is a
particularly complex and clouded issue. Until recently there was
seasonal migration of female workers from Egoalde to the tourist
facilities of Iparralde. Other young women went as far afield as Paris
in search of work as domestics. Young men also found seasonal
employment as timber cutters in the Landes and Alps regions of
France (Douglass 1976). In short, wages in menial occupations were
higher in France and there was a shortage there of manual labourers
for much of the post-World War II period.

Obfuscated by the macroeconomic reality, however, was the fact
that Egoalde was one of the richest, most industrialised and urbanised parts of Spain while Iparralde was one of the poorest, unin-
dustrialised and rural regions of France. The frontier, and all that it
represented, essentially accommodated the northward flow of
manual labour while precluding professional persons from each side
of the border from seeking employment on the other.

With the impediments now removed, however, Iparralde confronts
a challenge of major proportions. Formerly, it already experienced
grave difficulty in meaningfully absorbing its educated young people
into the local economy. There is a longstanding 'brain drain' that has
been lamented regularly, with some French Basque nationalists even
contending that Paris purposely kept its Basque region economically
underdeveloped in order to defuse possible political dissent by
forcing the intelligentsia, the most likely dissenters, to migrate elsewhere in search of employment. Furthermore, a centralised French
state bureaucracy regularly sent officials to the area recruited from
throughout the French hexagon.

In Europe's Brave New World without borders it may well be that
the most serious challenge to French Basque professionals will come
from their fellow ethnics to the south.[16] There is but an embryonic
attempt to create a university in Iparralde, whereas there are robust
private and public universities in Egoalde churning out thousands of
graduates annually for a job market that already has 20 per cent
unemployment. The competition for scarce jobs may well turn out to
be a truly divisive issue for all of the inhabitants of the Basque
borderland.

3. A somewhat related issue to the labour question is that of political and economic control. Given the considerable demographic and economic imbalance between Egoalde and Iparralde, how do scarcely more than 200,000 French Basques, with an underdeveloped economy, view the Basque behemoth to the south? The answer is with a fair degree of concern and suspicion. Their worst fears envision a French Basque economy controlled from Bilbo (Bilbao). Now that Iparralde and Egoalde are linked by a fine freeway it is a mere two-hour drive from Bilbo to Baiona (Bayonne). In Egoalde it has been common practice for wealthy urbanites to buy a farmstead for conversion to a weekend retreat or summer home. The demand far exceeds the supply, particularly given that many of the rural districts of Bizkaia and Gipuzkoa have become semi-industrialised and polluted. The bucolic villages of Iparralde beckon, and its real estate prices are a bargain by southern standards. Not surprisingly, there is already a discernible real estate boom in which French Basques are the sellers rather than the buyers. In the long run will this be a force for integration or a source of irritation?

4. When the border formerly functioned to curtail the free flow of goods through tariffs, quotas and other regulations it created marked economic differentiation *within* the borderland which translated into considerable entrepreneurial opportunity and activity on both sides of the frontier. Consumer perceptions regarding the relative cost, variety and quality of goods stimulated a two-way traffic of 'day-trippers', shoppers in search of bargains and choice. Regarding the issue of variety, the French market, with its easier access (at the time) to European and world markets, was a kind of bazaar of modern consumers' goods whereas the more closed Spanish market featured its own national products.

Thus, it was common for French nationals to purchase fresh vegetables, bakery goods, canned foodstuffs, alcoholic beverages and jewelry in Irun (priced considerably below the French market). The stores in Irun also offered Toledo ware, mantillas, fans, statuary (Don Quixote and Sancho Panza) and other souvenirs of Spain. The Spanish nationals sought small household appliances (perceived to be superior to Spanish manufactures and cheaper than when imported into Spain), coffee and confectioneries (perceived to be of better quality). For the Spanish nationals the French Basque area was an echo, albeit a pale one, of that grandest of Pyrenean borderland shopping destinations – Andorra. For the purchase of a major appliance it was worth the longer journey to that monument to twentieth-century consumerism. Needless to say, erasure of the border undermines the bases of such two-way bargain hunting, not to mention the venerable institution of smuggling.

5. During the Franco dictatorship the French–Spanish border functioned as a moral barrier between Catholic Spain and secular France. Spanish prohibitions on pornography and gambling created considerable traffic across the border of individuals seeking *Playboy* and similar publications, the opportunity to view a risqué film excluded or censored beyond recognition by Spanish officialdom, or an evening of gaming in the casino at Biarritz. Ironically, in the post-Franco period the situation has been reversed, since Spain now has one of Europe's most liberal drug codes and the legalisation and spread of gaming to San Sebastián has all but brought the Biarritz casino to its knees (it is currently undergoing a major renovation in an attempt to survive). A glance at the offerings of Spanish newsstands confirms that Spanish publications need not take a back seat to any other country regarding freedom of sexual explicitness.

6. There is the question of how obliteration of the border will affect the demographic mix of its populace. Formerly, the need to curtail contraband and a more conservative attitude towards patrolling the perimeter of nation-state sovereignty justified a substantial force of non-Basque French *gendarmes* and Spanish *guardias civiles*, as well as customs agents, in the western Pyrenean borderlands. These officials (and their families) resided in the villages and small towns on both sides of the border. More than one *gendarme* and *guardia civil* married a local girl.

On the southern side of the border, with its more extensive history of resistance against Spanish political hegemony, the border officials were more disdained than respected. Even after years of residence they were never embraced as community members. Should a *guardia civil* marry a local woman the union was more a source of embarrassment than pride for the bride's family and the couple usually relocated. On the northern side of the frontier there is greater acceptance of such outsiders, and the marriage of their daughter to a *gendarme* may even be viewed as a stroke of luck by her farming parents. Thus, historically within the borderlands the interaction between Basques and non-Basques was considerably more strained in Egoalde than in Iparralde.

Under the impending new order of a unified Europe communities on both sides of the border stand to lose their internal 'others'. It may well be that, at least with regard to everyday interaction, measures designed to increase contact and communications among Europeans, ironically, may well have the opposite effect in the borderland communities of not just the western Pyrenees but the whole continent.

Conclusion

The real lesson of this comparative exercise is that even when borders remain relatively static, as has been the case with the French–Spanish border (arguably the most stable in western Europe), the borderlands themselves are in a constant state of flux. This is true whether responding to internal conditions within a frontier's configuring nation-states, the transnational relations between them, or the ethnonationalist agendas within two borderland cultures differing substantively from their respective French and Spanish national ones. Thus, *how*, as opposed to *where*, north meets south is subject to constant negotiation. By comparing and contrasting their historical and contemporary developments, I have shown that north does not meet south in identical fashion in the eastern and western Pyrenees. Thus, the ways in which borderlands evolve *along* international frontiers is as much a historical (and ethnographic) question as how they articulate *across* them. In this regard it may be argued that Sahlins's innovative thesis with regard to the Cerdanya, may be of limited applicability even within the Pyrenean context.

Nor do these considerations exhaust the complexity of borderland realities. Donnan and Wilson (1994: 3) note that borderlands evince their own culture which, to at least some degree, link their inhabitants economically, socially and even politically across international borders. Thus, in defining borderlands as frontiers, they note,

Frontiers . . . are *zones of varying widths*, in which people have recognisable configurations of relationships to people inside that zone, on both sides of the borderline but within the cultural landscape of the borderlands, and, as people of the border, special relationships with other people and institutions in their respective nations and states. (1994: 8; emphasis added)

When, as is the case with the politicised Basques and Catalans, shared ethnicity ignores (or at least conditions) state boundaries, while distinguishing the borderlanders from the wider French and Spanish populations, there is a classic situation in which states meet at their internationally recognised borders while nationhood transcends them. It is also within such contexts that we begin to discern a multiplicity of borderland realities. I would argue, at least as a working hypothesis, that the width of Donnan's and Wilson's zones will tend to be greater when borderlanders share ethnicity across borders which differs from that of their dominant (and defining) respective nation-state populations. This, in turn, creates a situation in which the concept of 'the borderland' requires disaggregation into a multiplicity of borderlands according to whether the defining criterion is political, social or economic (in some contexts other criteria such as religion may be in play as well). The several borderlands are likely to overlap and be hierarchically ordered in terms of their importance for the borderlanders themselves according to their situation within the frontier's physical, as well as symbolic, space. An example would be the inhabitant of southern Araba who may, in terms of his/her commitment to Basque nationalism, be a borderlander in a political sense while totally insulated by distance from the border's social and economic consequences.

The Arabese example underscores another dimension of borderlander reality, namely that insofar as borderland status both confers upon and provides the inhabitants with elements that may inform the construction of social identity, from the individual's perspective the outcome of the process is far from predetermined. Rather, which elements are invoked or denied, displayed or concealed, is situationally determined. When receiving a team of visiting Basque-speakers bent upon 'raising the ethnic consciousness' of their highly hispanicised Riojan brethren, an Arabese Riojan might become politely 'Basque,' parochially 'Riojan,' provincially 'Alavese' (rather than 'Arabese') or contentiously 'Spanish'. Then there are his/her suitcase identities. When in Gasteiz/Vitoria to pay a local levy he/she is 'Arabese' at the provincial office. If on the same trip he/she should pass by an agency of the Basque Autonomous Government to apply for an available economic subsidy, the applicant becomes an 'Euskadian'. On an outing to Baiona, entailing a visit to that city's Musée Basque, the Riojan excursionist will most certainly assume his/her 'Basque Borderlander' persona. When in Logroño to attend a lecture on viticulture it will be as a fellow 'Riojan'. Finally, when in Madrid (or Paris for that matter) our Arabese Riojan visitor will likely wear his/her 'Spanish' identity with heartfelt pride.[17]

It should also be realised that the borderlands are simultaneously both highly structured and liminal zones.[18] They are structured in the sense that they are the symbolic and physical spaces where state hegemonies meet and accommodate. In the present case 'Frenchness' and 'Spanishness' are defined in formal, structured fashion at the Pyrenean border with each state literally patrolling its boundaries. 'Basqueness', however, is more of a liminal reality (at least at present) which transcends the statist definitions and, indeed, plays with and off them. Thus, if the structured border definition seeks to limit the horizons (physical and mental) of the borderlanders, the liminal perspective invites them to a more 'oceanic' view. In this regard, the individual can become its explorer, navigator and even pirate[19] (terrestially incarnate as the contrabandist). The attitude that any borderlander assumes towards the border is likely to be situationally conditioned and to vary over time. Depending upon historical conjunctures and contemporary realities, the same borderlander is capable of assuming patriotic (defender of the border) and piratical (violator of its rules) stances.

Finally, as a part of the recent deconstruction of anthropological discourse there is an overriding concern with *multivocality* within the discipline. This chapter is a contribution to the parallel, albeit much less developed, interest in *multilocality* – i.e. the multiplicity of meanings ascribed by human actors to space (Rodman 1992: 643). The chapter suggests that borderlands provide ideal contexts in which to study the human use of physical and conceptual space from a multilocal perspective.

In this regard, one line of suggested inquiry is how multivocality *from the borderlanders'* viewpoint intersects with multilocality. That is, within the western Pyrenean borderlands three languages (French, Spanish and Basque) collide and intermingle. Geographical features thereby assume more than one toponym and the use of any of the available ones in a particular instance immediately accesses a particular discourse that excludes competing ones. For example, to employ the French, Spanish or Basque toponym for a mountain peak is to invoke entirely different worlds. From French and Spanish perspectives the discourse is political, geological, etc., whereas from the Basque perspective it invokes the enchanted landscape of dolmens, cave paintings, witches' covens, summer pastures, the seasonal hunt for migratory birds and wild boars, and so on. We might expect to find borderlands to be particularly rich contexts within which to discern such overlapping, yet competing, views of the physical (and social) landscape.

Notes

1. In Sahlins's words, 'The historiography of nation-building in France has thus emphasised the extent to which the nation was imposed from the top down and from the centre outward' (this volume, p. 32).
2. There is also the question of the central Pyrenees. While some scholars argue that there is a basis for distinguishing a transnational borderland in the central Pyrenees (i.e. between Béarn and Aragón), others are uncomfortable with the notion. *De facto*, it is in the central Pyrenees that the mountain chain is at its highest and widest, thereby constituting a true barrier to transnational communication and transportation (Gómez Ibáñez 1975:

4–5). Nor is there the shared transnational ethnicity that is evident in the Basque and Catalan cases. For present purposes, therefore, the comparison will be limited to the western and eastern Pyrenees.

3. In this chapter I choose to respect the orthographic preferences of the autonomous regions in post-Franco Spain when referring to place names. Thus the three provinces of Bizkaia (Sp. Vizcaya), Gipuzkoa (Sp. Guipúzcoa) and Araba (Sp. Alava) formed the autonomous region of Euskadi. Navarra (B. Nafarroa) opted to constitute a separate region designated 'Navarra'. Egoalde is the Basque term which refers to all four southern, or Spanish, Basque provinces (i.e. Bizkaia, Gipuzkoa, Araba and Navarra), while Iparralde refers to the three French Basque regions of Labourd (B. Lapurdi), Basse Navarre (B. Benafarroa) and Soule (B. Zuberoa). I have similarly respected the Catalan usage of Catalunya, Lleida (Sp. Lérida), Barcelona (Sp. Barcelona), Girona (Sp. Gerona) and Tarragona (Sp. Tarragona).

4. Elsewhere in this volume, Sahlins underscores the conflicts over mountain pasturage in the Cerdanya (pp. 38–42).

5. Such a view ignores the existence of the Black Flag section of the *Estat Català* (Catalan State) party which, during the 1920s, planned attempts on the life of King Alphonse XIII (Payne 1971: 39). It also overlooks the faction *Terra Lliure* (albeit a small one) which, until 1990, espoused achieving Catalan independence through violent means if necessary (Conversi 1993: 261). Nor does it take into account Catalunya's history of class violence (McDonogh 1986). Delgado (1993) argues that there are many expressions of violence within Catalan culture and that the 'pacific' image of the Catalans is more an 'official' line promulgated by the political establishment and church authorities than the popular will.

6. In this regard Payne provides an alternative view which is a vintage example of essentialist reasoning. When discussing the fact that Basque ethnonationalism has been dominated by a single party (the PNV) while Catalanism has generated a plethora he tells us,

Basque nationalism has been primarily represented by one fairly continuous organization from 1893 down to the present. Its supporters attribute this to their own sense of unity, responsibility, and loyalty; a more plausible explanation might point to the practical, co-operative, non-individualist spirit of the Basques which in many ways contrasts with the hyper-individualist, sometimes quasi-anarchist, adversary-oriented features of much of Catalan society. (Payne 1971: 36)

7. As of 1980 Catalunya, with 6.3 per cent of Spain's total land area, had 15.8 per cent of the Spanish state's total population; the figures for Euskadi/Navarra were 3.5 per cent of the national territory and 7.1 per cent of Spain's population (Saenz de Buruaga 1983: 93).

8. Payne (1971: 33) notes: 'The unity of Basque and Castilian interests was such that there were never any Basque revolts against the Spanish crown under the old regime.'

9. I qualify this statement since Catalans manifest a sense of superiority with regard to other Spaniards (Bratt Paulston 1987: 50–1) while over time (usually measured in generations) outsiders do assimilate fully into Basque society. Indeed, one analysis of the surnames of known ETA activists

revealed that only about half were of 'full' Basque descent (Clark 1984: 147–8).

10. Both Iparralde and the Roussillon constitute less than 1 per cent of French national territory. In the late 1970s there were approximately 280,000 inhabitants in the Roussillon (compared with 5,360,000 in Catalunya) and 228,000 persons in Iparralde (compared with 2,600,000 in Egoalde) (Gras and Gras 1982: 19).

11. In his chapter in the present volume, Sahlins devotes a section to nationalism in the Cerdanya. However, the argument deals almost exclusively with the clash between French and Spanish nationalism. The fact that Catalanism is mentioned only in passing would suggest that it is insignificant.

12. Basque fishermen also use their vessels to run contraband with the exchange often taking place on the high seas.

13. Perhaps best epitomised in the popular novel *Ramuntcho* by Pierre Loti (1896).

14. There is, however, recent evidence of a fissiparous trend within Arabese politics as evidenced by the founding of a new party, *Unidad Alavesa* (Arabese Unity), emphasising Araba's historical foral rights within a Spanish national context. In the 1994 elections, UA garnered 18.8 per cent of the Arabese vote, which gave it five seats in the Basque parliament (versus 11 per cent and three seats in 1990).

15. It is one of the many ironies of modern Basque history that centralist France, less tolerant than Spain of regional political diversity, permitted the display of the colours of the *ikurrina*, or Basque nationalist flag, as 'folklore', while, under Franco, possession of a Basque flag was a crime.

16. Given its historical success in retaining a modicum of political autonomy *vis-à-vis* the Spanish state, Egoalde has been more successful in generating and employing an autochthonous intelligentsia.

17. For further discussion of the situational uses of the elements of ethnic identity see, for example, Lyman and Douglass (1975) and Douglass and Lyman (1976).

18. To illustrate the point I offer the rather sardonic tale about the German geologist I encountered while doing fieldwork in the Navarrese border community of Etxalar. He wanted to study a particular rock formation which 'meanders' back and forth across the French–Spanish border between Etxalar and Sare. He had petitioned both Madrid and Paris for formal permission to do so. He moved to Etxalar and daily grew more depressed as his requests went unanswered. Finally, halfway through the summer, I suggested that he might simply walk up to the border guards themselves, offer them a cigarette, joke around a bit and then get on with the project. It worked like a charm and he managed to complete several summers of research without interference.

19. It might be noted that Basques figured prominently in the ranks of both the corsairs and pirates of the New World.

References

Arana y Goiri, Sabino 1892. *Bizcaya por su independencia*. Bilbao: Amorrortu.

Bard, Rachel 1982. *Navarra. The Durable Kingdom*. Reno: University of Nevada Press.

Beer, William R. 1980. *The unexpected rebellion: ethnic activism in contemporary France*. New York: New York University Press.

Bleiberg, Germán (ed.) 1979. *Diccionario de historia de España*. 3 vols. Madrid: Alianza Editorial.

Bratt Paulston, Christina 1987. 'Catalan and Occitan: comparative test cases for a theory of language maintenance and shift', *International Journal of the Sociology of Language* 63: 31–62.

Capdeferro, Marcelo 1967. *Historia de Cataluña*. Barcelona: Editorial M. & S.

Clark, Robert P. 1979. *The Basques. The Franco years and beyond*. Reno: University of Nevada Press.

1984. *The Basque insurgents. ETA, 1952–1980*. Madison: University of Wisconsin Press.

1990. *Negotiating with ETA. Obstacles to peace in the Basque Country, 1975–1988*. Reno, University of Nevada Press.

Conversi, Daniele 1993. 'Domino effect or internal developments? The influence of international events and political ideologies on Catalan and Basque nationalism', *West European Politics* 16 (3): 245–70.

Costa, Joaquín et al. 1902. *Derecho consuetudinario y economía popular en España*. 2 vols. Barcelona: Manuel Soler.

Delgado, M. 1993. 'El 'seny y la 'rauxa'. El lugar de la violencia en la construccion de la catalanidad', *Antropologia* 6: 97–130.

del Valle, Teresa 1993. *Korrika. Basque ritual for ethnic identity*. Reno: University of Nevada Press.

Descheemaeker, Jacques 1950. 'La frontière dans les Pyrénées basques (organisation, antiquité, fédéralisme)', *Eusko Jakintza* IV: 127–78.

Donnan, Hastings and Thomas M. Wilson 1994. 'An anthropology of frontiers', in Hastings Donnan and Thomas M. Wilson (eds.), *Border approaches: anthropological perspectives on frontiers*. Lanham, MD: University Press of America, pp. 1–13.

Douglass, William A. 1976. 'Serving girls and sheepherders: emigration and social continuity in a Spanish village', in J. Aceves and W. A. Douglass (eds.), *The changing faces of rural Spain*. New York: The Halstead Press, John Wiley and Sons, pp. 45–62.

Douglass, William A. and Jon Bilbao 1975. *Amerikanuak. Basques in the New World*. Reno: University of Nevada Press.

Douglass, William A. and Stanford Lyman 1976. 'L'ethnie: structure, processus et saillance', *Cahiers internationaux de sociologie* 61: 197–220.

Elliott, J. H. 1963. *The revolt of the Catalans. A study in the decline of Spain (1598–1640)*. Cambridge: Cambridge University Press.

Fairén Guillén, Victor 1946. 'Contribución al estudio de la facería internacional de los valles del Roncal y Baretons', *Príncipe de Viana* 7: 271–96.

Giesey, Ralph E. 1968. *If not, not. The oath of the Aragonese and the legendary laws of Sobrarbe*. Princeton: University of Princeton Press.

94   *William A. Douglass*

Gómez-Ibáñez, Daniel Alexander 1975. *The western Pyrenees. Differential evolution of the French and Spanish borderland.* Oxford: Clarendon Press.
Goyheneche, Eugène 1961. *Notre terre basque.* Bayonne: Editions Ikas.
1979. *Le Pays Basque.* Pau: Société Nouvelle d'Editions Regionales et de Diffusion.
Gras, Solange and Christian Gras 1982. *La révolte des régions d'Europe occidentale de 1916 à nos jours.* Paris: Presses Universitaires de France.
Greenwood, Davydd 1977. 'Continuity in change: Spanish Basque ethnicity as a historical process', in Milton J. Esman (ed.), *Ethnic conflict in the Western world.* Ithaca: Cornell University Press, pp. 81–102.
Guiter, Henri 1973. 'Catalan et français en Roussillon', *Ethnologie française* 3 (3–4): 291–303.
Haliczer, Stephen 1981. *The comuneros of Castile. The forging of a revolution 1475–1521.* Madison: University of Wisconsin Press.
Hendry, Barbara Ann 1991. 'Ethnicity and identity in a Basque borderland: Rioja Alavesa, Spain', Ph.D. dissertation, Department of Anthropology, University of Florida.
Jacob, James E. 1994. *Hills of conflict. Basque nationalism in France.* Reno: University of Nevada Press.
Lefebvre, Théodore 1933. *Les modes de vie dans les Pyrénées atlantiques orientales.* Paris: A. Colin.
Loti, Pierre 1896. *Ramuntcho.* Paris: Calmann-Lévy.
Lyman, Stanford M. and William A. Douglass 1975. 'Ethnicity: strategies of collective and individual impression management', *Social Research* 40 (2): 344–65.
McDonogh, Gary W. 1986. 'A night at the opera: imagery, patronage and conflict, 1840–1940', in Gary W. McDonogh (ed.), *Conflict in Catalonia. Images of an urban society.* Social Science Monographs No. 71. Gainesville: University of Florida Press, pp. 33–53.
Parrish, Timothy 1985. 'Agrarian politics and regional class formation in La Rioja, Spain, 1868–1975', Ph.D. dissertation, Political and Social Science, New School for Social Research, New York.
Payne, Stanley G. 1971. 'Catalan and Basque nationalism', *Journal of Contemporary History* 6 (1): 15–51.
1973. *A History of Spain and Portugal.* 2 vols. Madison: University of Wisconsin Press.
Pi-Sunyer, Oriol 1983. *Nationalism and societal integration: a focus on Catalonia.* Occasional Papers Series No. 15, Program in Latin American Studies, Amherst: University of Massachusetts.
1985. 'The 1977 parliamentary elections in Barcelona: primordial symbols in a time of change', *Anthropological Quarterly* 58 (3): 108–19.
Rodman, Margaret C. 1992. 'Empowering place: multilocality and multivocality', *American Anthropologist* 94 (3): 640–56.
Rovira i Virgili, Antoni 1977. *Història de Catalunya.* 16 vols. Bilbao: Editorial La Gran Enciclopedia Vasca. [Originally published 1922–34.]
Saenz de Buruaga, Gonzalo 1983. 'Towards a new regional policy in Spain', in Dudley Seers and Kjell Öström (eds.), *The crises of the European regions.* New York: St Martin's Press, pp. 86–126.

Sahlins, Peter 1989. *Boundaries. The making of France and Spain in the Pyrenees.* Berkeley: University of California Press.

Salvi, Sergio 1973. *Le nazioni proibite.* Firenze: Vallechi Editore.

Sérant, Paul 1965. *La France des minorités.* Paris: Robert Laffont.

Shneidman, J. Lee 1970. *The rise of the Aragonese–Catalan Empire 1200–1350.* 2 vols. New York: New York University Press; London: University of London Press.

Weber, Eugen 1976. *Peasants into Frenchmen. The modernization of rural France, 1870–1914.* Palo Alto: Stanford University Press.

Woolard, Kathryn A. 1986. 'The "crisis in the concept of identity" in contemporary Catalonia, 1976–1982', in Gary W. McDonogh (ed.), *Conflict in Catalonia. Images of an urban society.* Social Sciences Monograph No. 71. Gainesville: University of Florida Press, pp. 54–71.

4 The 'new immigration' and the transformation of the European–African frontier

Henk Driessen

Introduction

In the past decade much has been written about the transformations of European frontiers. Much of this discussion has focused on the internal borders of the European Union, with rather less attention being given to its external boundaries. In many countries of Europe, however, it is precisely at these external boundaries that a sense of Europeanness is most visibly expressed and challenged. Thus, the celebration of '1992' in Spain was suffused with meaning, which sensitised people to many aspects of their national and regional identities. It made boundary problems manifest in many different ways, including the Basque and Catalan ethnonationalisms discussed by Sahlins and Douglass (this volume). Not only was '1992' a powerful symbol of European integration, in particular the projected date of the completion of the single European market promoted by Euro-politicians and the mass media, but it also referred to the commemoration of the 'discovery' of America, the celebration of the World Exhibition in Seville, the Olympic Games in Barcelona, the remembrance of the fall in 1492 of the Muslim kingdom of Granada, and the expulsion of the Jews from Spain. The Christian reconquest of Granada completely altered the political and cultural map of the Mediterranean world. The expulsion of the Jews and *Moriscos* became one of the largest 'ethno-religious cleansing' operations *avant-la-lettre* in early-modern Europe. Ironically, while these crucial moments from five centuries ago were being commemorated, North Africans were returning to Spain by the thousands, often through the backdoor. In 1992, the numbers of people travelling clandestinely in small boats across the Strait of Gibraltar from Africa to Spain broke all records.

Since Spain's incorporation into the European Union, its southern border has been transformed into a *European* frontier – a frontier re-marked and reinforced. Central issues of border ethnography in nation-states are the politics, economics and symbolism of inclusion and exclusion of newcomers. This chapter discusses the transformation of the border between Spain and Morocco as a result of political processes within the European Union. A local perspective is taken, focusing on African immigrants in Spanish and Moroccan border towns (see map 4.1). The relatively uncontrolled influx of immigrants exposes the vulnerability of the Spanish and Moroccan states and the identities of their citizens. Several categories of 'us' and 'them' are discussed in the context of events which took place in the early 1990s.

The 'new immigration'

Immigration, ethnic revival, racism and identity are increasingly being recognised as urgent topics for anthropological research in Europe (McDonogh 1993). Spain makes a particularly interesting case for a study of these issues for two reasons. First, the 1970s and 1980s saw a rapid process of Europeanization of Spanish culture and society. Second, given its fast economic growth and its close proximity to the Maghreb, Spain has recently become a country of immigration.[1] It offers a good illustration of the changing European patterns of immigration since the early 1980s (King 1993; Miles 1993). Refugee and clandestine immigration have increased considerably. New immigrants are of both sexes, young, without documents, and are employed in the booming service sector and in agriculture, where they are vulnerable or indeed lay themselves open to exploitation. Additionally, they face discrimination with regard to housing, health and education. Many of these immigrants want to be accepted as European citizens, but are continually reminded of their cultural origins. Their presence thus raises issues of identity and boundaries, issues which are obviously of central concern to anthropology. Yet refugee-related research in Europe is largely dominated by legal scholars, while studies of the 'new immigration' are often conducted by geographers and sociologists who are mainly interested in figures and trends, in which the cultural and human dimension is frequently absent.[2]

The apparent reluctance of anthropologists to become involved in refugee research may be due to the fact that standard fieldwork is not geared to the study of complex and politically sensitive contemporary processes.[3] The challenge for anthropologists has been how to preserve the strength and flavour of ethnography, which consists of its experiential perspective, and yet to go beyond the formats of the community study and the genre that has been called 'scoop ethnography'.[4]

Fieldwork on clandestine immigration is a delicate, difficult and at

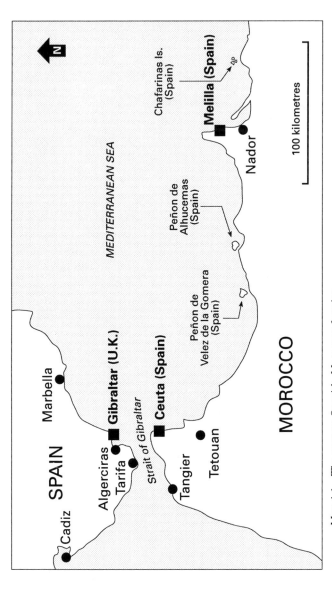

Map 4.1   The western Spanish–Moroccan frontier

times daunting endeavour. Yet a field approach is necessary in order to distinguish official policy, discourse and figures from attitudes and behaviour on the ground. Research must begin in the conceptual domain for two reasons. First, given the ideological and moral connotations of concepts used by politicians and the media, there is a need for a more neutral term to refer to those who enter western Europe and who often reside there without documentation. Although there is nothing more transient than the adjective 'new', I propose the term '*new* immigrants' as a viable, less pejorative, alternative to 'illegal immigrants'. This term is not meant to conceal a critical element of the new immigrants' position, i.e. that they are clandestine entrants, but rather to avoid an *a priori* stigmatisation of these people as criminals. Second, it is important to differentiate 'new immigrants' from earlier generations of labour migrants, because conditions in the countries of origin and destination have changed drastically over the past two decades (Lamphere 1992).

Combining fieldwork, life history and cultural analysis, I discuss how 'new immigration' and increased European integration are accommodated by people living on the Hispano-Moroccan border, people who are far removed from the centre of state power, ideology and control. How does the 'new immigration' influence the cultural construction of the 'wet frontier'? A local perspective will show that the Mediterranean frontier is as much constructed and contested from the inside out as it is from the outside in, a position broadly comparable to that which Kearney (this volume) adopts in relation to the US–Mexico border.[5]

Boundaries

Boundaries are clearly a central issue in any discussion of the 'new immigration'. There are several kinds of boundaries (Goody 1992: 30). In this chapter I focus on two forms: first, the symbolic boundaries between and among groups and communities in Spanish and Moroccan society; second, the political and legal boundaries between adjacent nation-states. My emphasis is on the construction of the Mediterranean Sea as a geopolitical and cultural divide between two countries, two continents, and two or more ways of life.

According to Braudel (1976), the Mediterranean 'Channel' never acted as a barrier between Spain and North Africa, but rather as a river that united more than it divided by making a single world of North and South. At the beginning of the sixteenth century, however, the Strait of Gibraltar became a political frontier for the first time in history. Since then, the degree of permeability of this wet frontier has varied with time and place. Recently, the 'Inner Sea' has become an area of friction between North and South; differences in income level, standards of living and economic development are on the increase. There is also a growing demographic gap, with population growth in the Maghreb ten times that in the European Union.[6]

The Mediterranean is not only a political, demographic and economic divide, but also an ideological and moral frontier, increasingly perceived by Europeans as a barrier between democracy and secularism on the one hand, and totalitarianism and religious fanaticism on the other. Francophone intellectuals of the Maghreb – who have acted as cultural brokers since the independence of Morocco, Tunisia and Algeria – are now caught between fundamentalist militants who label them as traitors and the European Union's restrictive immigration policy. Their European colleagues show little or no interest in them, while the distrust by North African intellectuals of their European counterparts has grown because of the Union's stance in the Gulf War and its hesitation in helping the Bosnian Muslims.[7]

The deepening of the Mediterranean divide is also linked to the accelerated process of integration in the European Union, the abolition of its internal borders and the reinforcement of the external frontiers.[8] However, the southern frontier of the European Union extends from Gibraltar to the Greek islands and covers tens of thousands of kilometres of coastline which makes immigration difficult to control.[9] On the European side there is mounting pressure to check the influx of immigrants. Political and economic refugees who enter southern Europe find it increasingly difficult to move to northern Europe. This exposes yet another divide: a gap between the northern countries which want their southern neighbours to settle the immigrants who arrive on their shores, and the southern countries which claim that they are unable to cope with this burden. For example, the Spanish authorities were unprepared to deal with the sudden increase in immigrants who stayed. In the 1980s large groups were more or less allowed to settle down illegally. Only in 1984 did the Spanish government take the first legal steps to contain immigration.[10]

As mentioned above, when Spain joined the European Union its southern border became a *European* frontier. The reinforcement and re-marking of this frontier have not only affected the political and economic relationships in the wider region but also the cultural categories used to divide people into 'us' and 'them'. The Inner Sea has increasingly become *the* spatial, political and cultural boundary between Europe and the 'Third World', much like the 'Border Area' between the US and Mexico discussed by Kearney (this volume). At the same time, the members of the European Union find themselves faced with growing ethnic minorities of diverse origin within their territories. New internal boundaries are being created between the majority and minority populations in southern Europe.

The external boundaries between Spain and Morocco have also been affected by recent global developments. Though Spain and Morocco are well-defined states that maintain ethnic, religious and linguistic boundaries with one another, these borders have never been stable or unequivocal. Even when borders remain relatively static, as has been the case with the 'dry' border between Spain and France (see Douglass, this volume), the borderlands themselves are in a constant state of flux. Both Spain and Morocco have had to deal with 'ethnic problems': Spain with ethnonationalisms and a growing population of Maghribian origin, and Morocco with a large Berber minority. The Spanish enclaves in northern Morocco are a source of conflict between Spain and Morocco, as are the fishing grounds in the Mediterranean Sea and the Atlantic Ocean.[11] Tension is also caused by the traffic in contraband and drugs and by unchecked border-crossings. Moreover, with 1.5 million expatriates (many of them Rif Berbers), Morocco has a sizeable presence in the European Union. In July and August 1993 almost 800,000 people – the vast majority of them Moroccans – passed through the port of Algeciras to spend a holiday in their native country.[12] This is only one instance of intense cross-border communication. Every year hundreds of thousands of Spanish and foreign tourists cross the Strait to Ceuta and Tangier as day-trippers on shopping and sight-seeing expeditions. Spanish travel agencies promote the crossing to Morocco as a trip to the Middle Ages. In fact, the tourist industry plays an important role in the commodification of cross-border differences.

The passage across the Strait to an imagined European paradise, attractive given the proximity of Europe but also hazardous, is a rite of passage to a new way of life – marked by ordeals inherent in such transitions. But there is no corresponding rite of incorporation on the Spanish shore. Like Kearney's Mexican migrants, the majority of these 'boatpeople' (or 'wetbacks', as they are often called in the media) enter a kind of permanent limbo in a submerged world set apart from the wider Spanish society.

In the early 1990s Spain's 'miraculous' economic growth came to a halt. 1992 was a year of tightened immigration rules and of serious racist attacks. In all these events cultural boundaries between established residents and newcomers were at stake, perhaps more so in Andalusia than in other regions of the peninsula. The events of 1992 forced Andalusians to face a dilemma. On the one hand, their region is dependent on the big money of the World Exhibition, European Union, tourism and – in a veiled way – on the clandestine labour of the new immigrants; on the other hand, they do not want their villages and towns being 'invaded', as many describe the experience of tourism and immigration, by outsiders, whether European or African, legal or illegal. They do not like the northerners turning their region into a pleasure garden for the European core, and neither do they applaud the presence of Africans who transgress – at least in the perception of many Andalusians – established cultural boundaries between 'us' and 'them'.

In sum, the Hispano-Moroccan divide has much in common with international borders everywhere, but is further complicated in its role as an external border of the EU, making it one of the frontiers between 'Europe' and 'Africa', 'North' and 'South', and 'First World' and 'Third World'. While much anthropological research at borders in the past has focused on the symbols which construct the boundaries of local communities, there have been few studies of international borders as frontier zones where the process of making nations into categories of 'us' and 'them' have their origins.

On the border

Tarifa (see map 4.1), the southernmost town of Europe, has always spoken to the imagination of western travellers as a gateway to the Orient, in particular to Tangier, the most northwesterly town of Africa. But only recently were the two ports linked by a daily ferry that covers the thirteen kilometres in less than an hour. From Tangier on a clear night you can see the lights of Tarifa across the Strait of Gibraltar. The main landmarks for the 'guides' who ferry immigrants to the promised lands of Europe are the bright lights of a petrol station along the national highway to Cádiz, two kilometres out of Tarifa. During preliminary research in Tangier in March 1992, local people took me to a street in the medina which they called 'la rue des nègres' where smugglers and passengers – referred to as *les loups* (wolves) and *les agneaux* (sheep) – met to haggle over prices for the nocturnal crossing (note a similar use of animal metaphors for smugglers and immigrants in the US–Mexican frontier case). Moroccan authorities turned a blind eye to this people-smuggling racket in which fishermen from Tangier and the Spanish enclave of Ceuta were heavily involved. The smugglers asked 50,000 to 75,000 pesetas per passenger.[13] One prospective migrant, a young man from northern Somalia, claimed to have walked through Ethiopia, Sudan, Egypt, Libya and Algeria before reaching Tangier, from where he knew 'it [was] easy to get to Europe'. He was living in a cheap boarding-house, working illegally in the building of tourist apartment blocks and hoping to save enough money to cross to Europe. It is doubtful whether he succeeded in realising his dream. In autumn 1992, after mounting pressure by Spain and the European Union, Hassan II declared war on illegal emigration, corruption and drugs. A new police chief was appointed in Tangier, thousands of soldiers were mobilised to guard the beaches, and black Africans disappeared from the streets. Indeed, there were few black people in the streets of Tangier when I returned there in June 1993. The number of soldiers patrolling the beaches had also been reduced.[14]

From the European side, the view of the Moroccan coastline is a constant reminder to the local inhabitants that there is a different world across the Strait. This view is exploited as a tourist image. One of the leaflets promoting Tarifa says: 'Tarifa: views on the Strait of Gibraltar, on the meeting point of the Atlantic Ocean and the Mediterranean Sea, and on the always attractive and mysterious African continent, to be reached by ferry within forty minutes.' Postcards show the mountains of Morocco from the ramparts of the old town.[15] Tarifa is also promoted as Europe's key to Africa, Tangier being the gate.

That a small physical distance can become a wide cultural gap became particularly evident in the second week of March 1992. While Tarifa was celebrating the excesses of Carnival, Morocco was fasting through Ramadan. A beach in Spain, which during the day was a venue for an international windsurfing competition, was at night a site for Africans entering Europe in search of a better life. In the daytime, tourists in pursuit of pleasure were ferried from Tarifa to Tangier for a day-trip, while at night Africans in pursuit of a living made their dangerous crossings in the opposite direction. During the summer of 1992 the arrival of immigrants on the beaches of Andalusia reached a climax. A Red Cross employee of Tarifa told me in 1993:

Last summer the weather was extremely calm. Boat after boat, jammed with immigrants, landed on the beaches of this area. They even came by daylight, not caring for the risk of being discovered. Most of those people cannot even swim. Yes, last summer they drowned by the dozens. I never saw such a thing before. Now it has become *tranquilo* (quiet), pressure from above, you know.

Who are these new immigrants? Compared with the 'old immigrants' who arrived in the late 1970s and early 1980s, and who frequently used tourist visas to enter Spain, the new immigrants are generally destitute. They lack the means to buy forged visas and a flight ticket to Madrid, Málaga or Barcelona and have to spend their last dollars on the nocturnal passage to Tarifa. Upon entering Europe by boat, these immigrants, predominantly men, own nothing but the clothes they are wearing. If they possess identity cards or passports, they often destroy them or leave them behind. They do so not only for tactical reasons (to make it more complicated for the Spanish authorities to send them back) but also because they desperately wish to begin a new life with a new identity. Having landed on the beach, they must reach Algeciras before dawn because their appearance makes them conspicuous to the Civil Guard who cruise the highway between Tarifa and Algeciras in search of 'new immigrants'. Sometimes they succeed in hiding until the following night, or in hitching a ride from a truck driver. From Algeciras they try to reach Málaga, Madrid, Valencia, Barcelona and France where they are less noticeable. Many of them know 'friends of friends of friends' who already live in Spain or France, though the only directions they carry are to 'Puerta del Sol' or 'Plaza de España' in Madrid, public squares where Africans gather.

In the early 1990s the situation in the Algeciras district grew so critical that a centre for clandestine immigrants had to be opened in Tarifa. It was the first refugee centre in Spain, and until 1993 the only official one. It is situated in a section of a building on the outer quay of the port, on the most outlying site of the town, literally on the edge of Europe.

When I arrived in Tarifa in early 1992, about seventy-five people were being held there in social and legal quarantine. The weather was calm after several days of Levanter storms. That weekend dozens of 'new immigrants' crossed the Strait. Thirty-five of them were caught at various spots in the municipal territory of Tarifa. When I approached the building where they were being held, the inmates attracted my attention, speaking to me in French through the barred windows where their laundry was hung out to dry, asking for cigarettes and information. A Civil Guard in the neighbouring office soon ordered me to leave. In early spring the 'inmigrantes ilegales acogidos en Tarifa', as they are called in the media, became an issue in the local and national political arena. Opposition parties in the Spanish parliament and in Tarifa's town council seized the opportunity to discredit government policy by denouncing abuses in the prison of Algeciras and the refugee centre of Tarifa. The fate of the African 'wetbacks' also attracted the attention of the international media.

Consider the case of Abdu, a man in his mid-twenties from Senegal. He grew up in one of the *bidonvilles* of Dakar, worked occasionally as a day-labourer, but remained unemployed for most of the time. His view of Europe was moulded by the glamorous television images of affluence and liberty which he saw in cafés. He began to dream of emigration ('l'Europe, c'est un rêve'). In December 1991 he sold his few belongings, borrowed money from his family and left his wife and children behind with his brother-in-law. In early 1992 he flew to Casablanca and travelled from there by bus to Tangier. It took him two weeks to arrange his passage to Spain. One night in February, Abdu and about twenty other immigrants set off from a beach not far from Tangier in a *patera*, a small fishing boat between four and eight metres long and some two to three metres wide, with an outboard motor. They became lost in fog, the boat began to take in water and only after four hours did they arrive at the rocks of Tarifa. Exhausted from bailing water, they abandoned the boat and swam ashore. Two of the passengers drowned and the others were picked up by the coastguards. Abdu spent forty days in custody at the Tarifa centre and was only released on the understanding that he would leave Spain within a month. When I met him (in Spain), he was trying to find work and obtain a residence permit: 'My family invested money in me. I have to find work and earn a living here. You know, we have a saying at home: "Suffering is part of life. He who wants to be successful, has to suffer first".' His story bears many similarities to those I heard from others seeking passage across the Strait.[16] According to an immigration officer in Algeciras, most of the immigrants come from Morocco, Algeria, Senegal, Mali and the Ivory Coast.

Tarifeños respond in various ways to these newcomers. Contrary to the tourist images sold in Tarifa, most of the local inhabitants live with their backs to Africa. The ferry from Tarifa to Tangier is almost exclusively used by tourists for brief organised shopping and sightseeing trips. Most local people are only indirectly confronted with the Africans, at best remaining indifferent, at worst becoming hostile. By the time of my second visit to Tarifa, they were becoming accustomed to the phenomenon of the 'wetbacks'.

Some men feared that the immigrants would become a threat to their standard of living: 'I tell you that the immigrants will take away our work', one of them said. Added to this anxiety is a general fear of otherness. Few residents were interested in the fate of the immigrants. Some older people with sharp memories of poverty, who had been emigrants themselves in the 1950s and 1960s, refused to report immigrants to the Civil Guard and helped them by giving them food, clothes and drinks. One man, a cowherd in his late fifties who lived on a small farm in Tarifa's hinterland, told me that he sometimes gave shelter to immigrants for a day or two: 'These people are not criminals, they are only desperate to leave poverty behind, like I was in the 1950s when I left for Germany to earn a living. We were treated there like gypsies, the same way the Africans are now being treated by most of us.'

Some organised help is offered by a small Refugee Aid Group based in Algeciras (*Algeciras Acoge*), which also counts some students from

Tarifa among its members. Their main work is to denounce abuses regarding new immigrants, in particular racism, and to provide information about the problem of illegality. However, many younger people, who grew up under better circumstances than their parents, are less accommodating. Some of the local workforce, being unemployed or unwilling to do the heavy and dirty work left to the immigrants, sometimes turn against the newcomers. One group paints anti-alien slogans on the walls of Algeciras and elsewhere. 'No a la inmigración de color a España', 'Moros no', 'Moros fuera', 'los españoles primero', 'STOP: Inmigración', and 'Mata negros' ('No to coloured immigration to Spain', 'No Moors', 'Moors out', 'Spanish people first', 'Stop immigration', 'Kill negroes') was just some of the graffiti in the Algeciras district.[17]

The fate of the 'new immigrants' is grim. During the first ten months of 1992 about 2,000 were caught on the beaches or along the coast of Cádiz province. More than 80 per cent were Moroccans, 5 per cent Algerians and the rest sub-Saharan Africans, according to figures provided to me by the immigration office in Algeciras. Those who escape the Coastal, Civil and National Guards or those released after forty days of detention, seek refuge in the large cities, where they constitute a floating underclass of non-persons. They work for less than minimum wages, or as street peddlers in the Costa del Sol, where ambulant trade is forbidden by most municipalities. Such street traders are constantly being chased by the local police, as I witnessed in Algeciras and Marbella. Nevertheless, many of these young men are not necessarily the passive, exploited figures presented in the media. They are often tough survivors full of stamina, good humour, flexibility and creativity.

Seku from Mali managed to create a niche for himself in Spanish society. I met him in Málaga, where he told me in Spanish that he had come to Spain three years earlier on a tourist visa, leaving his wife and two children behind. He began to sell watches and wood carvings for a 'friend' who already had a residence permit, operated a peddling network, and regularly flew back home to buy cheap goods. He said about this friend: 'Of course, he made a lot of money, whereas I was barely able to survive.' Eventually he found a job as a motor mechanic, the trade he had learned in his native country. In 1991 he applied for a residence permit in response to the limited amnesty programme for clandestine residents announced by the government. He likes to return to Mali for holidays and to see his family, which he hopes will join him one day.

Men like Seku are frontiersmen par excellence. Whereas many of their forebears crossed frontiers of chiefdoms and kingdoms for a variety of reasons – slave trade, poverty, persecution, war, adventure, famine – today young Africans cross international frontiers, partly for similar reasons in pursuit of what they now call 'freedom'.[18] They do not primarily use this notion in the liberal democratic sense (though many of them claim refugee status *vis-à-vis* the Spanish authorities), but rather in a general sense to refer to 'the good life'; that is, the liberty which results from what they see as a reasonable standard of living and a loosening of the tight social control of relatives and neighbours in their places of origin.

Crossing the frontier into Europe and finding a job is also a kind of initiation into manhood for young Moroccan men. They often work as undocumented day labourers in agriculture, picking olives in Jáen, strawberries in Huelva, and tomatoes and melons along the 'plastic coast' of Almeria and Málaga. Spanish market gardeners contract illegal labour, because they claim to be unable to find Spanish labourers willing to work in plastic hothouses at temperatures often over 50°C, and at wages below the legal minimum.

In his desire to taste freedom and a Western life style, Mustafa, who works as a day labourer on isolated farms in Málaga, occasionally visits the city to have a good time. For almost three years he has not been in contact with his natal family in the village of Beni Enzar at the border of Melilla. He likes to drink whisky and boasts of his Spanish girlfriend. He told me that other young men leave his country in order to escape military service. Some of them make money by smuggling small quantities of *chocolate* (hashish) and *kif* (marijuana). Cannabis grown in the Rif is worth three or four times its value if sold across the sea along the Costa del Sol.

Migration, however, is not as exclusively a male phenomenon as it was in the early 1980s. More and more Moroccan women now come to Spain. They enter domestic service in Málaga, Madrid, Seville, Valencia and Barcelona. Non-governmental agencies estimate that more than 50 per cent of all Moroccans in Madrid are women who work in the domestic service sector.[19]

Cultural categories and the frontier

Several categories of identity are used by the mass media, political agencies and citizens to mark the Euro-African frontier. When referring to immigrants, refugees and asylum seekers, politicians and journalists frequently use terms such as 'invasion', 'new invasion', 'flood', 'wave of mass migration', 'being deluged with refugees', and 'Spain under siege from an army of migrants' (all of which appeared as headlines in national, regional and local newspapers and magazines in 1992 and 1993). Even the liberal newspaper *El País* wrote about '*la imparable avalancha del Sur*'. These terms are derived from a vocabulary of natural disaster and war. It is a rhetoric that expresses and evokes fear. It is not only current in right-wing, nationalist circles but has gained a wider circulation in the media, in the streets, and in the cafés. Such expressions are frequently linked to the general notion of a demographic 'explosion' on the southern shores of the Mediterranean, a widespread fear of Islamic fundamentalism, and an 'invasion' of people from the Maghreb. Many Andalusians simply use the terms *moro* (Moor) and *negro* for all immigrants who cross the Mediterranean, regardless of their legal status and origin. These categories are often implicitly and sometimes explicitly linked by the media and citizens to criminality, smuggling and the use of drugs, abuse of alcohol and street fighting.[20]

There is a tendency in the Spanish media to exaggerate the number of immigrants. Moreover, they present an image of the immigrant population – male, young, illegal, African, living in poverty and being exploited in agriculture – which is valid only for a small proportion of foreign residents.[21] In presenting such an image, they contribute to the stigmatisation of the 'new immigrants'. For many local Spanish people, the typical immigrant is a young Moroccan male with criminal tendencies, loose morals and bad personal hygiene. Official figures, however, reveal a more complex immigration pattern, with women accounting for almost 40 per cent of illegal residents. Moreover, some 30 per cent of immigrants to the area are in fact wealthy western Europeans who reside illegally in Spain.[22]

I turn now to explore the role of markers such as 'Spain', 'Europe', 'Mediterranean', 'Muslim' and 'Christian' in the construction and transformation of the southern frontier. Spaniards in general, and Andalusians in particular, seem to be excessively preoccupied with 'Europe', at least when compared to people in Germany, Belgium or the Netherlands.[23] This is intimately related to cultural identity and the feeling among many Spaniards, not only intellectuals and politicians, that they must catch up with the rest of Europe after decades of dictatorship and underdevelopment. They are now eager to use 'corrupt', 'backward' and 'dictatorial' Morocco as a negative model to represent all that Spain no longer is. This attitude towards the southern neighbour and *moros* in general is outspoken and widespread. 'Europe' (as represented by the European Union) stands for democracy, rationality and a modern and prosperous way of life.[24]

However, the situation is more complex than a simple opposition between Spain and Morocco or Europe and Africa might suggest. The Spanish government not only embraces European identity but also cherishes its ambition to establish itself as a major Mediterranean power, a mediator between Europe and the Muslim world. Andalusia reflects this ambiguity. The non-European past of Spain is most visible here, and several new mosques have recently been built in the region. The old mosques of Granada, Seville and Córdoba are important sacred sites, increasingly visited by Muslim tourists and pilgrims. Wealthy sheikhs from the Gulf States have constructed their summer palaces in Andalusia, and some local Christians have converted to Islam.

There is considerable controversy among *andalucistas* (militants of the regionalist movement) and other Andalusians about the role of the Berber, Arab and Islamic heritage in the present regional identity. One faction, in particular *Liberación Andaluza*, sees a central place for this heritage, while the other faction tends to discard it as something alien and belonging to a distant past.

The position of Morocco towards the Spanish–African frontier is also marked by ambivalence. 'Europe' is part of daily Moroccan life, as both experience and image. Almost everyone has kith and kin across the Mediterranean. Crossing the sea is a dream for many young Moroccans. As one inhabitant of Tangier put it: 'In this country everybody talks about Europe and how good life is over there.' The image and dream are perpetuated by most *émigrants* through their conspicuous consumption and their tales of affluence when they are home for holidays. Few emigrants are willing to admit that they have failed. A man who worked for two years in the port of Rotterdam summarised his experience of the exodus as follows: 'We lived with many in small dwellings in old houses and spent our days poorly to save money in order to be able to boast when we were back for holidays. What was worst was the way your people [the Dutch] cold-shouldered us.' Moroccans who stay behind sometimes voice a rather negative image of the expatriates: 'They are greedy, selfish, ignore Islam, drink beer, and raise their daughters in a liberal fashion.' For their part, the *émigrants*, when they are abroad, tend to reproduce an outmoded view of Moroccan mores and thus reinforce the image of the Mediterranean as a chasm of cultural difference. In this regard, they resemble the makers of tourist images.

In Morocco the terms *urubbâ* (Europe), *urubbî* or *urubbiyûn* (European) belong to the vocabulary of newspapers and other media and are rarely used to refer to Europe and Europeans in daily life, except by a small minority of intellectuals. The common term for European is *nasrânî*, or sometimes *rumi*, which means 'Christian' just as

'Muslim' (*meslem*) and 'Moroccan' (*maghrabi*) are used interchangeably. The notion of being a European is inseparable from the notion of being a Christian. In Islamic terms 'Europe' stands for wickedness, impurity and greediness, whereas 'Morocco' is a symbol of spiritual superiority and purity. This is the vocabulary used by Islamist leaders and their followers among the young unemployed, schoolboys and students who hang out in the streets. On the other hand, for many young Moroccans 'Europe' is primarily a secular notion meaning 'the good life'. Numerous young men and women are so desperate to reach Europe that they are willing to risk their lives.

Mediterranean Morocco has been a forgotten frontier for centuries. The dominant image of this area in the rest of Morocco, especially in the Atlantic plains, is one of poverty, smuggling, *kif*, cut-throats, emigration and subordination (Zaim 1990: 5). But the category 'Mediterranean' is now also being used in a positive sense by an increasing number of young people in northern Morocco (and Rifians abroad), particularly those who are aware of and profess their Berber identity. These people employ 'Mediterranean' as a category of opposition to Arab domination. Some of them even celebrate the term *moro* as an honorary nickname in order to avoid the term 'Muslim' and its close association with Arab identity. Since many of the Rif Berbers are connected to Europe rather than Rabat, especially economically, they primarily present themselves as Berbers and Mediterraneans rather than as Moroccans or Muslims.[25] Gross (1993: 200) argues that the use of *Tamazight*, the Berber language, and its local dialect, *Tharifith*, is in itself an act of resistance to state power. Although it is spoken by an estimated 40 to 60 per cent of Morocco's population, it is not recognised as an official language of the state. The majority of state servants in the Rif are Arabic speakers from the Atlantic plains who are seen as corrupt parasites by the local population: 'Thus not to share a language with them is a kind of refusal of their authority and a way of establishing local solidarity' (Gross 1993: 200). As frontierspeople and bordercrossers, Rifians are more oriented towards Europe than towards Rabat. By seeking a living on both shores of the Mediterranean, they straddle the Mediterranean frontier like ethnic minority middlemen elsewhere and in the past.[26]

Conclusion

The Spanish state was built on a policy of ethnic, religious and cultural homogenisation which began during the Reconquista and culminated in the expulsion of the Jews in 1492 and of the Moriscos at the beginning of the seventeenth century. During this long period, the obsession with 'cleanliness of blood' (*limpieza de sangre*) and *casticismo* (purity of language, manners and customs) was particularly strong. Indeed, for almost four centuries Spain has been marked by a centralist policy that denied and repressed ethnic pluralism, a policy directed particularly at Basque and Catalan ethnonationalism, but also at the gypsies who have remained largely ostracised as an ethnic minority. Even now, the number of foreigners in the total population is small – 2 per cent – compared with other countries of the European Union. However, since the end of the Franco era, the boundaries and the power of the Spanish state have come under increasing pressure both from within (regional and ethnic movements) and from without (European Community, the 'boundless' world market, mass media and immigration).

In the 1980s Africans came to southern Europe in increasing numbers. Along with a re-definition of the Mediterranean frontier following the incorporation of Latin Europe into the European Community, new internal boundaries are being created between the majority and minority populations. In March 1993 the Spanish parliament approved a restrictive aliens policy and agreed on the introduction of an immigration quota. Since both Moroccan and Spanish authorities decided to tighten up border controls, the number of immigrants arriving on the beaches of Andalusia has diminished, at least for the time being. Yet, despite these restrictive measures on both sides of the Mediterranean Sea, immigrants continue to come without the necessary documents, to apply for asylum or simply to go underground.[27]

I have shown that the symbols and categories used to mark the Hispano-African frontier are multivocal, ambivalent and contested. There are contradictions between state ideology and frontier praxis, between the frontier as a categorical divide and the frontier as an interactive process. The immense changes in the political borders between nation-states in recent years make the time ripe for a shift in the anthropological gaze towards people and groups who live at and cross international borders, as well as towards the range of cultural experience in the transitional zones between states and continents.

Notes

This chapter is based on fieldtrips to Algeciras, Tangier, Tarifa, Ceuta and Gibraltar in March–April 1992 and June 1993, and represents a preliminary report on a continuing project about the cultural dimensions of the Spanish–Moroccan frontier. Since the chapter was completed, much new work has been published on refugees, borders and identities, though it rarely addresses precisely this combination of topics (see, for example, Alvarez 1995, Camino and Krulfeld 1994, Kearney 1995, Marcus 1995, Seremetakis 1996 and Stoller 1996).

1. There is little material available in English on the 'new immigration' and the 'alien problem' in Spain. In a recent overview of Muslims in western Europe there are ten lines devoted to the Spanish situation:

> In Spain, there is clearly a substantial presence of North African Muslims. Most of them are there, however, without documents, so little can be stated with any certainty. It appears that many may be temporary, working in the tourist industry on the Mediterranean coast. Spain is, of course, also a transit country for North Africans travelling back and forth to France. Individual Spanish Muslims have claimed that after the end of the Franco regime, many secret Muslims have declared themselves publicly, suggesting a tradition going back to the *reconquista*. (Nielsen 1992: 87)

Nielsen neglects the growing Spanish literature on the subject. Studies in Spanish, however, are mainly along legal and statistical lines. A recent example is the volume by López Garcia (1993), which offers statistical profiles of the Moroccans in Spain at the national and regional level with some case studies of city neighbourhoods based on survey research. The Italian case (Campani 1993; Montanari and Cortese 1993) and Portuguese case (Eaton 1993) provide comparative evidence for the Spanish case with regard to the sociological dimension of the phenomenon. For a general reflection on the problem of the new mass migration see Enzensberger (1992), and on the new Islamic presence in Europe, see Gerholm and Lithman (1990).

2. Anthropologists dealing with migration have always been interested in balancing out such studies by providing the cultural dimension (see, for example, Grillo 1973, 1985; Watson 1977; Werbner 1990).

3. Note, however, that since World War II the anthropology of Europe has contributed much to the development of alternative research strategies (see, for example, Wolf 1982; Cole 1977; Boissevain 1975).

4. Scoop ethnography is a kind of participatory journalism (Van Maanen 1988: 18–19, 135) which focuses on dramatic action and 'digging for data' so that the 'real story' can be told.

5. Moreover, the issue of boundaries is complicated by the fact that Spain's southern border extends across the Mediterranean Sea into the two enclave cities of Ceuta and Melilla. I have dealt with this geopolitical and cultural anomaly elsewhere (Driessen 1992; see also Rosander 1991; Carabaza and de Santos 1992).

6. See Sabagh (1993) on rapid demographic growth and its consequences for Morocco. From 1950 to 1990 the Moroccan population almost tripled, whereas in the 1980s the economic growth rate declined from 4.4 to 0.6 per cent per annum. More than half of the population is under the age of twenty. Almost one-quarter of foreign currency income is made up of migrant remittances (more than tourism and the production of phosphate together). The Moroccan Mediterranean frontier region, the Rif, has one of the highest population densities, and the highest rates of unemployment and emigration in Morocco. In Algeria the population almost tripled between independence in 1962 and 1990 ('L'Algérie à la dérive', *L'Express*, 17 February 1994: 24).

7. In Algeria FIS (Islamic Salvation Front) militants classify secular intellectuals as the *hizb fransa* ('French Party') and killed dozens of them during 1992 and 1993 (Brown 1993, Harbi 1993).

8. This abolition of internal borders should have been completed in January 1993. There have been several delays due to legal, technical and political reasons.

9. At many places the borders are porous. For instance, one can easily walk in and out of Melilla and Ceuta through the hills. Refugees use this route to leave Morocco and try to enter the Iberian Peninsula by ferry. Since most of them are sent back, refugees crowd the enclaves. In Ceuta they are aided by a Catholic relief organisation, whereas in Melilla they are left to their own devices. Hundreds of refugees from Zaire, Liberia, Nigeria, Ivory Coast, Burkina Faso, Somalia, Angola, Sudan, Chad, Ghana, South Africa, Lebanon and Palestine, who applied for asylum at the beginning of 1992, are living under deplorable conditions in the ancient hospital of the Red Cross (*El País*, 18 June 1993: 26).

10. The Spanish immigration policy consists of three strategies: more control at the entry points by the creation of a special Naval Civil Guard; more development aid to the countries of origin in order to curb the exodus; and integration programmes for foreign residents. In 1993 the entry quota was set at 20,000 workers, mainly Moroccans, who were employed in agriculture and domestic service (Puig de la Bellacasa 1992).

11. See LiPuma and Meltzoff (1994) on the effects of the European Union on Spanish fisheries.

12. In 1993, Spanish and Moroccan authorities coordinated the massive passage across the Mediterranean (called 'Operación Paso del Estrecho') in order to avoid the chaos and abuses of previous years in the ports of Algecerias, Ceuta and Tangier.

13. According to information provided by the Ministry of the Interior (see Puig de la Bellacasa 1992: 45).

14. These events received extensive, including international, press coverage. See, for instance, *L'Express*, 23 October 1992.

15. Some of the paintings by Delgado Guitart, an artist born in Tangier and raised in Spain, are inspired by views of Morocco from Tarifa, and from Tangier of Spain (Guitart 1993). He refers to the Strait of Gibraltar as a magic carpet.

16. Two Moroccans, one Algerian and a man from Mali told me their stories.

17. See Buezas (1992) for a survey of racist attacks in Spain. See also McDonogh (1992) on racism in Barcelona.

18. See Kopytoff (1987) for a discussion of migration across internal frontiers in pre-colonial Africa.

19. See the newspaper *El País*, 21 May 1991: 3.

20. Compare Stanton (1991) for the stigmatisation of Moroccan workers in Gibraltar.

21. I am aware that I also tend to emphasise this group. This is largely due to the fact that most of my research to date has been spent with young males from North and sub-Saharan Africa, these being the immigrants most frequently encountered in public places.

22. According to official estimates, there are 834,000 foreigners in Spain, 540,000 of whom are legal residents. A recent demographic study provides more realistic and reliable figures: 465,000 legal residents and between 88,000 and 132,000 illegal residents (see Izquierdo Escribano 1992). Compare the figures in Malgesini (1993). Non-governmental organisations estimate that approximately 300,000 foreign residents without documents remained in Spain after the 1991 legalisation (*El País*, 2 December 1991: 14–15).

23. It is, of course, difficult to measure degrees of preoccupation. One indicator could be the turnout at the recent European elections. The Netherlands had the lowest turnout (35 per cent) while Spain had a turnout of 60 per cent (*The Economist*, 18 June 1994: 30).

24. See Shore (1993) for a critical discussion of the Union's symbols.

25. I am grateful to Rashid Ahmed Raha for discussing this point with me. See also Moga (1993). On the status of the Berber language (*Tamazight*) in Morocco see Boukous (1992) and Gross (1993). The situation of the Kabyle Berbers in Algeria is very similar to that of the Rif Berbers in Morocco.

26. See Castile and Kushner (1981) on cultural enclaves and middlemen minorities.

27. After two years of intensified control at both sides of the Spanish–Moroccan border, the number of clandestine crossings is on the rise again in the Tangier–Tarifa–Algeciras area. In the summer of 1996 thousands of Africans landed on the beaches of Tarifa. It seems that the extremely calm summer weather and a slackening of control at the Moroccan side largely explain this increase. Smugglers of migrants now mainly operate from Larache.

References

Alvarez, R. R. Jr. 1995. 'The Mexican–US border: the making of an anthropology of borderlands', *Annual Review of Anthropology* 24: 447–70.

Boissevain, J. 1975. 'Towards a social anthropology of Europe', in J. Boissevain and J. Friedl (eds.), *Beyond the community: social processes in Europe*. The Hague: Department of Educational Science of the Netherlands, pp. 9–17.

Boukous, A. 1992. 'Quelques remarques sur la situation linguistique du Tamazight au Maroc', *Sharqiyyat* 4: 41–7.

Braudel, F. 1976. *The Mediterranean and the Mediterranean world in the age of Philip II*. 2 vols. Glasgow: Fontana/Collins.

Brown, K. 1993. 'Lost in Algiers, Ramadan 1993', *Mediterraneans* 4: 8–18.

Buezas, T. C. 1992. 'Actitud de los Españoles ante otros pueblos y culturas', in C. Moro (ed.), *Problemas culturales de la integración social de los inmigrantes: la nueva España y la cuenca sur del Mediterraneo*. Madrid: Fundación Humanismo y Democracia, pp. 77–105.

Camino, L. and R. Krulfeld 1994. *Reconstructing lives, recapturing meaning*. Gordon and Breach.

Campani, G. 1993. 'Immigration and racism in Southern Europe: the Italian case', *Ethnic and Racial Studies* 16: 507–36.

Carabaza, E. and M. de Santos 1992. *Melilla y Ceuta. Las ultimas colonias*. Madrid: Talasa Ediciones.

Castile, G. P. and G. Kushner (eds.) 1981. *Persistent peoples. Cultural enclaves in perspective*. Tucson: University of Arizona Press.

Cole, J. 1977. 'Anthropology comes part-way home', *Annual Review of Anthropology* 6: 349–78.

Driessen, H. 1992. *On the Spanish–Moroccan frontier. A study in ritual, power and ethnicity*. Oxford: Berg Publishers.

Eaton, M. 1993. 'Foreign residents and illegal immigrants: "Os negros em Portugal"', *Ethnic and Racial Studies* 16: 536–63.

Enzensberger, H. M. 1992. *Die grosse Wanderung*. Frankfurt am Main: Suhrkamp.

Gerholm, T. and Y. G. Lithman (eds.) 1990. *The new Islamic presence in western Europe*. London: Mansell.

Goody, J. 1992. 'Culture and its boundaries: a European view', *Social Anthropology* 1: 9–32.

Grillo, R. D. 1973. *African railwaymen: solidarity and opposition in an East African labour force*. Cambridge: Cambridge University Press.

1985. *Ideologies and institutions in urban France: the representations of immigrants*. Cambridge: Cambridge University Press.

Gross, J. 1993. 'The politics of unofficial language use: Walloon in Belgium, Tamazight in Morocco', *Critique of Anthropology* 13: 177–208.

Guitart, D. 1993. 'The dream', *Mediterraneans* 4: 185–90.

Harbi, M. 1993. 'Politics in other guises: Algeria 1980–1988', *Mediterraneans* 4: 25–31.

Izquierdo Escribano, A. 1992. *La inmigración en España 1980–1990*. Madrid: Centro de Publicaciones Ministerio de Trabajo y Seguridad Social.

Kearney, M. 1995. 'The local and the global: the anthropology of globalization and transnationalism', *Annual Review of Anthropology* 24: 547–65.

King, R. (ed.) 1993. *Mass migration in Europe. The legacy and the future*. London: Belhaven Press.

Kopytoff, I. (ed.) 1987. *The African frontier. The reproduction of traditional African societies*. Bloomington: Indiana University Press.

Lamphere, L. (ed.) 1992. *Structuring diversity: ethnographic perspectives and the new immigration*. Chicago: University of Chicago Press.

LiPuma, E. and S. K. Meltzoff 1994. 'Economic mediation and the power of associations. Toward a concept of encompassment', *American Anthropologist* 96: 31–51.

López Garcia, B. (ed.) 1993. *Inmigración Magrebí en España*. Madrid: Editorial Mapfre.

Maanen, J. v. 1988. *Tales of the field. On writing ethnography*. Chicago: University of Chicago Press.

Malgesini, G. 1993. 'Spain and the EC: sluicegate for Europe's labor market', *Middle East Report* 181: 25–30.

Marcus, G. E. 1995. 'Ethnography in/of the world system: the emergence of a multi-sited ethnography', *Annual Review of Anthropology* 24: 95–117.

116   *Henk Driessen*

McDonogh, G. W. 1992. 'Bars, gender, and virtue: myth and practice in Barcelona's *Barrio Chino*', *Anthropological Quarterly* 65: 19–33.
1993. 'The face behind the door: European integration, immigration, and identity', in T. M. Wilson and M. E. Smith (eds.), *Cultural change and the new Europe: perspectives on the European Community*. Boulder: Westview Press.
Miles, R. 1993. 'Introduction – Europe 1993: the significance of changing patterns of migration', *Ethnic and Racial Studies* 16: 459–67.
Moga, V. (ed.). 1993. 'Amazigh-Tamazight. Debate Abierto', *Aldaba* 19.
Montanari, A. and A. Cortese 1993. 'South to north migration in a Mediterranean perspective,' in R. King (ed.), *Mass migration in Europe. The legacy and the future*. London: Belhaven Press, pp. 212–34.
Nielsen, J. 1992. *Muslims in Western Europe*. Edinburgh: Edinburgh University Press.
Puig de la Bellacasa, F. 1992. 'Situación actual de la inmigración en España y politicas de actuación', in C. Moro (ed.), *Problemas de la Integración Social de los Inmigrantes*. Madrid Fundación Humanismo y Democracia, pp. 35–49.
Rosander, E. E. 1991. *Women in a borderland. Managing ethnic identity where Morocco meets Spain*. Stockholm: Stockholm Studies in Social Anthropology.
Sabagh, G. 1993. 'The challenge of population growth in Morocco', *Middle East Report* 181: 30–6.
Seremetakis, C. N. 1996. 'In search of the barbarians: borders in pain', *American Anthropologist* 98: 489–91.
Shore, C. 1993. 'Inventing the "people's Europe": critical approaches to European community "cultural policy"', *Man* 28: 779–800.
Stanton, G. 1991, '"Guests in the Dock". Moroccan workers on trial in the colony of Gibraltar', *Critique of Anthropology* 11: 361–79.
Stoller, P. 1996. 'Spaces, places, and fields. The politics of West African trading in New York City's informal economy', *American Anthropologist* 98: 776–88.
Watson, J. L. (ed.). 1977. *Between two cultures: migrants and minorities in Britain*. Oxford: Blackwell.
Werbner, P. 1990. *The migration process: capital, gifts and offerings among British Pakistanis*. New York: Berg Publishers.
Wolf, E. R. 1982. *Europe and the people without history*. Berkeley: University of California Press.
Zaïm, F. 1990. *Le Maroc et son espace Méditerranéen. Histoire économique et sociale*. Rabat: Confluences.

5 Transnationalism in California and Mexico at the end of empire

Michael Kearney

> Do not ask who I am and do not ask me to remain the same: leave it to our bureaucrats and our police to see that our papers are in order. At least spare us their morality when we write.　(Foucault 1972: 17)

> The geopolitical wound called 'the border' cannot stop the cultural undercurrents. The 'artistic border' is artificial. It shouldn't be there, and it is up to us to erase it.　(Gómez Peña 1986: 24)

This chapter has been stimulated by my ethnographic work on the US–Mexico border. My immediate problem in relation to this work is how to represent the social and cultural forms of an indigenous people – namely Mixtecs – who migrate in large and increasing numbers into this border area from their homeland in the state of Oaxaca in southern Mexico. This task of ethnographic representation is made complex not only by the spatial extension of the Mixtec community into the Border Area, but by the ambiguous nature of the Border Area itself, which has become a region where the culture, society and state of the United States encounter the Third World in a zone of contested space, capital and meanings. Furthermore, the problem of ethnographic representation of this community in this border region is made yet more problematic by a corresponding decomposition of what now, in the late twentieth century, can be seen as the 'classic' epistemological relationship between the anthropological Self and the ethnographic Other. In other words, exploration of these themes is prompted by the need not only to make sense of the ethnographic subject that presents itself in this complex field, but also of the changing boundaries and constitution of anthropology itself, that is, its sociology, epistemology and practice. This is so because anthropology, as an official discipline, is a constituent of the state, and as the boundaries and construction of the nation-state change so should we expect to find a restructuring of anthropology as a 'scientific field'.

When I speak of anthropology as a 'scientific field', I do so in Bourdieu's sense of scientific field not only as a field of study but also as a field of struggle (Bourdieu 1981) – a point to which I shall return below. Also with respect to terminology, I find it useful to distinguish between 'boundaries' as legal spatial delimitations of nations, viz. boundary lines, as opposed to the 'borders' of nations which are geographic and cultural zones or spaces, i.e. 'border areas', which can vary independently of formal boundaries.[1] Thus, whereas the 'boundary' between the United States and Mexico is an exact geometric line separating the two nation-states, the 'border area' is a broad, indistinct and fluctuating zone that overlaps both nation-states. The issues with which I am concerned in this chapter have to do with the lack of correspondence between the borders and boundaries of the nation-state.

Let me turn now to the question of changing boundaries and borders of the United States, which for convenience I periodise into two phases, the first of which I call the modern, and which corresponds to the growth and maturation of the United States as a 'colonial' nation-state.

The nation-state in the age of colonialism

The nation-state was necessary for the development of capitalism under modernity. As Corrigan and Sayer (1985) have shown, the maturation of modern capitalism necessarily entailed the formation of the nation-state as a cultural revolution, which over the course of several centuries put in place not only the bureaucratic and intellectual, but also the more general popular forms and practices which in their totality constituted the conditions for the development of capitalist society. Apart from these internal conditions, the modern nation-state is the product of two processes of global differentiation, one being the tension with other emergent absolute states, the second being the tension between the nation-state and its dependencies. I am primarily concerned here with the latter relationship.[2]

The modern period is thus coterminous with 'the Age of Empire', in which the colonial powers, constituted as nation-states, are clearly differentiated from their colonies (Hobsbawm 1987). This external oppositional dimension of the modern nation-state was predicated on a distinct spatial separation between it and its colonies, a structural feature which is integral to what elsewhere (Kearney n.d.) I call 'the Colonial Situation', and which provides the basis for the cognitive distinction between the coloniser and the colonised. Just as the task of the state is to consolidate internal social differentiation as national unity, so must nationalism as a force in modern history effect the differentiation of peoples on a global scale. Globally, the modern age was thus coterminous with the power of capitalism to spatially differentiate the world into developed, underdeveloped and de-developed regions. And in this modern differing it is the nation-state that emerges as the supreme unit of order, a social, cultural and political form which, as Anderson (1983) shows, is distinctive in having absolute geopolitical and social boundaries inscribed on territory and on persons, demarcating space and those who are members from those who are not. Thus, whereas absolute states achieved the consolidation of absolute power, it remained for the modern nation-state to construct absolute boundaries.

Since its inception until its formal national boundaries became fixed in the mid-nineteenth century, the United States enjoyed considerable territorial expansion at the expense of Mexico. During its period of territorial growth the United States rolled back Mexican society and sovereignty to its present south-western boundary (map 5.1). At a time when passports were devised and required for entry from Europe and Asia, movement across the south-western boundary was essentially unrestricted. Indeed, this lack of concern with firm demarcation of the boundary was a sign of its *de facto* categorical absoluteness between the two nations, born of military conquest.

This firm distinction between Anglo Self and Mexican Other was but one instance of a global system of distinction which was the fundamental structure of what I refer to above as the Colonial Situation, and which reached its apogee in the early twentieth century. This spatial and categorical distinction, this separation of Western nation from its colonies, provided the poles along which an axis of extraction and accumulation was constructed such that net economic value flows from the latter to the former. It was onto this spatial and economic distinction that social and cultural differences were inscribed. Thus the structuring of the colonial situation depended on the spatial separation of peripheral production and extraction of value and knowledge as raw materials from their consumption and transformation in metropoles, such that they could be reinvested back into the colonial project. It was within this systematic asymmetry that anthropology as a distinctive discipline assumed its 'classic' modern form as an intellectual enterprise structured by and structuring the lineaments of the colonial situation, such that the collection and consumption of anthropological knowledge became a permutation of the extraction, transformation and consumption of economic capital.[3]

As absolute boundaries are necessary for the construction of the modern nation-state, so is nationalism.[4] For a nationalism without borders and boundaries that can be defended and enlarged is impossible 'to imagine' – as Benedict Anderson (1983) might say. It is deemed

Map 5.1   Oaxaca and the US–Mexico border

'natural', therefore, that nationalism is the pre-eminent totemic sensibility of the modern age. In no other nation did this distinctly modern
sentiment have more power to offset other bases of collective identities
than in the United States, with its power to dissolve the ethnicity of its
huddled immigrant masses and to reconstruct it as 'American' and as,
inter alia, race and racism.

The fundamental project of the state – the inward task of the modern nation-state – is to elaborate and resolve the contradiction of differentiation and unity. The disciplinary power of the state must facilitate the reproduction of social and cultural differentiation within the nation, while at the same time perpetuating national unity. Thus, beyond the regulation (licensing, censusing, taxing) of the trades of the butcher, the baker, the candlestick-maker as they constitute a Durkheimian organic unity, the state must also ensure the reproduction of difference as social inequality, and this it does in large part by assuming responsibility for public education whereby it establishes a system of 'good' and 'poor' schools, and then 'grades' – in both senses of the term – students, such that they come to occupy the same social class position as their parents. I shall return to this theme later.

The nation-state and its borders in the age of transnationalism

What I wish to propose – and this proposition is suggested by the ethnography of the Border Area – is that history has passed beyond the 'modern age' as I have just described it with reference to boundaries of the nation-state. Such boundaries marked firm, absolute distinctions between national 'we' and distant 'they', and by the same token, between anthropological Self and ethnographic Other – between those who write and those who are written about. Whereas the modern phase was socially and culturally predicated on the nation-state, the present condition of the nation-state is aptly characterised as 'transnational'.

'Transnationalism' implies a blurring and reordering of the binary cultural, social and epistemological distinctions of the modern period, and as I am using it here, it has two meanings.[5] One is the conventional one having to do with forms of organisation and identity which are not constrained by national boundaries, such as the transnational corporation. But I also wish to load onto the term the meaning of transnational as post-national, in the sense that history and anthropology have entered a post-national age.

The border: Scene 1

Cañon Zapata is a deep north–south cleft between hills on the US–Mexico borderline where it runs along the edge of the city of Tijuana. Most of the canyon is on the California side of the boundary, but there are no tangible boundary markers except for an old monument and the broken strands of a wire fence on the hills to the east and west of the canyon. Down in the canyon there are no markers or wire at all. Up the canyon, well into the US side, are small food stalls made of scrap wood, covered with old sheet metal or boards for a little shade, and equipped with butane or wood stoves. Vendors of secondhand clothing and shoes have also set up their stalls. The canyon comes to life around three o'clock every afternoon as hundreds of people start to congregate, waiting until the right time to make an attempt to get to 'the other side'. They are, of course, already on the other side. What they must do, though, is get beyond agents of the Border Patrol who are on the hills overlooking the branches of the canyon above the town of San Ysidro. About a mile to the west of the canyon there is a large US customs facility which sits on the line between San Ysidro and Tijuana. This is the most heavily trafficked official international border-crossing in the world. Cañon Zapata is certainly one of the most, possibly the most, heavily trafficked unofficial crossings.

As the afternoon shadows move into the canyon, the assembled migrants eat their last taco, take a final swig of soda pop or beer, and possibly put on new shoes or a jacket which they have just bought. Then, in groups of five or maybe ten or twelve, they start to head out, up the canyon, and into its side branches. They walk in single file, each little group led by its *coyote*, the smuggler they are paying to lead them to a safe point and perhaps to arrange for transportation to somewhere yet farther north. Or perhaps there are experienced migrants in the group, who have made the trip many times and no longer need the expensive services of a smuggler.

When the sun is low, Border Patrol agents, the *Migra*, are silhouetted on the hills above the canyon. They scurry about in jeeps and on motorcycles and horses, responding to the probings of different groups, some of which are serving as diversions to draw the patrols away from others. The *Migra* almost never comes down into the base of the canyon where the migrants congregate, nor does the US government make any attempt to fence off or otherwise close or occupy this staging area.[6]

This same basic scenario is enacted at other sites where the borderline runs along the edge of Tijuana – and at many other places along the 2,000-mile border between Mexico and the United States.

The border: Scene 2

A few days before Christmas 1987, several green Border Patrol vehicles filled with agents swoop down into Cañon Zapata. The *ilegales* apprehensively move back towards the boundary line. Border Patrol agents pile out of the vehicles. One is dressed as Santa Claus and has a large bag of presents. The agents spread food and soft drinks on the bonnets of their vehicles, and call to the *ilegales* to come and get them. The Santa Claus hands out presents and a 'Christmas party' ensues. Then the *Migra* get back into their vehicles and drive away as the migrants prepare to attempt crossing 'to the other side' by avoiding surveillance and capture.[7]

The border: Scene 3

It is a moonless night. Two sleepy Border Patrol agents sit in an observation post that resembles a gun emplacement. The post is just on the US side of the boundary line where it runs through hills near the Pacific Ocean. Just behind the observation post is a wire-mesh fence that runs along the international boundary on the edge of Tijuana. The fence is old, bent and festooned with rags and scraps of paper impaled on it by the wind. It has many gaping holes through which 'illegal' border-crossers come and go almost as freely as the wind. The Border Patrol agents scan the hills around them and the fields below them with infrared nightscopes. Peering through these devices they see dozens of human forms, bent over, clutching small bags, parcels and sometimes children, silently hurrying along well-worn trails through the dry brush. Two days earlier, some eighty miles to the northeast, one of the agents had been sitting on a hilltop with binoculars scanning trails a two-day walk from the national boundary line.[8]

The nightscopes are but one component in a sophisticated high-tech surveillance programme that also includes motion sensors, search lights, television cameras, helicopters, spotter planes and patrols in various kinds of boats and ground vehicles, all coordinated by computers and radio communications. The fence described above has recently been repaired and a bank of high intensity lights installed. But the Immigration and Naturalization Service continues to be one of the most under-funded agencies of the federal government and also, according to charges made by its critics, one of the most mismanaged. The new fence and the lights are thus, in effect, symbolic measures which do little to reduce the basic porosity of the 2,000-mile long border. The fence has also recently been extended into the ocean to discourage international foot traffic along the beach. But in recent years there has been a notable increase of organised international maritime smuggling of aliens into the Pacific Coast of the United States.

The basic thesis concerning transnationalism that I wish to advance is that it corresponds to the political-economic and sociocultural ordering of late capitalism (Mandel 1975). Entailed in these new forms is a reordering of the capitalist nation-state. As a global phenomenon, the beginning of transnationalism corresponds to a historic moment that might be characterised as 'End of Empire'.[9] This characterisation is most literally apparent for Great Britain at the end of World War II, emerging as it did among the losers, or certainly as having lost its empire. Thus, the middle decades of the twentieth century saw the dismantling of the formal European colonial system and with it what had been in effect categorical distinctions between the Western nation-states, and between them and their colonies.

The modern age, the age of imperialism, was driven (according to Lenin, anyway) by the exporting of surplus capital from developed to underdeveloped areas of the world with subsequent destruction of non-capitalist economies and societies, processes which created wage labour – much of which was absorbed in these peripheral areas. The current transnational age is, however, characterised by a gross incapacity of peripheral economies to absorb the labour that is created in the periphery, with the result that it inexorably 'flows' to the cores of the global capitalist economy (Kearney 1986). This 'peripheralisation of the core' is now well advanced in Great Britain, whose colonial chickens have come home to roost, so to speak (Sassen-Koob 1982). The same is also true of former European colonial powers which are being 'overwhelmed' by former colonial subjects who are now 'guest workers': for instance, Algerians in France, Turks in Germany, and Guatemalans and Moroccans in Spain.[10]

A similar process is well under way in the decline of the US empire which is experiencing a comparable dissolution in the spatial and symbolic distinction between itself and its dependencies. Nowhere is this more apparent than in the south-western Border Area and in the cities of this zone which dramatically manifest a transnationalisation of identity in the culture, economics and politics of late capitalism.

In recent years the Border Area has, after a century of quiescence since the Mexican–American War of 1848, again become contested terrain. Now, however, it is not territory *per se* that is being contested, but instead personal identities, movements of persons, and cultural and political hegemony of peoples.[11] A Latino reconquest of much of the northern side has already taken place. But this Latino cultural and demographic ascendancy is not congruent with jural territorial realities, which are still shaped by continued US police power. This incongruity of cultural and political spaces makes of the 'border area', aptly named as such, an ambiguous zone. It is in this border area that identities are assigned and taken, withheld and rejected. The state seeks a monopoly on the power to assign identities to those who enter this space. It stamps or refuses to stamp passports and papers which are extensions of the person of the traveller who is 'required' to pass through official ports of entry and exit. But every day thousands of 'undocumented' persons successfully defy the state's power to control their movement into and through this space and in doing so contest not only space but also control of their identity.

Within official policy-making circles of the state, discussion of transnational subaltern communities is elaborated within a discourse of 'immigration policy', whereby the state attempts to regulate international migration. Rhetoric aside, and as noted above, the *de facto* immigration policy of the US government is *not* to make the US–Mexican border impermeable to the passage of 'illegal' entrants, but rather to regulate their 'flow', while at the same time maintaining the official distinctions between the 'sending' and 'receiving' nations, i.e. between kinds of peoples, that is, to constitute classes of peoples – classes in both the categorical and social sense.[12] Issues concerning 'migrant labour' are indeed at the core of the ongoing immigration debate, and here a major contradiction in official immigration policy appears. This situation results from the special nature of labour as a commodity that is embodied in persons and persons with national identities. Foreign labour is desired, but the persons in whom it is embodied are not desired. The immigration policies of 'receiving nations' can be seen as expressions of this contradiction and as attempts to resolve it. For the task of effective immigration policy is to separate labour from the jural person within which it is embodied, that is, to disembody the labour from the migrant worker.

This contradiction was notably apparent in the 1994 California gubernatorial campaigns in which the 'invasion of illegal aliens' became the primary issue as candidates for the governorship and other public offices sought to outdo each other in 'immigrant bashing'. The central issue became the costs to tax payers of welfare, education, law enforcement and such like due to the large and growing number of undocumented persons in the state. The current governor estimates that the total annual net cost to the state of such persons is US$2.4 billion. This figure is especially charged with emotion at present as the state staggers through a protracted economic depression, occasioned in large part by the decline of the defence industry. The base of the contradiction lies in the fact that the global competitiveness of many Californian industries depends on a productive, low cost labour force. Thus, for example, the major business in the state is agro-industry, which, while being the major contributor to political candidates, is also a major employer of 'illegal aliens'.

Immigration policy heightens the capitalist alienation of labour by geographically separating the site of the purchase and expenditure of that labour from the sites of its reproduction, such that the loci of production and reproduction lie in two different countries. This structure of transnational labour migration distinguishes it from the prevalent modern capitalist mechanisms for the appropriation of labour from subaltern groups: namely national labour markets, slavery and internal colonialism. Only in transnational 'labour migration' is there national separation of the sites of production and reproduction (see Burawoy 1976; Corrigan 1990a; Cohen 1987).

Modern capitalism has for several centuries relied in various degrees on transnational labour migration. But the point here is that transnational labour migration has now become a major structural feature of communities which have themselves become truly transnational. Official migration theory (migration theory informed by and in the service of the nation-state) is disposed to think of the sociology of migration in terms of 'sending' and 'receiving' communities, each of which is in its own national space. But the ethnography of transnational migration suggests that such communities are constituted transnationally and thus challenge the defining power of the nation-states which they transcend.

Elsewhere Carole Nagengast and I characterise the greater Mixtec diaspora and other widely extended subaltern communities as comparable to the transnational corporation and, accordingly, refer to them as transnational communities (Kearney and Nagengast 1989; cf. Rouse 1991). Both kinds of organisations engage in production orchestrated in two or more national spaces and so reproduce themselves. Thus, just as the transnational corporation in part transcends the Durkheimian power of the nation to impress itself as the basis of corporate identity, so do members of transnational communities similarly escape the power of the nation-state to inform their sense of collective identity.

To the degree that transnational corporations and transnational migrants escape the impress of the nation-state to shape their identity, so to a comparable degree must the native, non-ethnic 'white citizens' avail themselves of the only totemic capital that they have available to form an identity, from an inevitable dialectic of opposition with non-nationalist communities which are forming on and within their boundaries. And that totemic capital is of course nationalism (with a strong dash of racism). In areas of California, European-Americans have definitively lost control of much geographic space, of boundaries that have been 'invaded' by 'foreigners' and 'aliens'. But having lost control of geographic space in the Border Area, they have begun to take fall-back positions to defend social and cultural spaces where the state still has power to legislate identities and practices. Thus, a major part of the discourse on immigration currently centres on issues such as reinforcing English as 'the official language' (now so legislated in California, Arizona, Colorado and Florida).

These new forms of discipline correspond to a movement from an offensive jingoist nationalism to a nationalism on the defensive, a shift from a nationalism of expansion and domination to a defensive nationalism concerned with loss of control of its boundaries. To the degree that the modern nation-state and its associated culture are becoming anachronistic in the age of transnationalism, expressions of unease within the body politic – concerns with the integrity of its boundaries – are becoming apparent. As Gómez Peña aptly notes, 'For the North American the border becomes a mythical notion of national security. The border is where the Third World begins. The US media conceives [sic] the border as a kind of war zone. A place of conflict, of threat, of invasion' (Gómez Peña, quoted in Fusco 1989: 55). The current national obsession with 'foreign' drugs and 'crime' that are 'penetrating' into 'our nation' are also forms of transnationalism which similarly threaten the categorical integrity of the modern nation-state.

> One only need go down to this border just a short distance south of us to see how wildly out of control it is. And when we speak of out of control, we're not just talking about a few folks wanting to come in to get a job, we're talking about a torrent of people flooding in here, bringing all kinds of criminal elements and terrorists and all the rest with them.[13]

Such nativist sentiments as expressed in this quotation are symptomatic of the loss of spatial separation between developed and de-developed poles of transnationalism. A major way whereby this blurring of the modern and the 'traditional' is effected is via the spatial relocation of 'Third World' peoples into the core areas of the 'modern' capitalist West.

The transnational body and person

The border: Scene 4

Four Mixtec migrants are sitting around a table having their first meal in several days. For the previous four days they have been walking through the rugged mountains of eastern San Diego County. They are exhausted from cold, hunger and lack of sleep. Part of their trek was through snow; all of them are wearing light cotton clothing and two of them wear tennis shoes. They are talking with a Paraguayan peasant leader now in political exile, who is living in the house and who is astounded at their manner of entry into the United States. They tell him that when they came through these mountains they tried to sleep for part of the day and walk at night when it was too cold to sleep. But one night, they say, they became so cold that they had to stop and build a fire. One of them says that he was thinking as they were huddled around the small fire, hoping that it would not attract the attention of the *Migra*. He was thinking, he says, that he felt like a criminal, like someone who had to hide because they were doing some bad thing. But, he says, he could not understand what bad thing he was doing, for he is an honest man who comes to the United States only to work, to leave his sweat and earn some money. He says he is a father and husband and a good worker, and that is why his *patrones* always hire him. They do not think that he is criminal, but he says that he feels like he is a criminal and he cannot understand why. The other men agree that they feel the same when they are exposed to possible apprehension by the Border Patrol or by other police agents.[14]

As these sketches reveal, the US–Mexican border is riddled not only with holes but also with contradictions. In Scene 4 the Paraguayan, who is skilled in his own form of a pedagogy of the oppressed, proceeds to explain to the migrants why they feel like criminals, even though they know that they are honest productive workers. He startles them, engaging their attention by telling them that they run from the *Migra* and the police because, as he says to them, 'You pay the *Migra* to chase and persecute you.' 'How is that possible?' they ask. He then proceeds to elaborate on the accumulation of surplus value in the Californian farm labour market. These men will seek work as orange pickers in Riverside. The Paraguayan calculates the approximate wage that they will be paid for picking a pound of oranges. He then reminds them of the price of a pound of oranges in local markets, a price which differs greatly from what they will be paid. He explains how the difference is apportioned into costs of production, taxes and profits that are paid and earned by the grower. He then calls the men's attention to the taxes that the grower pays and how their taxes go towards the maintenance of the Border Patrol. Thus he proves his point that the migrants pay the *Migra* to pursue them like criminals. They, of course, then ask him why things are arranged this way, and by a Socratic questioning he elicits the answer from them: because they run scared all the time and are desperate to get work before they are apprehended and sent back to Mexico, they accept whatever wage is offered and then work like fiends and otherwise do what they can to satisfy their *patron*. In short, in a lesson that might have been taken from Foucault, he brings them to understand that the surveillance activities of the Border Patrol are not intended to prevent their entry into the United States to work, but instead are part of a number of ways of disciplining them to work hard and to accept low wages.

The contradiction in US immigration policy noted above is inscribed on the social person so constructed, the 'alien'. This 'alien' is desired as a body, or more specifically as labour power which is embodied in this person, by employers and indirectly by all who benefit economically and socially from this cheaply bought 'foreign' labour. But this alien as a legal person who might possess rights and prerogatives of a national, of a citizen of the nation, is the dimension of personhood that is denied. The ambiguity of the alien results from policy and policing which inscribe both of these identities – worker and alien – onto his person simultaneously (see Foucault 1977: 25–6). Being neither fish nor fowl and yet both at the same time, the alien is a highly ambiguous person.

As already mentioned, the 'border area' is a social and cultural zone of indeterminate extent, and some might argue that it runs from deep in Mexico to Canada. It is by passage into – but never completely through – this transnational zone that the alien is marked as the ambiguous, stigmatised, vulnerable person that he or she is. This border area is a liminal region into which initiates pass via what might punningly be called 'raites of passage', but from which they never emerge.[15] The alien exists in what appears to be the intersection of one of Leach's Venn diagrams (Leach 1964; cf. Turner 1964). And as we would expect from the anthropology of liminality, the initiate is reduced to a categorical state of non-human – in this case an 'alien'. In colloquial Mexican Spanish, 'illegal' border-crossers are pollos, or pollitos, that is, 'chickens' or 'little chicks'. This avian identity can be seen as a symbolism of initiation, of the twice born. Moreover, the pollos are defenceless creatures, vulnerable to the predators who prey upon them in the border zone. Indeed, the immediate border area is infested with predators who rob, rape, assault, murder, apprehend, extort and swindle the vulnerable pollos whose only advantage is their large numbers – most get through alive, although poorer.[16] And as Leach and Turner might have predicted, the hero of this liminal border is the supremely ambiguous and contradictory trickster and cultural hero of indigenous Mexico and North America, El Coyote (Melendez 1982). Ironically, but of necessity, the pollos must put themselves in the care of the coyote who may either deliver them or eat them.

We can now return to the Mixtec and ask how they respond to existence in this liminal transnational border area. Denied permanent residence in their homeland by economic necessity and denied naturalisation by the United States, Mixtec 'alien' migrants construct a new identity out of the bricolage of their transnational existence. What form does this transnational identity take? It coalesces as ethnicity, as an ethnic consciousness, which is the supremely appropriate form for collective identity to take in the age of transnationalism. In my research I have observed how Mixtec ethnicity arises as an alternative to nationalist consciousness and as a medium to circumscribe not space, but collective identity precisely in those border areas where nationalist boundaries of territory and identity are most contested and ambiguous (Kearney 1988; Nagengast and Kearney 1990). This situation conforms to Varese's analysis of how, under 'normal' conditions, the nation-state is able to supress other possible nations within it. 'Yet, sooner or later, it can no longer mask the development of the existing violent contradiction between the nations (that is the Indian ethnos) and the state' (Varese 1982: 35).

As Comaroff (1987: 307) notes, 'ethnicity has its origins in the asymmetric incorporation of structurally dissimilar groupings into a single political economy'. In this case, the single political economy is the transnational milieu of Mexico and the United States, where in both regions the Mixtec are construed as aliens. Denied their patrimony in Mexico, legally prejudiced in the United States, and otherwise used and abused in both nations, the Mixtec are marked as subaltern Other by the nations that reject them so as to exploit them. This transnational structured differentiation obviates the impress of nationalism as a basis for collective consciousness and thus opens the possibility for the ascendance into consciousness of ethnicity as a sign that marks difference, a sign that is recognised as such, both by those who are marked, and by those who mark them.[17] Moreover, those marked persons also remark on, and thus collaborate in the construction of, this system of difference.[18] The most outwardly visible form of Mixtec self-differentiation is the formation of various kinds of grassroots organisations in the United States and in Mexico that seek to defend their members as workers, migrants and 'aliens'.

As Mixtecs say, they come to the United States to leave sweat and take home some money. Sweat is a metaphor for *labour* which becomes disembodied from the 'alien' and as such contrasts with *work*.[19] Sweating for others in the United States contrasts with sweating for oneself in one's own community in Oaxaca. There, as it were, one's sweat falls onto one's own land and makes it produce *for oneself*, not for others. The community in Oaxaca is precisely that – a community, a social body which retains, more or less, its own sweat, its own labour in the form of work. To be an 'alien' is not only to experience the disembodiment of one's labour, but also to be socially disembodied, that is, to be removed from one's community to the degree that one's sweat, one's labour and identity, is soaked up in the United States. The individualised migrant is allowed into the US nation-state not as a citizen, but as an 'alien', not as someone to be incorporated into the social body, but as someone to be devoured by it. Migration policy/policing and resistance to it is thus a struggle for the value contained within the personal and social body of the migrant. The individual migrant resorts to micro strategies invented and reinvented by workers throughout the history of capitalism to retain economic capital embodied in their persons and desired by the *patron*. The worker seeks to be not just a machine or an 'animal' but a human being.[20] And as the individual worker seeks to defend his person and its embodied economic capital, so in a parallel manner the community attempts to defend the body social and its collective capital. It does so by converting some of that embodied capital into symbolic capital, and specifically symbolic capital in the form of markers of collective identity, expressions of which are noted by the state and by anthropologists as 'ethnicity'.

The Mixtec migrants are seemingly paradoxical in that they elaborate what appear to be signs of traditionality under conditions of modernity. But such inconsistency is only a spurious artefact of the discourse of nationalism and its intrinsic component of modernity. In other words, as the boundaries of the 'modern' nation-state dissolve under conditions of transnationalism, so does the opposition between tradition and modernity self-destruct and give way, grudgingly, to ethnicity as the primary form of symbolic capital expended in the construction of community in the age of transnationalism.

Disintegration and reconstruction of disciplinary boundaries

Deterioration of the boundaries of the nation can be expected to provoke a reconstitution of the state and its components, among which are its disciplines. Among the official academic disciplines, anthropology is unusual in the degree to which it has been assigned responsibility for articulating differentiation, and thus engaging in the intellectual/symbolic reproduction of differentiation, on a global scale, with respect to 'less developed peoples' as compared with 'us'. The fundamental epistemological structure of this 'classic' form of anthropology – it is classic compared with the 'baroque' anthropology of the present – was its firm categorical separation of anthropological Self from ethnographic Other, of those who undertook to know and those who were to be studied, known and, by implication (per Foucault), to be controlled. The modern period, as identified above, and which comes to an end after World War II, corresponds with this age of classic ethnography/anthropology.[21]

Anthropology – far from uniquely in the social sciences – is predicated primarily on the study of the alien Other, and has its own distinctive social epistemology of a knowing anthropological Self and a categorically distinct ethnographic Other that is to be known. This epistemological asymmetry of subject–object, of Self–Other, is in any ethnographic situation a reflection of a political asymmetry in which power, like the knowledge being discovered and produced, is unevenly distributed. Moreover, this differential production of knowledge is a differentiating production of power. Within capitalist society the social construction of reality occurs within the structured relations of classes of persons – those who study and consume the knowledge produced and those who are the objects, the raw materials of the knowledge. The dualism of bourgeois epistemology is predicated on this social duality and as such is inherited by all social sciences which acquire it as a basic disposition. But, as noted above, anthropology has its own social basis for epistemological dualism, which is given to it by the ethnographic distinction between Self and Other, which is so structured within the colonial situation and upon which colonial institutions erect parallel distinctions of class. Thus, given the double social origins of anthropology's epistemological dualism, it is – unlike that of, say, sociology – doubly determined.

As noted above, the mission of classic (modern) anthropology was contradictory: it had to humanise while it differentiated. We are all human, but we are all different. This is parallel to the contradiction which the nation-state must resolve. We are all one, but we are internally differentiated into classes, genders and races. In fulfilling this mission, anthropology applied the categories given to it by the ordering of official knowledge, especially the categorical distinction between Self and Other. Anthropological categories were established in the modern era which was associated with a robust nationalism. Now in the transnational era, this dualistic construction of classic anthropology, in both its positivist and interpretive modes, is inappropriate for the global, transnational differentiation of late capitalism in which the dualism of the colonial situation has been reconfigured into different spatial relationships. It is not that differentiation at the end of empire lessens, but that it involves a distinctly different spatial and temporal constellation of Self and Other and of the relationship between them. This categorical reordering of anthropological Self and ethnographic Other is most visible spatially in that they become interspersed, one in the geography of the other. Classic anthropology was done in communities of distinct Others; now, increasingly, the ethnographic Other is constituted in highly dispersed, interpenetrating transnational communities.

With the collapse of the categorical distinction between imperial Self and colonial Other, the basis was laid for the erosion of the social foundation of the modern nationalism of 'the West' and the emergence of new dimensions of global differentiation.[22] The imagining of this transnational condition has been reflected in several innovative 'antidisciplines'. These antidisciplines are antidisciplinarian in a double sense: they transcend the domains of the standard disciplines, and they tend to form themselves outside the official institutional body of the state, thus escaping the necessity of official scholarship elaborated as a constituting component of the nation-state. The project of *Annales* is one such case in point in that it displaced its vantage point outside national history and transcended historiography, seen as the history of nations as actors, to greater contexts and force fields within which the fates of nations are shaped.[23] Foucault's project too is an exemplar of antidisciplinary and antidisciplinarian scholarship. Foucault is the herald of the 'death of man', of the death of the Western subject in the post-modern age, which is to say in the age of transnationalism.[24] This disappearance of the subject/person of the classic social sciences and humanistic disciplines threatens these disciplines as they have been classically constituted. Accordingly, the dissolution of the disciplines which discipline the person/body can be assumed to run parallel to a corresponding reconstitution of disciplines.

As the 'alien' presents a challenge to the integrity of the US nation-state, the nation-state has responded by developing new disciplines to control its territorial boundaries and the cultural constructions upon which they are predicated. *This* discourse of nations and their boundaries is manifest, for example, in the current debates on North American university campuses over 'Western Civilisation' and 'Ethnic Studies' requirements. One can also note here the recent rise and institutionalisation of programmes of 'Border Studies', which are in some ways the academic counterpart of the Border Patrol. Other homologues of this tension in the boundary of the nation-state are the official language laws already noted and the national debate on immigration policy which was recently punctuated by the passage of the United States Immigration and Reform Control Act of 1986.

The dialectic of transnational exploitation and resistance takes place on the margins of nations and is both a symptom and cause of the progressive dissolution of the power of these nations to impress themselves as nationalities and as nationalisms on the subaltern peoples within their boundaries. One of the various dimensions of this challenge to the nation-state is the increasing refusal of transnational ethnic minorities to be the objects of study by the disciplines of the nation-state – it might be said that this is but one of a number of ways in which they refuse to be disciplined. As transnational subalterns increasingly penetrate into the cores of the world system, their presence there not only reorganises the spatial differentiation of development and underdevelopment, but also challenges the epistemological basis of classic anthropology in the manner already indicated. One result of this reordering is an increasing refusal of former ethnographic Others to submit to being taken as objects of investigation by the standard disciplines and a corresponding insistence on writing and speaking for themselves.[25]

Just as the borders and boundaries of the modern nation-state have become contested terrain, so increasingly is the power of official anthropology to describe peoples unilaterally and to form policies that affect them being challenged. In the case of Mixtecs this sensibility has manifested itself among various spokespersons and groups as a desire and an attempt to develop an autochthonous social science that can inform 'the community' about itself and its relationships with the powers which encompass it. This informing thus becomes literally part of the process of forming the ethnic community that is informed. In the

Mixtec transnational community this indigenous anthropology thus becomes a constituent of that which it seeks to study.[26] Such an anthropology, which is brought into being by the conditions of transnationalism and all that this term implies for the constitution of subaltern communities apart from the impress of national forces and for the dissolution of the traditional disciplining disciplines, is aptly referred to as a 'Practical Anthropology' (Kearney n.d.).

On the US side of the border, in California, the differentiating project of the state seems to be 'out of control'. This is most apparent demographically, with Los Angeles being simultaneously the largest city in California and, as pundits ironically note, the second largest city in Mexico. Clearly, Latin America does not stop at the border: a Mexican–Latino corridor now extends from Tijuana – the second largest city on the Pacific Coast, following Los Angeles – to deep within US territory, and here and beyond there is a large and growing archipelago of Latino peoples.[27]

Throughout this archipelago, practices of differing from below, born of forms of survival and resistance, proceed apace with official differing from above, and combine in a dialexis that defies modernism's ideology of the 'melting pot' (Corrigan n.d.). For generations, until the late 1970s, one of the main results of this dialexis was 'Chicano culture' in its various forms ranging from the more defiant and more or less conscious styles of resistance elaborated by 'pachucos', 'low riders' and 'home boys' with their distinctive argot to the persistence of more 'traditional' forms of Mexican culture such as Mexican language, music, folk medicine and cuisine. From the dominant European–American perspective, all of these 'alien' ways were simply Mexican. But to Mexicans – 'real Mexicans' – in Mexico, these things Mexican-American were *pocho*, that is ersatz and inferior. But in the late 1970s *el Chicano* was 'discovered' by Mexican intellectuals and cultural brokers. No longer seen as a bastard son, the Chicano became an icon of a particular kind of 'Mexican' creativity and resistance deep in the belly of the colossus to the north. In Mexican eyes, the Chicano has gone from a *pocho* to a cultural hero living in a region of occupied Mexico.[28] The border has thus taken on a different meaning for Mexicans than it has for European-Americans.

The recent dramatic revaluing of the Chicano and more generally of Mexico's relation to the north is doubtlessly related to the deep 'crisis' which Mexico has been experiencing since the mid-1980s in which real income of the middle and low sectors decreased by around 50 per cent, and official unemployment stood at around 40 to 50 per cent. Under these conditions, there is more pressure than ever on Mexicans to go to the United States to work. If the Mexicans living and working in the United States were to be repatriated into Mexico's supersaturated labour markets, all commentators agree that an impossible situation would result, aggravated by the loss of the sojourners' remittances which are no doubt Mexico's second or third most important source of foreign exchange. There are thus in Mexico deep structural reasons affecting perceptions of the national boundary. It has become more of an obstacle, a hindrance to getting to work and back, not unlike commuter problems elsewhere.

With respect to the necessity of the Mexican state to export jobs, a porous border is desirable. But as a modern nation-state, an assault on the integrity of its border is an assault on its power – its power to order and to differ. The border has thus become highly problematic for the Mexican state. Nowhere is this more apparent than in Tijuana which is, as Gómez Peña notes,

a place where so-called Mexican identity breaks down – challenging the very myth of national identity. The Mexican government has constructed this myth, which is that we have a univocal identity, one that is monolithic and static, and that all Mexicans from Cancun to Tijuana, from Matamoros to Oaxaca behave, act and think exactly the same. Of course this is a very comfortable myth for them to justify their power. By homogenizing all Mexicans and saying that, for example, Mexicans have a hard time entering into modernity, the Mexican state can offer itself as a redemptor of Mexicans, and the one who is going to guide them by the hand into modernity. So Tijuana is a kind of challenge to the Mexican government. (Quoted in Fusco 1989: 70)

Tijuana is in its own way as transnational a city as is Los Angeles, and indeed the two are inexorably fusing together into one transnational megapolis spanning the border. Another variant of this transnationalism is the immense demographic, cultural, emotional and very 'illegal' unofficial transnational bridge now in place between urban areas such as Los Angeles and Central America. As a result of US interventions in Central America, hundreds of thousands of refugees from that troubled area now live in the liminal world of the 'undocumented' who are *in* the United States but not *of* the United States. What has become apparent now at the end of the twentieth century is that imperial projects to differentiate the colonised Other promote indigestible differences within the colonising Self.

Conclusion

The Border Area is a liminal area where creative energies are released, creating signs and identities that are born outside of the national projects of the two nations which presume to control identities in this zone. This changing configuration of the border challenges the ability of the two nation-states involved to define the legal and cultural identities of their border populations, which transcend the official spatial and legal bounds. Two forms of this decay of the nationalist project are notable: one is the inability, born of contradictory desires, of the US state to 'document' the 'aliens' in its territory. The other is seen in the 'crisis of representation' in anthropology about which so much has been said. This is so because the epistemology of modern anthropology has been constructed as part and parcel of the dualism of the modern nation-state whereby it differentiates between its 'modern' Self and 'traditional' Others. In the Border Area this once spatial, categorical and very political distinction is becoming increasingly blurred. Whereas the past history of immigration into the United States has been one of assimilation, the ethnography of the Border Area suggests that its future history will be one of indigestibility, as the unity of national totemism gives way to the multiplicity of transnational ethnicity.

Notes

I wish to thank Paul Chace, John Comaroff, Philip Corrigan, Jean Lave, Carole Nagengast, Daniel Nugent, Mary O'Connor, Roger Rouse and Jonathan Turner for their helpful comments on an earlier version of this chapter.

1. These terms correspond to the notions of 'borderline' and 'frontier' respectively as set out in the editors' introductory chapter, which sees borders as consisting of three elements: the borderline, the structures of the state at the borderline, and the frontier (see this volume, p. 9).
2. For an illuminating discussion of the 'dialexis' of differentiation and dominance in general, see Corrigan (n.d. and 1990b). As used in this chapter, 'dialexis' refers to the shaping of cultural forms and social identities that results from the 'bottom-up' everyday productions and expressions of subalterns as they combine with and react to the 'top-down' constructions of cultural identity and social form that are imposed by the nation-state.
3. On economic capital and its transformations, see Bourdieu (1986).
4. Following Marx's distinction, it is useful to see bourgeois society as asserting itself outwardly as nationality and inwardly as state; see Corrigan and Sayer (1985: 1).
5. For a review of current anthropological theory and research on transnationalism see Kearney (1995).
6. Based on observations made by the author on various occasions between 1985 and 1988.
7. A description and photographs of this event were given to the author by Jorge Bustamante, President of *El Colegio de la Frontera Norte*, Tijuana, Baja California.

8. Observations made by the author on various occasions in recent years.
9. I have taken this term from a BBC television documentary series of the same name.
10. See Mandel (1989) for an illuminating discussion of the cultural politics of ethnicity and difference in the context of foreign labour migration in Europe.
11. Heyman (1991: 41) discusses and documents how 'the overall trend of US policy from 1940 to 1986 has been increased application of force at the border'.
12. As Cockcroft (1986) notes, in practice immigration policy is labour policy disguised as immigration policy. This interpretation of US policy re the US–Mexican border is supported by the research of Jorge Bustamante (1983), who has found an inverse relationship between economic indicators of the health of the US economy and the rate of apprehensions of undocumented Mexican migrants. In other words, as the US economy enters periods of expansion, the 'valve' is opened wider, allowing a greater 'flow' of Mexican labour, and then when the economy enters a recession associated with rising unemployment in the United States, the valve is partially closed to reduce the 'flow'.
13. James Turnage, Director of the Immigration and Naturalization Service in San Diego; quoted in Wolf (1988: 2).
14. Observed by the author in 1985.
15. *Raite* is a corruption of 'ride' and is pronounced 'RYE-tay'. One of the main services of coyotes is to arrange for *raites*, which is transportation to points north, or informal transportation in general. A person who provides such services is a *raitero*. Migrants sometimes punningly refer to *raiteros* as *rateros* (thieves). Passage for 'wetbacks' across the watery border between Morocco and Spain is also a 'rite of passage' through a dangerous space, the structure and sociology of which bears remarkable similarities to the US–Mexican border area and in which the counterparts of *coyotes* and *pollos* are 'wolves' and 'sheep' (see Driessen, this volume).
16. On collaboration of police and *coyotes*, police extortion and other human rights violations of Mexican migrants in the Border Area, see Nagengast, Stavenhagen and Kearney (1992).
17. On the consciousness of the transnational see Comaroff and Comaroff (1987).
18. John Comaroff comments on this dialectic of ethnic formation:

> The emergence of ethnic groups and the awakening of ethnic consciousness are . . . the product of historic forces which structure relations of inequality between discrete social entities. They are, in other words, the social and cultural correlates of a specific mode of articulation between groupings, in which one extends its dominance over another by some form of coercion, violent or otherwise; situates the latter as a bounded unit in a dependent and unique position within an inclusive division of labor; and, by removing from it final control over the means of production and/or reproduction, regulates the terms upon which value may be extracted from it. By virtue of so [doing], the dominant grouping constitutes both itself and the subordinate population as classes; whatever the prior sociological character of these aggregations, they are, in the process, actualized as groups *an sich*. (Comaroff 1987: 308)

19. On the distinction between 'work' and 'labour' see Comaroff and Comaroff (1987: 196–202).
20. A frequent observation of Mixtec migrants in the United States is that 'here we live and work like beasts'. And as one Mixtec farmworker recently remarked, 'The bosses treat their animals better than they treat us. They give their dogs, horses, and chickens houses to sleep in. But us they leave out in the rain. They even have barns for their tractors, but not for us.' The reference here is to the thousands of Mixtecs in California and Oregon who live outdoors in makeshift camps.
21. The 'classic' period of anthropology reached its apogee in the interwar period when the 'classic ethnographies' were written, e.g., those of Malinowski, Evans-Pritchard, Firth, Radcliffe-Brown, and their Boasian counterparts in the United States.
22. The rise of a differently constituted nationalism, a peripheral nationalism propelled by movements of 'national liberation', is an important part of this global shift to transnationalism, but cannot be dealt with here. See Chatterji (1986).
23. It is thus apparent that the objective reality of transnationalism, in both senses, has called forth a historiography which appears on the stage of history at its appropriate moment to reflect this transnational condition in consciousness: the project of the *Annales*, its global vision, is a reflex of the conditions of the moment of its appearance. And why the *Annales* group and not official scholarship? Bourdieu's (1988) work on the tension between ideas produced by intellectuals institutionalised within the official bureaucracies of the state versus those peripheral to it is instructive and suggests that the *Annales* was disposed to reflect transnational conditions because it was not assigned the task by the state of elaborating a historiography of nationalism, that is, a historiography which is a constituent of the nation-state. It is this sort of antidisciplinary scholarship which has given us the vocabulary to understand transnationalism as global history.
24. The modern subject, the individual 'actor' of capitalist society, whose demise Foucault announces, was and is a cultural construction born of two distinctly modern conditions. One of these was the power of commodification to create 'individuals' as distinct from the communities from which, by market forces, they were alienated and so formed. The other basis for the cultural construction of the modern individual was the modern distinction between colonial Self and colonised Other. The Western subject/Self only exists in *relationship* to an Other, and thus the collapse of the modern global categorical relationship between anthropological Self and ethnographic Other also occasions the 'death of man', of the subject as it was constructed in the modern age. (On the world-view universals of Self, Other and Relationship see Kearney 1984.) Foucault does not study the transnational age, focusing as he does on the modern age, but his method – the form of his work – personifies it, based as it is on Marx whose work was not, as is often observed, 'interdisciplinary' but transdisciplinary. More than the *Annales* and Foucault, Marx's transdisciplinary method pointed the way to transnationalism, denoted in his discourse as an 'internationalism', an idea that informed the subaltern counterpart of the transnational corporation,

namely 'The International'. This internationalism as a vision of global identity is a prescient sentiment that appears in the mid-nineteenth century at the apogee of the modern age and foretells the dissolution of its necessary sociocultural form, the nation-state.
25. See Harlow (1987) and *Latin American Perspectives* 1991 nos. 71 and 72, which are devoted to testimonial literature.
26. Numerous comparable instances exist among other 'traditional' groups which have recently assumed and been ascribed ethnicity (see Kearney and Varese 1995).
27. This image of Latin America as an archipelago is Gómez Peña's (Fusco 1989:73).
28. On *cholos*, *chavos* and punks on the border, see Valenzuela (1988).

References

Anderson, Benedict 1983. *Imagined communities: reflections on the origin and spread of nationalism.* London: Verso.
Bourdieu, Pierre 1981. 'The specificity of the scientific field', in Charles C. Lemert (ed.), *French Sociology: Rupture and Renewal Since 1968.* New York: Columbia University Press, pp. 257–92.
   1986. 'The forms of capital', in J. B. Richardson (ed.), *Handbook of theory and research for the sociology of education.* New York: Greenwood Press, pp. 241–58.
   1988. *Homo academicus.* Stanford: Stanford University Press.
Burawoy, Michael 1976. 'The functions and reproduction of migrant labor: comparative material from southern Africa and the United States', *American Journal of Sociology* 81: 1050–87.
Bustamante, Jorge A. 1983. 'The Mexicans are coming: from ideology to labor relations', *International Migration Review* 17: 323–431.
Chatterji, Partha 1986. *Nationalist thought and the colonial world.* London: Zed Press.
Cockcroft, James 1986. *Outlaws in the Promised Land: Mexican immigrant workers and America's future.* New York: Grove Press.
Cohen, Robin 1987. *The new helots: migrants in the international division of labour.* Aldershot, England: Avebury.
Comaroff, Jean and John L. Comaroff 1987. 'The madman and the migrant: work and labor in the historical consciousness of a South African people', *American Ethnologist* 14 (2): 191–209.
Comaroff, John L. 1987. 'Of totemism and ethnicity: consciousness, practice and the signs of inequality', *Ethnos* 52 (3–4): 301–23.
Corrigan, Philip n.d. 'Power/Difference', University of Exeter, unpublished Ms.
   1990a. 'Feudal relics or capitalist monuments? Notes on the sociology of unfree labour', in Philip Corrigan (ed.), *Social forms/human capacities: essays in authority and difference.* London: Routledge, pp. 54–101.
   1990b. *Social forms/human capacities: essays in authority and difference.* London: Routledge.

Corrigan, Philip and Derek Sayer 1985. *The great arch: English state formation as cultural revolution*. London: Basil Blackwell.

Foucault, Michel 1972. *The archaeology of knowledge*. New York: Harper.

1977. *Discipline and punish*. New York: Vintage.

Fusco, Coco 1989. 'The Border Art Workshop/Taller de Arte Fronterizo: interview with Guillermo Gómez Peña and Emily Hicks', *Third Text* 7: 53–76.

Gómez Peña, Guillermo 1986. 'A new artistic continent', *High Performance* 35: 24–31.

Harlow, Barbara 1987. *Resistance literature*. New York: Methuen.

Heyman, Josiah 1991. *Life and labor on the border: working people of Northeastern Sonora, Mexico, 1886–1986*. Tucson: University of Arizona Press.

Hobsbawm, Eric 1987. *The age of empire: 1875–1914*. New York: Pantheon.

Kearney, Michael 1984. *World view*. Novato, CA: Chandler & Sharp.

1986. 'From the invisible hand to visible feet: anthropological studies of migration and development', *Annual Review of Anthropology* 15: 331–61.

1988. 'Mixtec political consciousness: from passive to active resistance', in Daniel Nugent (ed.), *Rural revolt in Mexico and US intervention*. Center for US–Mexican Studies, University of California, San Diego, Monograph Series 27, pp. 113–24.

1995. 'The local and the global: the anthropology of globalization and transnationalism', *Annual Review of Anthropology* 24: 547–65.

n.d. 'Practical ethnography/practical anthropology'. Unpublished Ms.

Kearney, Michael and Carole Nagengast 1989. *Anthropological perspectives on transnational communities in rural California*. Working Group on Farm Labor and Rural Poverty, Working Paper #3. Davis, CA: California Institute for Rural Studies.

Kearney, Michael and Stefano Varese 1995. 'Latin America's indigenous peoples today: changing identities and forms of resistance in global context', in Richard Harris and S. Halebsky (eds.), *Capital, power and inequality in Latin America*. Boulder: Westview Press, pp. 207–31.

Leach, Edmund R. 1964. 'Anthropological aspects of language: animal categories and verbal abuse', in E. H. Lenneberg (ed.), *New directions in the study of language*. Cambridge: MIT Press, pp. 23–63.

Mandel, Ernest 1975. *Late capitalism*. London: New Left Books.

Mandel, Ruth 1989. 'Ethnicity and identity among migrant guestworkers in West Berlin', in N. Gonzalez and C. McCommon (eds.), *Conflict, migration, and the expression of ethnicity*. Boulder: Westview Press, pp. 60–74.

Melendez, Theresa 1982. 'Coyote: towards a definition', *Aztlán: International Journal of Chicano Studies Research* 13 (1–2): 295–307.

Nagengast, Carole and Michael Kearney 1990. 'Mixtec ethnicity: social identity, political consciousness, and political activism', *Latin American Research Review* 25 (1): 61–91.

Nagengast, Carole, Rodolfo Stavenhagen and Michael Kearney 1992. *Human rights and indigenous workers: the Mixtecs in Mexico and the United States*. Center for US–Mexican Studies, University of California, San Diego.

Rouse, Roger 1991. 'Mexican migration and the social space of postmodernism', *Diaspora: A Journal of Transnational Studies* 1 (1): 8–23.

Sassen-Koob, S. 1982. 'Recomposition and peripheralization at the core', *Contemporary Marxism* 5: 88–100.

Turner, Victor 1964. 'Betwixt and between: the liminal period in rites of passage', in *Proceedings of the American Ethnological Society*, Symposium on New Approaches to the Study of Religion, pp. 4–20.

Varese, Stefano 1982. 'Restoring multiplicity: Indianities and the civilizing project in Latin America', *Latin American Perspectives* 9 (2): 29–41.

Valenzuela, Jose Manuel 1988. *La Brava Ese*. Tijuana: El Colegio de la Frontera Norte.

Wolf, Daniel 1988. *Undocumented aliens and crime: the case of San Diego County*. San Diego: Center for US–Mexican Studies, University of California.

6   National identity on the frontier: Palestinians in the Israeli education system

Dan Rabinowitz

Introduction

Barth's concern, a generation ago, with the extent to which ethnic groups have boundaries (Barth 1969) has developed into a preoccupation with the extent to which cultures have borders and borders have culture(s). The boundaries of culture and the relationship of culture to territory are most significantly debated in the discourse of transnationalism, where enquiries into creolisation and hybridisation in border areas (Anzaldua 1987, Rosaldo 1988) have led to studies of diasporas (Clifford 1994, Boyarin and Boyarin 1993), and other interstitial phenomena. The initial tendency among anthropologists to look at border situations from the point of view of members of the marginal minority has also been supplemented by an enquiry into the perspective of the dominant majority (Rabinowitz 1994a).

The discourse of transnationalism is based on a productive critique of the inherent imperfections of traditional representations of nations, states and cultures as geographically discrete and politically pacific. It suggests a radically different definition of space and occupancy in which entities other than those defined by, contained within, or tantamount to states and nations become significant elements of the human experience.

The concept of the border zone – a place where, as Jon Simons (1995) put it, no one ever feels at home – challenges the primacy in Western culture of discrete borders and rigid boundaries. But while constantly moving away from this rigidity, the discourse of transnationalism remains dialectically dependent on it. If earlier traditions in geography, history and even anthropology were preoccupied with defining borders, redrawing and adjusting them, the current drive is an attempt to diffuse them. Studying communities which live across borders, survive despite them, routinely cross them and constantly network around them has become an indispensable aspect of the discourse.

This chapter is about a national frontier – that between Israelis and

142

Palestinians[1] – within Israel. Once labelled one of Israel's 'internal frontiers' (Kimmerling 1983), this demarcation line throws into relief some general characteristics of border areas and of the agency of those who find themselves living in them. This national frontier also extends into a number of states in the region, beyond Israel's state borders, reflecting not only the Palestinian experience of diaspora, but also Nazareth's location at the crossroads of a number of historical empires and states. Thus, although Israel may be a 'strong' state with rigid and effectively sealed off international borders, the national divide between Palestinian citizens of Israel and Israeli (Jewish) citizens puts all boundaries, internal and external, into perspective. The coherence of the state is systematically threatened by the internal cleavage. Moreover, the attachment of Palestinian citizens of Israel to other Arab groups across the border – a solidarity defined by culture, language, kin and destiny – plays a major part. Any attempt to analyse culture and society of Israelis and of Palestinians within Israel as separate from national boundaries, be they internal or external to the state, is futile.

This chapter is about education – a major aspect of nationalism (Gellner 1983) and a basic tenet of modern statehood. A state mono-poly, education is both a means to improve individuals and a tool in the service of the larger system. It homogenises language and bureaucratic skills, indoctrinates and shapes the individual for the advantage of collectives, ultimately of the state itself. The education system of the Palestinian citizens of Israel is sponsored and controlled by the state of Israel in a separate, clearly bound bureaucratic sub-system. Only rarely are the divisions between Israeli and Palestinian students, parents and teachers suspended. When they are, a metaphoric border zone emerges whereby the intimate and national collide. The case of nursery schools for Palestinian toddlers, administered by the all-Israeli staff of municipal officials of a new town which perceives itself as purely Jewish, is one such case.

Nursery schools are half-way spaces, whereby three- and four-year-olds, having left their homes for the first time, are being cared for exclusively by women. In fact the four main characters in this ethno-graphy are women: two mothers, two teachers, an Israeli and a Palesti-nian within each pair. Their roles as formal and informal emissaries, shouldering roles and duties ostensibly delegated to them from their respective national collectives, bring to the fore the agency of women on the national frontier. Gender thus emerges as a significant aspect of the national frontiers within the state of Israel.

Recent sociological and political science studies of Israel contribute important concepts to our understanding of the place of Palestinian citizens of Israel within the state and the society. Zureik (1979) sees these Palestinians as subjects of 'internal colonialism'. Smooha conceptualises their predicament as life on the receiving end of 'ethnic democracy' (Smooha 1989; see also Yiftachel 1992 for a critique of the model). Peled (1992) highlights the Palestinians' non-participation in what he terms the Israeli 'ethnic republic'. My present analysis of Palestinians occupying a border area attempts to dislodge their case from traditional state vs minority idioms and to examine it in the theoretical light of transnationalism. The social and pedagogic marginality of Palestinian toddlers admitted into an otherwise exclusive Israeli education system highlights the limitations of deeply divided border areas as zones of productive co-existence. The glimpses of pluralistic spirit usually expected and sometimes found in nursery schools stands in stark contrast to the rigidity, essentialism and exclusion inherent in segregated education. This suggests that rather than cultural hybridisation, creolisation and the gradual collapse of essentialist partitions between the dominant Israeli state and a subordinate Palestinian culture, the formal education system which the state imposes on the border in fact enhances a pluralist, liberal regime of neo-colonial cultural domination.

Natzerat Illit

The biblical village of Nazareth grew considerably after the beginning of the nineteenth century. Having become a full-sized town by the 1870s, Nazareth was one of the only Palestinian urban centres whose inhabitants stayed put during the war of 1948 (Morris 1991: 270–2). Ironically, the loss of other Palestinian communities in Galilee strengthened Nazareth, which ended up absorbing a large number of displaced Palestinian families. With a population of approximately 60,000, the town is now the main Palestinian urban centre in Israel and a focus of commerce and services for the entire region of southern Galilee.

The growth of Nazareth since the establishment of Israel in 1948, however, was coupled with serious territorial losses. Not least was that associated with the establishment in the 1950s of the Israeli town of Natzerat Illit, for which the central government allocated 15,000 dunams (approximately 3,700 acres) immediately east of Nazareth (see map 6.1). This move signalled the curtailment of the Palestinian town's main territorial hinterland for future development. Born out of the 1949 resolution of the Israeli cabinet to 'Judaise Galilee', and established as part of the third stage in this drive (Kipnis 1983: 723–4), Natzerat Illit was deliberately placed at the Palestinian heartland of lower Galilee. In this respect it is in line with other cases whereby multi-ethnic states

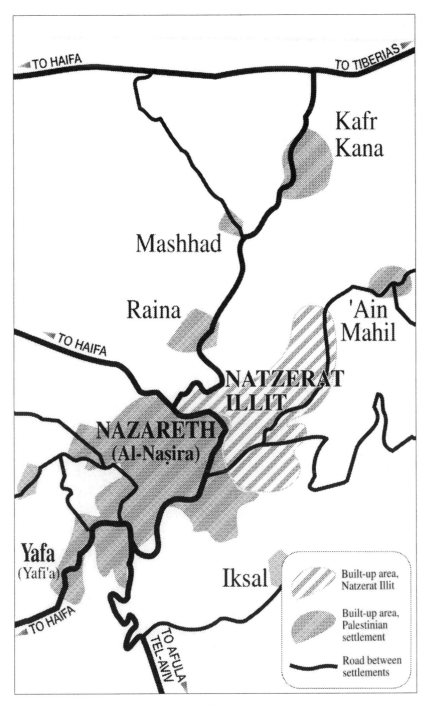

Map 6.1   Road map of the Nazareth area.

endeavour either to disperse minorities or to penetrate their homelands (Yiftachel 1994). Meanwhile, the growing scarcity of land in Palestinian Nazareth, together with asymmetric allocation of state resources to Palestinian local authorities (cf. Al-Haj and Rosenfeld 1990), uneconomic land-use patterns on the part of Palestinians and consistent reluctance on the part of central government to invest in public housing in Nazareth resulted in an ever-growing gap between heavy demand for housing and poor supply of actual units. Unable to afford to build or buy private homes in the Palestinian town, Nazarenes – particularly young families – in the 1970s began to rent and buy in adjacent Natzerat Illit. The Israeli town, by contrast, had considerable state investment in large-scale housing projects, creating by the late 1970s a growing surplus of residential units and an ailing real estate market.

Palestinians moving to Natzerat Illit in the 1980s were typically well-educated, professional, upwardly mobile Christian couples in their thirties and early forties (Rabinowitz 1997: 38–41). Their presence in the new town, beginning as a trickle in the late 1960s (Al Hamishmar 1984), became substantial in the late 1970s. It further intensified in the early 1980s (Bar-Gal 1986, Hefer-Rogovin 1987), growing to an unprecedented 800 households by the time I began fieldwork there in early 1989, when three-quarters of the residents were owner-occupiers.[2] Intended by the state to remain an exclusively Israeli settlement, the town was steadily becoming home to Palestinian families, much to the chagrin of Israeli residents. By the late 1980s, Palestinians constituted more than 12 per cent of the total population of Natzerat Illit.[3] The Israeli populace regarded this inflow as a serious problem, a feature which consistently reduces the town's reputation and its ability to compete successfully with other peripheral new towns in Israel.

Segregated education

Israel has a fully segregated educational system. Schools catering for Palestinian communities are run by a section of the Ministry of Education quite separate to that which operates schools for Israelis. This segregation, while not enshrined in state law, is meticulously maintained, not least in mixed communities such as Natzerat Illit. Palestinian residents of Natzerat Illit send their children to schools in adjacent Nazareth, a community where the long-term presence of Christian missions sponsored the development of a diverse and academically sophisticated educational system. The schooling system in Natzerat Illit, which caters exclusively for Israelis, is generally regarded as mediocre.

The one exception to educational segregation in Natzerat Illit is at nursery-school level. Nursery education for five-year-olds has been a formal part of compulsory schooling in Israel for decades, a provision extended to include four-year-olds in the 1980s. This immediately included Palestinian toddlers in the cohort which, according to the Israeli law of compulsory education, must be catered for by the municipal education department. With a high proportion of Christian Palestinian women employed outside the home, middle-class Palestinian families in Natzerat Illit have always needed affordable day-care facilities for toddlers. Unlike the excellent facilities for elementary and secondary schooling, Nazareth, the default choice for Palestinian families living in adjacent Natzerat Illit, had only a handful of overcrowded nursery schools by the late 1980s.

Palestinian parents in Natzerat Illit, on the other hand, have long had better options. The municipality of Natzerat Illit had almost forty nursery schools operating by 1989. Palestinian residents of the town had been attempting to enrol their children in these schools since the late 1970s. This attempt was made in spite of the obvious language barrier (the medium of instruction in nurseries in Natzerat Illit is Hebrew) and regardless of the realisation on the part of Palestinian parents (and their preference) that once nursery education was over, their children would join their peers in Nazareth for elementary school. Enrolment of Palestinian children in nursery schools in Natzerat Illit, however, remains scattered and sporadic. One reason is the policy of the all-Israeli education department in the municipal council of Natzerat Illit, which manipulates Palestinian applicants to ensure that they never exceed one or two per age group in a given nursery. Palestinian parents whose children are admitted tend to be submissive, often projecting an air of gratitude to the authorities for allowing their children the right to be there in the first place.

The pressure associated with the legal responsibility of the local authority for nursery education, however, created its own dynamics. In 1978, the department of education designated a nursery school in the northern section of town to admit Palestinian children. Five toddlers whose families resided in the neighbourhood were enrolled that year, joining a cohort of twenty-five Israeli children. The staff, which previously included a head teacher and an assistant, both of them Israeli women, was joined by a new recruit, a Palestinian woman whose job description was *ozeret safa* – Hebrew for 'language assistant'. Her task, as she put it to me a decade later, was 'to help out the Arab children, none of whom could speak any Hebrew when they first came to the nursery'.

Nicole, a professional employed by a welfare agency in Nazareth and mother of one of the Palestinian toddlers admitted into that first cohort, said in 1989 that the nursery had been perfect for her needs, and that she felt her daughter had been well taken care of. Her next-door neighbour Rutti, an Israeli, had her daughter at the same nursery, and the two girls were inseparable, playing together in the mornings at nursery school and in the afternoons at either of their homes.

This situation did not last long though. In early 1979 a number of the Israeli parents approached the council's education officers, demanding the removal of the Palestinian children from the nursery. Rutti, it soon became apparent, was a leading figure in this initiative. In 1989, embarrassed, she conveyed her version of the episode:

I really do not know what came over me, going to the council and placing that unjustified demand. I guess it was still the aftermath of leaving the Kibbutz. You see, it is not that our standard of living in Natzerat Illit was any lower than in the Kibbutz – in fact, our housing conditions improved remarkably once we moved. It was the general tatty appearance of things, and the feeling that the wholesomeness of being Israeli, of belonging to a place I loved – something I took for granted in the Kibbutz – was irreparably missing. This place, full of new immigrants with whom, apart from good will and idealism, I had so little in common . . . it was difficult. And then, on top of all this to have my daughter educated with Arabs . . . I guess for me it spelt another step away from the Israel I knew and loved, and the culture I was educated to believe in.

Nicole, not surprisingly, took her next-door neighbour's move as a personal betrayal. She initiated a confrontation, demanding an explanation from her friend and neighbour, forcing the truth home that the move initiated by Rutti was equally directed against her Palestinian self. 'Yes I am an Arab' she had to repeat to Rutti, who kept insisting that Nicole, who speaks impeccable Hebrew and has a fair complexion, 'was not'. Nicole then convened a meeting of the parents, accused them all of racism, a point which at least some of them apparently conceded. Rutti soon contacted the municipal council, asking them to drop the issue and to allow the nursery to go on as before. At that stage Nicole's husband, a well-known professional in his own right, stepped in and withdrew their child from the nursery. The newly elected Communist-led municipality of Nazareth had just established a day-care centre, where he had no difficulty securing a place for his daughter, who went on to attend primary, secondary and high schools in Nazareth. Her brother, some four years younger, attended a Na'amat (trade union women's section) day-care centre in Natzerat Illit between the age of two and three, then proceeded to primary and secondary schools in Nazareth. The couple's youngest daughter began attending a day-care centre in Nazareth in 1987, when she turned two. All three children ironically had Israeli child-minders when they were under two; as was typical among many families at that time, these were women of North African origin living nearby.

Decisions taken by Nicole and her husband suggest that like most Palestinians in Natzerat Illit, they draw a clear line between school education (including nursery schools), for which they turned to Nazareth, and child-minding and day-care centres, for which they chose Natzerat Illit, their town of residence. Nursery schools, with their more intensive pedagogic intervention and tighter administrative control, clearly represent the arbitrary and exclusive nature of the education system in a manner which day-care centres do not. At this juncture affiliation with the municipality of Nazareth – not only Arabic-speaking and Palestinian but also dominated by the communist party, so clearly disassociated from the state – became the natural choice.

Rutti, a liberal-minded person who regularly visited Nicole's apartment, became uneasy once the toddlers were enrolled at nursery school together. The nursery school was a part of the official education system, and so the situation was injected with new meanings. Matters now went beyond questions such as who plays with whom, where or when. The Israeli woman clearly found the public aspects of having her child educated with Palestinian toddlers taxing. Her own apologetic retrospective account invokes her need to feel 'a wholesome Israeli' – an experience she found impossible to keep compatible with liberalism.

Invisible school

The education department of Natzerat Illit took no further action regarding the mixed nursery school in 1979 or 1980. The next academic year, however, saw change: the mixed nursery ceased to admit Palestinian toddlers.[4] Instead, in 1980, the municipality set up two new nursery schools to cater exclusively for Palestinian toddlers. Located in a part of town where the majority of families were Palestinian, one school catered for three- and four-year-olds while the other, housed in an adjacent building, was designed for four- and five-year-olds. Both started out with Israeli head-teachers and Palestinian assistants.

One of the assistants was Na'ila, the language assistant at the old mixed nursery school. Having done well there, her relationship with the education department went from strength to strength. Finally, in 1984, she was promoted to become the first head teacher of a newly established nursery school designed exclusively for Palestinian children in the more fashionable southern part of town, where Palestinians were a minority. There she serves to date, aided by an Israeli assistant.[5]

The two schools situated in the predominantly Palestinian north-western section of Natzerat Illit are physically invisible to most Israelis, who simply never go there. Significantly, the nursery run by Na'ila, while located in the predominantly Israeli southern part of town on a residential street mostly inhabited by Israelis, is almost as invisible. The building is situated on an elevated terrace. Entering it from the street involves opening a little gate, climbing a flight of steps and walking around the side. The yard facing the street is narrow and untended, so all outdoor activities take place on the far side, virtually unseen from the street. Ironically, the only institution established by the council for Palestinians remains invisible to Israeli eyes.

The invisibility of the nursery is also reflected in its name. The official list for 1989 (Municipality of Natzerat Illit 1988–9) indicates that the thirty-six nursery schools which cater for Israeli children were named after (Hebrew) names of native flowers (nine schools), fruit species (four schools), trees and bushes (twenty schools), and geographical regions of the country (three schools). The three nursery schools which cater for Palestinian toddlers simply bear the names of the neighbourhood or the street in which they stand. The impression I had when I first saw the list was of a system forced to incorporate an entity it systematically refuses to recognise, let alone internalise.

Having been involved with nursery education for Palestinian children in Natzerat Illit for at least a decade, head-teacher Na'ila was highly regarded by the Israeli officials of the education department in the council. One of them described her as 'a self-made woman'. Another confessed that 'many [Israeli] people who know her wish there were many more Arabs as faithful (*ne'emanim*) as she is'. 'Faithful' in this context primarily implies identification with the state, coupled with loyalty to Israelis in the person's immediate work environment; in short, someone who is co-opted and pacified – the epitome of what Smooha, after popular usage in Israel, has labelled 'a good Arab' (Smooha 1992).

Officers in the education department were particularly impressed with the discipline and order Na'ila administers at her nursery school, so fundamentally at variance with the atmosphere in Israeli nursery schools. One official once attested how impressed he was with discipline and order in the Palestinian nursery, and with the differences between it and Israeli nurseries, which he described as 'chaotic'. Na'ila's nursery school is indeed a restrained environment. Children wishing to address either Na'ila or her assistant use *mu-'alamti* (my teacher), rather than the teacher's first name. Space is meticulously controlled. For example, when playing outside, children must seek the teacher's approval before re-entering the building to use the toilet.

Language

Na'ila's assistant Rosa is an Israeli of North African origin. More or less Na'ila's age, her official title, *ozeret safa* (language assistant), is identical to that which Na'ila herself held when she became involved with nursery education a decade earlier. Significantly, however, its meaning in the present context has been reversed. In the old mixed nursery, under an Israeli head-teacher, *ozeret safa* was a title given to a Palestinian assistant whose task was helping Palestinian children who spoke no Hebrew to fit into an alien environment. Rosa's task in Na'ila's nursery, where the medium of instruction is the children's native Arabic, is different. She is there to teach the Palestinian children Hebrew. 'Whenever I can, I switch to Hebrew with them', she once said, as though disclosing a clever ploy, evidently taking pride in the pedagogic responsibility invested in her. 'It is, after all, part of my job here – to make sure they learn some Hebrew.'

While Na'ila's role in the predominantly Israeli nursery school a decade earlier had been to help the Palestinian children understand what was happening around them, Rosa's role in the predominantly Palestinian nursery was to push forward the frontier of the dominant culture. Being a native Arabic speaker herself (albeit in a North African dialect), Rosa finds it easier and more efficacious to address the toddlers in Arabic, switching to Hebrew mainly for teaching Hebrew songs, or to impress a visitor. This, however, does not change the way she and her Israeli superiors portray her role in the nursery – always *ozeret safa* – 'language assistant', not merely 'assistant'. Her role as representative of the hegemonic order mitigates the danger that she should be perceived as an ordinary assistant to Na'ila, thus easing her structural disadvantage as an Israeli subordinated to a Palestinian (cf. Rabinowitz 1992). Rosa evidently cherishes this role. Enshrined in an official title, it establishes her as a frontier sentry on behalf of Jewish Israel, facing potentially dissenting and subversive Palestinians, however young. She is part of a system which nostalgically perceives transfusion to Palestinians of 'genuine identification with Israel' as an important and unproblematic aspect of the Zionist project.

By attending schools administered by Natzerat Illit's municipality, Palestinian teachers, parents and guardians acknowledge and reify what Bourdieu and Passeron (1977) have termed the power structure which underwrites the system's pedagogic authority. Rosa's competence in language is a central issue here, and an essential component of power. With Hebrew the dominant medium in the system, Rosa's agency and presence – one Israeli in an all-Palestinian environment – is a constant reminder that Israeli power permeates the pedagogic environment and dominates it.

Contents and curriculum

The absence of a systematic curriculum tends to obscure the mission and ideological thrust of nursery education. Clues must thus be sought in texts and practices which accompany occasions such as religious, national and personal celebrations – a project undertaken in Weil's (1986) account of birthday celebrations in Israeli nursery schools, and by Handelman and Shamgar-Handelman's (1990) account of kindergarten holiday ceremonies. Israeli holidays are celebrated either in the classroom or in public events in the community. In both cases, the programmes are ultimately supervised by local council officers. Teachers and principals are issued with recommendations for procedures in classroom affairs. Grander celebrations are often organised and conducted by school principals or by other officials on behalf of the municipal council. Natzerat Illit's education department, like those of other Israeli new towns, has always emphasised community events on public holidays. The calendar of centrally organised ceremonies includes strictly national events, Jewish feasts, and occasions which embody both. The way Palestinian toddlers are incorporated into these public events presents a fascinating case of exclusion through contrived inclusion.

Israel's Remembrance Day (Yom Hazikaron) comes one day before Independence Day (Yom Ha'atsmaut) in May.[6] Independence Day is a national holiday when all schools are closed, so Remembrance Day, occurring one day earlier, remains the obvious opportunity for staging formal school and town events. These events tend to highlight the solemnity associated with the memory of war heroes and the exaltation of the pinnacle of Jewish nationalism – the declaration of Israel's independence on 15 May 1948.

The venue for this and other holiday ceremonies in Natzerat Illit is the municipal football stadium, where school children arrive en masse in buses hired by the local authority. School children of all ages thus make up the bulk of the audience in what often becomes the major formal event of the day.[7] Local politicians and religious figures attend and speak. Teachers and pupils read poems, make music and sing. Wreaths of flowers are placed, torches lit and flags lowered to half mast.

The entire cohort of local school children is expected to attend the ceremonies, including the Palestinian toddlers. Like other nursery teachers, Na'ila and her Palestinian colleagues are issued with detailed operational guidelines and timetables, transportation schedules to and from the football ground, rules of conduct and other pieces of information required for a smooth event. Like Israeli toddlers, the Palestinians and their teachers dutifully arrive on site waving little flags of Israel, mumbling the songs laboriously taught by Rosa, presenting nicely packaged boxes of collectively purchased sweets to Israeli army representatives – a custom known as *shay lahayal* (Hebrew for 'gift for the soldier').

The nationalistic overtones of Israel's Remembrance and Independence Days are obvious. More than any other event this dual celebration embodies the exclusionary nature of Israeliness. It is the time when perceived common descent, citizenship and sentimental belonging are most vividly linked to blood: Jewish blood generally, and the blood of fallen Israeli soldiers in particular (Herzfeld 1993: 23–5; see also Kapferer 1988). It is, essentially, an event whereby non-Jews, albeit citizens of Israel, are categorically excluded. The very definition of the state, enacted in the ritual, hinges on the 1948 victory over the Palestinians and their allies in the Arab states.

One official happily remarked that 'the *shay lahayal* gifts which the Arab nurseries bring on Independence Day are always the nicest, the biggest and the most beautifully wrapped'. This observation was repeated to me a few weeks later when I visited Na'ila at the nursery. It was early afternoon, and parents were collecting their children. Na'ila and Rosa were busy tidying up toys and furniture around the playroom when an Israeli head-teacher of an adjacent nursery school walked in. Na'ila and the visitor had been colleagues for over a decade and there followed a genuinely amicable exchange of jokes and greetings. Then the visitor revealed the reason for her call. She had just realised that she was completely out of small flags of Israel, which she needed to decorate the nursery for an approaching end-of-year celebration, and hoped to borrow some from Na'ila.

Na'ila, as pleased to do a favour as she was flattered by the nature of this particular request, produced a bunch of blue and white flags from a drawer. The visitor was grateful, but not completely satisfied: she needed more. Na'ila moved fast and businesslike, disappearing downstairs to the school's store room and soon returning with a mail-bag full of clothes and garments. She opened it in front of her colleague, producing a large, tidily wrapped bundle of little triangular flags of Israel, all sown together on a long cord, ready to be hoisted. Smiling proudly at her own efficiency and tidiness, Na'ila handed the bundle to her colleague. The visitor was grateful and relieved. 'I knew that I could count on you', she said to beaming Na'ila.

The determination on the part of Israeli officials to drag the Palestinian toddlers through the elaborate motions of Remembrance Day, complete with its linguistic idiom and imagery which they can hardly comprehend, is intriguing. It is embedded, paradoxically, in the liberal tenets of the municipal bureaucracy. Palestinian toddlers are constituents of a system whose directives ostensibly apply to every individual regardless of religious, ethnic or national affiliation. It is only when directives are translated into motions on the ground, when rows of children begin entering the stadium mumbling songs whose meanings they cannot hope to fathom, that their exclusion becomes so apparent. When the flags are hoisted and the speeches sound, the Palestinian school children become mute witnesses to a foreign ceremony which signals their very marginality. The liberal officials who generously invite them in the first place are those who take a leading role in the stonewall which grows between them and the rest. Nominal inclusion notwithstanding, the hosts become indifferent to the difference of the guests, to use Herzfeld's (1993) suggestive term. The cruel overtones of exclusion grow tangible and inescapable.

Shavu-'ot (presentation of the harvest), in its contemporary Israeli guise, is a holiday premised on a medley of Jewish religious symbols and the Zionist idea of a return to the rural fatherland. Paramount amongst these icons is the notion of the seven plant species (*shiv'at haminim*) with which, according to the Pentecost, the land of Israel has been endowed, a notion which came into full play in the public ceremonies staged by the municipality of Natzerat Illit in June 1989. Once assembled on the football pitch, the thirty-nine nursery schools were divided into seven pre-arranged groups, each forming a circle on the pitch to represent one of the seven species. Like their Israeli peers, Palestinian toddlers too bring their collective 'harvest basket' to the ceremony every June. The performance was narrated in a syntax whose generative basis was not only profoundly Jewish, but also clearly nationalistic. It took the form of a dialogue: a teacher relayed questions from the stage, the children responded in unison from the floor. The first few questions, including 'what festival are we celebrating today?' and 'how many species, children, has our land been endowed with?' established the essential features of the situation, settling two key issues which hence will go unquestioned: whose land this is, and whose festival is being celebrated. This set the scene for a procession in which members of each of the seven groups were called to publicly present their 'harvest' of fruit – or graphic representations thereof. Each presentation was accompanied by an appropriate Hebrew song, describing the merits and uniqueness of the species presented.

Local council officials seemed proud of the incorporation of Palestinian toddlers into the ceremony. On one occasion, a senior council official produced photographs of the previous year's Shavu-'ot event, pointed at a circle of four-year-olds seated on the grass and said: 'Look at those Arab children and their teacher here. You couldn't really tell the difference between them and the rest, could you? Ever so well behaved, obedient, clean and calm.' The official was genuinely proud to recollect and demonstrate success in what appears to be the worthy project of having all children of whatever creed and colour join the action. The highly exclusionary aspect of the affair was simply not registered. It was neither problematised on the day, nor pondered on the occasion of its photographic reconstruction a few months later.

A third occasion in which Palestinian school children in Natzerat Illit join Israeli children is the mass tree-planting event of Tu-bishvat in January. Tu-bishvat has a rather obscure mention in the Mishna as 'new year for the trees'. In modern Israel, however, it has become a nation-building celebration, complete with mass tree-planting as token participation in the Zionist transformation of the land. Its narrative focuses on the national duty and privilege to 'redeem' the land (geulat haa'retz). Trees are not planted merely for timber, shade or as a means to combat soil erosion. Rather, planting creates new social space. The motto is represented in a famous nursery rhyme:

> Du-nam po vedu-nam sham,
> Ama nikhbeshet,
> kahmig'al admat ha'am . . .
>
> (an acre here, an acre there,
> land is being conquered,
> thus we redeem the nation's soil . . .).

On a wet and muddy day in January 1989, the Palestinian nursery children, accompanied by staff, diligently attended, dutifully planted, and numbly listened to the sound of songs and recitation they could barely understand.

Jewish and national Israeli holidays do not feature significantly in the classroom of the Palestinian nurseries. Rosa may teach a Hebrew song or two, primarily so that the children can reproduce them on public events, but not much more. For them attendance at the public ceremonies remain isolated, at best insignificant events.

The majority of children in the three nursery schools for Palestinians in Natzerat Illit are Christian.[8] So are all five Palestinian women teachers and assistants. When it comes to Christian holidays, the teachers are encouraged by the education department to model celebrations on patterns known in church-run nursery schools in Nazareth.

Thus, unlike schools for Israeli children which operate six days a week and close on Saturdays, the nurseries for Palestinian toddlers in Natzerat Illit are closed on both Saturdays and Sundays. Friday, the Muslim holiday, is a normal schoolday.

The special holidays are Easter and Christmas, both celebrated in the nursery complete with nativity play, a Christmas tree, presents, Papa Nawal (Santa Claus), Easter eggs and the appropriate array of carols and hymns sung in Arabic. Both occasions involve an early evening ceremony attended by the parents, for which the children and the staff prepare laboriously. Senior council officials are often present at the Christmas ceremony as guests of honour, to be presented with Christmas presents by the teachers. If an official fails to attend, the presents are promptly delivered to their home or office. At least one official displays these presents in her office, referring to them as tokens of the 'good relations with the Arab nurseries' and 'their smooth incorporation into the educational system of the town'.

Conclusion

The Palestinian citizens of Israel are marginalised twice over. Citizens of Israel, they are members of a racialised minority perceived by many Israelis as potentially disloyal and subversive – an adequate justification for many Israelis to withhold state resources and certain rights from Palestinians for almost fifty years. Currently representing one-eighth of the entire Palestinian people, the Palestinian citizens of Israel have an ambiguous position within their parent ethnie too. Implicated by their residence and citizenship in Israel, and by their growing acculturation into Israeli life, they tend to be suspected and marginalised by Palestinians elsewhere and by Arabs generally. The double bind in which they live turns the borders of the state of Israel into a demarcation line between their two evils: being second-class citizens within their state of citizenship and being suspect members of their own nation. The Palestinian citizens of Israel thus represent what I would like to call a 'trapped minority', trapped between a host but hostile state which reluctantly offers them citizenship and an absent, scattered mother nation with little political and economic weight.

A microcosm of Israel, Natzerat Illit presents some fine examples of the strains exerted by their predicament on Israeli liberals and liberalism (Rabinowitz 1994a, 1994b). The Israeli officials in charge of the educational bureaucracy in Natzerat Illit find themselves in an awkward situation. Lacking real knowledge of or, for that matter, genuine interest in Palestinian or Arab culture, and having little inclination to cope with

Palestinian clients in any serious manner, they are forced by the bureaucracy to manage a cohort of Palestinian toddlers. Herzfeld's (1993) characterisation of bureaucracies struggling to keep people out takes a fascinating turn here: Natzerat Illit officials cater for those forced in by the system, clients they personally see as aliens.

The ad hoc solution adopted by the municipal bureaucracy is based, in the first analysis, on a liberal ethos of individuality. The Palestinian toddlers are to be treated just like anybody else. They are designated an equal patch in the stadium on Remembrance Day, have an equal footing along the rows of planters on Tu-Bishvat and assume an equivalent role at the presentation of the harvest on Shavu-'ot. Paradoxically, however, this very insistence on individualised equality is what eventually produces grotesque marginalisation: four-year-olds attending ceremonies which are not only culturally irrelevant to them but also fundamentally political in terms of their exclusion.

Elsewhere (Rabinowitz 1992, 1994a, 1997) I describe how the Palestinian presence in Natzerat Illit is viewed by Israeli residents not only as a drawback for the town, but, more significantly, as a hiccup in the 'natural' course of local history. The educational system of Natzerat Illit was consistent with this spirit in as much as it could not find the strength to treat the toddlers as a collective with a separate perspective. Rather than accepting them as members of a group whose narrative is legitimately incongruent with that of mainstream Israel, the system attempted to reform them by subjecting them to loaded occasions with strong nationalistic overtones. This, after all, is the nature of state-inculcated education: to level clients under the burden of mainstream ideology, often disguised as heritage or culture.

Nursery education, in Israel and almost everywhere, is de facto gendered. Women predominate in a setting which is seen by many as extending the motherly care which young children should and do have at home into their first encounter with the formal education system. In both Israeli and Palestinian cultures, women are still very much associated with the private sphere, a stereotype accentuated in the case of nurseries by the role of teachers as out-mothers. The political dimension of nurseries designed and run by the Israeli municipality for Palestinian toddlers is thus mitigated by the centrality of women. An arena constructed and maintained by women, it is easily marginalised and hidden. The impact of 'Palestinian' nursery schools on the way Israelis might redefine the town's relations with the Palestinian community is effectively blocked. The only officially recognised middle ground within Natzerat Illit where Palestinian and Israelis meet is thus largely sterilised and made less threatening. The type of 'loyal' Palestinian woman selected to control it, and the relationship constructed by the system between her and her Israeli assistant, arrest potential change. The stereotype and role model of women as keepers of tradition and stability is deployed to keep the national frontier from becoming a real meeting place.

The in-but-out predicament of Palestinian toddlers in the Israeli system in Natzerat Illit is linked to the marginality associated with being members of a trapped minority. Education is a right (or duty) granted to (or forced on) citizens by law, so nominal inclusion in the system had to be granted to Palestinians by virtue of their citizenship. This notwithstanding, once included in a system geared primarily for Israelis, obvious inconsistencies between the system's pedagogic aims of nation/culture-building and their identity as Palestinians were inevitable.

The reformist spirit displayed by the Israeli system becomes subdued, however, when it comes to events perceived by the officials as strictly 'cultural', such as religious ceremonies in the Palestinian nursery school. Christmas and Easter are not only observed: they are celebrated in the proud presence of Israeli officials in a public display of respect for authenticity and heritage. Trinh points out that unlike the colonial period, when cultural differences signalled primitiveness and called for the Eurocentric civilising mission, neo-colonialism regards lack of differences as a loss of cultural heritage. This, she argues, creates a link between 'planned authenticity' and 'separate development' (Trinh 1989: 80–9). Spivak (1988) argues that the notion of cultural difference is central to the attempts of the First World to keep cheap labour (in the 'authentic' Third World) at bay. It would appear that the line between colonialism and neo-colonialism in the case of pedagogic policy for Palestinian toddlers runs between events which represent mainstream Israeli nationalism and ones which celebrate Christianity, which Israelis seem to view as a harmless cultural trait.

National frontiers, within states or across international borders, must be understood as peripheries shot with inequalities, hegemonies and power structures emanating from the centre. Nimble, vital and subversive as minorities can be in terms of penetrating the dominant culture, the advantages possessed by states and majority nations in their struggle to keep Others excluded and thus protect themselves are powerfully resistant.

Parts of the discourse of transnationalism, particularly those which focus on hybridisation and creolisation, sometimes imply an easy, optimistic way out of border situations, with subalterns in both dominant and dominated groups working together to form grass-roots subversions of the asymmetric power structure, scoring triumphs for the human spirit. The case of Palestinians at the territorial and political periphery of Israel constructively problematises such optimistic analysis of the agency and destiny of human contact in border situations. Rather like recent critiques of Gramsci's seminal ideas on subaltern resistance (critiques which, incidentally, also come from anthropologists researching interstitial situations – for example, Kaplan and Kelly 1994, Comaroff and Comaroff 1991, Abu-Lughod 1989), I too believe that celebration of the borderlands as loci of constructive coexistence in spite of dictates on the part of the metropolis is premature.

The rapidly expanding vocabulary of non-essentialism, with its emphasis on hybridity and mixtures – of blood, traditions, ideas, theories and more – must not obscure the inevitable proximity found in many border situations between members of opposing, often hostile groups and nations. Uneven power distributions, projections of deep political turmoil and old rivalries are there even once creolisation has started to unfold. The presence of a state, a dominant nation and the machinery which serves them make border situations into significant peripheral extensions of power balances stemming from the centre. Hybridisation notwithstanding, the frontiers between dominant state and subordinate nation, at borders or deeper into the state, remain major fault lines upon which states may stand or fall.

Notes

1. 'Palestinian citizens of Israel' is preferred throughout this study to 'Israel's Arabs', 'Israeli Arabs' or even 'Arabs in Israel'. For a more thorough exposition of the issue of labelling the Palestinian minority in Israel see Rabinowitz (1993).
2. My survey of 247 Arab households in Natzerat Illit was conducted in early 1989, and included several questions on housing. The inquiry regarding ownership of residence (242 valid cases) reflected 75.7 per cent owner-occupation, 20.6 per cent rentals and 1.6 per cent 'key-money' lease arrangements (in which the landlord collects a third of the property value when the lease is signed, rent is relatively low and tenants may use the property for their lifetime).
3. These proportions changed considerably with the arrival in Natzerat Illit in 1990 and 1991 of 7–10,000 new Jewish immigrants from the crumbling Soviet Union.
4. It carried on as an all-Israeli school for a number of years, then was phased out until its final dissolution in 1987, not least because of dwindling demand in an ageing part of town. By the late 1980s the buildings were serving as the headquarters for the regional fire brigade.
5. The two Israeli head-teachers in the nursery schools established in 1980 in the northern part of town have since been replaced by Palestinian teachers.

6. Dates for holidays in Israel are determined by the Jewish calendar. In terms of the Western calendar, events may shift from year to year.
7. Natzerat Illit, like most communities in Israel, has at least one other public event staged in the late afternoon of Remembrance Day. Held near the main memorial for natives of the town who had been killed in wars, it is a smaller, more solemn event.
8. In 1988–9 only five of the thirty-five children attending Na'ila's nursery were Muslim.

References

Abu-Lughod, Lila 1989. 'The romance of resistance: tracing transformations of power through Bedouin women', *American Ethnologist* 17: 41–55.
Al-Haj, Majid and Henry Rosenfeld 1990. *Arab Local Government in Israel.* Givat Haviva: The Institute of Arab Studies (in Hebrew).
Al Hamishmar (daily paper) 1984. 'Natzerat Illit – the Real Side of the Coin', 11 January, pp. 3–4 (in Hebrew).
Anzaldua, Gloria 1987. *Borderlands/La Frontera: the new Mestiza.* San Francisco: Spinsters/Aunt Lute Books.
Bar-Gal, Y. 1986. 'Penetration and colonization of Palestinians in Natzerat Illit – early evidence', in A. Sofer (ed.) *Residential and internal migration patterns among the Palestinians of Israel.* Haifa: University of Haifa (in Hebrew).
Barth, Fredrik 1969. *Ethnic groups and boundaries: the social oganization of culture difference.* Oslo: Universitetforlaget.
Bourdieu, P. and J. C. Passeron 1977. *Reproduction in education, society and culture.* London: Sage.
Boyarin, Daniel and Jonathan Boyarin 1993. 'Diaspora: generational ground of Jewish identity', *Critical Inquiry* 19 (4): 693–725.
Clifford, James 1994. 'Diasporas', *Cultural Anthropology* 9 (3): 302–38.
Comaroff, Jean and John Comaroff 1991. *Revelation and revolution: Christianity, colonialism and consciousness in South Africa.* Chicago: University of Chicago Press.
Gellner, Ernest 1983. *Nations and nationalism.* Oxford: Blackwell.
Handelman, Don and Lea Shamger-Handelman 1990. 'Holiday celebrations in Israeli kindergartens', in Don Handelman (ed.), *Models and mirrors: towards an anthropology of public events.* Cambridge: Cambridge University Press.
Hefer-Rogovin, Orit 1987. 'The distribution of Arab residents in Natzerat Illit', M.A. thesis, Dept of Geography, Tel-Aviv University.
Herzfeld, Michael 1993. *The social production of indifference.* Chicago: University of Chicago Press.
Kapferer, Bruce 1988. *Legends of people, myths of states. Violence, intolerance, and political culture in Sri Lanka and Australia.* Smithsonian Institution Press, Washington and London.
Kaplan, Martha and John D. Kelly 1994. 'Rethinking resistance: dialogics of "disaffection" in colonial Fiji', *American Ethnologist* 21 (1): 123–51.

Kimmerling, Baruch 1983. *Israeli state and society*. New York: State University of New York Press.

Kipnis, Baruch 1983. 'The development of the Jewish settlement in Galilee, 1948–1980', in A. Shmueli, A. Sofer and N. Keliot (eds.), *The lands of Galilee*. Haifa: The Society for Applied Social Research, University of Haifa (in Hebrew).

Morris, Benny 1991. *The birth of the Palestinian refugee problem, 1947–1949*. Tel-Aviv: Am-Oved (in Hebrew).

Municipality of Natzerat Illit 1988–9. 'Report of the Department of Education', mimeograph.

Peled, Yoav 1992. 'Ethnic democracy and the legal construction of citizenship: Arab citizens of the Jewish state', *American Political Science Review* 86 (2): 432–43.

Rabinowitz, Dan 1992. 'Trust and the attribution of rationality: inverted roles amongst Palestinian Arabs and Jews in Israel', *Man* 27 (3): 517–37.

1993. 'Oriental nostalgia: how the Palestinians became "Israel's Arabs"', *Teorya Uvikoret* 4: 141–52 (in Hebrew).

1994a. 'To sell or not to sell?', *American Ethnologist* 21 (4): 823–40.

1994b. 'The common memory of loss: political mobilization among Palestinian citizens of Israel', *Journal of Anthropological Research* 50: 27–44.

1997. *Overlooking Nazareth: the ethnography of exclusion in Galilee*. Cambridge: Cambridge University Press.

Rosaldo, Renato 1988. 'Ideology, place and people without culture', *Cultural Anthropology* 3: 77–87.

Simons, Jon 1995. 'The feminist coalition in the Border Areas', *Teorya Uvikoret* 7: 20–30 (in Hebrew).

Smooha, Sammy 1989. 'The Arab minority in Israel: radicalization or politicization?', *Studies in Contemporary Jewry* 5: 59–88.

1992. *Arabs and Jews in Israel*, vol. 2: *Conflict and change in a mutual intolerance*. Boulder: Westview Press.

Spivak, Gayatri Chakravorty 1988. 'Can the subaltern speak?', in Cary Nelson and Lawrence Goldberg (eds.) *Marxism and the interpretation of culture*. Urbana: University of Illinois Press.

Trinh, T. Minh-ha 1989. *Woman, Native, Other*. Bloomington: Indiana University Press.

Weil, Shalva 1986. 'The language and ritual of socialisation: birthday parties in a kindergarten context', *Man* 21 (2): 329–41.

Yiftachel, Oren 1992. 'The concept of ethnic democracy and its applicability to Israel', *Ethnic and Racial Studies* 15 (1): 121–36.

1994. 'Regional mix and ethnic relations: evidence from Israel', *Geoforum* 25 (1): 41–55.

Zureik, Elia 1979. *The Palestinians in Israel: a study in internal colonialism*. London: Routledge and Kegan Paul.

7 *Grenzregime* (border regime): the Wall and its aftermath

John Borneman

Heidi

Heidi recently turned fifty. She is beginning a new life, in a reunited Germany, in a 'Europe without borders'. Born in 1944, in Cottbus, eastern Germany, she was an unplanned child of the former German Democratic Republic (GDR), one of those women on whose labour the socialist state had staked its future. As early as 1949, the year of the founding of the East German state, GDR leaders concluded that it was in the state's interest to take seriously the socialist ideology of *Gleichberechtigung*, equal rights for men and women. They included an equal rights guarantee in the constitution. They opened the educational system to women a generation before the West German regime did. They engaged in a kind of affirmative action for women, not only encouraging them to take part in *Aufbau*, the rebuilding of the economy and society, but also making it difficult for women to remain, in the language of the time, 'only housewives'. The regime suspected that there would be much resistance from older women like Heidi's mother, who had never worked outside the home before the war, as well as from adult men, who were unaccustomed to treating women as equals. Indeed, throughout the 1950s, the promise of higher pay, a better standard of living, and more freedoms enticed large numbers of skilled East German men (and some women) to the capitalist markets of the West, which, at that time, favoured labour by men (and housework by women) – with the result that the GDR's future was increasingly tied to its women.

Under these circumstances, Heidi and her mother and her brother stayed in the East. Heidi would be educated in the new schools. She and her brother would benefit from being children of proletarian parents, members of the class that, according to official propaganda, was to take over leadership – sometime in the future. This would make them loyal to the state, so the new state thought. And, indeed, her brother remained loyal, making a stellar career as a member of the socialist party and manager of a state-owned Kombinat, trust company. Soon after completion of her studies, Heidi began despising this state, and her hatred grew over the years. Her status as a 'chosen' person, and her ambivalence about it, distinguished her from all West German women of her generation, who were not 'chosen' but had to contend with the officially sanctioned reassertion of patriarchal social conventions and a phallic state ideology after the war, who had to organise a social movement to fight against the state for a personal stake in the future (for a statistical comparison of women's statuses, see Geißler 1992: 236–63).

When Heidi was eighteen months old, her father died. Eleven years later, she left her mother to live in a boarding school and to study mathematics, a 'male' discipline. Heidi says that her experience in the boarding school was formative. It replaced the nuclear family romance, already impaired by her father's early death, with a peculiar Oedipal triangle of 'State, mommy, me'. In this triangulation, the state differed from all prior forms of phallic authority in that it initially tried to increase its visibility; it struggled to establish a legitimate authority not in private, behind closed doors, but in public discussions, on a world stage. Heidi knew exactly where her support and where the Law were coming from, and precisely because of this knowledge she experienced no sense of awe or lack with respect to the state.

West German feminists frequently criticise East German women for lacking a critique of patriarchy, for allowing men to 'exploit' them by not demanding of men an equal contribution to childcare, or for unselfconsciously becoming mothers. But because the East German state initiated the critique of patriarchy, women there were not forced to develop their own movement to oppose it. And even though an extremely large percentage of East German women became 'mothers', they were never forced into marriage in order to support their children, as was frequently the case in West Germany. Moreover, in East Germany divorce had been made cheap and easy, whereas in West Germany legal divorce was expensive and possible only after a property settlement. Heidi took for granted her significance to this state and its laws, to the new order; her critique of it did not grow out of an understanding of gender(ed) oppression.

The GDR was, after all, a revolutionary state. It invoked as the condition of its legitimacy not traditional authority but a future Communist order in which Heidi was to be an integral part of the imagined new centre. Marx and Engels may have been iconic fathers of the new state, but this was to be no normal nation-state. In contrast to the legitimation strategy of the Federal Republic of Germany (FRG),

Rechtsstaatlichkeit, rule of law, was never a fundamental principle of the GDR's authority. Indeed, the GDR appealed to 'socialist legality': the conditions of rule were neither fixed nor firm but considered merely a means to achieve a more just, socialist order. The GDR represented itself as an historical alternative to patriarchy, specifically to the patriarchal authority of West Germany, which in turn represented itself as the successor state of the Third Reich – with the accompanying benefits and burdens. The sovereign was not the Verfassung, the constitution, as in the West German Rechtsstaat, but the 'dictatorship of the proletariat' as interpreted by the ruling Socialist Unity Party (SED). The GDR constantly drew attention to the contingent and constructed nature of its own powers, emphasising its newness, denying any continuity with prior German states, rewriting both its civil and criminal code several times, revoking laws within days after passing them, and undermining the power of all mythical origins and all fathers. In an effort to create new forms of authority, the state improvised, continuously redrawing borders and boundaries, renaming persons and things, endowing it with an aura of provisionality. Since its dissolution in October 1990, the GDR is often reduced, both colloquially and in formal legal discourse, to its *Grenzregime*, border regime – to the entire system of rules and regulations intended to demarcate East Germany from its West German counterpart, to enclose, bound and reconstitute its 'people'.

Heidi remembers her boarding school experience as one of unending debate, discussion and critical reflection about the present and future. Her best friend at the school, who was preparing for a career in international trade, is still her best friend today. Back then they talked about everything, Heidi said, until the wee hours of the morning, everything except for the fact that he liked men, something he only told her twenty-nine years later, after he had married and divorced, and changed his career several times, always because his homosexuality got in the way. Though he tried to keep his sexuality secret from his ever-inquisitive state employers, they either suspected or came to know. Up to 1969, the official line was that homosexuality did not exist in the socialist, family-friendly GDR; it was a perverse 'condition' and product of capitalism, existing on the other side of the Great Divide, which, of course, one should not, or could not, cross (see Borneman 1991b). Heidi still does not forgive him for not sharing this secret with her, nor does she forgive herself for not having known earlier, for having missed all the conspicuous signs that he had tried to hide from her. 'It would have been so much easier with all my men' – she was married twice – 'if I could have said to them that he was homosexual. They were very jealous of us and never accepted my friendship with him, that we had such complete confidence and trust in each other.' To Heidi, this relationship represented an explicit openness and reciprocity that could countenance no boundaries. In contrast to her relation with the state, which was built on a series of public secrets, she understood private secrets about the past or present to be a violation of trust; everything had to be acknowledged and discussed.

When the Wall was erected, in the early morning hours of 13 August 1961, Heidi knew nothing of her friend's 'condition'. She was still in boarding school, still filled with a youthful enthusiasm about postwar reconstruction. It took six weeks to complete the Wall, and, while Heidi watched with concern the political events and controversy surrounding it, she did not experience them as a delimitation on her freedom. As part of a generation designated heirs to the Idea of Communism, Heidi fully identified with the perceived need to secure the border and protect the nascent state. She had already visited West Berlin many times and had witnessed the smuggling of precious East German goods at the border. Therefore, at first she agreed with the leaders of her vulnerable state that the border and its effect of containment was a precondition for her further growth. Yet, for the next twenty-seven years, she had to endure the twelve kilometres of 1.25 metre high concrete slabs along with 137 kilometres of barbed wire that encircled West Berlin, with an equally well-policed barricade constructed to separate East from West Germany (see map 7.1). As Heidi grew into adulthood, her experience of this encirclement changed.

Containment

No border in the modern period has received more of the world's attention and been the source of more fantasy and fear than *die Mauer*, the Berlin Wall. Leaders of the self-proclaimed 'Worker and Farmer State', the GDR, justified its construction as necessary to realise an idea, this-worldly-Communism, and to secure their own rule, in the name of the people. Officially designated an 'anti-fascist protection barricade', the Wall had little to do with fascism but a great deal to with protection. It was supposed to halt the further sabotage of a haemorrhaging East German economy by preventing the workers, who had been fleeing to the West in massive numbers, from leaving. This economy, organised around socialist principles of collective ownership, central planning and just redistribution, proved unable to keep pace with the general prosperity provided by its West German, capitalist counterpart.

The Wall became the material symbol of the Cold War division of the world into two moieties within a single city and within a formerly

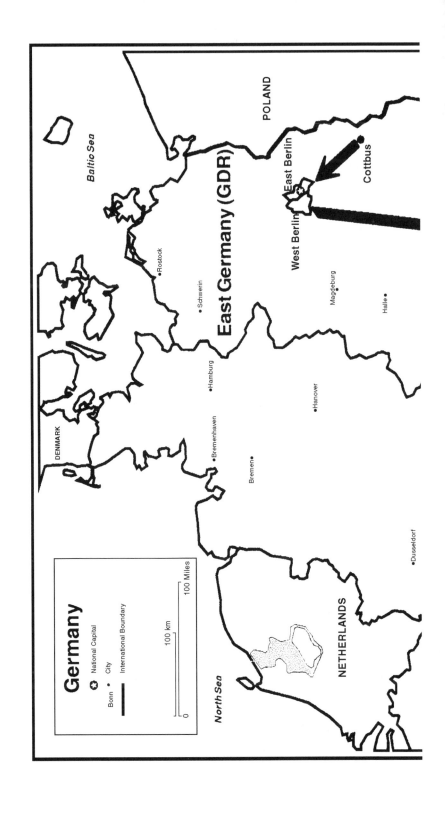

Germany

⊛ National Capital Bonn
• City
— International Boundary

0 — 100 km
0 — 100 Miles

DENMARK

Baltic Sea

North Sea

NETHERLANDS

East Germany (GDR)

POLAND

West Berlin
East Berlin

Cottbus

•Rostock

•Schwerin

Magdeburg

Halle•

•Hamburg

•Hanover

•Bremenhaven

Bremen•

•Dusseldorf

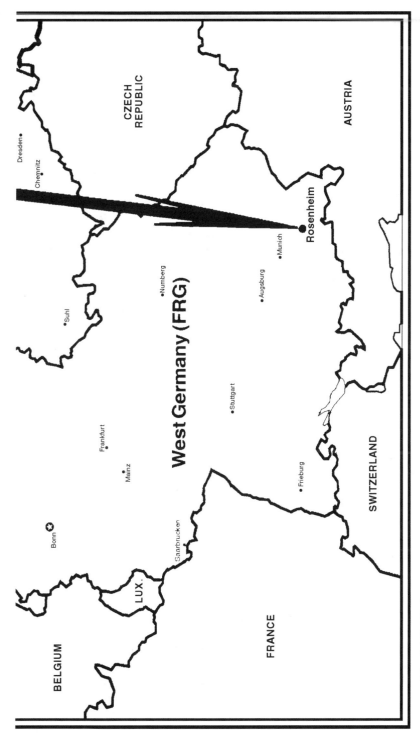

Map 7.1 Heidi's journey.

unified territorial state. It served mythical ends as a twofold functioning sign – icon and symbol – embodying, enacting and standing for the opposition between capitalist and communist alliance systems, between 'plan' and 'market', between 'security' and 'liberty'. It prefigured the memory of the GDR as a Grenzregime.

'Containment' as both concept and practice played a special and ironic role in the life of the Wall. As a concept and strategy, 'containment of communism' originated in Britain and the United States in the late 1940s to deal with a Communist enemy thought of as contagious, or irresistible, and likely to set off a chain reaction of ideological and political conversions, similar to falling dominoes, in countries that came into contact with it (Gaddis 1982). But events took a cruel twist and the supposedly contained East German state internalised this strategy, constraining itself and its own citizens as well as being confined and isolated by the West. For a variety of reasons, ranging from fear of the state to belief in socialism, most GDR citizens initially cooperated with this strategy.

West Germany effectively practised the British and American strategy of 'containment of communism' on East Germany, which had the effect of exaggerating and dramatising the East German citizen's experience of confinement and enclosure. The Hallstein Doctrine, formulated in 1955, established the principle that the Federal Republic was the sole sovereign representative of all of Germany; any state that granted political recognition to or established diplomatic relations with the other Germany would be declared an enemy and penalised with sanctions. Unable to enter into full diplomatic and economic relations with most of the world's states, East Germany remained an economically innocent member of the community as it did not (could not) engage in exploitative relations with countries in the so-called Third World. Instead its leaders tried to become self-sufficient. Long before the idea of 'generic' items became a new form of commodity differentiation in the West, the state's planners distributed products under single names: peas were sold as 'Tempo-erbsen', detergent became 'Spee', coffee houses were called simply 'Espresso'. Instead of producing pride in self-sufficiency, the lack of product differentiation and choice in the East came to be associated with uniformity and conformity and tended to reinforce the image of the West as more developed and dynamic, more diverse, more colourful. Only a few intellectuals, who often had limited but coveted access to Western goods, seemed to take a perverse satisfaction in the standardisation and lack of choice in commodities.

Despite the protective space that the Wall provided for East German goods, this respite lasted less than a decade. By the 1970s, the mixed economy, which had never been totally socialised, had deteriorated to the point that it needed major injections of capital from the West – which it got during the period of detente. As the younger citizens of the GDR grew increasingly impatient with the experience of containment, including, of course, the inability of the economy to keep pace with Western standards, pressures to cross the border mounted. The 1980s saw a small-scale proliferation of social protest groups under the protection of the Protestant church, organised around issues of environmentalism, sexuality, liberty and social justice. Late in the evening of 9 November 1989, Günther Schabowski, a member of the ruling Politburo, assured the world press that restrictions on visas to Western countries were in the process of being lifted. On guard against double-talk, a journalist pounced: Did the new travel law also extend to the West Berlin border? Schabowski wavered. He had received the new regulation just minutes before. 'Yes,' he said, 'it says here Berlin (West).' Within minutes several hundred young citizens had gathered outside a Berlin border crossing. The border guards were taken aback. The Wall was about to open (Borneman 1991a: 1–4). Without *die Mauer*, neither the East German state nor the Cold War could be sustained. Within a couple of months, the so-called 'domino effect', which had hypothesised the fall of capitalist countries to communism, worked in reverse, as the governments of the entire Eastern bloc, with the exception of Albania, fell. And a year later, even the Albanian regime capitulated.

Our relationship

During my initial East Berlin fieldwork in 1986, Heidi's boarding-school friend, now a gay man, introduced us. I became acquainted with many women like her, of her generation, of her social situation, women who had professional identities and were not dependent on men. This dependency on men, specifically on fathers and boyfriends/husbands, for money or jobs or emotional completion, or even as an antithesis for self-definition, seemed, by contrast, to mark all West Berlin women whom I knew. Not that Heidi rejected men; only once in her adult life, for several years after the birth of her second daughter, did she live without a man. But I always sensed in Heidi an integrity, or the search for such an integrity, independent of her relationship to a man, to a husband, to a father, to a provider. It was clear to me that the assertion of this integrity had its costs, that Heidi had to struggle without a role model and against social conventions (the status of the law notwithstanding) that defined her solely in terms of other family members. She had to overcome nagging self-doubts about her own worth and her own right to liberty. I suspect (and here I am undoubtedly overly systematic) that I represented to her an intimacy and freedom made possible by three kinds of productive ambiguities: (a) I did not project onto her a *gender* that was the opposite of mine – and, in turn, she did not need this opposition, (b) the erotics of our relationship were not tied to *sexual* expectations, (c) because of my own working-class origins, I was only partially identified by a *nationality* belonging to the First World or the Golden West. Because these ambiguities blurred conventional boundaries, Heidi never identified me with the phallus, as an authority who indexed her own lack of freedom, material goods, education and taste – 'inadequacies' directly tied to nearly every East German's self-esteem.

Moreover, there was a way in which Heidi appealed to and affirmed my desires to challenge the very boundaries that seemed to define me. She also provided me with the opportunity to work through certain idealist projections which she embodied. I had seven siblings in the United States, including six sisters, who, unlike Heidi, had not been able to transcend or even fundamentally alter the role of 'woman' as defined by their working-class origins; I was a gay man from the West who had experienced some of the limitations of liberalism's exalted liberties while Heidi had experienced the limitations of socialism's security. We asserted no essential difference to each other, though in practical terms it was obvious that we lived in radically different worlds and that our worlds were in some fundamental sense closed to each other. What fascinated me was that my lack of access to her experiential world did not translate into my exclusion from it. Although she was a mother, Heidi in no way lived through her daughters when we met, but treated them as special relationships which were also open to me, if I wished to establish relationships with them. She said that for her motherhood was initially the pleasure in feeling a child's skin, the sensuousness of a child's touch – hardly experiences that most parents felt comfortable sharing with me. She also understood socialism's fundamental aporia: a celebration of the working class, which is supposed to transcend its conditions of origin and simultaneously reproduce itself as working class, to aspire to petty-bourgeois ends without then becoming 'bourgeois'. And, although I was a graduate student from Harvard University, she did not reduce my identity to matters of my career, which is what many people do when they find out that I am gay – I become, for them, only 'an anthropologist'. Instead, Heidi seemed to take genuine delight in understanding how I stood with respect to class, sexuality and profession, and how those structures articulated in me. We sought each other out neither because of a desire for completion nor for domination/submission. We provided access to alternative worlds that were beyond the domain of experiences open to us personally. Our relationship has sustained itself on mutual curiosity.

Heidi's separation

On 11 November 1989, two days after the opening of the border with West Germany, Heidi moved to Rosenheim, a large but sleepy Bavarian village nestled in the mountains midway between Munich and Salzburg. She refers to this radical move simply as *das Wechsel*, the change. Three years later, she decided to separate from her second husband, Sieghard, a medical doctor with whom she had lived for sixteen years. I arrived at their home two days after Christmas 1993, on the evening that Sieghard moved out.

Sieghard has never had any close friends – one of Heidi's strongest criticisms of him – and therefore he had to rely on 'the family', meaning Heidi's two oldest daughters, Peggy and Greta, along with Greta's boyfriend, to help him move the heavy furniture. The youngest daughter, Franzi, who is twelve and Sieghard's only daughter-by-blood, has such a strong aversion to her father that she refused to help in the move. On that evening, Sieghard ran into Franzi in the hallway and asked if she wanted to take a vacation with him sometime the next year. Offended that he would pose this question at this parting moment, as if he had taken no note of the years of coldness on his part and avoidance on hers, Franzi silently turned away and withdrew to her bedroom. The other two daughters remained amiable with Sieghard throughout the move, only too pleased, they told me, to get him out of the house, as well as the family, something they had encouraged Heidi to do for years. Without complaint, they lifted furniture twice their own weight the entire evening. I offered to help, but Peggy said that Sieghard would have problems accepting the help of a male stranger visiting her mother. The oldest daughter, Peggy, is 27 and works as a midwife in Hamburg. The middle daughter, Greta, is 22 and in an apprenticeship programme to become a potter.

I hid in the kitchen during that part of the evening, reading a book that Heidi had just given me, about the Treuhand, the agency set up to administer and privatise state-owned property in the former GDR, estimated in early 1990 to be worth 650 billion DM. Heidi was impressed by the book's documentation of how this valuable property, instead of being sold and the profits distributed (in 1990, estimated at around 40,000DM ($25,000) per East German citizen), was either undervalued and sold or given away to Western firms by the Treuhand. Rather than distribute any money to former citizens of the GDR, the

Treuhand single-mindedly pursued privatisation. This entailed elimi-
nating around 30 per cent of all jobs in eastern Germany. The outcome
seemed obvious and predictable to me, the outsider with no personal
investment in the outcomes of unification. Though Heidi was now an
enthusiastic resident of the western part of Germany, she had not
become a complete insider, a full Wessi. At some very basic level, she
still identified with the fate of Ossis: the former citizens of the former
GDR.

As I read, Sieghard moved out. Over the previous eight years Heidi
and I had had regular telephone conversations, but we had been
together only twice before, and I had visited her and her family just once
prior to this visit, in 1986 in Cottbus. At that time, Heidi seemed to me
extremely angry: critical of her neighbours, of her colleagues at the
college where she taught mathematics, of the people of Cottbus, and of
the state. They all wanted her to keep quiet and uncritically accept her
role as a small-town teacher, wife and mother, according to Heidi. Only
some of the students seemed to respond positively to her endless energy
and engagement. Sieghard appeared as a shadow of a person, someone
to whom Heidi also could not turn for support; he left little, if any,
impression on me.

Like many of her compatriots, Heidi experienced the final years of the
GDR as a social death. Her professional life was blocked, and worse, for
her, she was asked to teach lies in her job at the local community college
– about the market, the economy, the health of the state. She clearly saw
the state going bankrupt, the economy getting worse, but material
wealth had never been that important to Heidi. She wanted something
else. Although the state had propagated a 'unity of career and motherhood', Heidi had never been able to realise that unity to her satisfaction
in her own life. The state's pronatal and pro-women policies had
produced mixed results. To be sure, Heidi had been able to give birth to
and raise three daughters without consistent support from any of the
particular men she had lived with, and without giving up her career. For
that she was thankful. And many women, unlike their male counterparts, stayed in the GDR, unwilling to leave their mothers behind and
appreciative of the training and education they could not have obtained
in the West. Yet the demands of raising three girls, a task of which Heidi
is proud and in no way regrets, consistently placed restrictions on her
occupational advancement, leading her ultimately to settle for a minor
teaching post. By the mid-1980s her marriage had become merely a
habit and stymied her personal development, though Heidi admitted
this to me and to her daughters, and perhaps to herself, only recently.
Her daughters had not experienced the enthusiasm and intensity that

Heidi had had in the boarding school in the *Aufbau* years; they lacked any sense of attachment to Cottbus or to their friends.

By 1988, Heidi had made up her mind to leave the GDR, it was only a matter of when and how. Sieghard went along with her decision, but, disturbed by the spectre of unemployment and financial insecurity in West Germany, he would have preferred to stay in the East. The obvious way to leave was to obtain approval to visit a relative in the West: *Familienangelegenheiten* (family occasions) were one of the priority grounds listed by the state for travel. Heidi selected her aunt's eightieth birthday in 1989. The date for the planned trip was 11 November. After about a year of paper-shuffling through the labyrinth of bureaucracies, both she and Sieghard obtained permission, first from their employers, then from the state and the state's security apparatus, to travel with the entire family to Rosenheim. Heidi told only one person, her gay friend from the boarding school, that she did not intend to return. She and her family told none of their neighbours, nor any of their colleagues at work or school. Silently, working conspiratorially as a family unit, they discreetly sold a few large items of furniture and the automobile but planned to leave all the rest behind – photo albums, clothes, china, their entire material history – for fear that the approval to travel would be denied if it appeared that they were leaving for good.

From the time of the building of the Wall to 1964, travel of East Germans to the West was restricted to prominent persons or to *Reisekader*, those officially approved as trustworthy. An agreement reached in 1964 allowed retired persons to visit West Berlin or West Germany once a year. Not until the late 1960s, when former Social Democratic Chancellor Willy Brandt initiated *Ostpolitik*, did the GDR begin expanding the limited opportunities available for some of its citizens to travel to the West. His strategy of *Annäherung durch Wandel* (change through rapprochement) contrasted sharply with the prior Christian Democratic strategy of *Abgrenzungspolitik* (politics of demarcation). The category of visits regulated by an agreement between West Berlin and the GDR, signed on 20 December 1971, referred to *dringende Familienangelegenheiten*, pressing family events. Possible grounds for visits included baptisms, marriages, life-threatening illnesses, death of parents, siblings, and children, wedding anniversaries and birthdays. These familial categories created an entirely new dynamic between citizens and the state, as well as constituting a form in which the desire to cross the Wall was legal.

In the following decade, however, pressure to travel or, alternately, to leave, grew so intense that the GDR expanded its system of selling disgruntled citizens to the Federal Republic. In 1974, for example, it doubled the number of ransomed political prisoners, to 1,100, from the 630 ransomed the year before. By 1984, it again came up with a new strategy, not only of doubling the number of ransomed political prisoners (from 1,105 in 1983 to 2,236 in 1984) but also authorising a mass release of would-be migrants (from 7,729 in 1983 to 37,323 in 1984) (Wendt 1991: 390). This emigration (including isolated cases of coerced exile) did not, however, function as the state intended, as a so-called 'social safety valve'. Ridding itself of its most unhappy citizens did not relieve the state of the pressure to make its borders more permeable. Instead, each successive exodus created visible absences in friendship circles and work units within the GDR, and thus generated dissatisfaction among those who remained. This pressure for expanded movement was also not relieved by increasing the number of permissible visits per year, nor by enlarging the category of people permitted to travel to the West and to return. These permissible visits did not exceed 60,000 until 1986, when, in the liberalisation coinciding with Erich Honecker's first visit to the West, 573,000 visits were allowed. The number of visits increased to 900,000 in 1987, with the category 'family' often broadly and arbitrarily extended by officials to friends and acquaintances (Borneman 1992a: 142–6, 305–10). Under the rubric 'family', Heidi applied to visit her mother's only sister on her birthday. Although they had exchanged letters over the years, they had never met before. Not attaching any particular importance to blood ties, Heidi had no idea what to expect.

I held these visits and this travel policy to be cruel jokes. It was the ultimate absurdity that the GDR, a state founded on socialist principles of universal brotherhood, would attempt to 'liberalise' policy in this way to meet both the rising expectations of its own citizens to travel as well as to comply with provisions of international agreements on 'bringing families together' that it had signed in return for international recognition, culminating in the Helsinki Accords of 1975. This 'liberalisation' was not only a betrayal of its earlier principles of fairness and inclusion based on need and performance, but also an affirmation of the principle of *jus sanguinis*, blood-based descent, a racist categorisation that had served the National Socialist government particularly well in its extermination policies, and remained the legal principle of FRG citizenship (Senders 1996: 147–76). It was also the legal rationale behind West Germany's insistence that all GDR citizens had an automatic right to FRG citizenship, since they, too, were Germans by blood. Heidi knew all this, but, despite her moral reservations, she also knew that her blood-based membership was the only legal category available that might make it possible for her to leave.

Two weeks before the scheduled trip, Heidi's mother died.

The trip to my aunt then took on added significance. I don't know how I made it through that week. I also had to do everything for Sieghard, I knew he wouldn't have the strength to organise the move himself. And I had to arrange for the funeral of my mother, her death hit me real hard, I'm still working through this loss. I swear I didn't sleep the whole last week before leaving. On the day after the Wall opened I was teaching. A few of the students took the day off to go to West Berlin, but most were still there. We had a marvellous, open discussion about the future. Suddenly all the barriers were gone. And my colleagues! Those who had been most ideological were suddenly very insecure, as if overnight they could see their futures change.

Heidi's aunt lived alone, widowed and childless. Yet, she feared the visit of Heidi and her family, or at least that is what Heidi sensed. She feared that this visit would change something. 'What do they want from us?' was the refrain that Heidi suspected played repeatedly in her aunt's mind. 'We didn't accept a single thing from her', Heidi told me.

And now I'm her best friend. She relies on me for everything – she has no one else. And it is *so* hard for her to accept help from me, from an East German relative. But I'll make her take it, she has no choice. She has no one else to turn to.

For Heidi and her family, then, the opening of the Wall came unexpectedly and suddenly, in the very middle of an exodus that they had planned for over a year. It did not, however, make this planning superfluous.

When we arrived in the West, I said we would do it all ourselves. We got 250DM from the state and that's it. We didn't stay in a camp. We didn't ask for anything. And things were tight. We barely got by. A friend gave us a small loan that we paid back as soon as we got work. I was so ashamed by the behaviour of the other East Germans, in the camps and before the authorities who were trying to assist us. They demanded, 'Where are the cigarettes?' 'I want some beer!' As if it was their right! They hadn't earned those things. They were gifts. It was Bavarian money, not theirs!

And then, how they would always insist they were Ossis – in order to get special privileges, or to explain away their ignorance! If they wanted to travel somewhere, they'd just get on the train, and when caught without a ticket, they'd say, 'I'm from the East.' I never ever said that, and nobody, not once, has ever suspected that I come from the East. The same holds true for my daughters. If someone asks me something and I don't know, I don't say, 'I'm from the East.' I just say, 'I don't know.'

I asked Heidi if people assumed that Sieghard comes from the East.

He's a wonderful doctor, you cannot fault him there. But, oh yes, they know he's from the East. And he's not done with that history yet. It's very hard for him here. He emphasises his East Germanness, his helplessness. I think he longs for the security he had in the East, but that's no real option for him, he won't return. He had no friends there either. I was everything for him: cook, bedpartner, maid, I bought his clothes. But he never knew me, and what he knew he didn't like. I waited until he received a secure job contract before asking him for a separation. And his reaction? Nothing. I gave him a chance to change. Nothing affects him. He's totally closed. Now he's got a good job, a permanent one, and he's planning his retirement, waiting for death. He wanted to plan my retirement, too, but I want to live, finally, for myself, to find out what I really want.

The decision to move West was easy for Heidi. The only question she still asked herself was why she had waited so long. As with all things in her life, she takes time, she thinks things over, and over, and over. She talks things through in a kind of self-therapy, and then talks through them again, and again, and again. Sieghard hated this thinking and he hated this talking. He told her he hated the way she used her hands when talking. 'That's me', she told me.

He didn't like me. How could I live all those years under that pressure? He functioned like a black cloud when he entered a room! Franzi would run when she saw him coming. I finally moved out of the bedroom into the basement. He told me something was wrong with me sexually. Something was wrong with *me*! But I knew my problems with him had started long ago, right at the beginning of our relationship. Very early on something just wasn't right. Still, I held out, because of the children, I couldn't just leave.

I remember Heidi telling me eight years earlier about what initially attracted her to Sieghard. They were both attending a Kur, a quasi state-sponsored health spa, and in that atmosphere of health and recovery, they became sexually involved. Heidi said that sex there with Sieghard was novel in that, for the first time, she had sex standing up. He lifted and held her so she could sit on him, and that, she explained, was an experience she had never had. It was also another kind of border-crossing, a violation of norms, an expression of liberty, and one that did not repeat itself once they got married.

During breakfast on the morning after Sieghard left, Heidi said she wanted to say something. I thought it was private, and got up to leave, but she said, 'Stay, you can use it for your research.' Surprised and somewhat embarrassed, I sat back down. There we were, the three daughters, myself, Heidi, and Klaus, Heidi's West German business partner of the last several years and lover as of the last six months. She had not told Sieghard about him. 'It would have been too much for him', she explained, 'and if he'd known he would never have separated from me. Besides, I'd made up my mind long before Klaus and I got involved. It took me a long time to convince myself that Klaus was really interested in me' – he is 17 years younger than she, married, and has two children.

I just wanted to wait until Sieghard had job security so that leaving him wouldn't harm him. When I told him I wanted to divorce, his reaction was, 'Well, are you sure you can survive alone?' No emotion whatsoever.

What Heidi wanted to say that morning at breakfast was that there were problems with Sieghard's leaving that were not yet, in her words, *bewältigt* (reckoned with/come to terms with). She told us how, at this point in her life, she desired above all freedom for herself. She also wanted the girls to be independent of her, and, she said, she wanted to talk about the consequences of this divorce, its effects on the girls. She had new projects that she was pursuing, one of which is to help Russian and Ukrainian artists who write children's books and draw comics. The disintegration of the Soviet Union has resulted in the collapse of these particular state-supported industries. Rather than see them employed as street cleaners, Heidi is now employing some in her business, as well as subsidising them in their free time. She is doing this out of conviction and does not expect to make any money from it. Her long soliloquy lasted about a half an hour. At the end, Franzi got up and quietly walked out. Peggy, her oldest daughter, began crying. And Greta, the middle daughter, sat in the middle, mediating rather unsuccessfully between the fronts.

Heidi's daughters

At that breakfast, Peggy complained that Heidi was admonishing her for not getting involved in the divorce and separation. She insisted that the divorce was Heidi's affair and not hers, that Heidi should have separated from Sieghard long ago. Peggy supported Heidi in whatever she did, but, she added, she would never have put up with sixteen years of marriage to Sieghard. She also felt that her mother was too strong for her, that Heidi's strength was overwhelming, and therefore she had to distance herself from Heidi's affairs. The same, she said, was true of her birth-father, a doctor and former high official in the Socialist Party, who insisted that Peggy's affairs were always of concern to him – and this, despite having dumped her and Greta on her mother after their divorce. For six years Peggy had had no contact with her father; yet, when Peggy turned eighteen and suggested that she wanted to leave the GDR, her father told her not to go because it would endanger his career. 'In early 1989', said Peggy bitterly, 'he was the first one [of us] to go to the West when he obtained the privilege [as Reisekader].'

Heidi felt wounded by what she understood as Peggy's withdrawal. She thought that Peggy was drawing the wrong conclusions from her own marital failures. Peggy said her conclusion was that she would never get in a situation where someone could use and demean her like Heidi's two husbands had done to Heidi.

I have known Peggy since she began her education as a midwife. She is giving that career up now to return to school to study ethnology. She explains her fascination with other cultures as partly due to her years of being unable to travel outside the GDR, but also, she had always sought out international friends, whom she finds more interesting than fellow Germans. She does not plan on marrying, nor on making the same mistakes with men that her mother did, but instead likes to think of herself as open to experiments in life style. Upon resettling in the West at the same time as the rest of her family, Peggy initially found work in Heidelberg; but she found the city too small and provincial and has since moved to Hamburg. All of her friends are now people born and raised in the West, and Peggy never tells people that she was raised in the East. 'Why tell them?' she explained to me. 'It would only provide certain stereotypes for them to think about me. They never suspect that I come from the East, and I don't offer the information.'

Both Greta and Heidi accuse Peggy of thinking herself superior to them. Greta has been involved with a man from Rosenheim several years older than her for the last three years. She broke off the relationship once, though, because she doubted his commitment to her. Within a couple of months he begged to get together again, insisting that she was the one for him. Greta admitted to me that she dominates the relationship, does all the initiating and planning, which, she said, is true of all the women she knows well. She and her boyfriend plan on staying in Rosenheim. 'It's not an exciting place', Greta explained, 'but we're happy here. It's beautiful. There's work.' Peggy accused Greta of remaining with this friend only because she could not find someone better, not because she really wanted to be with him. Greta responded by accusing Peggy of arrogance, and ultimately, said Greta, addressing Peggy's criticism, 'that is why people get and remain together anyway'.

I, along with Klaus, sat in silence during the accusations and counter-accusations, the tears, the pain. At times we were asked to intervene, which we staunchly refused. Later, I tried to sort out the influence of division and unification on this family, the limitations and possibilities opened for them due to their peculiar positioning. Certainly, division initially worked to Heidi's benefit, in that she had access to and support for education unavailable to most women in the West. But was Heidi's divorce a necessary consequence of not just the move, but of German unification? Did the dissolution of the two-state structure create the possibility for more diverse personal trajectories among the East Germans, including separate developments within and not merely between families? Should one view this divorce, therefore, not only as a loss for Sieghard, but also as a rare opportunity for a middle-aged woman? And what were the reasons, other than birth-order, behind Heidi's passions, Peggy's need for autonomy, Greta's accommodations and Franzi's obliviousness?

Security and liberty

The Berlin Wall and the border between East and West created a modern historical anomaly: two moieties out of a single city, two political-economic-cultural systems out of one. Anthropologists have been slow to recognise that the creation of systems of difference and opposition was a basic generative principle of the Cold War, a product of modernism and not a phenomenon found only among vanishing or 'traditional' societies. Before I went to study the divided Berlin, several generations of ethnographers had been studying non-Western moieties during moments of their disintegration, with no access to an historical explanation of their genesis. After three years of research, however, I realised that I had been witnessing a similar situation, though larger in scale: I, too, was documenting not the construction but the final collapse of a global 'dual organisation'. I had been living through the implosion of a matching, asymmetrical classification of the universe.

Like all boundaries, this border divided, contained, restricted and limited. It was also extremely productive of desire: it created monsters, heroes, traitors, yearnings, love and hate. The territorial borders of the state were the most powerful of both the delimiting and productive boundaries that emanated from the Cold War, but they were not the only borders created by the state. The state's delimitations created novel and unanticipated conditions of envy of those who could cross, and of fear of those who had crossed. Once a *drüben*, an other side, was created, someone had to represent this other side. But who was to represent it and how, since few were allowed to see it? Having seen the other side, would someone be content to return to live among the contained? In propaganda and reportage of competing East and West media available on the evening news, this other was always represented not as a wayward child of Germanness but as something that must be abjected or exorcised from the character and organisation of Germany. East Germans had to weigh personally the official media images against the stories told by people who had actually been 'there'. The confusion of images, I would argue, worked to the benefit of the East German state until the 1980s. At that time, the West German television programmes became more widely available in the East, and, by the late 1980s, the GDR began granting large numbers of people the opportunity to travel and experience personally the other side. As the West's version of Germanness became authoritative, it came to dominate the perceptions of East Germans, including the idea that their own experiences could better be represented by the West Germans than by themselves. The authoritativeness of the West German media also enhanced its influence, through selective coverage, on the sequencing of the 1989 demonstrations in Leipzig, as well as on the consequences of the opening of the Berlin Wall. The GDR's own coverage of these events was never taken very seriously as a set of legitimate counter-representations.

Cradle-to-grave security is what the regime in the East had promised. In order to provide this security, it had built the Wall. But this security state was increasingly experienced in terms Heidi would describe as suffocation, as the antithesis of freedom. While most citizens made their peace with confinement, a few tried to escape. These escapes were well publicised in the West as heroic flights to freedom. In November 1989, most published accounts stated that 197 East Germans died or were shot in attempts to cross one of GDR's borders (what the GDR had criminalised as *Republikflucht*, flight from the Republic). By 1992 this number had risen to 372. Recently released documents indicate that 588 people died in their attempt to escape East Germany. The number of dead is likely to increase to around 600 as new accounts begin to include, for example, more of those who drowned in the Baltic Sea swimming to Denmark, or Soviet soldiers shot defecting to West Berlin. Currently the victims include 290 East Germans who were killed while trying to cross land borders into West Germany, 172 who were killed trying to cross the Berlin Wall, 81 who perished in boat attempts to escape across the Baltic, and 20 who were killed while fleeing into Hungary, Czechoslovakia or Bulgaria. An additional twenty-five East German border guards were killed by their fellow guards as they sought to flee to the West.

Death was only the most dramatic and tragic of the effects of the deployment of the Wall to provide the bliss of security. Another major effect of the Wall was that large numbers of citizens, especially youths, increasingly measured happiness largely in terms of what they most lacked: liberty. And this liberty was measured by one's ability to travel 'abroad', of experiencing what was beyond the Wall and the borders of the state. This experience found its most common expression in 'tourism', as it does in the West, and was less a search for something new, for adventure, than a method of distancing oneself from the weighty present, of shedding one's skin. The desire to travel abroad has not been clearly articulated as a right or a liberty by social theorists or social protest movements, which instead, especially with regard to the former Eastern bloc, have focused on free speech, freedom from arbitrary government, and rights to organise. By 1989, a clear majority of citizens, Heidi and her family included, expressed a desire for more of this sort of liberty, articulated in terms of the right to travel to the other side, wherever that site may be located, even at the cost of personal security.

The aftermath

The collapse of the Wall has perhaps permanently changed the terms in which the historical tension between liberty and security are perceived and experienced. While removal of the border has indeed created more liberty for nearly all East Germans, it has also introduced tremendous insecurity into the world of work and the personal lives of many people, which in turn has exacerbated many of the old divisions among former East Germans as well as spawned many new ones. These divisions go beyond the well-publicised stories of *Stasi* complicity and personal betrayals, of family spy scandals where the spy alternately protected someone and limited their advancement (see Borneman 1993c, Segert 1993). To 'come to terms with history', as Heidi proposed to her daughters, would mean pausing and reflecting on ways in which complicity, betrayal and opposition were lived as part of a hierarchical system of role allocation, to clarify the personal gains and losses incurred living in the Cold War system of national (in)security states. On the other hand, the new opportunities opened to Heidi and her daughters are available to the extent that they have distanced themselves from their histories and place in the former GDR, to the extent that others no longer identify them with their pasts. Given their own alienation from the East as a home, a place, a culture, this distancing was easier for Heidi and her daughters than for most others, like Sieghard, and it explains to some degree their success. Indeed, they have never returned to Cottbus for a visit, and even refuse to visit West Berlin. The adjustments are also made easier in that their yearning for liberty was never very cleanly mapped onto a desire to travel abroad, and their disdain for boundaries extended well beyond those of the territorial state. Also, their relative unconcern for security is in accord with the demands of the enlarged Federal Republic of Germany, which, freed of the competitive pressure from the socialist East, is now limiting and even dismantling many welfare state policies, especially those necessary for internal national security, which were enacted during the Cold War (cf. Lemke and Marks 1992).

When I asked Franzi, who is now sixteen, what she plans to do when she leaves school, she replied that she would go to university, perhaps in Bavaria or Switzerland. She, too, is already looking away from her past, to the West and South instead of East and North. I asked her if she still had contact with any old friends in Cottbus. 'No', she replied. Did she miss anyone or anything there, I asked. 'No', she said, with a kind of nonchalance that seemed to me unstrained.

Perhaps her generation's sentiment was best expressed in the outcome of a meeting in Naumberg, eastern Germany, of 120 students between the ages of 11 and 18 from eastern and western Germany in the spring of 1994. They attended what was heralded as the first 'German–German Student Meeting'. The central question posed by the organisers was, 'We were foreign to one another – are we still?' Students responded in a variety of forms, writing newsclips and speeches, making videos and collages, staging musical or theatrical performances. According to the *Frankfurter Rundschau*, the fundamental message was reflected in the observation of one of the fourteen-year-old participants, 'I believe that the mental Wall is thicker among adults than us.' Indeed, the Cold War experiences that divided the two Germanies are no longer a part of the world of these students. But perhaps more revealing of the state of mind of this generation is the statement of one student: 'We were desperate to come up with something so we could discuss how we are still foreign to one another or are supposed to be' (TWIG, 17 May 1994: 7). In other words, how these young people come to terms with division will largely depend on how they react to the framing of current expectations by their elders. Lacking any direct experience with either the early passions behind Cold War division, the disillusionment at its end, or the euphoria turned to bitterness and cynicism at unification, they are at a loss for a framework that might account for their differences. They are, much like all children, left to work with the passions and disillusionment of other generations (see Borneman 1992b, 1993a).

Some of these elders are now frequently displacing the fantasies and fears provoked by Cold War borders onto an empty space of a shared, amorphous Germanness that is counterposed sharply to asylum seekers, Turks and would-be immigrants. What ties these particular groups together is their function as a counterconcept to a new nativism. For some Germans, the foreign is no longer the other Germany, but the non-native. This pan-Germanism does not, however, eliminate the use of distinctions between East and West; it merely makes them more difficult to highlight and in some contexts makes them taboo. Many others reject altogether a space of Germanness as opposed to the non-native, and instead try to identify with 'Europe', or 'the West', or even 'the world'. Since many former West Germans, being well travelled and cosmopolitan, are much more capable of representing themselves as European or Western or even world citizens than are their East German compatriots, this kind of Euro-gloss often works to accentuate East–West differences. And even if West German cosmopolitanism is a thin veneer that, under the competitive global pressures resulting from unification, is often transformed into an arrogant neo-nationalism, this arrogance is something that the East Germans cannot (yet) afford to display. Moreover, most East Germans valorise this West German identity by desiring to occupy the space of Westernness, however that may be defined, whether cosmopolitan or nationalist. For now, the operative definition of foreignness is unstable as the significance of borders is increasingly defined less territorially than economically, politically or culturally, with no clear locations of, or demarcation between, any of these domains.

Gender, sexuality, nationality

The dynamics of gender, sexuality and nation in former socialist countries, like East Germany, is frequently oversimplified by observers from countries in the West who think that they recognise prior versions of themselves in the East. One popular version of these dynamics is that while time generally stood still in the East, women did change some, men not at all (Borneman 1993b). The logic goes that while western Europe promoted positive nation-building and cultural change during the Cold War, socialist regimes suppressed nationalist sentiment and all forms of social movements. Therefore, according to this version, the eruption of suppressed nationalist sentiment, or the re-assertion of traditional gender norms and behaviours, or the proliferation of sexualities, was to be expected once the Iron Curtain came up (for a refutation of this thesis as regards Romania, see Verdery 1991). We might begin correcting this version by taking into account the complex and changing nature of differentiation during the Cold War, the interplay of gender, sex and nation as three loosely articulated systems of difference. This interplay was by no means the same in each of the east European countries. Certainly, the socialist 'bloc' existed at the state level, but within that bloc the dialectic between security and liberty was inflected by divergent lived histories. For example, socialist ideology did not have the same impact on the radically different gender systems in the north (for example, Poland) and the south (for example, Serbia); sexual practices changed significantly in East Germany but the whole subject remained relatively taboo in Romania; nationality was a very difficult and schizophrenic identity in East Germany but obtained added coherence in state policy in Poland and Bulgaria. In the case of the divided Germany, Cold War oppositions worked to exacerbate all three systems of difference.

The German–German border influenced both men and women, neither was left standing still in time. Oppositional nation-building processes provided a meta-framework in which social identities unfolded (see Cheater, this volume). Arguably, with the death of Hitler and the 'unconditional surrender of the nation' (or, the 'collapse', as it is still frequently designated), the Law of the Father no longer held. (One might even date this authority shift to the death of Hindenberg.) But to lose this father-function did not necessarily harm 'men'. Many men also fought for women's rights, especially in the 1950s in certain social classes in the East, and in the 1970s as part of a generation conflict in the West. Many men also either had lost their fathers in the war or they grew up hating them, and therefore worked just as hard as women to kill the Father, to eliminate vestiges of the authorial system that traced power from *Gottvater* to *Landesvater* to *Familienvater*. On the other hand, loss of the father-function did alter fundamentally what it means to be a 'man', as it also changed the conditions under which 'women', like Heidi, developed. Heidi's first husband tried to preserve his father-function and the power inherent in that position. Whatever gains this may have meant to his career were counterbalanced by his loss of a relationship not only with his wife but also with his daughters. Heidi's second husband, Sieghard, had a more ambivalent, if not passive, relationship to the Father; but he, too, failed to construct a positive alternative for himself to prewar notions of German masculinity and sexuality, and he, too, paid dearly for his lack of imagination.

For both men, notions of male (and female) sexuality seem to have changed even less than notions of gender. With respect to the relation of the loss/death of the Father to the experiencing of alternative sexualities, East and West differed considerably. The intense generation conflict of West German men and women in the 1960s often revolved explicitly around a 'reckoning with the past', meaning the death of the Father, and around sexual experimentation as social provocation (Borneman 1992a: 237–83). In the East, sexual experimentation was primarily a private and relatively depoliticised activity and did not become part of a generational confrontation as in the West. Heidi explains her attraction to a young West German man who has benefited from this sexual experimentation as part of a historical dynamic largely in terms of his refusal to assert traditional forms of 'male' authority.

Memory of the Wall

'1989' marked the end of a period that began in 1945, one characterised in double-speak as both a 'postwar' and a 'Cold War' era. It was indeed a 'cold' rather than 'hot' struggle in that it was fought – despite both sides' rhetoric of progress towards MAD (mutually assured destruction) – over quotidian life, as a war of attrition, less to destroy the other than to lame it and to fix the terms of its future. This drama of reaching the final historical form of human society – in the case of the GDR, a scientifically driven utopia – concluded, according to some, not with the collapse of the Eastern bloc but with the spread of liberalism to that traditionally illiberal region. As predicted, capitalist markets and parliamentary democracy were immediately exported to the East. But contrary to many early prognoses, these key symbolic systems of the victorious West have not provided an end to history, for the meaning of 'markets' and 'democracy' has changed steadily, as do all export models when they come into contact with actual consumers. It is increasingly clear that liberalism functions much like other utopias, including GDR Marxism: in the name of a universal humanism, it functions more to reproduce a particular regime of tolerance and property distribution than to support any abstract group interests or humanity taken as a whole. Instead of the end of history and the crowing of Liberalism, we have the end of belief in a universal 'man', with the result that the meaning of 1989 and of the Wall (our most recent past) remains open to multiple interpretations and rereadings, depending on the position and interests of the observer.

The Berlin Wall itself continues to exert pressure on history, no longer as a border – with their usual thoroughness, German officials have nearly totally removed remnants of the Wall from around Berlin – but as a trinket, a museum piece, a global commodity. In these forms the Wall now has a fixed, 'free world' meaning: any part can substitute for the former whole Cold War and bring forth a memory of freedom and its denial. Land along the eastern side of the Wall, which had been expropriated by the GDR, has either been returned to its last owner or is being fought over in court. One can now buy from Turkish dealers throughout Berlin stones painted to look like chips of the graffiti-signed, western side of the Wall, to wear around the neck, or to hang on the ears, or to display on a living-room mantel. Some sections of the original Wall have been preserved and repainted in scenes symbolising freedom, or its converse, oppression, and then sold or donated to groups and individuals in at least seventeen countries. Several slabs that were repainted by self-proclaimed international artists in 1990 still rest in their old spots in what is now called 'East Side Gallery'. One section stands near the demilitarised zone that separates North and South Korea, several stand in front of the United States presidential libraries honouring JFK, Ronald Reagan and George Bush. Even the CIA headquarters in Langley, Virginia, has adorned itself with a panel from the Wall – no doubt less to evoke 'freedom' than to reinforce a view lacking any historical evidence, a memory that claims that the CIA – despite its endless blunders – contributed to the final victory over Communism. The one association completely missing in any of these material commemorations is the relation of Cold War borders to 'tourism' – that peculiar interpretation given liberty by most of those East German border-crossers who prompted the opening of the Wall on 9 November 1989.

Within two years of the border's demolition, people in several places in Germany began rebuilding it. For example, a 130 metre (426 foot) part of the fence between the eastern town of Geisa in Thuringia and the western town of Rasdorf in Hessen has been reconstructed. Though the entire border was torn down in 1990, three years later mayors of both communities wanted the fence as a memorial to the decades-long compulsory division. Originally 2 kilometres of the border fence were to remain standing as part of an artistic project that would include reclaiming Point Alpha, a former American base at this site. By 1987, the Rainbow Association, which was founded to build bridges between East and West, had proposed to the government of the GDR the construction of an international meeting site, complete with a rainbow spanning the former border crossing to serve as a visible sign of reconciliation – but the GDR rejected the idea. But in July 1993, artists from the former East and West finally met at Point Alpha to address the theme 'Living Without Borders'. Presently the accommodation at Point Alpha is being used to shelter asylum seekers, whose number in Germany increased dramatically with the opening of the Wall. Needless to say, asylum seekers have become a prototype for post Cold War international border-crossers. The category includes an extremely heterogeneous group of people, impossible to classify according to a single geographic, political, cultural or economic criterion. Most seek both liberty and security; all want a 'better' life (or in some cases, simply a life) elsewhere.

Rebuilding the Wall to keep certain memories of division alive has not prevented former Communists – who one still associates with the era of Cold War borders – from returning to power in most of the former Eastern bloc states, including in some of (the new) eastern Germany's provinces. It must be noted, however, that none of these former Communists promise a return to Cold War borders, though many appeal to a redrawing and reassertion of borders, mostly along nationalist or economic lines (for the position of former East German Communists, see Bisky et al. 1993). The opposition politicians who initially replaced the Communists also contributed to their own demise; most have been unable to maintain popular support by offering liberty and free markets alone, nor have they been able to project their problems onto an external enemy, as was the case with both sides during the Cold War. Where this externalisation of problems has been tried, as in Chechnya or Yugoslavia, xenophobic and genocidal nationalism has been the accessory deployed by politicians to stay in power. Indications that something has been learned from the experience of the Wall's division are isolated, and those few politicians who dare to acknowledge the simultaneity of people's needs for security and liberty, variously interpreted and balanced, have frequently been isolated within their own political parties.

Grenzregime

In explanations of '1989' and events leading to the collapse of East European Communist regimes, including the dissolution of the GDR, two basic approaches in the social sciences prevail: either one begins with a theory or model and finds examples to prove or disprove it, or one begins with specific histories and looks for ways to account for them. I have chosen the latter approach, preferring the richness and complexity of experiential history to the parsimony and elegance of a model. In this choice I have followed a long anthropological tradition of explanation that, as Clifford Geertz has written, 'substitutes complex pictures for simple ones while striving somehow to retain the persuasive clarity that went with the simple ones' (1973: 33). The question for me, as an anthropologist, is not whether certain experiences or events lend themselves to serve a particular model (to prove or disprove) but from what perspectives might one account for and do justice to particular experiences and events. In other words, social science is put less in the service of itself than of the objects it seeks to constitute and explain.

The authoritative account on which most social scientists tend to do their modelling of Eastern European revolutions has been that of

Timothy Garton Ash (1989; 1990). For the East German revolution, Ash listed a compendium of factors, including the development of an opposition that provoked repression, a lack of will on the part of Egon Krenz (Honecker's replacement as head of party and state), the influence of West German television and Gorbachev's warning. The attempt to weigh these factors has produced a wide variety of models, such as Karl-Dieter Opp's sociological proposal for 'a micro-model specifying a broad set of individual incentives to participate; then we contend that political events and changes in the social context together with existing co-ordinating mechanisms produced the large-scale demonstrations of 1989' (1993: 659); or Sidney Tarrow's political science model which suggests that the 'rebellions' were a result of an 'opportunity for ordinary citizens to express and expand [their] demands' (1991: 15); yet others attribute events to intellectual dissent and the peace movement (Allen 1991), or 'the element of surprise' (Kuran 1991). These factors are all undoubtedly important, but importance says little about significance, and significance is always relative to the perspective from which one wishes to explain. Yet this perspective from which one speaks is rarely itself examined and made a part of the analysis. A reflexive sociology that would include in a description of the object examined the measures by which value and significance are attributed is all too frequently preached but not practised.

Perhaps the most popular model used to explain the monumental event in the history depicted in this essay – what Heidi calls simply 'the change' – has been 'exit, voice and loyalty', initially formulated and applied to the life of firms by Albert Hirschman in 1970. The question often asked is which East Germans were exhibiting 'voice': those who demonstrated to stay (and thereby also could be classified as 'loyal') or those who opted for 'exit' by fleeing to other East European embassies. Since the original model posits the three behaviours as mutually exclusive and leading to different behaviours on the part of the firm, application of the model to East German events, and the collapse of the GDR, has reduced the behaviour of actors to a single choice between three categories. The inability to acknowledge multiple (and often contradictory) actions of individuals and the state has resulted in confusion. But who or what is confusing, one must ask, the actions and events or the model? In subsequent work, Hirschman has consistently complicated his own model and warned against overextending his original elegant framework to other contexts. He has done the same in a recent article accounting for the 'fate of the German Democratic Republic', warning of 'the risk of making too much of a theoretical construct', admonishing us against the search for 'mysterious, if pre-

ordained, processes that dissolve all contrasts and reconcile all opposites' (1993: 202). After deftly sketching the events leading up to
November 1989, he concludes that 'exit can cooperate with voice, voice
can emerge from exit, and exit can reinforce voice' (1993: 202). So
much for simple cause and effect.

In this spirit of theoretical modesty, I have offered a description of
one woman, Heidi, and of those close to her, hoping that her story
might act as a lens to reveal new patterns and connections in the
construction and collapse of borders. I have also fashioned Heidi's story
to address the peculiarities of balancing liberty and security while living
in a Grenzregime during the Cold War and its aftermath. Any explanation of Heidi's 'change' after 1989 must substitute a more complex
understanding for a simpler one, since this change cannot be explained
in terms of a parsimoniously defined set of isolable factors such as voice,
exit, lack of the ruler's will, increased citizen opportunity, dissent and
spontaneous cooperation, or surprise. If we disentangle these factors
and assign them significance as dependent and independent variables,
we are forced *a priori* to ignore the vast majority of facts, the excess, that
make Heidi's abstract case into a human story. Through this reduction,
we necessarily lose in this modelling the historical specificity and
complexity of what is to be explained, the singularity of the object.
Borders, even an overdetermined one like the Berlin Wall, are the
products of ambivalent and multiple inputs; they are fortuitously
constructed and dismantled because of contradictory processes that
usually simultaneously support and undermine their continued existence. To focus on the life of one person – and someone marginal to the
processes one usually labels as 'history' (as in fact we all are) – can shed
light on only some parts of the story of the Wall and its aftermath. Yet
Heidi's life, precisely because of its fundamentally indeterminate nature
and marginality, reveals to us a decentred perspective on some of the
particularities of the patterned unfolding of the history of a Grenzregime: this series of events at this time in this place. That I have used
social theory only insofar as it explains her story, rather than made her
story serve theory, reflects my preference for keeping method and
theory sensitive to the historical exactness and density of human life.

References

Allen, Bruce 1991. *Germany East*. Montreal: Black Rose Publishing.
Ash, Timothy Garton 1990. *The magic lantern: the Revolution of '89 witnessed in Warsaw, Budapest, Berlin, and Prague*. New York: Random House.
1989. 'The German Revolution', *New York Review of Books* XXXVI (20): 3–14.

Bisky, Lothar, Uwe-Jens Heuer, Michael Schumann (eds.) 1993. *Rücksichten: Politische und juristische Aspekete der DDR-Geschichte*. Hamburg: VSA Verlag.

Borneman, John 1991a. *After the Wall: East meets West in the new Berlin*. New York: Basic Books.

(ed.) 1991b. *Gay voices from East Germany*. Bloomington: Indiana University Press.

1992a. *Belonging in the two Berlins: kin, state, nation*. Cambridge: Cambridge University Press.

1992b. 'State, territory, and identity formation in the postwar Berlins', *Cultural Anthropology* 7 (1): 44–61.

1993a. 'Uniting the German nation: law, narrative, and historicity', *American Ethnologist* 20 (2): 288–311.

1993b. 'Time-space compression and the continental divide in German subjectivity', *New Formations* 3 (1/Winter): 102–18.

1993c. 'Trouble in the kitchen: totalitarianism, love, and resistance to authority', in Sally Falk Moore (ed.), *Moralizing states and the ethnography of the present*. Washington, DC: American Ethnological Society Monograph Series.

Gaddis, John Lewis 1982. *Strategies of containment: a critical appraisal of postwar American national security policy*. New York: Oxford University Press.

Geertz, Clifford 1973. *The interpretation of cultures*. New York: Basic Books.

Geißler, Rainer 1992. *Die sozialstruktur Deutschlands*. Opladen: Westdeutscher Verlag.

Hirschman, Albert O. 1993. 'Exit, voice, and the fate of the German Democratic Republic: an essay in conceptual history', *World Politics* 45 (1): 173–202.

Kuran, Timur 1991. 'Now out of Never: the element of surprise in the East European Revolution of 1989', *World Politics* 44 (1): 7–49.

Lemke, Christiane and Gary Marks 1992. *The crisis of socialism in Europe*. Durham: Duke University Press.

Opp, Karl-Dieter 1993. 'Dissident groups, personal networks and spontaneous cooperation: the East German revolution of 1989', *American Sociological Review* 58 (October): 659–80.

Segert, Dieter 1993. 'The state, the Stasi and the people: the debate about the past and the difficulties in reformulating collective identities', *The Journal of Communist Studies* 9 (3): 202–15.

Senders, Stefan 1996. 'Laws of belonging: legal dimensions of national inclusion in Germany', *New German Critique* 67 (Winter): 147–76.

Tarrow, Sidney 1991. 'Aiming at a moving target: social science and the recent rebellions in Eastern Europe', *Political Science and Politics* XXIV (1/March): 12–20.

The Week in Germany (TWIG), 17 May 1994, p. 4.

Verdery, Katherine 1991. *National ideology under socialism: identity and cultural politics in Ceausescu's Romania*. Berkeley: University of California Press.

Wendt, Hartmut 1991. 'Die deutsch-deutsche Wanderungen', *Deutschland-Archiv* 24 (April): 390.

8 Transcending the state? Gender and borderline constructions of citizenship in Zimbabwe

A. P. Cheater

> The frontiers are there, the frontiers are sacred. What else, after all, could guarantee privilege and power to ruling elites?
> Yet the peoples, it would seem, see matters differently . . . The frontiers, for them, remain a foreign and unwarranted imposition . . . So that even while a 'bourgeois Africa' hardens its frontiers, multiplies its frontier controls, and thunders against the smuggling of persons and goods, a 'peoples' Africa' works in quite another way. For if the smuggling of goods and persons appears perverse and wicked when seen by governments in place, peoples in place can evidently find it right enough, and even natural.
>
> (Davidson 1986: 43, 44)

Introduction

Zimbabwe, like most newly independent states, is still attempting to construct its populist nationhood,[1] now under the dominating ideas of a black male elite. But not all of its citizens, especially women and non-blacks, construct their identities and relationships to the state in ways that are congruent with the state's contemporary construction of a national identity for its citizens. In the ongoing political fight to delimit citizenship, reflecting differing ideological notions about the 'proper relationship between the individual and society' (Blackburn 1993: 1), these competing definitions of citizenship seem to be regarded as 'borderline' constructions by the social categories who do not accept them. In this chapter, I explore discrepancies between the Zimbabwean state and a particular category[2] of its internationally mobile citizens over the construction of citizenship as identity in the 'cultural mindset' of transborder traders, a mindset that seems not to be anchored in the territory of any nation-state, but does respond to the laws of the state of citizenship.

The Zimbabwean state's view of citizenship coincides with Radcliffe-Brown's (1950: 43) idea that 'a continuing social structure requires the aggregation of individuals into distinct separated groups, each with its own solidarity, each person belonging to one group'. Following this premise, Zimbabwe sees itself as having inalienable rights to its own citizens and no obligations to any others. Its Minister of Home Affairs has explicitly noted the corollary of the state's position: 'it is not possible for a person to have complete allegiance and loyalty to two sovereign States at the same time'.[3] This male view of the patriline, extrapolated to the state (cf. Herzfeld 1992: 42), is incompatible with the life experiences of exogamously married women in a patrilineal system. It also presents difficulties for globally dispersed and ethnically mixed mobile families. Finally, while its emphasis on single nationality acquired through descent is shared by many other countries, the Zimbabwean state's explicitly patrilineal view conflicts with changing international understandings of citizenship entitlements and their transmission through women and to children, via the principle of bilineal descent. Over the past couple of decades, citizenship in many countries has become more inclusive. Zimbabwean citizenship rules, however, as Gaidzanwa (1993) has already noted, have become more exclusive since independence.

Turning to the perspectives of Zimbabwean citizens, I do not deal here with those who live near territorial boundaries and regularly 'jump' them without passports to visit family on the other side. Zimbabwe and its neighbouring states are considering introducing special 'border passes' to award themselves some degree of putative control over such movement,[4] recognising that people are unlikely to travel hundreds of kilometres through an official border post in order to visit kin who live within walking distance across an international boundary.

Instead, my concern here is with the construction of citizenship among hundreds of thousands of individual members of internationalised networks, who, from different parts of the country and speaking different home languages, regularly cross Zimbabwe's borders legally in what is called *going out* of the country. Those who *go out* nominally total over 10 per cent of Zimbabwe's population, although multiple journeys imply that their absolute numbers may be smaller. Perhaps a majority comprises black women traders from both urban and rural localities who travel hundreds of kilometres by rail and bus to cross into neighbouring states. Their trade is publicly trivialised as 'shopping' across state boundaries. Unlike the Hausa cross-border traders described by Cohen (1969), who by-passed customs posts and ignored the bureaucratic requirements of the states whose borders they crossed, or the Mexican 'illegals' described by Kearney (this volume), polyethnic Zimbabwean women 'shoppers' usually adhere to state requirements while crossing international boundaries to pursue collective interests at odds with those of the state. Their 'trading culture' transcends both ethnicity and nationality, but involves attitudes, values and organisational behaviour (engaging with the state as the territorial locus of the citizenship on which their mobility rests) that perhaps constitute a novel form of 'corporate culture' in the 'informal sector'. I briefly contrast the activities of these predominantly women traders with those of the staff of Zimbabwe's national airline, who shop in more exotic places. The behaviour of the cross-border traders reflects popular views of what Zimbabwean citizens ought to be able to do with their lives, in contrast to the state's narrowing definition of citizenship.

Mobility and the construction of citizenship in a developing economy

Constructing citizenship is, like state formation, a problematic, ongoing process of defining boundaries and identities. That Zimbabwe's identity is problematic is hardly surprising. This state is only just over 100 years old. From 1890 to 1923, Southern Rhodesia was part of Rhodes's British South Africa Company. For the next thirty years it was an independent colony of the United Kingdom, then spent ten years as a one-third partner in a federal dominion that collapsed, before unilaterally declaring itself independent and spending fifteen years in the international political wilderness. Over these nine decades, the tiny ruling minority of white settlers created a nationalism separate from that of the colonial metropolis, conceptualising their state and themselves as an independent-minded frontier of Western civilisation.

Notwithstanding this 'independence' of settler thought, the country's colonial legislation on migration, nationality and citizenship shows remarkable similarities to that of other Commonwealth countries also influenced by British templates. In 1980, however, following Britain's formal recognition of the country's independence, Zimbabwe, under indigenous control, redefined itself first as a 'developing nation' and later as a 'newly industrialising country', switching its approach to citizenship into what Gellner (1983: 81–2) classifies as 'counter-entropic late nationalism', based on black experiences of racial exclusion during the colonial period. As Barbalet (1988: 44) indicates, the struggle of black Zimbabweans for citizenship has been 'the struggle against exclusion' from the *political* (more than civil or social) rights of citizenship. The outcome of this struggle by black males has been a *jus sanguinis* view of citizenship as depending on ascribed descent, which has replaced the earlier settler-determined territorial or *jus soli* model based on individual mobility and contractual achievement. But, perhaps surprisingly, this new approach also shows continuity with legislative decisions based on the 'late' nationalism of white settlers in the 1960s and 1970s.

Colonial Southern Rhodesia, like most British colonies and dominions, was a society based on imperial mobility. Although colonial settlers never comprised as much as 5 per cent of the total population, settler immigration was encouraged. European, Asian and African immigration created a society with limited social contact across racial categories, but one which defined the major legal cleavage as distinguishing all immigrants, irrespective of their colour, from indigenous Africans. The number of non-European immigrants was usually limited – though when local labour was not attracted by local wages such immigrants were sometimes given assisted passage. The colonial state offered temporary work permits, but all immigrants received permanent residence rights on arrival and sometimes tax remissions too. However, the colonial state also assumed that immigrants would not necessarily stay forever and that decisions about residence and citizenship would be made in accordance with individuals' economic interests.

Until 1984, Zimbabwe permitted multiple citizenship. From 1899 to 1949, British citizenship could be acquired by birth in the colony or by naturalisation. This citizenship was available initially after one year's domicile and could be held in tandem with those of other countries which were held prior to naturalisation, but later naturalisation elsewhere resulted in its forfeiture.[5] From 1950, when Southern Rhodesian citizenship first became available, one year's continuous residence prior to application was necessary plus a total of four years in the previous seven;[6] from 1970 three years' and from 1984 five years' continuous residence were required.[7] Citizenship gave access to employment in the civil and uniformed services, and to government scholarships, plus the rights to vote and to a passport, in addition to the rights of permanent residence. Since very few blacks met the educational and property qualifications required to register on the separate African voters' roll, the political rights of citizenship were relevant mainly to white settlers. However, as a civil right, passports were readily available even to unskilled non-voters who wished to work elsewhere.

Political control of the economy in a new state

In this history of ongoing state-formation in a country which has offered its own citizenship for less than half a century, the 1965 Unilateral Declaration of Independence (UDI) had a particular and lasting impact on the permeability of the country's borders and its citizens' choices of identity, especially in commercial situations. Before and during the UDI period (1965–80), the increasingly nationalist settler state developed a very tight system of economic control[8] to facilitate its expanding but by then (under the United Nations trade embargo) illegal international trade. Based on the proportion of international trade in its total trade, UDI Rhodesia nonetheless developed one of the most open economies in the world. Paradoxically, this openness depended on extensive state regulation, where until the 1960s it had simply reflected participation in a much wider market. And the international trade itself, especially involving Europe and North America, depended on citizen traders with multiple nationalities travelling on foreign passports, since those issued by the unrecognised government of Rhodesia were accepted only by South Africa and, until 1975, Portugal. Passports from states which refused to recognise illegal Rhodesia were an important resource used very successfully in the expansion of Rhodesia's state-dominated UDI boom economy. In these circumstances, dual citizenship and multiple passports were useful to both state and individuals. Such identities did not conflict with one another, not least because the other citizenships were seen as instrumental to the achievement and protection of an autonomous Rhodesian nationality. Ironically, Zimbabwe seems to worry now that its own citizenship may function as a similar 'identity of convenience'[9] for dual nationality, non-indigenous Zimbabweans – particularly economically powerful whites.

In 1980, the newly independent state of Zimbabwe inherited the complex colonial system of economic control, extended it, and began to use it to effect greater distributive justice between blacks and whites. Import quotas and foreign exchange allocations were increasingly allocated to 'emergent businessmen' rather than to those whose enterprises had earned it. The agriculturally driven economy faltered, not least because of recurrent droughts; the value of the Zimbabwean dollar was driven inexorably downwards;[10] replacing capital and acquiring imported raw materials to keep factories operational became increasingly difficult; employment – already low – fell even further. Imported electronic goods, for business or domestic use, became virtually unobtainable on the local market. A new word entered the national vocabulary: *forex* (foreign exchange, or hard currency). As tourists and other visitors offered the opportunity to acquire much-needed forex or goods illegally in 'street deals', established capital and unemployed work-seekers alike had every incentive to evade the state's economic controls. Corruption developed quickly among all bureaus involved in the state-controlled system (import licensing, customs, police) as well as in the private sector (see also Gaidzanwa 1993: 54), until the forex control system was rapidly dismantled, as part of structural adjustment, in 1993–4.

The 'black' economy which developed against the independent state offered opportunities for windfall gains, but also reflected white capital's determination to retain economic power despite having relinquished political authority. In this struggle, black politicians and bureaucrats tried to control economic behaviour, especially of capital, by using the state. If we regard this as a class conflict, then citizenship rights have certainly been involved in it, perhaps supporting Barbalet's (1988: 10) observation that 'class conflict may possibly be about the nature and scope of citizenship rights'. And for Gaidzanwa (1993: 50), 'trading and speculation in scarce goods and commodities' has become a specific locus of class struggle between bourgeois men and poor women in Zimbabwe which is 'articulated in the rhetoric relating to citizenship, patriotism and entitlement'.

After independence, the state laid down minimum wages and conditions of employment, politicised industrial relations, and bureaucratised aspects of everyday life previously regarded as private (Cheater 1992, 1995). It also used state definitions of identity (nationality, citizenship) to control access to economic opportunities. Permanent residence no longer comes automatically, nor does residence confer the right to work. Temporary residence permits are granted only in association with temporary employment permits issued to contract workers in specific jobs,[11] and to their spouses and dependants who are not permitted to seek employment at all. While not actually speaking the language of the social rights of citizenship, Zimbabwe nonetheless defines employment *generally*, not just in the state sector, as a scarce resource reserved for Zimbabwean citizens and the dwindling category of permanent residents (Gaidzanwa 1993: 46).

Citizenship and identity

In keeping with the trajectory of mid-twentieth-century Rhodesian nationalism,[12] newly independent Zimbabwe has continued moves[13] to define the citizenship status under its control as sole, sacrosanct and unambiguous, in contrast to the early colonial acceptance of multiple national affiliations as normal. Perhaps oddly, but like its predecessors and similar British-influenced legislation in many Commonwealth countries, Zimbabwe's 1984 Citizenship Act did not define citizenship, nor its rights and obligations. Instead, minimalist definitions exist in the text of the declaration of allegiance, which used to be read aloud by newly registered citizens from prompt-cards collected at the end of the ceremony. But even these definitions are not normally available to citizens, and there is no teaching on issues of citizenship within the state educational system.

Citizenship matters thus appear to be subject to administrative decision, and administrative behaviour suggests that the Zimbabwean state does not distinguish civil, political and social rights of citizenship in the way that the literature following Marshall (1950) does. Nor does the Zimbabwean state seem to regard citizenship as the virtues of 'co-operation, altruism, responsibility and consideration of broader social interests' (Gaidzanwa 1993: 39) exercised through 'active involvement in the affairs of the community' (Vogel 1991: 59); nor yet as a set of rights and obligations exercised by individuals in relation to itself. Instead, the state appears to view citizenship as a form of ownership over individual citizens, reflected in an apparent reluctance to encourage their free mobility abroad. In Gaidzanwa's (1993: 53) view, the new state assumes 'unmitigated temerity' among its citizens who apply for passports as 'documents they are entitled to get from the state'.[14]

During its enactment, the 1984 Citizenship of Zimbabwe Act was publicised as enforcing Zimbabwean identity in an undivided loyalty to one state. The 'Conditions of Issue' (p. 56) for Zimbabwean passports issued after 1990 specify that 'A citizen of Zimbabwe who is eighteen years of age or above may not be a citizen of any other country. A citizen of Zimbabwe who makes use of the passport of another Government commits an offence.' The Zimbabwean state used the media to convince its citizens that they would automatically commit an offence for which they could be stripped of their Zimbabwean citizenship and passport should they abuse Zimbabwean rules or travel on the passports of other states. However, the Citizenship Act[15] actually states that

Any citizen of Zimbabwe who, without the written permission of the Minister, makes use of a current passport issued in his[16] name by the government of a foreign country shall be guilty of an offence: Provided that it shall be a defence to a charge under this sub-section for a person to prove that, when he made use of the passport concerned, he was entitled in terms of section nine to be a citizen of the foreign country concerned.

Section 9(7) states that

A person who becomes a citizen of Zimbabwe by registration while he is a citizen of a foreign country shall cease to be a citizen of Zimbabwe one year after such registration unless, on or before the expiry of that period, he has renounced his foreign citizenship in the form and manner prescribed.

This renunciation must be made to Zimbabwe, *not* to the state of citizenship.[17] The recurrent emphasis in the Act on 'the form and manner prescribed' suggests that what was demanded was more a one-off symbolic renunciation of identity than a permanent and enforceable surrender of rights to a legally competent authority.

When the renunciation was first required, in 1985, there was some speculation among both blacks and whites that few whites with dual or multiple citizenships would forgo the passports of 'advanced economies' when forced into this choice, given that their rights of permanent residence in Zimbabwe were guaranteed in the legislation.[18] It seemed to be assumed that blacks would comply, simply because they were *black* Zimbabweans living under a black government with which they could (and should?) identify. But there was open scepticism among both blacks and whites about the duration and legal value of the guarantee of permanent residence in the longer term, together with indignant assertions of Zimbabwean identity among whites. The long queues to surrender other identities lasted for months, right up to the deadline. They included the infirm aged, or kin acting on their behalf. But they certainly did not include all black Zimbabweans with multiple citizenships. Ultimately some 20,000[19] passports were handed (illegally) to the Zimbabwean state, which returned them to their issuing authorities. The United Kingdom, having publicly advertised that any action taken in Zimbabwean law has no validity in British law, returned them to their legitimate holders. Mono-citizenship is in fact enforceable by one state only when all other states also enforce it, as Zimbabwe's 1984 Citizenship Act rightly recognises. But the 'partner' states involved may refuse to enforce it, thus rendering it impossible to eliminate dual citizenship. Countries, such as Australia, which share Zimbabwe's monopolist view of citizenship recognise this problem publicly and do not attempt to bully their citizens into ill-informed compliance with their own state-determined preferences. Many Commonwealth and European states do not share the view that mono-citizenship is desirable, and even in Australia, the question has legitimately been asked:

In this world in which we now live, with heightened connections between countries and a sense of community reaching beyond national borders, . . . is the sense of loyalty to one country, and one country only, so important for citizenship? (Rubenstein 1994: 43)

Contradicting egalitarian understandings of citizenship (Hindess 1993: 38f.), but in accordance with its switch to *jus sanguinis* as the guiding principle of its nationality, Zimbabwe has begun to exercise its exclusionary powers against certain of its citizens. Like its predecessor states, Zimbabwe continues to distinguish citizens by birth and descent from citizens by registration. But now citizens by birth get passports valid for ten years, while the passports of registered citizens are validated only for five years. This provision is argued not to be discriminatory but rather protective, merely ensuring that registered citizens do not leave Zimbabwe for so long (seven years) that they automatically lose their citizenship,[20] even though it may seem odd that the state which authorised this provision apparently guards against its activation in issuing passports. Moreover, since 1984 birth in the country in itself has carried no guarantee either of citizenship or residence rights. Even a citizen by birth and descent who formally rescinds or has rescinded her or his citizenship and then emigrates, on trying to return will find that s/he has no residual residence rights, contrary to article 13(2) of the UN Universal Declaration of Human Rights and the more generous colonial provisions which made it impossible to remove the right of domicile from those born in the country.[21] These practices increase the probability of statelessness, but under its own law,[22] the Zimbabwean state may not withdraw citizenship if that action renders a person stateless, unless the responsible minister 'is satisfied that it is not conducive to the public good that the person should continue to be a citizen of Zimbabwe'.[23] Again, this is a continuation of colonial legislative provision[24] with parallels in many other Commonwealth states.

I therefore argue here that the Zimbabwean state has used its authority to define citizenship status in ways intended to strengthen the state against its citizens, collectively and with respect to specific sub-categories, rather than to ensure the individual rights, freedoms and entitlements conferred by citizenship in older-established nation-states – including, somewhat exceptionally in the Third World, Thailand (Sompong Sucharitkul 1990).

The state's view of citizenship is not lost on the citizenry, some of whom act in ways that suggest social constructions of 'citizens against the state' or, in Skalnik's (1989) phrase, citizens 'outwitting the state'. Or, perhaps, an 'amoral' view of the state as there to be manipulated whenever possible to the citizen's advantage, without too much regard for what the state, as just another recently established stakeholder in the economy, has sought to delimit as its rights against legitimate market competition from individual citizens and corporations.

Regional mobility

Southern African territorial boundaries arbitrarily divide a large, integrated region, for which Gaidzanwa (1993: 47) has argued, from a gendered perspective,[25] that existing rules of citizenship should be replaced. Part of the region's integration has been institutionalised in the post-colonial period, through the Preferential Trading Area (PTA) and Southern African Development Community (SADC). But as Gaidzanwa (1993) indicates, perhaps most of this integration is informal, deriving from colonial and even precolonial patterns of mobility, especially among blacks, and is seen very clearly in the pattern of cross-border mobility between Zimbabwe and all of its neighbouring states.

Zimbabwe has an easily permeable international frontier of over 3,000 kilometres, but only eighteen official border posts, four of which are located at international airports well inside the country (see map 8.1). Official Zimbabwean statistics for cross-border flows, especially departures, are known to be 'incomplete'.[26] Comparing the official figures for arriving residents and temporarily departing residents, it appears that Zimbabwe *gained* 1,462,666 returning residents – some 15 per cent of its total population – between 1988 and 1992.[27]

Of Zimbabwe's four neighbours, Zambia and Botswana require passports but no visas from Zimbabwean visitors, whereas both Mocambique and South Africa require visas as well as passports. The major cross-border flows are to South Africa and Botswana. Zimbabwe's official count of 42,091 visitors to Botswana in 1991 contrasts dramatically with the annualised extrapolation of 547,000, based on 1,500 crossings per day through the Plumtree border post alone which were reported by the Zimbabwean press during a period not notable for extraordinary movement.[28] Moreover, as table 8.1 shows, there is considerable unexplained annual variation in the official number of visitors to Botswana. Turning to South Africa, Zimbabwean statistics from 1988 to 1990 suggest that between 22 and 56 per cent of all South African single-entry visas issued to Zimbabwean residents were not used, whereas the South African estimate[29] of non-use (based on scrutiny of passports) was between 8 and 12 per cent. From 15 July 1991 to 1996, South Africa routinely issued to Zimbabweans multiple-entry visas with a normal validity of six months. Computerised records for only one South African border post, Beit Bridge, for the first eight months of 1993,[30] showed over 1 million visits by Zimbabwean passport holders. The 1993 ratio between visas issued (for the whole year) and visitors admitted from Zimbabwe (from January to August) extrapolated from the South African figures, is 1:4, a major contrast with the ratio of 1:1.4 derived from South African visas issued in 1992 and the Zimbabwean outbound figures for that year. Since fewer South African visas were issued in 1993, it is unlikely that this discrepancy was a result of increased travel.

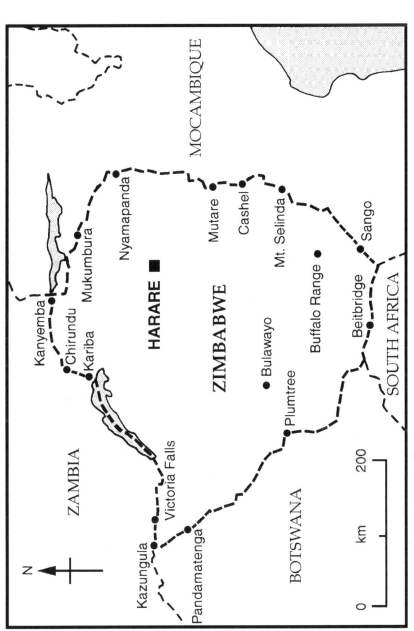

Map 8.1 Zimbabwe's international border posts.

Table 8.1. *Temporary border crossings from Zimbabwe to neighbouring states*

Year	Botswana	Zambia	Mocambique	South Africa	South African visas issued
1988	4,322	11,697	4,761	68,583	n.a.
1989	14,880	16,744	8,429	78,710	179,352
1990	6,166	18,977	10,347	110,133	236,535
1991	42,091	20,784	12,855	213,347	274,297
1992	7,411	24,568	19,760	377,415	268,848
1993	n.a.	n.a.	n.a.	>1,000,000	264,227

Sources: Central Statistical Office Dec. 1992 *Monthly Migration and Tourist Statistics*. Harare: CSO (table 5.2, p. 30); South African Trade Mission, Harare.

Regional trade: Zimbabwe's mail-order equivalent

1987, Saturday 8.30 am. The peace of our quiet close in the wealthy northern suburbs of Harare is shattered by the insistent rattling of my locked wrought-iron gates. There stands an attractive black woman in her mid-to-late twenties, dressed in a smart green suit, stockings, medium-heeled black court shoes, matching handbag, perfumed and expertly made-up, demurely releasing my gates.

Good morning madam. We are the ladies who travel to Botswana. Is there anything you would like to order? Shoes? Clothes? Microwave? Steam iron? Computer? Video? Disks? Fax? . . . You don't have to pay now. Just tell us what you want. It will take about a month, and we will bring it here and you can pay then. You don't need forex, just pay in Zimdollars. The prices are quite reasonable, and you don't have to use your holiday allowance.[31] We provide everything. You just pay us when we deliver exactly what you order.

As Gaidzanwa (1992, 1993) has already detailed, in a faltering post-independence economy Zimbabwean women have proved to be innovative, resourceful risk-takers in their attempts to hold their families together by contributing to or generating a household income. Informal cross-border trade (initially to Botswana and more recently to South Africa) dates from the mid-1980s and is firmly in female hands. It is part of a larger, composite network of women traders in the region, but is not, apparently, linked to male-dominated cross-border smuggling of restricted or prohibited goods, including ivory, rhino horns, gemstones, weapons, stolen luxury vehicles and drugs.[32] Little is known of Zimbabwean women's links with Zambian and Mocambiquean women who, in the 1990s, have traded second-hand clothing,[33] originating as aid donations to their countries, into local markets in Zimbabwe. But by mid-1993, some Zimbabwean women traders were travelling to Zambia and Mocambique to source their own supplies of such clothing.[34]

In passing, I should also note that not all women in the import–export trade necessarily travel to neighbouring countries to buy or sell goods. Some women, at least in the Bulawayo area, handle goods imported (personally, on holiday trips, or by rail freight or post) by their male relatives (brothers, sons) working in South Africa (Werbner 1991: 178–85).[35] Others, probably throughout the country, opportunistically send craft-goods to and receive trade-goods from related trade-partners as far afield as Cape Town, using trusted road or rail travellers[36] who are prepared to deliver extra luggage to specific addresses.

The informal trade across Zimbabwe's southern borders is substantial in its volume and requires not only financial acumen, but also a knowledge of bureaucratic procedures and ways around them in at least two countries. Yet my 1987 visitor, obviously expert in canvassing wealthy potential customers, was not typical of the women involved. In the 1980s, most were relatively poorly educated, spoke English haltingly, and presented themselves – in old dresses, canvas shoes and head scarves – as coming from tough peasant or working-class backgrounds. Such traders elicited derision from (male) customs officials when insisting that their imports were for personal use. 'Mama, you say you are going to use this fax in Chitungwiza? You don't even have electricity!' More recently, the state has restricted items that individuals can import without licences in an attempt to protect registered import–export businesses against informal female competition (Gaidzanwa 1993: 53–4).

One ultimately unprovable account of the origins of the cross-border trade involving such apparently unsophisticated women locates it in the desperation of white capital. *All* Zimbabwean citizens are entitled to holiday allowances, even though during the colonial period these were used almost exclusively by whites. So forex-starved businessmen allegedly organised many women with low lifestyle demands to *go out* for twenty-four hours to claim their duty-free import allowances. The businessmen are supposed to have helped the women complete applications for passports and their holiday forex; and then paid for the forex (retaining the traveller's cheques themselves) and train or bus tickets to take the women to a collection point, where the women countersigned their traveller's cheques and took delivery of the goods. The businessmen allegedly paid the women minimal living expenses for the trip and on the women's return, collected the goods. Or so some local rumouring – perhaps constructed by the new black male controllers of the state – has it. I am not able to assess its accuracy, but should this rumour have any foundation in fact, it would reflect the post-1984 structural convergence of settler and female interests against their control and exclusion by the redefined emphasis on patrilineal descent as the basis of Zimbabwean citizenship. It would, moreover, be a truly ironic inversion of the colonial collusion between white and black men against the civil rights of black women, which both Gaidzanwa (1993: 43) and myself (Cheater 1986a), like Schmidt (1992), have previously noted.

Not surprisingly, then, Gaidzanwa (1992: 10–11) offers an alternative explanation based on her research findings in the mid-1980s among a very small group of these women; namely, that they had sufficient business sense to see that they could sell their craft-goods in neighbouring countries for hard currency to buy trade-goods for local resale. Such business acumen may have been stimulated by an unsuccessful attempt by the state's Department of Women's Affairs, in the early 1980s, to organise an export market for such craft-goods. This attempt failed because the state's financial accounting requirements conflicted with the need (especially among rural women producers of these craft-goods, who still have no access to banking facilities locally) for speedy payments in cash.

There is also a second trading network through which scarce, high-value goods enter Zimbabwe and neighbouring countries, organised by the staff of the region's airlines. Different airlines fly different regional and international routes, thus permitting 'niche marketing'. In the early 1990s there were some surprising travellers on Air Zimbabwe: young people of both sexes, unemployed school leavers with a somewhat insecure fluency in English and a distinct reluctance to talk even in Shona, travelling to Frankfurt for a weekend in December or January in thin cotton clothes and canvas shoes, with no hold baggage. They were relatives of staff, travelling on rebated fares at 10 per cent of normal cost and mobilised to do so for their forex and duty-free import allowances. In one of the more spectacular Air Zimbabwe scandals,[37] the airline confirmed that on one flight in 1989 scores of potential full-fare passengers were turned away while 95 out of the 139 passengers travelled on rebated fares.[38]

Press constructions of 'unpatriotic citizens'

Very shortly after Air Zimbabwe started flying beyond South Africa, its staff recognised the potential of rebated fares for sideline fiddling in 'vulture' and 'wolfpack' modes (Mars 1982). In 1984 the Zimbabwean press identified a 'lucrative colour-television smuggling racket', when over 100 sets belonging to airline staff were impounded by Customs. Hundreds more were reported to be awaiting cargo shipment in AirZim's European destinations.[39] Press editorials briefly indicted pilots, cabin crew, affluent Zimbabweans and government officials for their alleged abuse of 'jobs providing special opportunities to cheat the state', despite public denial of their involvement by the white-dominated Pilots' Association of Zimbabwe.[40] But these issues were never revisited by the national press. Again, the press rightly asked 'where are the smugglers getting the foreign currency from?' but reported only the state's apprehension of stewardesses flying out with small amounts of unauthorised forex and of a 'top official' on a Z$15,000 forex charge.[41] The roles of ancillary and Customs staff at the airport were not pursued in print. No link was drawn with the newspapers' own 1983 and 1986 reports of air crews being charged with importing marijuana into the United Kingdom,[42] or with the ministerial reinstatement of one stewardess convicted on such a charge and fired by the airline's management.[43] In short, despite one class-oriented swipe at informal 'imports' by airline personnel, the Zimbabwean press did not conceptualise this internationalised activity as 'shopping', much less stigmatise it in the manner later reserved for the higher-volume regional trade conducted by lower-class black women. As Gaidzanwa (1992: 9) has noted, the illegalities of middle-class and elite purchases in politically acceptable places were ignored, while much middle-class work was invested in trying to identify illegalities among working-class 'shoppers' dealing in middle-class goods purchased in the then pariah state of South Africa.

The first press reference to women 'shoppers' was a letter to the major Sunday paper shortly after the plane crash which killed Samora Machel, denouncing the women for trucking with the regime responsible for his death.[44] Early in 1988, women defrauded by a local black travel agent were reported to have seized his office property and held his wife hostage in their search for recompense.[45] From 1990, when, as table 8.1 shows, the trade to South Africa really took off, press denunciations of the women 'shoppers' became more frequent. Late in 1990, the Ministry of Home Affairs issued a press statement on South African reports of Zimbabwean 'shoppers' dying from violence and exposure in South Africa and the Zimbabwean press reported on local women being mugged in Johannesburg – ironically, by Zimbabwean men.[46] By 1991 the women were being subjected to vaginal searches by Customs (Gaidzanwa 1992: 9), and a vice-president was urging 'shoppers' to acquire 'skills' instead of making 'exorbitant' profits from crossborder trade and 'contributing to a drain of badly-needed foreign currency'.[47] In 1991–2, the reports were of 'shoppers' being raped. A letter alleged that they prostituted themselves for 'free' accommodation in South Africa and were giving all Zimbabwean women an international reputation as prostitutes.[48]

By 1993, the press had targeted alleged illegalities in the women's behaviour. A Zimbabwean diplomat in a neighbouring state and a government minister appealed to 'shoppers' not to flout state law in foreign countries (mainly by trading without locally required permits), and to remember their 'patriotic duty to be the country's ambassadors'.[49] From mid-year, the litany of shoppers' illegalities focused on their behaviour in Zimbabwe. In July 'volatile women' travelling home from South Africa 'hijacked and hotwired' their own hired bus after 'overzealous' Zimbabwe Republic policemen tried to impound it and its driver 'for failing to keep to the [non-existent] timetable'![50] In August they were accused of smuggling;[51] in October of involvement in the drug trade;[52] in November of organising abortions (illegal in Zimbabwe) for married shoppers who had become pregnant on their travels;[53] and of what was called 'pawning' to foreigners their allegedly lost and stolen Zimbabwean passports, in order to obtain new passports without South African immigration restrictions stamped in them, and to stay on in that country.[54]

These reports in the state-owned press have systematically constructed women cross-border traders not merely as dangerously anti-social, but also as a multiplex threat to state authority. Yet in one lone report at the end of 1993, it also became clear that some of these women are immensely important public figures. Over 2,000 mourners from three countries were reported to have attended the funeral at Beit Bridge of two women traders killed (with many others) in a bus crash while they were returning from South Africa.[55] So if the state had hoped, by this negative publicity and attempted shaming, to control the women's activities, it had taken on an adversary of considerable proportions.

But the state has also employed other means of control. The Harare passport office has long – and perhaps unfairly – been reputed to be the nation's least efficient issuing office: it deals with the largest demand. In 1991 this office physically ran out of new passports; and during the previous five years, applicants had had to wait between 6 and 18 months for their applications to be processed. Officials hinted privately that women cross-border traders illegally maximised their access to holiday allowances through multiple passports held in different names. (With few exceptions, Zimbabweans are officially permitted only one passport, and much to their chagrin have to wait two years for a replacement if it is mislaid.) Some Zimbabweans speculated that the Reserve Bank had instructed the passport offices to limit the demand on holiday allowances while the Open General Import Licence (OGIL) system was being introduced and its impact on forex demand was still unknown, but anticipated to be very high. 'As a matter of policy', the Reserve Bank refused to divulge its forex allocations to the press when asked how much forex the women traders used.[56] However, if 250,000 holiday allowances had been claimed annually, the demand would have totalled over Z$112 million. This is, of course, a massive sum under the independent control of women lacking formal education and employ-ment as the twin foundations of a 'modern', male-dominated state, and the economic significance of the trade is attested by the promptness with which the South Africans have issued visas. Finally, the state attempted – unsuccessfully – to run the women out of business in its 1991 Z$8 million 'trinkets allocation' of forex to the newly formed Zimbabwe State Trading Corporation.[57]

Gaidzanwa (1993: 54) also sees structural adjustment policies as part of male bourgeois strategy in their class war against poor women. But the state's freely expressed hope that, following the lifting of currency restrictions, import saturation would 'spell the demise of the individual trans-border shopper'[58] was probably premature, if not misplaced.

Constructed threats to the state and the symbolic control of gender?

Why have female cross-border traders been constructed by the Zimbab-wean press and state as problem citizens? For Gaidzanwa (1993: 52–3), this is a result of the gendered dispute over state resources and who should have access to them. These press constructions began very shortly after the state's emphasis (in its 1984 Citizenship Act) on patrilineal descent as the basis of eligibility for Zimbabwean nationality and citizenship. They could, therefore, be interpreted as supporting Gaidzanwa's (1993) argument that Zimbabwe's approach to citizenship deliberately attempted to resubordinate women, perhaps against other legislation which very creditably reformed women's rights after 1980 (Stewart and Armstrong 1990, Cheater 1993). There is no doubt that ideologically Zimbabwe remains a patriarchal state, as re-emphasised in its 1984 Citizenship Act and failure to outlaw in the Constitution discrimination based on gender.[59] Against public debate, until 1996 it steadfastly refused to grant women the right to transmit residence rights to foreign spouses, or even citizenship to their own children, on the same terms that apply to Zimbabwean men (Citizenship of Zimbabwe Act 1984, Galvin 1991, Gaidzanwa 1993)[60] and in the same ways that are today common, mainly but not exclusively in Western countries.

I would go further than Gaidzanwa, however, to argue that the female cross-border traders, so vilified in the state-owned press, challenge male Zimbabweans' ideological construction of womanhood as ultimately dependent on men. The 'transborder culture' of mobile women traders not only undermines existing ethnicities and transcends differences of nationality in economic cooperation, but also threatens male Zimbabwean notions of the proper order of female dependency. These women survive well financially, dealing in hi-tech goods with uses that baffle many men. They develop business relations with wealthy and more powerful consumers. They shrug off the dangers of rape in developing board and accommodation networks in foreign lands with previously unknown distant and classificatory kin and unrelated strangers. They use state entitlements against all expectations. They know their way around complex state and banking bureaucracies, without the benefit of high levels of formal education or personal relations of (male) patronage. Like other Zimbabweans, including most young people, these pseudo-cosmopolitans expect, as of right, to hold passports as they shuttle between countries. They are long-distance migrants of a very different kind to the role defined generations ago by men as labour migrants in Southern Africa.

The women are, then, anomalous. The disorder of anomalies must be brought under symbolic control (Douglas 1957), in this case by their ritual public denunciation as dangerous citizens, who consume their entitlements as citizens without due regard for – perhaps even in opposition to – the male-dominated state which uses its symbolic boundaries to produce these entitlements. This public denunciation has clear structural parallels with accusations of witchcraft levelled against women marrying into exogamous patrilineages, and perhaps also with those levelled against women traders in West Africa (Nadel 1970).

Conclusion: counter-constructions of citizenship

In this chapter, I have tentatively tried to capture conflicting constructions of the identity of Zimbabwe's female cross-border traders in their act of transcending state boundaries, symbolic and territorial. The existing literature on nationality, citizenship and identity boundaries has been of little help in what seems to me to be relatively uncharted anthropological territory. Without further research, it is impossible to say whether these women traders self-identify as Zimbabwean citizens in all three contexts in which they operate: at home, as sellers of trade-goods imported ostensibly for personal use; in transit, as cross-border travellers; and in neighbouring states as sellers of craft-goods and retail buyers of trade-goods. The Zimbabwean state-controlled media have ignored these locational specificities in presenting 'shoppers' as disgracing the nation, and writings on mobile traders generally describe their activities either in their home territory, or in foreign cities, sometimes explicating shifts in identity in foreign contexts (e.g. Cohen 1969). My concern is somewhat different. Crossing the Zimbabwean border, the women traders are its citizens, perhaps with a range of identities and passport options; yet in transit between border posts and end-destinations, individual identity choices may also include citizenship options. This simultaneous clarity and ambiguity of identity while crossing the border perhaps relates to the jealous guarding of its citizenship and travel documents by the Zimbabwean state.

Given the structural parameters of the Zimbabwean state's approach to citizenship, those whom it denounces as 'unpatriotic citizens'[61] unworthy of its passports and protection could be predicted to be mainly internationally mobile women – and diaspora migrants, whom I have chosen not to consider here. The acquisition of multiple identities and passports, possibly even citizenships, by women pursuing their economic interests, supports Handler and Segal's (1993: 6) point that '"national identity" implies an autonomy and "self-determination" which are now more than ever merely, though powerfully, rhetorical'. Contradicting the Zimbabwean state's view, these citizens do not experience any noticeable conflicts of interest arising from their multiple identities. The state apparently has a problem in understanding the principle of situational selection as a 'shifting of [segmentary] levels of solidarity', which it finds 'inconceivable' (Herzfeld 1992: 113), but Zimbabwean people do not. Moreover, those who control the Zimbabwean state assume that political and economic citizenship should converge, in contrast to popular experience of the results of recent state policies.

I have argued that this popular attitude or cultural mindset is related to the historical precedent of UDI economic nationalism, as well as to pre-colonial traditions of 'voting with one's feet' against oppressive or intrusive chiefly or state power. In becoming members of regional socioeconomic networks that are not contained within state boundaries, Zimbabwe's women who trade across these frontiers are more attuned to globalising trends than are its menfolk who adhere to cultural concepts of the state and citizenship that are rapidly undergoing global displacement.

Notes

1. '[T]he distinguishing feature of populistic nationalism [is] its equation of "the nation" and "the people"'. (Stewart 1969: 183)
2. 'Category' is used here in accordance with its sociological meaning of people sharing one or more common attributes, in preference to 'group', which implies that social relationships link those in question. Zimbabwe's internationally mobile citizens (and ex-citizens) fall into a number of differing social categories, and I shall deal with only one of these here. As will become clear later, 'network' is a more appropriate description of the women traders concerned, but in this particular context is an awkward usage.
3. Parliamentary Debates, House of Assembly, 14 August 1984, col. 800.
4. *Herald*, 23 November 1993.
5. Southern Rhodesia 1899 Order in Council; Southern Rhodesia 1939b Naturalisation Act, s. 7.
6. 1949 Southern Rhodesian Citizenship and British Nationality Act (which took effect from 1 January 1950), s. 8(2)(b).
7. 1970 Citizenship of Rhodesia Act; 1984 Citizenship of Zimbabwe Act, s. 4(1)(c)(ii).
8. 1964 Reserve Bank of Rhodesia Act; 1964 Exchange Control Act (which took effect in mid-1965) and subsequent regulatory amendments.
9. *Herald*, 11 January 1994, editorial.
10. By 1997, Z$1.00 was worth between 5 and 6 pence sterling, compared with 75 pence shortly after independence in 1980.
11. Such jobs cannot be changed without invalidating the TEPs associated with them.
12. Southern Rhodesian Citizenship and British Nationality Act, no. 13. of 1949; Citizenship of Southern Rhodesia and British Nationality Act, no. 63 of 1963; Citizenship of Rhodesia Act (Cap 23) (1970).
13. None of which have been subject to any form of public discussion, even within the Legislative Assembly. Parliamentary Debates, 14 August 1984, vol. 10, no. 17, cols. 799–805.
14. Some citizens have been reminded personally by state officials that Zimbabwean passports are held on withdrawable privilege, not by right.
15. Section 21 (3).
16. That language connoting male persons applies also to females, was laid down in section 8(1) of the Interpretation Act (Cap. 1, 1962).
17. This demand gives the appearance of not understanding what is legally involved in terminating citizenship in its intrusion on the prerogatives of other states.
18. Citizenship Act, sections 9(9) and 9(10).
19. Zimbabwe recorded their receipt but officially did not count them.
20. Section 13 of the 1984 Act permits the state to remove citizenship after a registered citizen's continuous absence of seven years. This provision first appeared in section 22(1) of the 1963 legislation, extending the previous three-year time limit on absence written into section 29 of the 1949 Act, and was recorded in the parliamentary debate 'for administrative reasons'

relating to data capture as being 'completely ineffective' even then (Legislative Assembly Debates, 21 November 1963, col. 334).

21. Southern Rhodesian Immigrants Regulation Act (Cap 60) (1939), s.8(f); *Herald*, 8 October 1993.

22. Citizenship Act, section 11(3)a.

23. Citizenship Act, section 11(3)b.

24. Dating from the Southern Rhodesian Citizenship and British Nationality Act, no. 13. of 1949, s. 27(4).

25. A more generalised critique of gendered citizenship is provided by Vogel (1991).

26. 'In the main this is because of: (a) The omission on [sic] cross-border movements at points other than the official ports, and (b) Evidence that some residents who declare that they are leaving for less than twelve months in fact stay away permanently or rather longer than a year' (Central Statistical Office 1993: 1).

27. Central Statistical Office 1992: 30–1 (tables 5.2 and 5.3).

28. *Herald*, 24 September 1991.

29. Given by the South African Trade Mission in Harare.

30. Information provided by the South African Trade Mission in Harare.

31. A 'holiday allowance' is an annual entitlement to purchase forex to take a holiday outside Zimbabwe. Previously miniscule, in 1994 it was set at US$2,000 (then Z$17,000) and more recently was raised to US$5,000.

32. From press reports in Zimbabwe, however, it would appear that the women's trade attracts at least as much police interest as male smuggling and a good deal more adverse press publicity.

33. For many decades, the market for second-hand clothing has been underdeveloped in Zimbabwe. However, since independence an increasing proportion of the population has been impoverished, and Zimbabwe's textile and garment industries have sought external markets in order to remain in business (Cheater 1986b: xv, 19–20). As a result, many Zimbabweans can no longer afford to purchase new clothing, and second-hand imports have been very profitable for traders.

34. *Herald*, 20 July 1993.

35. Werbner (1991: 178) appears not to have understood fully the Zimbabwean referent of 'going out'.

36. Baggage limitations mean air travellers are less suitable for this task.

37. There have been many, and an official Commission of Inquiry.

38. *Herald*, 16 June 1989.

39. *Herald*, 5 January 1985.

40. *Sunday Mail*, 8 January 1985; *Herald*, 9 January 1985, 24 January 1985.

41. *Herald*, 24 June 1984, 5 January 1985, 18 February 1985.

42. *Herald*, 20 July 1983, 4 February 1984, 18 July 1986.

43. Interim Report, p. 37.

44. *Sunday Mail*, 2 November 1985.

45. *Herald*, 10 January 1988.

46. Press statement 16 November 1990; *Herald*, 7 December 1990.

47. *Herald*, 9 March 1991.

48. *Sunday Mail*, 12 May 1991.

49. *Herald,* 24 April 1993; 4 June 1993.
50. *Sunday Mail* 18 July 1993.
51. *Herald,* 14 August 1993.
52. *Herald,* 23 October 1993.
53. *Herald,* 6 November 1993.
54. Some fifty people per week were then applying to Zimbabwe's Trade Mission in Johannesburg for emergency travel documents to replace mislaid passports (*Sunday Mail,* 14 November 1993).
55. *Herald,* 20 December 1993.
56. *Sunday Mail,* 8 December 1991.
57. *Herald,* 13 September 1991.
58. *Herald,* 16 June 1993.
59. Section 11 of the Constitution of Zimbabwe (revised in 1996) still limits gender equity to those individual freedoms specified in the declaration of rights. In section 23, the legislation concerning marriage, divorce and other family matters, as well as the whole of customary law, is specifically exempted from Constitutional regulation.
60. Following a High Court ruling on an appealed test case, all foreign spouses are now treated as foreign husbands used to be.
61. Herzfeld (1992: ch. 5) notes that confrontations between states and patriotic citizens are not unusual.

References

Barbalet, J. M. 1988. *Citizenship.* Milton Keynes: Open University Press.
Blackburn, R. (ed.) 1993. *Rights of Citizenship.* London: Mansell. (Introduction, pp. 1–11).
Central Statistical Office 1992. *Monthly migration and tourist statistics.* Harare: CSO (December).
1993 *Quarterly digest of statistics.* Harare: CSO (September).
Cheater, A. P. 1986a. 'The role and position of women in colonial and pre-colonial Zimbabwe', *Zambezia* 13 (2): 65–80.
1986b. *The politics of factory organization.* Gweru: Mambo Press.
1992. 'Industrial organisation and the law in the first decade of Zimbabwe's Independence', in A. P. Cheater (ed.), *Industrial sociology in the first decade of Zimbabwe's independence.* Harare: University of Zimbabwe Publications.
1993. 'Ambiguities and contradictions in the political management of culture in Zimbabwe's reversed transition to socialism', in C. M. Hann (ed.), *Socialism: ideals, ideologies and local practice.* (ASA 31) London: Routledge.
1995. 'La bureaucratie comme mode de vie post-coloniale au Zimbabwe', in J.-L. Balans and M. Lafon (eds.), *Le Zimbabwe contemporain.* Paris: Karthala and Institut Français de Recherche en Afrique, pp. 201–12.
Cohen, A. 1969. *Custom and politics in urban Africa.* London: Routledge and Kegan Paul.
Davidson, B. 1986. 'On revolutionary nationalism: the legacy of Cabral', *Race and Class* 27 (3): 21–45.
Douglas, M. 1957. 'Animals in Lele religious symbolism', *Africa* 27 (1): 46–58.

Gaidzanwa, R. B. 1992. *The ideology of domesticity and the struggles of women workers: the case of Zimbabwe.* ISS Working Paper Sub-Series on Women's History and Development, no. 16. The Hague: Insitute of Social Studies.

——— 1993. 'Citizenship, nationality, gender and class in Southern Africa', *Alternatives* 18: 39–59.

Galvin, T. M. 1991. Socio-cultural sources of stress in marital decision-making among Zimbabweans married to foreigners. Unpublished D.Phil. thesis. Harare: University of Zimbabwe.

Gellner, E. 1983. *Nations and nationalism.* Oxford: Basil Blackwell.

Handler, R. and D. A. Segal 1993. 'Introduction: nations, colonies and metropoles', *Social Analysis*, 33: 3–8.

Herzfeld, M. 1992. *The social production of indifference.* Chicago/London: University of Chicago Press.

Hindess, B. 1993. 'Multiculturalism and citizenship', in C. Kukathas (ed.), *Multicultural citizens: the philosophy and politics of identity* (CIS Readings 9). St Leonard's (NSW): Centre for Independent Studies, pp.31–45.

Mars, G. 1982. *Cheats at work.* London: George Allen and Unwin.

Marshall, T. H. 1950. *Citizenship and social class and other essays.* Cambridge: Cambridge University Press.

Nadel, S. F. 1970 [1952]. 'Witchcraft in four African societies', in M. Marwick (ed.), *Witchcraft and sorcery.* Harmondsworth: Penguin.

Radcliffe-Brown, A. R. 1950. *African systems of kinship and marriage.* London: Oxford University Press for International African Institute.

Rhodesia 1964a. *Reserve Bank of Rhodesia Act* (no. 24). Salisbury: Government Printer.

——— 1964b *Exchange Control Act* (no. 62) (Cap. 170). Salisbury: Government Printer. (Amendment: 1970.)

——— 1970 *Citizenship of Rhodesia Act* (cap. 23). Salisbury: Government Printer.

Rubenstein, K. 1994. 'Constitutional issues associated with integration: the question of citizenship', *BIPR Bulletin* 11: 41–3.

Schmidt, E. 1992. *Peasants, traders and wives.* Portsmouth, New Hampshire: Heinemann; Harare: Baobab; London: James Currey.

Skalnik, P. (ed.) 1989. *Outwitting the state.* New Brunswick: Transaction Publishers.

Sompong Sucharitkul 1990. 'Thai nationality in international perspective', in Ko Swan Sik (ed.), *Nationality and international law in Asian perspective.* Dordrecht, etc.: Martinus Nijhoff Publishers, pp. 453–91.

Southern Rhodesia 1899. *Order in Council: Naturalisation.* (Gazetted 28.4.1899)

——— 1939a. *Immigrants Regulation Act* (cap. 60). Salisbury: Government Printer.

——— 1939b. *Naturalisation Act* (cap. 66). Salisbury: Government Printer.

——— 1949. *Southern Rhodesian Citizenship and British Nationality Act* (no. 13). Salisbury: Government Printer.

——— 1962. *Interpretation Act* (cap. 1). Salisbury: Government Printer.

——— 1963a. *Legislative Assembly Debates* (27 November, cols. 323–39). Salisbury: Government Printer.

——— 1963b. *Citizenship of Southern Rhodesia and British Nationality Act* (no. 63). Salisbury: Government Printer.

Stewart, A. 1969. 'The social roots', in G. Ionescu and E. Gellner (eds.), *Populism: its meanings and national characteristics*. London: Weidenfeld and Nicolson, pp. 180–96.

Stewart, J. and A. Armstrong (eds.) 1990. *The legal situation of women in Southern Africa*. Harare: University of Zimbabwe Publications.

United Nations 1948. *Universal Declaration of Human Rights*. New York: General Assembly.

Vogel, U. 1991. 'Is citizenship gender-specific?', in U. Vogel and M. Moran (eds.), *The frontiers of citizenship*. New York: St Martin's Press, pp. 58–85.

Werbner, R. 1991. *Tears of the dead*. Edinburgh: Edinburgh University Press; Harare: Baobab Books.

Zimbabwe 1984a. *Parliamentary Debates: House of Assembly* (14 August, vol. 10, no. 17, cols. 799–805). Harare: Government Printer.

Zimbabwe 1984b. *Citizenship of Zimbabwe Act* (no. 23). Harare: Government Printer.

Zimbabwe 1996. *Constitution of Zimbabwe* (Revised edn). Harare: Government Printer.

Zimbabwe 1987. *Interim Report of the Commission of Enquiry into Parastatals: Air Zimbabwe Corporation*. Harare: Government Printer.

9 Borders, boundaries, tradition and state on the Malaysian periphery

Janet Carsten

One of the more embarrassing memories from my fieldwork on the island of Langkawi concerns a trip that my relatives in the village of Sungai Cantik planned to make by fishing boat across the border to southern Thailand. Pulau Langkawi forms part of the northern Malay state of Kedah. It lies off the west coast of the Malay peninsula, just south of the border between Malaysia and Thailand. The purpose of the trip was to do some cheap shopping, to visit friends and relatives, and to stay for a few days of enjoyment before returning loaded up with bargain Thai merchandise. The excursion was planned with consider-able excitement – this was an out of the ordinary event, although not altogether unheard of – and I was invited to go along. Without thinking too hard about what might be involved, I accepted.

In the following days, doubts about the trip itself – on an overcrowded fishing boat – were reinforced by doubts of a more bureaucratic kind. Were there risks involved? What about my status as a foreign researcher if we were apprehended without proper documentation – visas, licences, passports? I demurred at the last moment, on the pretext of feeling unwell. The puzzlement and disappointment of my relatives, and particularly my foster mother's look of scepticism over my supposed illness, still bring back a sense of embarrassment and inadequacy undoubtedly recognisable to most anthropological fieldworkers.

These personal recollections connect with some issues of wider relevance in the ethnography of Southeast Asia. Central to these issues is the notion of the border. My anecdote is about crossing an inter-national border between two nation-states – Thailand and Malaysia. It is notable that the villagers I lived with were not particularly concerned about this border. Indeed, on this occasion and on others, they ignored as far as possible the bureaucratic implications of moving across a modern international frontier.

During fieldwork, I was often struck by the pleasure which villagers in Langkawi derive from making trips, from travelling for the sake of it, or for the purpose of visiting relatives, shopping, attending a ceremony or a celebration, or seeing to some administrative matter. Hann and Bellér-Hann (this volume) note a similar kind of pleasure afforded by 'trader tourism' on the north-east border of Turkey. When the missed excursion to Thailand was over, the travellers returned full of stories of what they had done, and loaded with goods which they had acquired on the trip. The excitement was not unusual. Villagers often make trips to the mainland, and ferries to and from Langkawi are crowded with passengers carrying fresh produce and other consumption goods; adults are often accompanied by children who are there just for the fun of it.

A delight in travel for its own sake is well documented in the literature on Southeast Asia. The Iban *bejalai* (Freeman 1970) is an occasion not just of temporary migration to make a living, but one which is central to gaining a reputation, acquiring prestige goods and becoming a man. The Sumatran phenomenon of *merantau* (Kahn 1980, Kato 1982) appears similarly central to personhood and sociality. In Langkawi, as elsewhere in the region, it is usual for young men to engage in migrant work for a few years between leaving school and marriage. In these various ways, villagers in Langkawi make trips of short or long duration to the mainland or further afield. Mobility underlies social life in Langkawi in another, more fundamental, way. A substantial proportion of the population of Sungai Cantik is made up of migrants, or the direct descendants of migrants. Migration appears to have occurred in a more or less continuous trickle from at least the mid-nineteenth century until the present. I will discuss this phenomenon in more detail below. Here, I merely underline that many villagers have links with kin in different areas of the mainland, or in southern Thailand or Indonesia. Their world has for a long time extended beyond the island of Langkawi, the state of Kedah and the borders of the modern Malaysian nation-state. The social life of Sungai Cantik straddles many borders.

The story I began with also concerns another kind of border, that between the fieldworker and those she temporarily lives among. In this chapter I will argue that there is a connection between these two borders. In order to see this connection we must investigate the notion of 'the border' itself. More than twenty years ago, Benedict Anderson argued that anthropologists and others need to understand Southeast Asian notions of power in indigenous terms rather than in Western ones, and he showed the implications these notions held for the traditional state (*negeri*) in Southeast Asia. That the borders of the *negeri* were qualitatively different from those of the modern nation-state was a crucial aspect of his theory. Borders, like power, must be understood in local terms. We should not assume in advance that we know what kind of entity it is we are dealing with when we talk of the border.

As I will show, international borders between nation-states and boundaries between persons are not necessarily entirely different sorts of phenomena. For this reason, at points in this chapter I slip from a discussion of international borders to what might be considered to be more 'symbolic' boundaries between kin and non-kin, or between persons. In an analogous way, Stokes (this volume) discusses how Arabesk provides a way of thinking about notions of masculinity, difference and hierarchy, and by extension national borders and ethnic difference on the southern border of Turkey. In treating international borders and boundaries between kin and non-kin, or between persons, as if they were the same sort of phenomena, I am not only asserting that in the context which I describe here there is a strong correspondence between them. I would go further than this. Anderson (1983) has alerted us to the symbolic power of the concept of the nation. I make no apologies for treating the political 'reality' of an international frontier as no less symbolic – or more 'real' – than boundaries between persons and between kin.

The traditional state in Southeast Asia

The traditional Southeast Asian state, or *negeri*, was a different kind of entity from the modern nation-state. Its borders were shifting and permeable. As Anderson (1990: 41) has written,

The territorial extension of the state is always in flux; it varies according to the amount of Power concentrated at the center . . . the kingdoms were regarded not as having fixed and charted limits, but rather flexible, fluctuating perimeters. In a real sense, there were no political frontiers at all, the Power of one ruler gradually fading into the distance and merging imperceptibly with the ascending Power of a neighboring sovereign.

Anderson has shown how this kind of boundary was a corollary of notions of power in Southeast Asia. Delineating an ideal type, he argues that, in contrast to Western notions, power in Java was perceived as something concrete, homogeneous, constant in quantity, and without inherent moral qualities (1990: 23). Like a cone of white light cast down by a reflector lamp, power was both undifferentiated in quality and fused or concentrated in form. It was at its most concentrated at the centre of the kingdom, where it was embodied in the person of the ruler and in various kinds of heirloom objects which the ruler tried to collect around him, and it diminished towards the periphery (1990: 36). The traditional concept of power depended on a 'syncretic and absorptive' centre realised in the person of the ruler (1990: 38).

As Anderson makes clear, these notions imply a direct contrast with the meaning of the frontier in a modern nation-state. Ideally at least, the frontiers of the modern state mark an absolute shift: on one side of it the government has as much power as at the centre, or in the capital city; on the other side it has no power whatever (Anderson 1990: 41–2). The extent to which this is empirically the case is, of course, questionable. As Peter Sahlins argues (this volume), local notions of identity were not necessarily superseded by national ones during the process of state formation; indeed, in the case of the borderland between France and Spain local boundaries and notions of difference provided a basis for the construction of a sense of national identity (see also Sahlins 1989).

Anderson, Tambiah (1976), Wolters (1982), Errington (1989) and others have discussed the nature of the traditional Southeast Asian polity. In Southeast Asia the traditional state was defined by its centre not by its boundaries. In this case, however, it seems that the empirical reality was closer to the ideology of power than in the case of the modern nation-state. Thus Gullick (1983: 56) has described how the boundaries of mid-nineteenth century Kedah were not clearly defined; the state was made up of a central core zone and an imprecise outer zone. In fact, the power of a ruler was revealed not so much by the extent of his kingdom, but in the number of people he controlled. Victorious rulers might augment their power during periods of dynastic conflict by moving large numbers of people to the centre (Anderson 1990: 43). Thus the sociology of power hinged on ties of fealty between persons, not on the unambiguous mapping out of space.

Those who lived at the periphery of the kingdom were least subject to the control of the sovereign. This is very clear in the case of the hill tribes, whether they were swidden cultivators or hunters and gatherers. The history of groups like the Kachin of highland Burma (Leach 1954) or the Buid of Mindoro (Gibson 1986) is one of continual attempts to avoid domination by the lowland states. To a lesser extent the same processes seem to have characterised relations between rulers and their peasant subjects in the lowlands. As Adas (1981) and others have argued, if the exactions of rulers of the pre-colonial state were too great, peasants might well move from the centre to peripheral areas. Adas describes how peasant rebellions in Java and Burma increased when colonial powers imposed the bureaucratic measures associated with a modern nation-state. These included the substitution of permeable border zones by fixed frontiers, and consequent restrictions on peasant mobility.

The Malay state of Kedah, of which Langkawi is part, conforms in many respects to Anderson's description of the *negeri*. Important for several hundred years as a trading centre, Kedah's history can be read as a continuing interplay between attempts by external powers to wrest control over trade from its indigenous rulers, and the latter's struggle to preserve their political and economic independence. This was frequently achieved by playing off Siam against Burma, or either against the successive interests of the Portuguese, Dutch and English.

Kedah's political structure was typical of the Malay *negeri* as described by Gullick (1958). This structure, which has been glossed as feudal, was headed by the sultan or raja who led a coalition of territorial chiefs who had control of local administration, defence and revenue collection. These chiefs were represented in the villages by local leaders. The use of rivers for communication and trade was central to the state structure, and control of these, and hence of trade revenue, was an important aspect of political power. Territorial chiefs levied taxes of which a share went to the sultan. Both the population and their produce were at the command of the raja and the territorial chiefs (Bonney 1971: 8–11).

Kedah's history has been shaped by its geographic location (see map 9.1). Its strategic position on the northern perimeter of the Malay peninsula and at the south-western seaboard of the Isthmus of Kra meant that it was a focus for the rival interests of Burma and Siam (see Bonney 1971: 3). Kedah's importance was enhanced by its role as an entrepot for land routes to other areas of the peninsula (Bonney 1971: 7).

The founding of a British settlement at Penang in 1786 heralded a profound change in the nature of the economy of Kedah. It is estimated that trade revenues fell by about a third as Penang's importance as a trading centre grew. From the end of the eighteenth century Kedah's economic base shifted from mixed entrepot trade and self-sufficient agriculture to one in which agriculture dominated. Peasant agriculture expanded, and rice, exported to Penang, mainly to feed the growing population there, became Kedah's most important export commodity.[1]

Intermittent fighting between Burma and Siam meanwhile continued, and in 1821 the Siamese claimed that the Sultan of Kedah had been making overtures to Burma. Siam responded by invading Kedah and deposing the sultan who fled to Penang.[2] The invasion of Kedah caused immense devastation. In its aftermath the population of the mainland state is estimated to have halved, with massive migration to adjacent areas (Zaharah 1972: 196). Langkawi is mentioned in accounts of the sultan's subsequent unsuccessful attempts to regain control of Kedah, and as suffering further Siamese assaults, indeed it seems to have been a particular centre of resistance (see Hall 1964: 483; Hill 1977: 49–50; Winstedt 1936: 181–4; Bonney 1971: 157; Gullick 1983: 44).

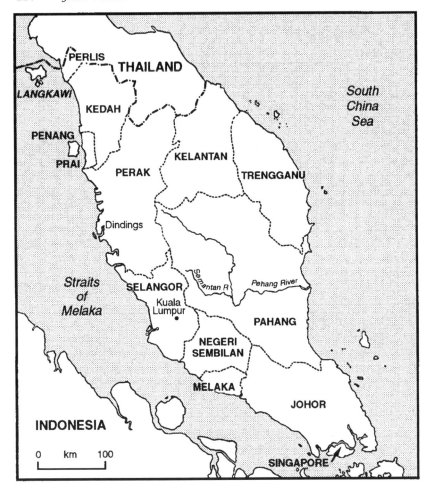

Map 9.1   Langkawi and Peninsular Malaysia (based on Andaya and Andaya 1982).

In 1824, war between Britain and Burma led the former to approach Siam as a possible ally. Two years later the British entered into an agreement with Siam under which they guaranteed to prevent the sultan from attacking Kedah (Winstedt 1936: 383–5; Hall 1964: 484–6). By the 1850s the population in mainland Kedah was restored to its pre-invasion level (Zaharah 1972: 96). It is probable that there was a similar movement back to Langkawi. In the seventeenth century Langkawi had been a major centre of pepper cultivation, but by 1850 pepper was no longer an important export commodity (see Bonney 1971: 6; Sharom

1970b: 124), and was not being grown on Langkawi (Hill 1977: 50). It may be inferred that the island was by this time less significant economically in relation to mainland Kedah than it had been in the past. Topping describes how the Langkawi islands, 'do not yield Rice in sufficient quantities for the inhabitants' (1850: 42).

Under the Anglo-Siamese Treaty of 1909 Siam abandoned her sovereign rights over Kedah, as well as Kelantan, Trengganu and Perlis (thereafter known as the Unfederated Malay States). Britain appointed Advisors to these states (see Cowan 1961: 258–60; Hall 1964: 536–7). The Japanese invaded Malaya in 1942 but Langkawi's peripheral location and economic insignificance meant that the island was less affected by the Japanese occupation than many areas on the mainland. However, villagers have vivid memories of food shortages and occasional atrocities from this period.

Kedah's border location, the economic importance of trade, the mobility of people and commodities, and the competition for control over people and trade revenues were all highly significant factors in shaping the history of the pre-colonial and colonial state.

Population mobility

I have mentioned how people in Langkawi often make journeys to the mainland, and how they take pleasure in travel almost for its own sake. Young men's engagement in migrant work after leaving school means that their social world includes areas of the mainland. I also mentioned how mobility is an aspect of people's lives in a more profound way in that many residents of the village where I lived are themselves migrants, or the direct descendants of migrants to Langkawi (see Carsten 1995a).

The importance of demographic mobility is indicated by the fact that about one-fifth of the 260 adults in Sungai Cantik whose life histories I obtained were not themselves born in Langkawi. Of the 212 who were born in Langkawi, 48 (nearly a quarter) had either one or both parents who originated from elsewhere. These people mainly came from nearby areas on the mainland: many from Kedah, significant numbers from Pulau Pinang, southern Thailand, Perlis and Perak. A few came from areas of the peninsula still further away: Johor, Trengganu, Negeri Sembilan. Others came from Aceh, Minangkabau, Java, India or Hong Kong. Villagers' accounts suggest a great mixture of origins and influences.

According to villagers' accounts, the main motivating force behind migration has been economic. When villagers talked about how they or their ancestors came to Langkawi, they often said, 'we came destitute, as migrants' (*kita mari bangsat*). Many told me how they had no land or other property, and came to Langkawi to look for work, especially to work as fishermen. Although other reasons are sometimes cited – quarrels with kin, fighting or warfare such as that in Aceh, Kedah and Siam in the nineteenth century, or the difficult conditions of the Japanese occupation in the 1940s – the chief concern was to make a living.

As already mentioned, there has been a steady trickle of migrants into Langkawi since the mid-nineteenth century onwards. This migration does not have any single dominant pattern. Men and women described to me how they, their parents or their grandparents came to the island as children accompanying their parents. Sometimes such a family group might be followed by one or other spouse's parents or an unmarried sibling. Others came as unmarried young men, on their own or with a brother, and married and settled on the island. A child might be taken by an uncle or aunt as a foster child to grow up on Langkawi. A young man or woman from the mainland might marry someone from Langkawi and come to live there. People of all ages came. Some life histories show several movements back and forth between the mainland and Langkawi which are often linked to particular marital histories.

We can gain a clearer understanding of this mobility in the light of the historical and political context which I outlined above. Such mobility should not be viewed as atypical of a region in which land and resources in outlying areas were more abundant than near the centres of power on the mainland. As is clear from Anderson's account of the *negeri*, control over people was of greater significance to the ruler than control over land. If the boundaries of the state tended to fluctuate, then what was important to the ruler was to maintain a population sufficient to produce a surplus and maintain an army.

Adas (1981) has argued that peasant tenants or labourers in pre-colonial and colonial Southeast Asia would often transfer their allegiance to alternative rulers, or simply move further from the centre, when the demands made of them in taxation and corvee labour became too great (see also Tambiah 1976: 120–3). Focusing on Burma and Java, Adas suggests that these wholesale migrations were a form of 'avoidance protest' (1981: 217) in a context of low population density and refuge zones of unoccupied lands in outlying areas (1981: 219). Kratoska (1985) has argued that peasants in late nineteenth-century Malaya were not particularly attached to their land and might readily abandon it if they could move elsewhere and if their livelihood was uncertain. It thus seems that the possibility of peasant cultivators moving to pioneer areas on the periphery was a serious constraint on the power of rulers.

Sharom Ahmat (1970a, 1970b) has shown how the economy of Kedah at the end of the nineteenth century was based on rice cultivation. The power of the sultan depended on control of economic resources through taxation. But Sharom argues that, in contrast to other Malay states, the political and economic structure in Kedah was highly centralised. The limited resources and small population of Kedah meant that an elaborate administrative apparatus was unnecessary.

These factors encouraged political stability in Kedah at this time. The revenue of the state depended on the ability of the *raayat* ('the masses') to cultivate rice without major upheaval. Kedah's rice was largely exported to Penang, and it was thus in British interests too to maintain political stability. Sharom's argument is particularly relevant, because he makes a special point of the importance to the state of rice cultivation remaining undisrupted (see Sharom 1970b: 121). The contemporary comments of a British administrator reinforce this point:

In a Malay state, the exaction of personal service from the rai'yat is limited only by the powers of endurance of the latter. The superior authority is obliged, from self-interest, to stop short of the point at which oppression will compel the cultivator to abandon his land and emigrate. (Maxwell 1884: 104–9)

Sharom emphasises the efforts made to minimise this exploitation. Where local leaders were the subject of complaints for their corruption or excessive use of forced labour, they might be replaced (Sharom 1970b: 121). Although it appears that the population was rather stable during this period (Sharom 1970b: 120–2), the seriousness with which the problem was taken by the sultan demonstrates the disruptive potential that migration was perceived to have.[3] Nor was this stability wholly consistent. Sharom cites two cases of groups of villagers migrating in the 1880s, which resulted in the administration taking measures to prevent movements from recurring (1970b: 121).[4]

Discussing these themes, Banks (1983: 9–44) has argued that nineteenth-century Kedah was a 'frontier society' characterised by two styles of life. One, on the plain, near to the royal court, was highly stratified. Peasants were subject to heavy demands of forced labour, military service and taxation. This, together with the fragmentation of land-holdings, led to migration to the periphery where the second style of life operated. In the isolated areas to which these peasants migrated they were somewhat freer from the exactions of the sultans, there were less marked wealth differentials, and a more egalitarian social order. Banks's discussion refers to Sik, a hill district of northern Kedah, but would also seem to fit Langkawi, situated as it is on the north-west fringe of the state of Kedah.

So far, I have focused on the historical conditions which made population mobility a significant aspect of social life in the Southeast Asian *negeri*. It is also clear that this mobility persists today in the rather different conditions of the modern nation-state. In so far as this mobility is confined within the borders of the Malaysian state, it raises no particular bureaucratic problems. Indeed, from the Malaysian government's point of view it is to be encouraged, since it lends a considerable flexibility to employment patterns which is highly advantageous in the context of rapid economic development. However, where migration is transnational the situation is somewhat different.

Many of the villagers I know have kin in southern Thailand. Life histories which I collected indicate that this has been an important area for migration to Langkawi. As economic conditions in Malaysia become significantly better than in Thailand for peasants and fishermen, controls over the flow of people crossing the Malaysian Thai border have been imposed more stringently. However, villagers' perceptions and practices with regard to the movement of people and merchandise indicate that they still regard southern Thailand as very much part of their social world. Apart from the kind of excursion which I described at the beginning of this chapter, it is common for villagers to visit their kin on the other side of the border particularly to attend marriages and funerals. Kinship ties across the border are constantly re-established. In the early 1980s, it was not considered unusual for marriage or fostering to result in a young person from southern Thailand coming to live in Langkawi. But villagers were of course aware of the bureaucratic complications that might ensue.

The absorptive centre

Anderson's description of the traditional *negeri* with its 'absorptive centre' has recently been developed by Errington (1987, 1989) who proposes a comparative model of Southeast Asian societies. Errington discusses a range of societies in the region in terms of their 'houses', marriage systems and concepts of siblingship. She draws a distinction between societies of 'Eastern Indonesia', such as the Rotinese and others, which have asymmetric alliance and are underlain by a thorough-going symbolic dualism (see Fox 1980), and those of the 'Centrist Archipelago', like Langkawi, which have cognatic kinship and endogamous marriage.[5] The societies of the Centrist Archipelago exhibit a strong centripetal tendency. Here,

the 'Houses' or social groupings tend either to coincide with the whole society, and hence be wishfully complete and autonomous as in the Indic States, or to be centered on an Ego or set of full siblings and to stretch indefinitely from that center, with no clear boundaries. (Errington 1987: 405)

In the Centrist Archipelago, cross-sex siblings epitomise unity and similarity. The hierarchical states conceive themselves in an image of encompassment and unity, which is often envisaged in terms of sibling-ship. Unity, however, is threatened by the outside: the centrist societies are shot through with dualism between 'us' and 'them'. As Errington puts it, 'Eastern Indonesia postulates unity but institutes fracture', while the Centrist Archipelago 'institutionalises unity but is haunted by duality' (1987: 435).

In Langkawi the image of unity and encompassment is, as Errington suggests, projected in an idiom of siblingship. Siblings are perceived to be closer than any other kin both in terms of shared bodily substance and the emotional tie between them. Growing up together and sharing food from the same hearth, they embody the unity of the undivided house. Indeed, they stand for kinship itself – the term for 'kin', *adik beradik*, is derived from *adik* which means 'younger sibling'.

Siblingship is also the model for proper, moral 'kin-like' behaviour between neighbours or co-villagers. In local perceptions, siblingship is not restricted to full brothers and sisters. It extends out to encompass cousins in Ego's own and his or her children's generations, and the siblings of parents and grandparents in previous ones. Children are always encouraged from a very young age to call their cousins by appropriate sibling terms. The world of kin can be thought of as made up of layers of past, present and future siblings (see McKinley 1981). Further, this world is not one in which kin and non-kin are rigidly divided off from each other. Instead, kinship operates along a con-tinuum from the close to the more distant. In most circumstances it would be insulting to imply that a co-villager was not, in some vague way, loosely connected by kinship.

We can see how this image of siblingship not only connotes closeness and unity, but always has the potential, depending on circumstances, to encompass other kin, neighbours, people of the same community and fellow Malays from other areas. It is clear that these perceptions of kinship imply rather fluid boundaries between kin and non-kin, those who are familiar and strangers. In fact, such fluidity is central to processes of kinship, because it means that unrelated people can become 'kin' quite easily.

One way in which non-kin may become kin is through marriage. I have described kinship in Langkawi as 'endogamous'. But it is impor-tant to understand the meaning of endogamy here. Villagers in Sungai Cantik describe the ideal marriage as occurring between people who are 'close' (*dekat*). By closeness they may imply genealogical connection – second cousins are thought to be of about the right sort of distance for marrying. But villagers may equally well be thinking of closeness in terms of geographic proximity, social status, religiosity or even appearance. They do not necessarily distinguish the criteria they are using. Ideally, spouses should simply be similar to each other, and this is what 'closeness' is all about. Whether a couple was genealogically connected before marrying or not, once they marry and have children, their two sets of parents are thought to become kin to each other. Husbands and wives thus produce new kinship, both in the past through the connection they establish between their respective parents, and in the future in the form of the new sibling set which is constituted by their children.

In this way, marriage continuously redraws the boundary and merges the distinction between kin and non-kin. But marriage is not the only way in which this may occur. I have described elsewhere how fostering, living together, sharing food from the same hearth, and hospitality can have the same effects (Carsten 1991, 1995b). In local perceptions, living and eating together over time create shared bodily substance and relatedness just as marriage and having children do. These are ways of bringing strangers closer, and incorporating them into the world of kin.

On the boundary

I have shown how kin and non-kin are not rigidly separated categories in Langkawi. The boundary between them is permeable. It has been necessary to examine how kinship is perceived to understand the significance of this permeability. The gradual dilution or concentration of siblingship through more or less intensive sociality (hospitality, eating and living together, marriage) allow non-kin to become kin and vice versa in a continuous process.

This outline of notions of kinship in Langkawi may have given the impression that local people are simply rather vague about where to draw the line between kin and non-kin, or that they are quite uninterested in doing so.[6] Such a view is misleading. There are many circumstances in which distinctions between kin and non-kin or between kin and affine are tremendously important. For example, villagers discriminate against close kin when engaging in purely commercial transactions (see Carsten 1989). But particular designations of kin or non-kin can also change quite dramatically. Villagers are quite capable of switching rapidly from a mode of speech and behaviour which stresses that 'we are all kin here' to one in which quite elaborate distinctions are being drawn. The main context for making such distinction is during disputes, when the fact that someone is 'only related by marriage' – but who previously was always referred to as kin – suddenly becomes very important. Individuals often simultaneously occupy a number of different kinship categories *vis-à-vis* each other. One can be sister-in-law and cousin to the same person. Which description is deemed relevant in a particular context may be highly significant.

Nor is it the case that villagers are necessarily vague about the nature of their genealogical connections. Although they may tend to 'forget' irrelevant and distant ancestors who have long since died, they often have a strikingly precise knowledge of their connections to distantly related cousins – especially when these live close by and interact frequently (see Carsten 1995a). Far from simply being uninterested in the question of where to draw the boundary between kin and non-kin, this question is actually highly salient for villagers. But its salience is not at all straightforward.

The permeable boundary between kin and non-kin can be likened to those of the traditional state which Anderson described in similar terms. Here too, a process of concentration and dilution, depending on whether one moves towards or away from the centre, is at work. In this case it is the ruler's power which gradually fades as one moves towards the periphery. At the border this power simply fails to exert any pressure and merges with that of a neighbouring ruler. In the world of kinship the analogy would be the strength of ties of relatedness which gradually fade as Ego moves away from the house and hearth and the close kin with which he or she is associated. When moving to another village or another region, ties of kinship may be almost imperceptible or non-existent. However, new kinship ties can be established very easily, and these are vital to the absorption of migrants in the communities where they settle.

This analogy may appear less far-fetched if we look again at the link between the two constructs, kinship and the state. In drawing a likeness between them I have described both in terms of mobility. On the one hand, the lessening power of the ruler is experienced by the subject who moves away from the centre of the state towards the periphery. On the other, the diminution of the force of kinship is felt when villagers move away from their home village to a different one in an unfamiliar region.

We have already seen that these two processes, one 'political' the other 'familial', were actually linked historically. The traditional Southeast Asian state was one in which people did move. The history of Kedah which I have outlined here shows the macro political forces that encouraged mobility among the rulers' subjects: trade, rival interests of foreign powers, warfare, taxation, poverty. My own research shows how such mobility was experienced by these subjects, and how any understanding of their notions of kinship must take account of this mobility. In a context in which migration is not a rare occurrence but part of the way of life in village communities, the rapid conversion of strangers into kin has played an important role in the establishment and reproduction of village communities. Conversely, when kin move away, they tend to become irrelevant quite rapidly. Unless the immediate descendants of such out-migrants intermarry, succeeding descendants will ignore or forget any genealogical connection.

These processes of accretion and loss are still at work under the conditions of the modern nation-state where a substantial degree of migration occurs between the states which make up the federation of Malaysia. Newcomers are still easily incorporated into the world of kin through fostering and marriage. The rigid boundaries of the modern nation-state have thus had only a very partial impact on this aspect of villagers' lives. Although the historical conditions which gave rise to population mobility have changed, some of the practices and perceptions associated with these conditions persist. In particular, I suggest that the notions of kinship I have described are ones which are likely to change rather more slowly than political and economic conditions. In this context it is worth examining more closely the notions of boundary which are fundamental to kinship.

Boundaries between persons, between houses and between villages

In Langkawi a concern with boundaries and where they should be placed is in fact a common theme which underlies, in a complex and subtle way, a number of different aspects of social life. This concern emerges particularly clearly in notions of personhood, and in ideas about the house and about the village. It is not possible to do justice to all these ideas here, but in this section I briefly outline some of them in order to substantiate the connection I have made between notions of kinship and the *negeri*.[7]

Ideas about the person emphasise both the boundedness and uniqueness of the individual, and simultaneously the connectedness of individuals to others – particularly siblings. Individuality is emphasised in the idea that each person has their own fate or destiny and an individual 'soul', *roh*. Men may have a more clearly defined individual identity than women, and this is expressed in nicknames which are not normally given to women. Men's nicknames refer to some singular event in their lives or to a unique and idiosyncratic character trait. For example, 'Tok Udang' (Grandfather Prawn) is so named for his intense liking for prawns; 'Pak Gerek' (Uncle Bicycle) is named for the occasion he fell off his bike in particularly amusing circumstances.

As well as this stress on the individual, notions of personhood also emphasise the fact that each person is part of a more or less indivisible sibling set. Once again, this is expressed in names. Birth-order terms for a group of siblings are perhaps the most common way of addressing or referring to co-villagers. These terms place each individual in their sibling group and refer to a knowledge of the complete sibling set.

People, in common with other living things as well as houses and boats, are thought to have a 'vital essence' or 'soul stuff' (semangat). The semangat is not simply an individual entity. Villagers say that it is one, a unity, but that this unity has a seven-fold quality: 'it is seven but only one holds'. The seven-foldness is in fact indivisible, and it is envisaged in terms of siblingship. People say that the semangat consists of seven siblings, but these siblings have no individual identity: they are seven, but at the same time only one.[8]

In these ways as well as others, villagers emphasise that personhood is not only about individuality, but that it encapsulates relatedness. And this relatedness is perceived in terms of siblingship which we have seen is at the heart of notions of kinship. The boundedness of the person is both acknowledged and at the same time compromised by notions of indivisible siblingship.

Just as people have semangat, so too do houses. Once again, this spirit or essence is believed to occur in the form of an indivisible, seven-member sibling set, and these members have no separate identity. This is not the only way in which houses are associated with siblingship. There is also a very clear connection between the house and the set of siblings who are born in it and grow up together sharing food from the same hearth (see Carsten 1995c).

The unity and boundedness of the house is simultaneously marked and unmarked. Co-residents of one house are expected to cook and eat full rice meals together on a daily basis, and this food sharing is at the heart of co-residence. It also creates kinship, since eating rice from the same hearth creates shared bodily substance. Children are normally actively discouraged from eating in houses where they do not live, and one way of imputing immoral behaviour, particularly to adult men, is to claim that they regularly eat in other houses.

The unity of the house and its members is also emphasised in the way agricultural land, water, clothes and money are shared and made to appear indivisible between household members (see Carsten 1987,

1989, 1995c). But this unity is simultaneously contradicted by the way that the boundaries of houses are continuously or at least partially transgressed within the compound (*kampung*).

The compound is a group of houses situated on undivided village land. Residents of one compound usually have close social relations with each other, and are often the most frequent visitors to each others' houses. These visits are conducted with marked informality. Such close neighbours tend to use the entrance to the house that otherwise only household members themselves would use. They are not treated with any particular politeness or respect during their visits, and may or may not be given a snack or coffee, whereas visitors from further away would always be shown more formal hospitality. Women often send dishes of cooked food to neighbouring houses in the same compound, and this is one way in which the unity and integrity of the individual house hearth and the commensality of those who live in one house is compromised.

Co-members of one compound often own rice land together. This is a consequence of the way houses subdivide to form compounds. When siblings grow up and marry, some will establish new houses in the locality of their spouse's parents, others on new land, and some will build a new house on the same plot of land as their parents' house. Eventually, the original couple die, and houses of one compound come to be headed by members of a sibling set and their descendants. Thus the establishment and growth of compounds is a consequence of the reproduction of a group of siblings. The ties between their houses is perceived to derive from siblingship, and this is central to their closeness.

There is a sense, then, in which the compound can be seen as an enlarged house. The informality of social relations within the compound, the sharing of food and property, can be thought of as being derived from behaviour in the house. And if we move from the compound to the wider neighbourhood, and from the neighbourhood to the village as a whole, we can see the same gradual shifts of behaviour. It is notable that the compound (even if it has only one house on it), the neighbourhood and the village are all denoted by the same term, *kampung*. I have argued elsewhere that in many respects the village community is envisaged in the image of the house – it is the household writ large – and this is particularly clear in the organisation of communal feasts (*kenduri*) which celebrate marriages (see Carsten 1987, 1995c).

The elusiveness of boundaries between houses, compounds, neighbourhoods and villages is expressed in the symbolism of food sharing. Eating a full rice meal together defines the limits of the house. But it is also what defines the village community. The *kenduri* is the ceremonial occasion par excellence in which the whole village participates.

Members of the community prepare and partake together of a particularly lavish rice meal.

But the fluidity of boundaries is not restricted to food symbolism. When walking through the village, it is very striking how difficult it is to perceive where one compound begins or another ends. The boundaries of plots of land are unmarked. Different compounds flow into another just as different hamlets, and even different villages often seem to merge with each other with no perceptible marker between them.[9] This of course brings to mind the similar blurring of distinctions between kin and non-kin which I discussed earlier. Once again, however, appearances may be deceptive. In many circumstances villagers have a strong interest in precisely where the boundaries between one plot of land and another lie. Indeed, just as the boundaries between kin and non-kin can suddenly emerge and become marked in a dispute, so too the sudden and rather anomalous construction of a fence between two houses is usually a clear indication that the two sets of residents have fallen out with each other.

The point is not that these distinctions are simply not made or irrelevant. On the contrary, they are the subject of immense concern. It is precisely because the drawing of boundaries is problematic, because where they should be placed may be uncertain and subject to change through the processes of expansion and absorption which I have described, that people hesitate to make such definitive statements. In the last analysis, to make such distinctions may simply be rude – just as it would be rude to imply that a distant relative is a stranger, or that one would like one's own plot of land to be clearly separated from one's neighbour's.

In Langkawi it is always difficult to make hard and fast distinctions between people or localities without permanently excluding certain people from social intercourse, as happens between the Malays and the Chinese. Within the Malay community, boundaries remain fluid.

Conclusion

I began this chapter by evoking the importance of mobility to the lives of people in Sungai Cantik. People regularly move over short or long distances between the mainland and Langkawi. They go on brief excursions, on longer visits to kin, engage in temporary migration, and sometimes permanently settle in areas which are far from their natal homes. I have linked this mobility both to historical conditions and to the geographic location of Langkawi, an island on the fringe of a northern Malay state whose 'border' status between Siam and Burma has been central to its history.

Anderson's analysis of Southeast Asian notions of power and their implications for the traditional state in Southeast Asia have proved very fruitful. That the borders of the *negeri* were qualitatively different from those of the modern nation-state was a crucial aspect of his theory. It implied the need to examine the meaning of the 'border' in indigenous terms and in local contexts. The political ideology of the traditional state in Southeast Asia seems to have corresponded rather more closely to empirical reality than is suggested for the modern European case examined by Peter Sahlins. Sahlins's analysis suggests that notions of identity on the borderland between France and Spain had an important impact on nation-building at the centre. In the Southeast Asian case considered here, it is not so much that what happened on the periphery shaped the centre, but that the ideology of the polity involved particular relations of power *between* centre and periphery. Power of the ruler faded from the centre outwards; at the border it merged with that of neighbouring sovereigns. The permeable border was a corollary of notions of power; it was also an empirical reality.

The permeable borders of the traditional *negeri* have continued to mark aspects of social life in the modern nation-state. People are still relatively mobile under different political and economic conditions. Their mobility has been only partially affected by the rigidity of international frontiers.

Further, I have argued that the permeability of boundaries between different categories of people is not just a matter of political importance. It is central to local ideas about kinship. Notions of kinship which correspond well with certain aspects of the traditional state continue to flourish. Partly because this kinship involves a very remarkable degree of flexibility (as many ethnographers have noted), it may have changed rather more slowly than surrounding economic and political conditions.

The permeable boundary is a theme which underlies many different aspects of life in Langkawi, and possibly of Malay culture more generally. It connects personhood, kinship, the house, community and the wider polity – areas that anthropological analysis tends to separate. A corollary of this argument is that the political 'reality' of the international border is placed in question. Political boundaries have a symbolic importance (as Anderson has emphasised), and this symbolism may correspond to that of boundaries between persons or houses or villages.

In the introduction to the chapter I suggested a possible connection between villagers' attitudes to the international border between Malaysia and Thailand, and to the boundary between themselves and me. This simile, which brings together the personal and the 'political' may seem more comprehensible in the light of the preceding discussion. Villagers of Sungai Cantik were as enthusiastic about crossing an international border as they were to encompass and incorporate me, and this can be understood as two aspects of one cultural phenomenon. My hesitation in both these spheres was equally part of my own cultural baggage. Paradoxically, given the purpose of fieldwork, while they embraced movement and sought to encompass, I found myself maintaining more rigid boundaries.

The links I have drawn between spheres seemingly as widely separated as 'personhood' and 'the state' are not at all coincidental. They speak of an underlying congruence between kinship and history which many Southeast Asianists might regard as at the core of the region's unity. At the same time, we are dealing with a phenomenon which is at the heart of the region's other most obvious feature – its diversity. For it is the very permeability of the border, the impossibility of making hard, permanent distinctions between the similar and the different, between the inside and the outside, which gives social life its flexibility. Boundaries are drawn only to be erased or redrawn in another place, and this has been at the heart of historical processes of expansion, encompassment and change.

Notes

The fieldwork on which this chapter is based was conducted between 1980 and 1982 in a fishing village on Pulau Langkawi which I have called 'Sungai Cantik'. Fieldwork was financed by a studentship from the Social Science Research Council (now ESRC) with additional funds from the Central Research Fund of the University of London. Further fieldwork on the history of migration was conducted in 1988–9, financed by the British Academy, the Wenner-Gren Foundation and the Evans Fund of the University of Cambridge. I am grateful to Jonathan Spencer for his comments and suggestions.

1. For a fuller account of these processes see Sharom (1970a: 15–16), Hall (1964: 474, 483), Banks (1983: 16–17, 21, 23), Bonney (1971: 66), Hill (1977: 50–1, 54–9), Gullick (1985: 111).
2. For a detailed account of the relation between Kedah, Siam and the British at this time see Bonney (1971); also Hall (1964: 483).
3. It was for this reason that the sultan relaxed the obligations of the *raayat* to perform forced labour (*kerah*) (Sharom 1970b: 121). However, Gullick (1983: 66) links a heavy *kerah* burden in mid-nineteenth-century Kedah to the low population. See also Gullick (1985: 116).
4. One case involved a group of sixty families who intended to migrate to the Dindings in Perak, and the other a group of peasants from Yen who moved to a neighbouring district. See Scott (1985: 245–6) for a discussion of flight as a means of resisting oppression on mainland Kedah. Syed Hussein Alatas

(1968: 584–5) has described how this means of avoidance rather than defiance conformed with peasant values.
5. Errington (1987: 404) notes that this distinction does not operate within strictly defined geographic boundaries.
6. This kind of view seems to underlie many ethnographic descriptions of kinship in Southeast Asia. Thus Embree (1950) characterised Thailand as having 'a loosely structured social system'; others have stressed flexibility and adaptive potential in different circumstances (see Freeman 1961).
7. The importance of boundaries has been relatively unexplored in the literature on Malays. One exception is Endicott's *An analysis of Malay magic* (1970), which may be read as a subtle account of notions of boundaries as reflected in spirit beliefs and ideas about personhood. For a fuller analysis and description of notions about the house and the person in Langkawi see Carsten (1987, 1995b, 1995c).
8. For a fuller account of the *semangat, roh* and Malay beliefs concerning the soul see Endicott (1970).
9. Lim (1987: 93) has commented on how Malay 'house compounds flow into each other', boundaries between them are indistinct, and space is 'free-flowing'.

References

Adas, M. 1981. 'From avoidance to confrontation: peasant protest in pre-colonial and colonial Southeast Asia', *Comparative Studies in Society and History* 23 (2): 217–47.
Andaya, B. W. and L. Y. Andaya 1982. *A history of Malaysia.* London: Macmillan, Asian Histories Series.
Anderson, B. 1983. *Imagined communities: reflections on the origin and spread of nationalism.* London: Verso.
 1990 [1972]. 'The idea of power in Javanese culture', in B. Anderson, *Language and power: exploring political cultures in Indonesia.* Cornell: Cornell University Press.
Banks, D. J. 1983. *Malay kinship.* Philadelphia: Institute for the Study of Human Issues.
Bonney, R. 1971. *Kedah 1771–1821: the search for security and independence.* Kuala Lumpur: Oxford University Press.
Carsten, J. 1987. 'Analogues or opposites: household and community in Pulau Langkawi, Malaysia', in C. Macdonald (ed.), *De la hutte au palais: sociétés "à maison" en Asie du Sud-Est insulaire.* Paris: Editions du CNRS.
 1989. 'Cooking money: gender and the symbolic transformation of means of exchange in a Malay fishing community', in J. P. Parry and M. Bloch (eds.), *Money and the morality of exchange.* Cambridge: Cambridge University Press.
 1991. 'Children in between: fostering and the process of kinship on Pulau Langkawi, Malaysia', *Man* 26: 425–43.
 1995a. 'The politics of forgetting: migration, kinship and memory on the periphery of the Southeast Asian state', *Journal of the Royal Anthropological Institute* 1 (2): 317–35.

1995b. 'The substance of kinship and the heat of the hearth: feeding, personhood and relatedness among Malays in Pulau Langkawi', *American Ethnologist* 22 (2): 223–41.

1995c. 'Houses in Langkawi: stable structures or mobile homes?', in J. Carsten and S. Hugh-Jones (eds.), *About the house: Lévi-Strauss and beyond*. Cambridge: Cambridge University Press.

Cowan, C. D. 1961. *Nineteenth century Malaya: the origins of British political control*. School of Oriental and African Studies, University of London: Oxford University Press.

Embree, J. F. 1950. 'Thailand: a loosely structured social system', *American Anthropologist* 52 (2): 181–92.

Endicott, K. M. 1970. *An analysis of Malay magic*. Kuala Lumpur: Oxford University Press.

Errington, S. 1987. 'Incestuous twins and the house societies of Southeast Asia', *Cultural Anthropology* 2: 403–44.

1989. *Meaning and power in a Southeast Asian realm*. Princeton, NJ: Princeton University Press.

Fox, J. J. 1980. *The flow of life: essays on eastern Indonesia*. Cambridge, MA: Harvard University Press.

Freeman, J. D. 1961. 'On the concept of the kindred', *Journal of the Royal Anthropological Institute* 91: 192–220.

1970. *Report on the Iban*. London: Athlone Press.

Gibson, T. 1986. *Sacrifice and sharing in the Philippine highlands: religion and society among the Buid of Mindoro*. London: Athlone Press.

Gullick, J. M. 1958. *Indigenous political systems of Western Malaya*. London: Athlone Press.

1983. 'Kedah 1821–1855: years of exile and return', *JMBRAS* 56 (2): 31–86.

1985. 'Kedah in the reign of Sultan Ahmad Jajuddin II (1854–1879)', *JMBRAS* 58 (2): 102–34.

Hall, D. G. E. 1964. *A history of Southeast Asia*. (2nd edn) London: Macmillan.

Harris, H. (compil.) 1764. *Navigantium atque itinerantium bibliotheca or a complete collection of voyages & travels*, vol. I. London.

Hill, R. D. 1977. *Rice in Malaya: A study in historical geography*. Kuala Lumpur: Oxford University Press.

Kahn, J. S. 1980. *Minangkabau social formations: Indonesian peasants and the world-economy*. Cambridge: Cambridge University Press.

Kato, T. 1982. *Matriliny and migration: evolving Minangkabau traditions in Indonesia*. Ithaca: Cornell University Press.

Kratoska, P. 1985. 'The peripatetic peasant and land tenure in British Malaya', *Journal of Southeast Asian Studies* 16 (1): 16–46.

Leach, E. 1954. *Political systems of highland Burma*. London: Athlone Press.

Lim, J. Y. 1987. *The Malay house: rediscovering Malaysia's indigenous shelter system*. Pulau Pinang: Institut Masyarakat.

Maxwell, W. E. 1884. 'The law and custom of the Malays with reference to the tenure of lands', *JMBRAS* 13: 75–220.

McKinley, R. 1981. 'Cain and Abel on the Malay peninsula', in M. Marshall (ed.), *Siblingship in Oceania: studies in the meaning of kin relations*. Lanham: University Press of America.

Sahlins, P. 1989. *Boundaries: the making of France and Spain in the Pyrenees.* Berkeley and Los Angeles: University of California Press.

Scott, J. C. 1985. *Weapons of the weak: everyday forms of peasant resistance.* New Haven: Yale University Press.

Sharom Ahmat 1970a. 'The structure of the economy of Kedah, 1879–1905', *JMBRAS* 43 (2): 1–24.

1970b. 'The political structure of the state of Kedah, 1879–1905', *Journal of Southeast Asian Studies* 1 (2): 115–28.

Syed Hussein Alatas. 1968. 'Feudalism in Malaysian society: a study in historical continuity', *Civilisations* 13 (3): 579–92.

Tambiah, S. J. 1976. *World conqueror and world renouncer.* Cambridge: Cambridge University Press.

Topping, M. 1850. 'Some account of Quedah', *Journal of the Indian Archipelago* 4.

Wolters, O. W. 1982. *History, culture, and region in Southeast Asian perspectives.* Singapore: Institute of Southeast Asian Studies.

Winstedt, R. O. 1936. 'Notes on the history of Kedah', *JMBRAS*, 14(3): 155–89.

Zaharah Mahmud. 1972. 'The population of Kedah in the nineteenth century', *Journal of Southeast Asian Studies*, 3 (2): 193–209.

10 Markets, morality and modernity in north-east Turkey

Chris Hann and Ildikó Bellér-Hann

. . . consider two ethnographic maps, one drawn up before the age of nationalism, and the other after the principle of nationalism had done much of its work.

The first map resembles a painting by Kokoschka. The riot of diverse points of colour is such that no clear pattern can be discerned in any detail, though the picture as a whole does have one. A great diversity and plurality and complexity characterizes all distinct parts of the whole: the minute social groups, which are the atoms of which the picture is composed, have complex and ambiguous and multiple relations to many cultures . . .

Look now instead at the ethnographic and political map of an area of the modern world. It resembles not Kokoschka, but, say, Modigliani. There is very little shading; neat flat surfaces are clearly separated from each other, it is generally plain where one begins and another ends, and there is little if any ambiguity or overlap. Shifting from the map to the reality mapped, we see that an overwhelming part of political authority has been concentrated in the hands of one kind of institution, a reasonably large and well-centralized state. In general, each such state presides over, maintains, and is identified with, one kind of culture, one style of communication, which prevails within its borders and is dependent for its perpetuation on a centralized educational system supervised by and often actually run by the state in question, which monopolizes legitimate culture almost as much as it does legitimate violence, or perhaps more so. (Gellner 1983: 139–40)

Like all ideal types, Gellner's depiction of the age of nationalism invites empirical investigation and critique. Other contributors to this volume point out that, in many modern situations, the cultural boundaries between nation-states are not necessarily as sharp as he supposes. However, in the case study that we shall present in this chapter, Gellner's ideal type comes unusually close to the current empirical reality. The virtually complete closure of a border for half a century played a decisive part in bringing about this situation. We shall concentrate on the consequences of the recent re-opening of this border. Our argument is that the 'modernist fiction' that is the Turkish nation-state, crucially buttressed by Islam, has triumphantly succeeded the diversity of the agrarian age, and is not yet seriously threatened by the new diversity of 'post-modernist' fragmentation. It may, however, be threatened from within by anti-modernist reaction: moral revulsion from the proliferation of petty trading and prostitution has strengthened the position of Islamic forces, who have assumed power in many parts of this region in recent elections.

Following a modern anthropological convention, the unit of inquiry is defined somewhat arbitrarily.[1] The contemporary Turkish administrative provinces of Artvin and Rize in the north-east corner of the country are part of the transitional zone where Anatolia blends into the Caucasus (see map 10.1). Neither the state boundary that separates Artvin from Georgia nor the provincial and district boundaries on the Turkish side respect linguistic or other cultural differences. On the contrary, all these lines have been subject to frequent political and administrative manipulation. The state boundary has been fiercely contested. It shifted on several occasions in the late nineteenth and early twentieth centuries, when European imperial powers (including the British) intervened actively. But the coastal frontier has been fixed since 1921, and there was virtually no movement across it between the beginning of the Stalinist period in 1929 and the re-opening of the frontier (though only for bilateral tourism and commerce) in 1988. Having begun fieldwork on the Turkish side in 1983, and having revisited the region in 1988 at the time of the re-opening, we were well placed to assess the impact of this change during more recent work in 1992–3.[2]

Pre-modernity

The lands that surround the Black Sea provide a good illustration of Gellner's characterisation of agrarian society. Much of their cultural diversity was provided by the trading communities of the coastal zones, as well as by agriculturalists and pastoralists of the various interiors. These lands were intimately tied to classical Mediterranean civilisations. Greeks were prominent in many parts of the Black Sea as traders, and in some areas they also provided the nucleus of substantial agricultural populations. Some of the earliest documented accounts of unequal cultural encounters, forerunners of later anthropological encounters, can be found in Greek accounts of the 'Other' they discovered in the area which is the main concern of this chapter, the south-east corner of the Black Sea. The classical geographers and historians tended to exoticise the people they called *ethnoi*, the term from which our modern

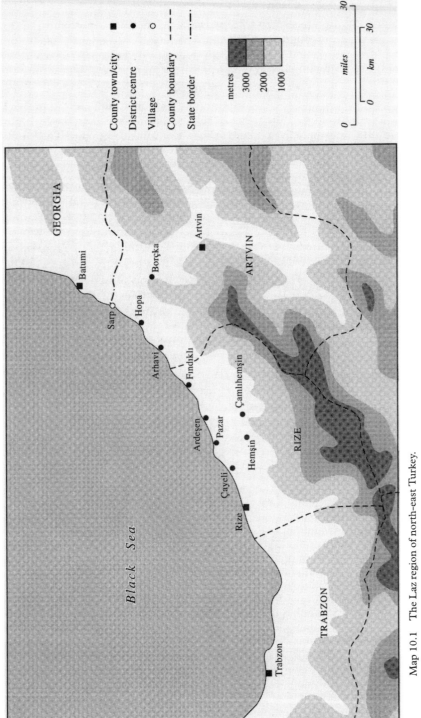

Map 10.1   The Laz region of north-east Turkey.

'ethnic group' has derived, but which for them approximated to 'barbarians'. Anthony Bryer quotes Apollonius of Rhodes as follows on the Mossynoekoi: 'Whatever is right to do openly before the people or in the market place, all this they do in their homes, but whatever acts we perform at home, these they perform out of doors in the midst of the streets without blame'; and Strabo informed his readers that they lived in tree huts, from which they would ambush travellers (Bryer 1966: 175). These people lived in and around Colchis, and the term Colchians is still sometimes used by scholars as a very loose label for the inhabitants of the region. Historical sources are extremely thin until the period in which the Byzantine Empire provided a rather loose political integration throughout Anatolia. But the Rize-Artvin coastal zone lay on the periphery of this and other early polities, and none of them ever bothered with it particularly. Even the late Byzantine Empire with its capital at Trebizond (Trabzon) does not seem to have established very effective controls over lands barely a hundred miles from this city. The main areas of Greek settlement soon petered out in the less favourable topography east of Trebizond. With the foothills of the Pontic Alps descending all the way to the coast and impeding land communications, and the hazards of malaria, this zone between the Greek-dominated Pontos and the adjacent Georgian-dominated section of the Caucasus contained no large cities. Thanks to the relatively abundant sources for the Pontos, scholars have been able to trace the parallel processes of Turkification and Islamisation which progressed rapidly after the region was formally incorporated into the Ottoman Empire in 1461.[3] However, the persistence of substantial groups of Greek-speaking Muslims down to the twentieth century indicates the complexity of these processes. In the Rize-Artvin zone it seems likely that most people, since at least medieval times, spoke a language related to Georgian, *Lazuri*, and called themselves *Lazi*.

But who are these Lazi or Laz, as they have come to be known in Turkish? They are first mentioned as a 'people' in documents from the sixth century, when they were Christians, but converted to Islam around the end of the sixteenth century (Bryer 1966: 181; see also Bryer and Winfield 1985). In more recent times they have themselves struck other citizens of Anatolia as radically different, strange, bizarre, less civilised. For most Anatolians the stereotype of the Laz can be applied to the entire eastern Black Sea region. Within this stretch of several hundred miles of coastline, only the inhabitants of the final section before the Georgian border identify themselves nowadays as 'ethnic' Laz. We have no sure way of knowing how they identified themselves in past centuries. Outside Rize and Artvin the stereotype is used loosely to refer to populations further to the east of themselves who exhibit alleged 'Laz' characteristics, and not in any strict 'ethnic' sense. Nor did the bound-aries of the Laz in this ethnic sense coincide with the larger adminis-trative entity known as Lazistan in the late Ottoman and early Republican periods. Thanks in part to the policies of successive Turkish governments, most contemporary Turks, including many of the inhabit-ants of Rize and Artvin, are unaware that the zone adjacent to the Georgian border is occupied by people who continue to speak a non-Turkic language, related to Georgian.[4]

Although the Laz were probably the most numerous group through many centuries in Artvin and Rize, many others were present alongside them, just as Gellner's model would suggest. In addition to Greeks and Turks, the interior contained large Georgian-speaking communities, and also groups of Hemşinli, whose own language was related to Armenian. These groups are still present in the region today. The Hemşinli are split into two distinct areas. Their old language is only barely alive in the eastern group. It died out some two centuries ago in the western group without this having direct repercussions for their 'ethnic' distinctiveness. These groups are all Muslim today, though people do not agree as to the time of their conversion. There was considerable geographical mobility, much of it by ship since the difficult topography inhibited land communications in the coastal zone. Many inhabitants of this region found work in Batumi or in other Black Sea ports of the Tsarist Empire.

The advance of Imperial Russia into the Caucasus forced a retreat on the part of the Ottomans, who ceded substantial territories, including the city of Batumi, at the Congress of Berlin in 1878. Many Muslims migrated to more central areas of the Empire rather than come under Russian rule. During World War I, Russian and trans-Caucasian forces penetrated deep into Anatolia and occupied the coastal strip, including Trebizond. This army was pushed back by Ottoman forces early in 1918, and non-Turkish Muslims fought with these forces in successful campaigns that led to the recapture of Batumi (Lang 1962: 203). In 1921 Georgia's short-lived period of independence ended with a Bol-shevik coup. The city of Batumi was again ceded by Turkey, but substantial areas of the interior around Artvin with a non-Turkish population remained in Turkish hands. The frontiers of Atatürk's new 'nation-state' were determined by (geo)political and military factors. The weakness of the trans-Caucasian and Russian (later Soviet) forces ensured that no significant numbers of 'ethnic Turks' would be left outside the new border in this region (in contrast to the situation in Thrace, for example, where substantial numbers of Turkish-speaking

Muslims were left outside the new borders). On the contrary, there were rather few Turks in Artvin and the eastern districts of Rize: Laz, Georgians and Hemşinli were all more numerous. Though each of these was linguistically distinctive, the vast majority shared the same Muslim religion. The frontier adjustments did not force further large-scale population movements at this point. However, the region's ethnic diversity was reduced as a result of the so-called population exchanges, which eliminated virtually all the remaining Greek communities of the Pontos.

Modernity

Modernity in Gellner's sense refers to a new type of society, quite different from the dynastic empires and cultural heterogeneity characteristic of the agrarian age. The nation-state is a product of altered material conditions, in which the modernisation efforts of new elites require standardised educational systems and the monopoly of a uniform high culture. In this corner of the Black Sea the emergence at virtually the same moment in history of the Soviet Union and the Kemalist Republic inaugurated a series of far-reaching, comparable changes on both sides of the border. All forms of interaction across the border were now strictly controlled. The coastal frontier, now located at a stream running through the Laz village of Sarp, was effectively closed in 1929. With Stalin's triumph in the power struggle that followed the death of Lenin, the original internationalist goals of the Bolshevik revolutionaries were replaced by the programme of 'socialism in one country'. This closure was paralleled in the capitalist but state-directed ('étatist') programmes adopted by Kemalist Turkey (Keyder 1981).

After World War II communist regimes were also established in predominantly Christian Bulgaria and Romania. The southern shore, its population by now overwhelmingly Muslim, was the only section of the Black Sea littoral that belonged to the political West. Turkey became a valued partner in the North Atlantic Treaty Organization, and from 1950 was officially committed to democratic multi-party politics. The development of a capitalist economy also progressed rapidly. But progress in both economic and political realms was uneven and regularly interrupted. The state maintained tight control over many key sectors of economic life, and the military intervened on several occasions to uphold their own interpretation of Kemalist Republicanism (cf. Gellner 1994).

The Kemalist modernisers took their legal codes from the Swiss and their model for state administration from the French. Citizenship rights were bestowed universally on individuals according to enlightenment ideals. The Kemalists also followed the French model rather than the Swiss in emphasising the consolidation of national identity as Turks. They had no category 'national minority'. Like other peoples, notably the Kurds, the Laz were considered to be Turks. Their language, for instance, was not written down or studied, and its use was officially prohibited. Even referring to the existence of such groups was enough to justify a charge of seeking to fragment the state (*bölücülük*). At no time do there seem to have been any stirrings of ethnic separatism in this region. The situation in the Soviet Union was more complex, since the Georgian Republic was officially multinational. Abkhazia was an 'autonomous republic' associated with a specific minority group. The corner of Georgia relevant here, that part adjacent to the border, was also an autonomous republic: but Adzharia was created not on the basis of a minority ethnic group but on the basis of Islam, a minority religion in the Georgian context. Despite official recognition of minorities (including a tiny group of Laz) and the explicit denial of assimilation strategies, Georgian nationalism flourished within this socialist system. The Georgian language was the prime medium of communication, and Georgian civilisation was presented as defining the unity of the entire country from time immemorial (Chinchaladze 1993). This was similar to the view presented by the Turkish authorities of the role of Turkish civilisation throughout Anatolia. In the control they exercised over education and culture, the Ankara regimes closely resembled their socialist counterparts. Thus the school curriculum presented a distinctive view of a glorious Turkish past, and Atatürk played the same role in public life and ritual as did Lenin (and more briefly the great Georgian himself, Joseph Stalin) within the socialist countries. Prominent in the ceremonies devised by the sovereign state for its legitimation purposes were annual commemorations of the defeat of occupying foreign armies: in this region of the Black Sea the anniversaries of the victories of the early months of 1918 were occasions for patriotic celebration, along with Republic Day, and other secular holidays. The main features of these developments in Turkey and Georgia were replicated in the other countries bordering the Black Sea, and fit squarely within the overall framework of 'modernity' in Gellner's sense. Whereas Rize and Artvin had once formed part of a 'fuzzy' transition zone, extending roughly between Trebizond and Batumi or even beyond, now there was a sharp line on the map, a map which was itself widely deployed in the symbolism of the Turkish 'nation-state'.

The over-riding concerns of these countries throughout the twentieth century have been to modernise their economies and transform their

fundamentally peasant populations into urbanised, industrialised societies on the model of the successful states of the West. The political
frameworks varied significantly and were susceptible to change through
time. Turkey adopted a multi-party system in the very same period that
Bulgaria and Romania passed from dictatorships of the right to dictatorships of the left. Economic programmes also varied: Turkey never
embarked on collectivisation programmes to compare with those of the
socialist world, and the scope for the petty bourgeoisie widened considerably after 1950 (Keyder 1987). But the state was always the
dominant force in economic accumulation, and neither Turkey nor the
Black Sea socialist countries were significantly integrated into the world
economy; nor, in spite of some limited COMECON initiatives, were the
economies of this region closely linked to each other. Above all, there
are close similarities throughout this region in the ways in which a
homogenised national society was produced through the state's monopoly over 'legitimate culture'. Generations grew up aspiring to mobility,
both social and geographical, within frameworks of possibility delimited
by their 'nation-state'. Social structures throughout the region under-
went massive transformation as industrial investments expanded and
communications were transformed. In all these respects the countries of
the Black Sea formed a hotbed of modernism, in contrast, for example,
to the 'stagnation' that was perceived in adjacent areas of the Middle
East.[5]

The most significant contrast between Turkey and its socialist neighbours in the Black Sea region lay in the field of religion. Several versions
of Orthodox Christianity formed the dominant religious tradition in all
the countries that became socialist (though other religions were also
present, including Islam and Judaism). The general pattern seems to be
that these traditions did not stand up well to militant atheism, and the
Black Sea socialist societies – including Islamic Adzharia – became
highly secularised. In Turkey the pattern is more complex. In some
areas, including Rize, in spite of or perhaps because of its diverse ethnic
profile and relatively late conversions, the secularism of Atatürk evoked
gestures of resistance from local *imams*. In practice, official secularist
codes came to be combined with recognition of the special status of
Islam as the religion of the overwhelming majority of Turks. The
gradual development of this 'Turkish–Islamic synthesis' allowed for the
integration of Islam into the new national identity, a fusion that has now
been well documented (see Tapper 1991). The area around Rize has
retained its nationwide reputation for unusually strong levels of commitment to Islam.

The people of the coastal zones of Artvin and Rize were historically poor and isolated from the major centres of political power in Anatolia and the Caucasus. Their marginal, peripheral position was radically transformed after 1950 through the development of tea as a cash crop (Hann 1990). The state had a monopoly in the purchase and processing of the crop, and its generous support prices made tea popular: it rapidly assumed the character of a monoculture, as households abandoned the less remunerative cultivation of hazelnuts and in many cases converted even the bulk of their subsistence plots to tea bushes. The new industry created jobs for men in the processing factories and confirmed the position of women as the major providers of field labour. Many families became prosperous and hired day labourers or used sharecroppers to harvest their tea. The value of coastal land, some of which had previously been uncultivated and malarial, soared to some of the highest rates in the country after the successful introduction of tea. The publication of such indicators (largely hypothetical, since there was never a very active market in land) encouraged inhabitants to associate themselves with the rapidly developing western parts of Turkey, and certainly not with the economically backward regions of eastern Anatolia. Arhavi, for example, the penultimate town before the border, liked to cultivate its reputation as the 'little Istanbul'.[6] The success of the tea industry led to spin-offs for other sectors of the regional economy, including private construction and commerce. The penetration of the state was also responsible for the creation of hundreds of new jobs in local administration and in the provision of health and educational services. Quite apart from welcoming the new services, local people also valued these jobs very highly because they offered long-term security, including a state pension, in a region from which previously most men had been constrained to emigrate to find employment.

During the modernist era these processes of national consolidation on either side of the border at Sarp proceeded quite separately. The Laz community here remained divided. Even close family were unable to visit each other (though some travellers' accounts report that a distinctive form of communication through singing developed among the villagers; see Pereira 1971). The frontier was heavily manned by the military on both sides. Although tea was grown by villagers in close proximity to the border, the area was out of bounds to foreign visitors and the main road itself was not maintained. For most practical purposes, communications ceased at the port of Hopa, the last Turkish administrative centre, some ten miles from the border. The great majority of residents in this part of Turkey, including hundreds of thousands of Georgian speakers, had little or no idea what was happening to the people of Georgia and the other components of the Soviet

Union, people who were soon to appear – often very literally – on their doorsteps. The expression 'iron curtain' was regularly used in Turkish journalism, and we think it encapsulates popular Turkish attitudes to the 'socialist Other'. The Chernobyl nuclear explosion of 1986 was the one event which brought the Soviet Union vividly into the imagination: it served to confirm stereotypical images of the inefficiency and general incompetence of socialist economic systems.[7] The very existence of the heavily guarded, closed frontier confirmed the images of political repression and 'totalitarianism'. Near the small town where much of our fieldwork was conducted, the threat was reflected in the presence of a NATO early-warning station in the foothills of the mountains. This military base was known simply as 'the radar', and its garrisons were catered for in the centre of the town by a military recreational establishment known as the *gazino*. They had become part of the scenery in this small town, and people associated them with the communist threat (we never heard any suggestion that a military presence might be required in this region for any other reason).

A small minority of locals, mainly teachers with left-wing political sympathies, had a radically different and much more positive image of communist society; this too was a stereotype that had developed as a product of political and ideological debate in Turkey, and it was not based in any experiential awareness of communist conditions.

Post-modernity?

The scholarly literature on the alleged crisis of modernity has tended to emphasise questions of culture and the politics of identity. On the whole, rather less attention has been paid to changes in political economy.[8] This region of Turkey, though geographically peripheral, has not experienced cultural fragmentation. Although Georgian and Lazuri have persisted as spoken languages in Rize and Artvin, they have not served to mobilise any resistance to the centralised modernist state. This state, whose commitment to modernisation was exemplified in its protection of the infant tea industry, came under great pressure from the 1970s onwards. Political and economic instability increased throughout the country. Rising expectations among the tea growers were disappointed as increases in the price paid for tea leaf failed to keep pace with the general rate of inflation. The industry had difficulty in maintaining quality controls and was obliged in 1981 to introduce quotas to control the quantity of leaves supplied by growers at peak periods. As a consequence of these policies, at the time of our fieldwork in 1983, there was deep resentment towards the state-controlled Tea Corporation.

People felt that the region had become excessively dependent on one crop, for which the remuneration was now inadequate. Many men felt that, even if they were able to secure a job in one of the processing factories, their income from four months' seasonal employment was hardly a satisfactory alternative to long-distance migration.

These tensions contributed to local support for a new political party at the elections of 1983. A commitment to remove state bureaucratic controls over economic life was one of the main attractions of the Motherland Party (*Anavatan Partisi*), led by Turgut Özal.[9] The eastern Black Sea coast became one of the Party's strongholds, particularly after 1987 with the appointment of Mesut Yılmaz, a Rize deputy, as foreign minister, and later prime minister. In the decade of Thatcherism and Reaganomics, Özal and Yılmaz (who both had strong links with American business economics) wanted to make some quite radical modifications to the étatist, protectionist structures of the Kemalist state. However, any attempt to introduce the conditions of 'pure competition' into this sector, both internally and externally, would almost certainly (given the low quality of the Turkish product by international standards) have led to a general collapse of the industry. In the end the government's decison to abolish the state's monopoly was a carefully judged compromise. There was no privatisation of the Tea Corporation, with its network of factories throughout the region, but the Corporation was exposed to private sector competition. The second half of the 1980s saw many new factories built, a few of them large and capable of matching the state's factories, but the majority small-scale and controlled by local entrepreneurs. As a result of this expansion, growers were spared the inconvenience and – in many cases – financial penalties which they had suffered following the Tea Corporation's quota arrangements.

Consistent with his general economic orientation, and motivated also by the political factors that prevented him from building closer links with the European Community, Özal was the main force behind a late 1980s initiative to promote Black Sea economic cooperation. As with the evolution of the European Community, it would seem that the initial emphasis was mainly placed on economic policy, with little if any consideration being given to questions of political or cultural integration. At this time every other country invited to participate was still socialist. One of the earliest concrete outcomes of this initiative was an agreement to re-open the border crossing at Sarp.[10] This was implemented with modest ceremonies in September 1988, but the change had little immediate impact. The volume of traffic in both directions remained low for the first two or three years. Although the inter-government agreement envisaged the development of tourism and petty trading, both sets of authorities made their passports and exit visas expensive and bureaucratically difficult to obtain. These obstacles have not been significantly amended on the Turkish side, so that the numbers of Turks visiting Georgia have remained small. However, following the political and economic disintegration of the Soviet Union in 1991 the numbers of former Soviet citizens entering Turkey at Sarp have increased very dramatically.

Most of these visitors came with short-term tourist visas, but their real purpose was trade. They came in battered family Ladas, roofracks stacked high with goods for sale or spare cannisters of fuel (which might also be offered for sale). Others came in organised parties on ancient buses bursting with whatever merchandise people could lay hands on. They sold this merchandise at the regular market places of the small towns along the coast. They also sold it by the roadside, on pavements and in small restaurants. Some local authorities made efforts to regulate this trade, but for the most part there were no effective controls over the goods sold (which included pets and perishable foods, and also fire-arms), nor over the locations of the market activity. This lack of regulation is perhaps the chief characteristic of the new situation: in contrast to the controlled stability of the age of modernity, exemplified by 'formal sector' commerce in the shopping streets of the rapidly expanding urban centres, the phase of post-modernity is characterised by the chaotic and essentially uncontrollable 'informal sector' associated with the trader-tourists.

The visitors themselves emphasised their economic motivation: even tiny quantities of dollars would take them a long way, given the extent of economic disintegration in their home regions. For them, Sarp was a gateway to the world of capitalist market economies. It seems unlikely that many traders saw Sarp as their entry-point to the West in any deeper cultural sense. Some of them made it no further than the small towns of Artvin and Rize, though others proceeded as far as the bright lights of Trabzon, and a few ventured even beyond, as far as Istanbul. Few traders spoke negatively (at least to us) about their Turkish customers, though some complained about the chaotic conditions at the border crossing, the lack of effectively regulated public transport and the dreadful state of the road between Sarp and Hopa. Some women commented adversely on the 'uncultured' behaviour which they sometimes experienced from Turkish males (see below). But the visitors were more prone to devalue other groups of foreigners: for instance, small traders from the border zone would condemn the bribery and strong-arm tactics of the Tbilisi 'mafia', while those from Tbilisi would repeat such criticisms, but direct them against the much bigger mafia of Baku, and so on.

Local attitudes towards this new commerce varied widely. Perhaps those left-wingers who had previously upheld a rather utopian stereotype of the Soviet Union were the most confused in their reactions. Some sought to deny that these traders were in any way representative of the former communist society. However, at least in the initial phases, the markets were regularly frequented by people in virtually every social group. They provided an occasion to go out and socialise (*gezmek*). People usually did this in single-sex groups, often with no serious intention of making purchases. For instance, women would pause to unfurl drapery materials quite different in style to those available in Turkey, while men pored over collections of second-hand tools, and their children sampled the wide array of toys. Richer families with nothing better to do at the weekends would make trips to the other small towns of the region in the hope of spotting some attractive commodities. For all concerned the 'Russian market' (*Rus pazarı*), as it was quickly – though from the point of view of its ethnic composition inaccurately – named, was a source of fun and entertainment.

Some people condemned the markets because, they said, the goods offered there were of bad quality and they took business away from honest local Turkish traders. This comment was fairly unusual, though predictably it was a point made forcefully by certain shopkeepers themselves. Others, however, were able to benefit from picking up raw materials cheaply on the *Rus pazarı*, and then selling them on at a profit through their shops. Some were able to forge more permanent links with foreigners, both as suppliers and as customers. A great many items brought in by these trading tourists were attractive to the townspeople and villagers in this region of Turkey. These included luxuries, such as silk scarves or antique carpets, but also a range of more basic consumer goods which had been available more cheaply under socialist rule than in capitalist Turkey. Hence many people welcomed these markets for economic reasons. They were seen as beneficial, for example because they made available some goods at low prices to people who would not otherwise be able to afford them, or because they gave local children a far wider selection of toys than was traditionally available through local shopkeepers.

Most people in the town where we were living and its hinterland fell between these extremes in their evaluations of the markets. There is no question of a blanket condemnation of trade itself as a bad thing, in the tradition of Aristotle which is inclined to view any abandonment of household self-sufficiency as a moral peril.[11] The people of the eastern Black Sea coast have been producers of commodities for a long time. Many of them, in conversation, expressed warm human sympathy with the plight of the trader-tourists, forced to endure these peddler expeditions in often quite ignominious conditions in order to survive in their native country. At the same time, although both sellers and buyers are also heirs to religious traditions which emphasise a concept of the 'just price', most people threw themselves into haggling without any regard for the niceties which would govern transactions between fellow Muslims in a local shop, or even transactions with a local Muslim market trader. Thus the buyers in these new marketplaces, in a clear demonstration of what Sahlins (1974) calls 'negative reciprocity', seemed to go all out to achieve the best possible deal for themselves from these strangers, unencumbered by moral considerations. In short, there was a kind of overall moral endorsement for this market space in which all economic agents can engage in 'free', 'amoral' individualist exchanges – maximising their utilities according to the standard assumptions of neoclassical economics.

But if the marketplace exchange of ex-socialist goods for capitalist currency at the best rates one can obtain is viewed as basically legitimate, as part of the moral economy of these communities, another aspect of the impact of the new 'open-door' economic policies in this corner of Turkey was classified differently. This has hitherto been a highly conservative region, both in its self-image and in the perceptions of many other Anatolians. Most local women, including the women of the market towns, keep their heads covered. Village women seldom visit town with their husbands, and the sexes do not often work together, or eat meals together in public restaurants. In this setting, some highly conspicuous foreign women, often exaggerating their distinctiveness through their clothes, hair styles and the use of make-up, took advantage of the opening up of this part of Turkey to cash in on opportunities to provide services for which men previously had to travel as far afield as Ankara.[12] Prostitution has provoked general moral outrage and affected perceptions not only of the trader-tourists but of all foreigners.

Rumours and salacious stories abounded during our fieldwork in 1992–3. Older men spoke in sorrow about the behaviour of sons who had sold their last gold chain in order to consort with a foreign woman. Some younger women who previously had not worn even a headscarf took to covering themselves, sometimes more drastically, lest they be treated as a foreign woman and subjected to leers and staring. Some older women spoke with anger about their husbands' behaviour, and everyone seemed to agree that the divorce rate had risen sharply (though this was denied by local lawyers and state officials). Other women attempted to organise petitions and letters of protest to the provincial governor. Since most of the money spent on the *Rus* women originated from the tea industry, they also petitioned the directors of major factories. Pressure was put on local hoteliers not to accept foreign women: one businessman, also active in local politics as a leading member of the Motherland Party, abandoned a large new hotel investment rather than face accusations that he was making profits out of the immoral behaviour. Regional and national newspapers gave considerable attention to the few cases where a prostitute was brought before the courts. But the police were unable to deal with the problem effectively, and to judge from the media reports, it seems that they were powerless even to stop women who were deported following conviction from returning to Turkey and resuming their highly profitable activity.

All these issues were presented as aspects of the *Rus pazarı*, where women were generally more active and conspicuous in the wheeling and dealing than the male trader-tourists. Soliciting did not take place at the marketplaces and few of the prostitutes bothered with the petty forms of trading. They picked up their customers on the streets and more especially in the restaurants in the evenings. A number of new entertainment centres opened along the coast, usually known as *gazino* or *müzikhol*. They sold alcohol and provided live entertainment: typically, a middle-aged female Turkish singer was accompanied by a small band. The prostitutes sat together around a large table, consuming only soft drinks, until they received propositions: sometimes for dancing and food, sometimes directly to action elsewhere. Prices started at around 300,000 Turkish *lira* (about 30 dollars), though the women might initially demand 1 million Turkish *lira* so that the bargaining process resembled that of the marketplace. Even in the smaller towns, the phenomenon quickly became highly visible.

The consequences of the trade and prostitution for images of the self and of the Other were considerable. People used metaphors of military invasion and occupation, and said that their region (*memleket*) was 'finished'. A similar idea was expressed in Lazuri with a pun: the clapped out *Lada* that came to symbolise the trade resembles the word *lata*, meaning 'crushed'. Assessments of the women themselves were revealing. Many people in Rize and Artvin, men and women, agreed that some of the foreign women were genuinely attractive. According to this aesthetic the pale, blonde Slav women were much preferred to the darker women from Georgia and Azerbaijan (and they therefore gravitated towards the larger urban centres where they could charge much more money for their services). These women were referred to as *Beyaz Rus* (*Beyaz* means white). When this term was applied to women from southern Russia or the Ukraine our initial diagnosis was an error in political geography. We later realised that this conforms to the traditional positive associations of whiteness in Turkish Islamic culture. Local women were hard put to explain why their men should wish to consort even with the decidedly less attractive prostitutes from neighbouring parts of the Caucasus. The most common face-saving explanation was that the women of the eastern Black Sea coast carried excessive labour burdens and were unable to take appropriate care of themselves physically. Some of the most active female campaigners against the activities of the *Rus* women, self-described feminists, drew the conclusion that local women should try to emulate the foreigners in personal style and appearance (see Bellér-Hann 1995).

Male behaviour has changed significantly as a consequence of prostitution. Whereas in 1983 a foreign woman could walk around the small towns of Rize and Artvin without being hassled in any way, by 1993 the risk of molestation was ever-present. Men who did not threaten women physically were nonetheless likely to express their aggression in other ways: patronising or making fun of them when they entered shops, and proclaiming loudly as they left that all foreign women were *pis* (filthy). Adults and even young boys regularly used the name Natasha, or alternatively the Georgian word *gogo*, meaning woman, as insolent forms of address for every foreign woman. The widespread assumption was that every *gogo* was associated with prostitution.

This assumption was not universal: a few people took a different approach and blamed the sordid spectacles on the backward character of this part of Turkey. Those who established business partnerships with Georgians and Russians deprecated the usual stereotypes. Even fewer people made the journey across the border, but several small businessmen accomplished successful trips without falling foul of the much touted mafia. Some of these people commented favourably on the orderly (*düzenli*) quality of the Georgian towns, in mitigation for the undeniable dearth of goods in their marketplaces.

The moral panic engendered by the prostitution needs to be placed in the wider context of recent developments in this region and in Turkish society generally. By the early 1990s the climate in the tea industry had again turned very sour. Numerous factories were closed down, and virtually all the private owners were criticised by growers for protracted delays in payment for leaves supplied to them. Fieldwork in 1992–3 uncovered a familiar sense of frustration concerning the region's dependence on tea; but this time, instead of the blame being attached to a remote and overly bureaucratic state power, it was attached more to the abuses and corruption of private-sector operators, many of whom, it was alleged, had drawn on state credits to set up their factories, and made a handsome profit out of their so-called 'bankruptcies'.

The Motherland Party's free-market orientation also had far-reaching 'Westernising' effects on the whole of Turkish society. Nowhere was this more evident than in the media, where the State Corporation was exposed to virtually uncontrolled commercial competition. Television in particular was transformed, and many people commented on the high sex content of many Western programmes, including films transmitted at hours which would certainly be considered unsuitable for such material in a country like Britain.[13] These films may themselves have played a part in inducing some men to seek sexual excitement outside traditional confines. Combined with sensational coverage in the popular press, it may also have had the effect of encouraging both men and women in this region to imagine the extent of the depravity associated with the *Rus pazarı* to be much greater than was in fact the case.[14]

Anti-modernity

Turgut Özal and many of his younger followers, including Yılmaz, his eventual successor as party leader, liked to present themselves as modern leaders, who wished above all to promote Turkey's integration into a global culture and trading system in which the products of Europe and North America are perceived to dominate. At the same time, Özal's own stance towards religion and traditional morality was complex and perhaps deliberately ambivalent.[15] It is possible to interpret his policies as a clever attempt to narrow the 'centre–periphery gap' so characteristic of this society in the past. Analysis of some recent survey data has suggested that 'the values associated with urban, educated elites are commonly shared by much wider strata in Turkish society' (Toprak 1993). From this point of view the liberalism of the Motherland Party is in the Kemalist tradition, in as much as it promotes social integration along secular lines. From other angles, however, the policies pursued over the past decade represent not so much a logical extension of the country's modernisation drive as a threat to the delicate synthesis that underpins it. The gap between the secular elites of Ankara and the rural and small town inhabitants of the eastern Black Sea coast seems to have widened rather than narrowed in recent years. District governors explained to us that both the physical filth and chaos currently associated with the petty traders and the moral filth and chaos associated with the prostitutes were only temporary phenomena, which in due course would be brought under more effective public controls (in the case of the markets) or eliminated (in the case of prostitution). This has not satisfied or convinced everyone, and certainly not the groups of local women who have clamoured for more effective police action to curb the sex trade.

The kind of scenario being played out at village level is illustrated in the following story. Cemil is the eldest son of a relatively poor family we have known since 1983. His grandfather had a few years education in an Islamic school and travelled regularly to Batumi for work in the last years of the Ottoman Empire. His father graduated from a secular primary school, later acquired a clerical job in the health centre in the local town, and is now a pensioner. His mother, who is not literate, looks after a few acres of tea bushes, vegetable gardens and livestock. Cemil's two sisters have made arranged marriages and now live in Istanbul and Ankara. A younger brother is unmarried and works seasonally for the state road services. All four children are *lise* (high school) graduates. However, in contrast to many of his contemporaries, who like him failed in their attempts to enter higher education, Cemil could not rely on family wealth or connections to set him up in employment. His father has met the more vital cultural norm by providing him with a wife, by whom he has two children, but they still share accommodation and have little prospect of separation from the parental home. Cemil has worked for four private tea factories in recent years, but either the factory went bankrupt or the conditions were so exploitative that he left. He then invested family savings, supplemented by a large loan, and acquired a car for work as a chauffeur. Since men prefer to mix with *Rus* women at night away from their home district, vehicles have become an even more highly valued resource. Cemil soon discovered a social world of thrills never before available to villagers. He befriended a group of Georgians and, to the dismay of his whole family, disappeared across the border one summer for over a month. By his own account he spent the whole time partying, returning to Turkey only when his money ran out. Meanwhile, his wife had no option but to remain with her in-laws and her children. The car has been sold to pay off his debts. With his father's support Cemil has opened a modest shop in his village, where he is obviously an example to other villagers whose contacts with the *Rus* are limited to occasional haggling in the marketplace. He says that he sees the error of his ways and is now a reformed character. He also says that he owes his salvation to Allah.

Indeed, the most obvious political beneficiaries of this situation have been the forces of religion. It is important not to overstate the case: we knew some *imams* who were regular patrons of the *Rus pazar* (i.e. they bought some household goods there because they represented good value for money). Some of those traditionally unsympathetic to religion (such as many local teachers) alleged that plenty of 'bearded ones' themselves take more than a passing interest in the foreign women, though we never saw the slightest evidence to confim this familiar anti-clerical jibe. Most religious specialists were vociferous in their condemnation of this latest threat to Islam and the purity of family life. Although the *Refâh Partisi* (the religious party) managed only fourth place in the region in national elections during the 1980s, by the early 1990s it was expanding and had already become the major force in several villages in the district of Pazar where we were based. In the local elections of spring 1994 this party swept to power in many more parts of the region. It is worth exploring further the ambiguities and elisions that lay behind these successes. I have already implied that part of the explanation may lie in disillusionment with what the established secular parties have done for the region, and in particular the apparent cul-de-sac to which dependence on tea seems to have led. But the *Refâh Partisi* has focused less on the future of the tea industry and possible alternative strategies of economic development, and much more on the moral issues associated with the *Rus pazarı*. It proved itself the only party capable of mobilising large audiences for public meetings during our fieldwork. We were observers at one meeting in which much of the passionate rhetoric seemed designed to confuse the precise source of the complaint locally (prostitution in the wake of a collapsed communist empire) with the more general threat posed by Western capitalism, with its alleged complete disregard of family values. Women clad from head to foot in black carried banners protesting against plans to build more hotels for the trader-tourists. One of the most eloquent slogans read 'OTEL – MOTEL – AIDS!' Another proclaimed: *'Bu turizm değil, rezalet.'*[16]

At one level what seems to be happening at present in this corner of Turkey is the very familiar process of stereotyping an 'Other' which is devalued, and to whom the Self can therefore feel superior. Citizens of modern Turkey can agree to disparage the goods of the *Rus pazarı* in much the same way as Poles view the equivalent goods in Warsaw, or Germans the comparable merchandise, controlled by Turks and Poles, in Berlin. As the early writings of Max Weber on Polish migrant workers testify, such attitudes among Germans go back a long way.[17] Perhaps the most conspicuous feature of the contemporary stereotyping is the 'mafia' allegation, which certainly seems widespread throughout the ex-communist regions. But the contemporary situation on the eastern Black Sea coast is much more complex than this, partly because the state frontier was completely closed for so long, and partly because, in spite of the similar ways in which they pursued modernity, the forms of society on each side of this border were culturally distinctive.

In their appearance and personal habits, and in the conspicuous independence of their women, these new visitors seemed to emulate Westerners; yet most of them were visibly poor, they were pitiful imitations of the real thing, as known through the mass media. Turks are by and large accustomed to being on the receiving end of negative stereotypes from 'Westerners': they sum up what they perceive to be the Western image of the Turk with words such as *berbat*, 'rotten', or *barbar*, 'barbarian'. But now they were in the position of the Westerner, possessed of the full trappings of a market capitalist economy and political democracy, while their poor visitors were in the role of the *barbar*. But because this combination of capitalist democracy is poorly rooted in Turkey, and because of all the recent disappointments in the tea economy, the arrival of these new outsiders gave an opportunity to forces which range beyond the patterns of conventional national stereo- typing, and move instead into the realm of demonizing. For the forces of religion, all those associated with the *Rus pazarı* were the agents of evil, out to attack the moral foundations of Islam. The anti-Western rhetoric of the *Refâh Partisi* here fell on especially fertile ground. The fact that those who represented the West were not really Westerners at all but came from the geographical east and had fewer contacts with Europe than Turks themselves was a key factor. It was precisely because local Turks could feel superior, in the stereotypical manner described above, that they could also proceed to demonise the *Rus* women in a way that they did not demonise European and American women (such as those they might admire in the privacy of their homes in popular television programmes).

Although many local people, men and women, did indeed make the prostitutes the main focus of their anger and passion, this demonizing did not focus exclusively or even principally on the women. It was often deflected to communism itself, and its presumed impact on human nature. Previously dismissed as inefficient and authoritarian, com- munism was now condemned as totally degenerate and corrupt. Com- munist society had always run entirely on sex and alcohol. It had made people heartless (*gönülsüz*), and less than fully human. Cemil, the villager referred to above, explained that the women were not actually very good at sex. The reason, in his view, was that their menfolk had not taught them properly. The reason for that was drunkenness, which in turn was the responsibility of the state for not allowing a private enterprise economy. Demonic associations were also present in wide- spread popular commentaries on the marks on the facial features of Mikhail Gorbachev: these were readily identified with the marks of Satan and with malevolent spirits (*cinler*). But perhaps the most graphic marker of this demonizing trend was the small poster widely displayed by the public health authorities, warning in the anodyne language of medical science about the dangers of sexually transmitted diseases. This did not mention the AIDS threat explicitly, but incessant media coverage made this the prime association.[18]

Conclusion

This chapter presents a provisional analysis of a complex and still unfolding situation in north-east Turkey. We have drawn a distinction between 'normal' processes of stereotyping the 'Other', and specific processes of demonizing that 'Other', as observed in contemporary Rize and Artvin following the recent re-opening of the state border with Georgia. Stereotypes can assume a wide variety of forms, from the exoticising of tribal peoples by ancient Greek writers on the peoples of this region to the contemporary images of 'Western' sexuality as spread by the technologies of globalisation. A fuller discussion of the stereotypes held within this region would have to be much more nuanced. For example, there are the (extremely fluid) boundaries that separate townspeople from villagers. There are also significant differences within the region in terms of the strength of religious commitments: broadly, these can be summed up as a decline in religiosity as one moves east. The inhabitants of Arhavi or Hopa, closest to the border, may feel they have rather little in common with the more devout Muslims of Pazar and Ardeşen. But there is a basic uniformity about the reaction to the *Rus pazarı* and the prostitutes in the early 1990s: it has not completely broken down the more local boundaries, but for a large majority it has heightened awareness of a more significant and more alien Other.

What impact has the open frontier policy had on ethnic and cultural identities and stereotypes within the Rize-Artvin region? An embryonic ethnic movement has emerged in the last few years among the Istanbul Laz diaspora, with substantial inputs from Wolfgang Feurstein, a scholar based in Germany (Hann 1997). Feurstein has devised an alphabet for *Lazuri* that relies for the most part on modern Turkish characters. The activists have been careful not to make any claims that might be interpreted as claims for political separatism, but have urged only that action be taken to defend *Lazuri* and Laz culture more generally. However, in 1992–3 there was little sign that these intellectual activities in the diaspora were affecting notions of self and identity in the homeland. We found no evidence that the opening of the border had created any new sense of cultural distinctiveness and a related ethnic consciousness, either among Laz or among any other group (there remain substantial numbers of Georgian speakers in this region). The small numbers of Laz who crossed the border regularly as traders obviously enjoyed certain advantages: a few had renewed old family ties and were looking to expand business partnerships. But others were doing the same with Georgians and other non-Laz, and Laz traders were not considered to be any different to others. One does find among some Laz a sympathy with the economic plight of the traders. But this is found among other inhabitants of the region as well, and is by no means limited to Laz. The vast majority of Laz share the general attitudes described in the preceding section. The fact that Laz can converse quite fluently with Mingrelian traders does not lead to any sense of shared identity: the primary distinguishing mark of the Mingrelians is the Christian religion, and in this context the Laz identify firmly with the Muslim Turks. Thus, far from the opening of the border leading to any weakening of Turkish identity through the development of new ethnic identities, or to the emergence of some higher common identity as 'people of the Black Sea', it seems instead to have led to greater solidarity and cohesion *within* the boundaries of the nation-state. Even those peripheral groups with potentially strong links to groups across the boundary have been induced instead to heightened awareness of the links that make them part of modern Turkey.

We therefore reach conclusions somewhat different from those drawn by Stokes in his investigation of Turkishness in the frontier area of the Hatay (Stokes, this volume). We argue that the rulers of modern Turkey have been extremely successful in creating a highly standardised and homogenised culture, one with which the vast majority of the inhabitants of a diverse region can strongly identify. On the eastern Black Sea coast the arrival of nation-state modernity was kick-started with the deportation of the Greeks in the early 1920s. Since then integration and assimilation have proceeded without force, though all aspects of social life, economic development as well as cultural and educational policies, have been very much under the control of the Kemalist state. However, the delicate synthesis underpinning this state has been threatened in the period since the accession to power of Turgut Özal in 1983. The consequences of his Westernising, free-market economic policies have been accentuated in this region by dependence upon one crop which requires generous support if it is to continue to satisfy the aspirations of local people. All this has contributed to the expression of a common identity *vis-à-vis* the ex-socialist Other, unseen for fifty years. However, increasingly this common Turkish identity seems to be rooted in Islam rather than Kemalism. In conditions of severe economic deterioration, where elite policies seem designed to promote the overtly sordid and immoral in all areas of social life, the future seems more uncertain than at any period in the previous history of the Republic.

Notes

1. Leach (1954: 5) was a faithful if reluctant follower of Radcliffe-Brown in this respect. Both accepted a territorial definition of the unit of inquiry in terms of 'any convenient locality'.
2. Every phase of this fieldwork has been carried out jointly. It has been supported throughout by the Economic and Social Research Council (formerly SSRC; research grants HR 8790/1; R000 221022; R000 233208). It was hoped that the most recent phase of this research in 1992–3 would include a visit to Georgia and some preliminary inquiries into perceptions of this border from the Georgian side. Unfortunately, conditions were far too unstable to permit such a visit, and the present account is therefore restricted to observations and materials gathered in Turkey.
3. For further detail see Bryer (1966) and Meeker (1971, 1972). Because of its distance from the centre and the relative inaccessibility of its valleys, the region retained a high degree of autonomy from the Ottoman state. As late as the mid-nineteenth century the relationship between the Ottoman authorities and the local lords of the valleys remained a loose one (Meeker 1972: 240). The region wavered between two larger political entities, Russia and the Ottoman empire, in the early twentieth century (Marr 1910). In this respect, Ottoman rule in the eastern Black Sea region is comparable to the traditional Southeast Asian state (*negeri*) as described in this volume by Carsten.
4. Further discussion of these Laz stereotypes in Turkish popular culture can be found in Meeker (1971) and in Hann (1990). We are currently preparing a further ethnographic study of the Laz-speaking region.
5. See, for example, the assessment of David Lang (1962), which in the light of the events of the last few years was over-optimistic: '. . . when one contrasts the dynamic economic and industrial system of Georgia with the chronic instability of some modern countries of the Middle East, or with the deplorable stagnation and effeteness of others, there is no denying the positive side of Russia's work in Georgia. The Soviet formula for a federation of European and Asiatic peoples under the domination of Russian Communists is not a perfect one, especially as it takes absolutely no account of the personal preferences or political aspirations of each national group. But at least it ensures that when at last the day comes for Georgia and other smaller peoples of the Soviet Union to enjoy a larger measure of free speech, genuine democracy and a wider self-determination, they will do so without drifting back into a vicious circle of ignorance, poverty and disease, and be able to stand on their own feet economically and industrially in this competitive modern age' (1962: 273–4).
6. These evaluations do not correspond with state practice in one further matter of great importance to many local people. The state requires various

categories of civil servant to carry out a tour of duty in a province that is classified as 'eastern'. Artvin is the only province of the eastern Black Sea region that qualifies for this purpose.

7. Some of these images of bureaucratic incompetence on the part of non-accountable, remote state authorities were later transferred to their own governmental authorities in Turkey as a result of their handling of radiation problems associated particularly with tea production. Scandals concerning the Tea Corporation's willingness to market contaminated tea continued to arouse public concern well into the 1990s.

8. This sweeping generalisation seems to us defensible, though a number of recent texts such as Robertson (1992) and Friedman (1994) seek to provide integrated accounts of various aspects of political economy and global cultural change.

9. The gendering of the name of the new party is, of course, consistent with the rhetoric of the nation to be found in many other modern national movements; in this case it may be more significant, in the light of gender-specific attitudes to foreigners to be discussed below. *Anavatan* is a modern word, as is the related term *vatandaş*, citizen. It fits with the party's self image as an agent of modernity, seeking to extend an essentially Western conception of citizenship rights to all individual members of Turkish society.

10. Turks, significantly, do not speak so much of a frontier or border (for which the words are *hudut* or *sınır*) as of a 'gate' (*kapı*). The opening of the Sarp gate became more widely known throughout Turkey in 1992–3 thanks to a popular song by Erkan Ocaklı concerning the Russian prostitutes who entered through it: see further discussion below, and also Bellér-Hann (1995).

11. However, moral considerations were applied more strictly to certain 'commodities' in the recent past, sometimes along ethnic lines. According to Feurstein (1983: 36) the Laz people, unlike their Hemşinli neighbours, did not buy and sell milk. The persistence of traditional sentimental attachments is evident today in the virtual absence of a land market in most rural parts of this region. Some families who have left their villages struggle to retain their land, even when income-maximising strategies would suggest a sale.

12. Apparently there was once a brothel at Trabzon, but this was suppressed several decades ago; and although some men spoke of having used facilities at Çorum, most indicated that the usual place for a man to lose his virginity was in one or other of the many specialist establishments of the capital or in Istanbul.

13. It is tempting to compare these contemporary images of the West, and especially Western women, with the representation of Middle Eastern women in the cultural products of generations of Western 'Orientalists' (cf. Said 1978). In both cases we can observe the popular dissemination of stereotypical images that bear little connection to social realities. But contemporary technologies do make this 'Occidentalism' a rather different phenomenon from classical Orientalism. It is unhelpful any longer to oppose the Orient to the so-called advanced countries of north-west Europe and North America. One of the most popular soap operas in Turkey during

our recent fieldwork was produced in Mexico. In this sense, we are indeed dealing with the culture of post-modernity, or 'globalisation'.

14. To gather accurate data about prostitution was clearly difficult. It was clear that a high proportion of the men who patronised these establishments were not permanent local residents. They included migrant workers holidaying in the region (holidays might be frequent, and last until resources ran out), or locals who would drive to other towns in search of women, rather than risk damaging their reputation in their own.

15. Özal aroused the wrath of loyal Kemalists in other political parties with a number of concessions to the forces of religion, including the spread of religious education inside the state-controlled education system. Özal's close family members, as represented in the mass media, were very demonstrably committed to Islam.

16. 'This is not tourism, it's a scandal!' On the moral weighting of the term *rezalet*, see Stokes (1992: 224–5).

17. As Bendix has commented, Weber was worried that '. . . the higher civilization of the Germans was being jeopardized by these inroads from the barbarian east' (1959: 20).

18. There was general agreement among local doctors that the incidence of sexually transmitted diseases had increased in the region. However, as of summer 1993 not a single AIDS case had been recorded in this region.

References

Bellér-Hann, I. 1995. 'Prostitution and its effects in north-east Turkey', *European Journal of Women's Studies* 2 (2): 219–35.

Bendix, R. 1959. *Max Weber; an intellectual portrait*. London: Methuen.

Bryer, A. 1966. 'Some notes on the Laz and Tzan (part one)', *Bedi Kartlisa*, 21–2, 174–5.

Bryer, A. and D. Winfield 1985. *The Byzantine monuments and topography of the Pontos*. 2 vols., Washington, DC: Dumbarton Oaks Research Library and Collection.

Chinchaladze, N. 1993. 'Ethnic conflicts in Georgia', paper presented at the Amsterdam conference, 'The anthropology of ethnicity', December 1993.

Feurstein, W. 1983. 'Untersuchungen zur Materiellen Kultur der Lazen' unpublished Magisterarbeit, Albert-Ludwigs Universitat, Freiburg.

Friedman, J. 1994. *Cultural identity and global process*. London: Sage.

Gellner, E. 1983. *Nations and nationalism*. Oxford: Blackwell.

1994 'The new circle of equity', in C. M. Hann (ed.), *When history accelerates: essays on rapid social change, complexity and creativity*. London: Athlone.

Hann, C. M. 1990. *Tea and the domestication of the Turkish state*. SOAS Modern Turkish Studies Programme, Occasional Papers 1, Huntingdon: Eothen.

1997. 'Ethnicity, language and politics in Northeast Turkey', in C. Govers and H. Vermeulen (eds.), *The politics of ethnic consciousness*. London: MacMillan, pp. 121–56.

Keyder, Ç. 1981. *The definition of a peripheral economy: Turkey 1923–1929*. Cambridge: Cambridge University Press.

1987. *State and class in Turkey.* London: Verso.

Lang, D. M. 1962. *A modern history of Georgia.* London: Weidenfeld and Nicolson.

Leach, E. R. 1954. *Political systems of highland Burma: a study of Kachin social structure.* London: G. Bell.

Marr, N. 1910. 'Iz' poezdki b' Turetskiy Lazistan', *Izvestiya Imperatorskoy Akademii Nauk' (Bulletin de l'Académie Impériale des Sciences de St. Petersbourg)*, pp. 547–632.

Meeker, Michael E. 1971. 'The Black Sea Turks: some aspects of their ethnic and cultural background', *International Journal of Middle Eastern Studies*, 2 (4): 318–45.

1972 'The great family aghas of Turkey: a study of a changing political culture', in R. Antoun and I. Harik (eds.), *Rural politics and social change in the Middle East.* Bloomington: Indiana University Press.

Pereira, M. 1971. *East of Trebizond.* London: Geoffrey Bles.

Robertson, R. 1992. *Globalization: social theory and social culture.* London: Sage.

Sahlins, M. 1974. *Stone age economics.* London: Tavistock.

Said, Edward W. 1978. *Orientalism.* London: Routledge.

Stokes, M. 1992. *The Arabesk debate: music and musicians in modern Turkey.* Oxford: Clarendon Press.

Tapper, R. (ed.) 1991. *Islam in modern Turkey: religion, politics and modern literature in a secular state.* London: I. B. Tauris.

Toprak, B. 1993. 'The role of religion in secular Turkey', paper presented at the Manchester conference on 'Change in Modern Turkey: politics, society, economy', May 1993.

11 Imagining 'the South': hybridity, heterotopias and Arabesk on the Turkish–Syrian border

Martin Stokes

Borders create problems for those whose lives they frame. These problems have two dimensions. The first concerns the efforts of the modern state to coerce or persuade local populations to accept its jurisdiction, political and economic decisions, notions of a unitary national culture and the dubious benefits of its military protection. These efforts are often acute in border regions. Here, the power of the nation-state and its symbolic apparatus do not fade out, but intensify, as a number of contributors to this volume point out (in particular, Sahlins; Hann and Bellér-Hann). This often places inordinate demands on minority populations, for whom a border often cuts across pre-existing and culturally more relevant ties with others excluded by these borders. Majority populations may apparently reap the benefits of such arrangements, but suffer the longer-term consequences of living with problematic 'others' in their midst.

The second is born of the contradiction between nationalism and globalisation. Realignments within the remains of the modern nation-state system have aggravated the tendency of borders to cut across formerly undifferentiated territories, and even through the middle of metropolitan centres (as in Sarajevo, Nicosia and Jerusalem). In part, this is due to the fact that borders are no longer capable of separating people in quite the same ways. Today, the symbolic apparatus of the nation-state is overtly contradicted by a flow of commodities, capital, labour and media messages across borders according to the dictates of political-economic realities which are transnational and global. The state, as Appadurai has frequently pointed out, has relinquished much of its meaning-making to transnational industry (Appadurai 1993). The sociology of globalisation seems to be divided between writers such as Gilpin, who see nation-states retaining their grip in an increasingly global political order through military power or through the increasingly strong hand of some nation-states in newly emerging transnational blocs (see, for example, Gilpin 1981), and those who would argue, for various

263

reasons, with Appadurai, that the nation-state is inexorably on the wane. It is perhaps more accurate to say that what has emerged is a new set of contradictions, or, to use Hall's phrase, a new 'articulation' between global, national and local orders (1992: 304). The apparatus and cultural language of the nation-state no longer allows people to deal with the situations in which they find themselves.

As migration moves newly underprivileged people away from border areas, or as separatist struggles seek new targets beyond heavily militarised border zones, the problems that borders create are often felt some distance away. While these problems are not geographically restricted, they are, however, particularly acute in border areas, entailing a great deal of cultural 'work' from people in border localities to make life there socially, economically and politically manageable. Lavie's (1990) description of a community of Bedouin in the Negev whose life has been chronically problematised by ever-shifting borders focuses on 'allegories' of identity, that, to paraphrase her own account (1990: 39–40), transform the paradoxes of their lives. She stresses the ways in which the problems of fragmentation, hybridity and rupture are worked out through all manner of cultural performance and, in particular, narration. While I find Lavie's use of the concept of allegory extremely useful, it tends to privilege the domain of the spoken, and to underplay the non-verbal. It is in the non-verbal domain that people are often able to embrace notions of hybridity and plurality which are often unsayable; this domain is consequently a vital cultural resource in the management of border lives. In it, one finds the expression of something resembling Foucault's 'heterotopia', an 'impossible space' containing a 'large number of fragmentary worlds' (cited in Harvey 1989: 50). Heterotopic spaces are, in this context, doubly 'impossible'. First, the nation-state is committed to co-opt or eradicate plurality in the pursuit of a unitary national culture; this process renders unthinkable the fractured, partial worlds that many, if not most, people inhabit within the categories that it propagates. Secondly, the means we have as anthropologists of conceptualising 'culture' (the product of theories which were born alongside the nation-state) lead us to privilege in our explanations activity which is stable and bounded, and to have difficulty with what is not. An exploration of this 'heterotopic' space, therefore, has the dual aim of delineating aspects of a border culture and of shifting the anthropological focus onto crucial, or, to use Foucauldian terminology, 'productive', aspects of culture which are shifting, fragmentary and 'nomadic' (cited in Harvey 1989: 44).

This chapter looks in particular at the production and use of a form of popular culture and music called 'Arabesk' in the Hatay province of

Turkey.[1] The southern and eastern boundaries of the Hatay province constitute a significant part of the Turkish–Syrian border, significant not only in terms of its length, but also in its somewhat ambiguous status for both countries (see map 11.1). While it was excluded by the Ankara Agreement of 1923 from the National Pact (*Misaki Milli*) drawn up by Mustafa Kemal three years earlier, and became part of the French mandated territories of Syria, it was effectively handed back to Turkey in 1939 as a result of changing priorities in the region on the part of the colonial powers in the run-up to World War II. The Syrian state which emerged from the remaining French mandate in 1946 saw the annexation of the Hatay as an act of treachery on the part of the French, and aggressive territorial expansion on the part of the Turks, and Syrian nationalists have not entirely given up their claims on this area to this day. The late addition of this province to the modern Turkish state, together with its large heterodox Arabic-speaking population, mark it out as something of a peculiarity to most Turks, and Turkish diplomacy in this region is marked by a certain delicacy. Syrian claims to the area are vociferous, but also marked by a certain ambiguity. Older Syrian maps show the Hatay unambiguously as a part of Syria, and some also show a 'Greater Syria' which extends to include the city of Adana and its hinterland, the Çukurova plain. More recent maps incorporate the province by showing it in the same colour scheme as Syria, or including contours or town names where these are omitted outside Syria, but differentiate it by marking its border with a dotted (as opposed to continuous) line, indicating that it is not, in practice, a part of Syria 'proper'. The Syrian government was persuaded to remove the Hatay from its maps in order to ensure Turkish participation in the Mediterranean games in Latakia in 1986.

The ambiguity of the Hatay in national terms is perceived in the region in various ways. Incoming Turks, whether military personnel, workers and managers in the heavy industry of the coastal strip or local government employees tend to have little enthusiasm for the area; even after lengthy stays, they find themselves ill at ease with the damp heat, the constant thundering of trucks and lorries, the time and expense involved in getting to Istanbul and Ankara, and the all-pervasive sounds of the Arabic language and the 'Arabic' sounds of the Hatay Turkish dialect. The explanation of the negative qualities of the place, as far as outsiders are concerned, is focused with remarkable consistency on a form of popular culture known, appropriately enough, as Arabesk. Arabesk is primarily a musical form, considered by many to be a hybrid Turkish version of Arab popular song, but it is also associated by its Turkish critics (and there are many) with an all-embracing kitsch anti-culture

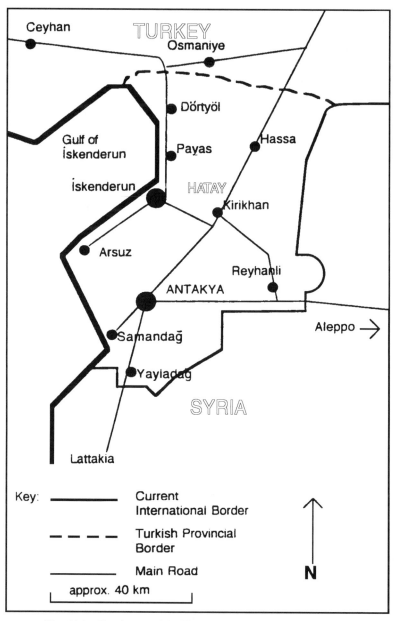

Map 11.1   Sketch map of the Hatay.

which stretches from films and other low-brow pleasures associated with squatter-town life, to corruption, cynicism and sleaze in party politics. For those Turkish outsiders in the area, the association of the place with Arabesk focuses both their feelings of alienation, and an uneasy sense of difference. The subject of Arabesk in the Hatay was constantly on the lips of outsiders in the region, who would use it to share a moment of gloom, on the assumption that I held the same views as them on both issues. A brief anecdote will exemplify this point. When I arrived in the area after an overnight bus journey, I was taken to eat a kebab in a transport cafe whose paper-thin walls were festooned with pictures of Bülent Ersoy, the transsexual Arabesk star. My host, a teacher from north-west Turkey who had lived in the region for some years, waved his hands around him with a resigned and depressed air, and the words 'This . . . is a real Arabesk place (*burası . . . tam arabesk bir yer*). What's there to do here?' These were practically the first words I heard, and I often heard them repeated.

A gendered border

Arabesk is widely associated with a generalised notion of the south of Turkey. This association has a mythic dimension, in the sense that it organises the production and consumption of Arabesk, and is constantly evoked in spoken language to organise and narrate notions of honour, shame, moral and political order and disorder. 'The South', in these terms, evokes notions of a pervasive, deeply rooted and pernicious principle of hybridity and 'oriental' chaos lying at the heart of Turkish society, and has been constructed by its critics in political debate as a moral panic, reminding the Turkish population that the modernist republican legacy demands an ongoing battle and constant vigilance against the forces which threaten to undermine it. The association which is made outside the area between the Hatay and Arabesk also involves pervasive tropes of nationalist historiography and its cultural and symbolic apparatus. This association hinges on the way in which the Turkish–Syrian border is symbolically 'gendered'. That is to say, it is the product of classificatory schemes which produce both gender difference and nationalist historiography, among other things. Borders, as Carsten suggests elsewhere in this volume, have to be understood as part of a continuum of boundary-making and boundary-crossing activities, ranging from the domestic to the international.

As a symbol, the border itself condenses a number of ideas for Turks concerning the nature of Turkish and Arab identity, the present and the past, the nation-state and Islam. These ideas have been framed by the ideology of Turkism, one of a number of nationalist ideas which emerged in Ottoman elite bureaucratic circles in the late nineteenth century in response to the disintegration of the Empire. Mustafa Kemal spent his life establishing the apparatus of the modern nation-state on the ruins of the Ottoman polity in accordance with his own particular version of Turkist thinking. He did this through a peculiarly effective combination of ideological persuasion (through, for example, education and language reform) and through force, where persuasion failed. The thrust of his revolutionary reformism was directed at symbols of identity, in particular through language, dress, music, urban and domestic architecture and monumental sculpture, all of which explicitly stated that Turkey had shed the debilitating cultural load of its 'Arab' past. The models for these symbols of identity were sought in Anatolia and sometimes Central Asia, wherever the pernicious influence of Arab 'civilisation' was deemed to have had least effect. Turkishness was then defined according to this essentially negative process. In this view, what was Turkish was what remained when one took away what was demonstrably 'Arab' from Anatolia's rural culture. The border which separates Turkey from the rest of the Muslim world is in ideological terms, then, the line that separates Turkey's present from its past, order from chaos. What lies beyond is considered to be evidence of the turmoil from which the modern Turkish state has been dragged on its journey towards a modernity which is by definition western European. In this sense, Turkey's southern border is much more of an ideological issue than the north-eastern borders discussed by Hann and Bellér-Hann (this volume); the socialist 'other' being far less relevant to the construction of Turkish nationalist mythology than the Arab.

The creation of the national borders in the National Pact of 28 January 1920 and the popular imagery of this act draws heavily on notions of soil and paternity in rural Turkish life. As Delaney has argued (1991), rural patriarchy is articulated through a series of interlinked metaphors relating women to unproductive soil. This unproductive soil is brought into productive use by the male act of claiming, ploughing, scattering seed and protecting it. Delaney is particularly concerned with how these metaphors connect farming practice to ideologies of patriarchal authority in the household, village, state and a cosmos created by a male God. In the different context of this discussion, one could argue along with Delaney that all acts of boundary making, and the acts of propriety involved, imply a male process of division, protection and control of an unbounded femininity. Kemal's act of drawing up the borders of the modern nation-state continues to be widely and easily understood in Turkey in terms of an act of paternity.[2] For this reason he was given the title of Atatürk, the 'father Turk', a title by which he continues to be known in Turkey. Through his seminal act of defining and englobing Turkish soil, he brought it into politically 'productive' use (Stokes 1994). As Carsten (this volume) notes, borders are often understood in a kinship idiom, by relating them to more localised notions of morality and exchange. Here, however, in stark contrast to Carsten's Langkawi experience, which permits ambiguity and inclusion, the Turkish kinship idiom involves notions of property and exclusion; its boundaries are impermeable.

The significance of the Hatay in the Turkish ideological scheme lay in the fact that it was left outside the process of border definition by Mustafa Kemal. Like an unmarried woman, it had not been claimed, protected and brought into productive relations with others. Subsequent contributors to the Atatürkian myth (see, for example, Kinross 1964) stress the fact that the Hatay was part of Atatürk's original plan. As a realist and a strategist, however, he recognised the fact that he would have to bide his time in order to claim it for the new Turkish state. The Hatay historian, Mehmet Tekin, in a similar vein, remarks that the Ankara Accord of 13 July 1921 (which established the quasi-autonomous Sanjak[3] of Alexandretta as part of the French Mandate) was signed under protest from the Turkish delegates (Tekin 1993: 117). In addition, the Turkish position had been undermined by a prior agreement between the Turkish foreign minister and his French counterpart on 11 March of that year, to which Mustafa Kemal had not given his agreement (Tekin 1993: 111). In both Kinross's biography and Tekin's history of the Hatay, the story ends with the establishment of the independent Hatay Republic on 2 September 1938, the prelude to the Turkish annexation ten months later, and Atatürk's death shortly after. This conclusion unambiguously stresses the fact that the incorporation of the Hatay into the *Misaki Milli* was a final act of paternity on Atatürk's part (and not the agency of foreign powers). Having completed it, he was able to die in peace. The opening lines of an 'Independence March' for the Hatay composed by an anonymous Turkish soldier in 1939 makes the patriarchal and gendered relationship of the province to the Turkish state absolutely clear:

> *Antakya, İskenderun Türkün iki kızıdır*
> *Bayrağında biri ay, biri de yıldızıdır. . .*
>
> Antakya and İskenderun are the two daughters of the Turks
> On its flag it has one moon and a star . . . (cited in Tekin 1993: 247)

It is true that he died soon after the incorporation of the Hatay state, but one cannot avoid the conclusion that the Hatay was ceded to Turkey as a result of wider power structures in which the leaders of the new Turkish state played an extremely minor role. Whatever else it was, it was not the act of decisive self-determination of which the other *Misaki Milli* borders were undoubted evidence. To extend the logic of this gendered nationalist historiography, there is, as it were, a crucial flaw in the masculinity of the border, and this flaw is responsible for the steady flow of an Arabness corrupting the Turkish political body, and a femininity which corrupts the vigorous masculinity of the Turkist political principle. The ready association that Turks from outside the region make between Arabesk and the Hatay has a great deal to do with the fact that some of the most conspicuous icons of Arabesk are also people whose masculinity is either suspect or blatantly transgressed. The high sobbing vocal textures of Arabesk, the film personae of Arabesk singers as figures shorn of their manly honour and dignity, and the presence among their number of gay and transsexual singers point to what is widely seen as the expression of a compromised, flawed masculinity. At the level of these ideologically organised metaphors, Arabesk is readily associated with this southern border region.

Arabesk

In other ways, however, the myth of the South and its borders explains very little about Arabesk, which must be seen more in terms of the centres of cultural production in Turkey than the peripheries.[4] The term Arabesk has a long history in the context of Turkish art music, and was later applied and somewhat vaguely used to describe newer currents in the art music genre brought in by Turkish composers who had some connection with the Egyptian film industry in the 1930s, such as Sadettin Kaynak and Suat Sayın. However, the term became firmly attached to a genre of popular music after 1969, with the growing commercial significance of the 45 rpm disc (and later audio-cassettes) in Turkey's metropolitan centres, and the entrepreneurial experiments of musicians such as Ahmet Sezgin and Orhan Gencebay in Istanbul's *gazino* clubs. Orhan Gencebay's 45 rpm single *Bir Teselli Ver* was released in 1968, achieving mass sales by the standards of the time, and is conventionally thought of as the first Arabesk recording, in spite of the fact that Gencebay repeatedly denies his association with the genre. It mixed elements of Turkish art, folk and Western rock with some elements of Arab popular styles, and constructed through the sobbing lyrics a subject who is torn apart by violent desires for a remote and manipulative love-object. This form, established through Gencebay's experiments in club and recording studio, continued to dominate commercial song production in Turkey throughout the 1970s and 1980s.

Even in musicians' circles in Istanbul, I found it difficult to disentangle discussions of the history of the genre from discussions of Turkey's southern underbelly. One recurrent argument offered by my own music teachers and mentors in Istanbul in explanation of Arabesk was that it was simply 'southern' music which kept alive memories of the homeland for the millions of southern migrants in the big city. For them, the area was one of a partial and compromised Turkishness. Their own view, largely shaped by the state's media system, based in turn on the ideology of Turkism formulated by Ziya Gökalp at the turn of the nineteenth century, defined an essential and pre-eminently rural Turkish culture (*hars*) in opposition to the Arab civilisation (*medeniyet*) of the Ottoman cities. In the south, where Turks constituted a minority among predominantly Arab and Kurdish populations, this distinction was held to break down. 'Arab' urban art musics and 'Turkish' rural folk musics consequently coexist in a confusing and unstable mix, from which Arabesk inevitably emerged. According to this view, the music served the useful function of softening the cultural blow for those travelling from the hybrid peripheries to the Turkish centre.

In these kinds of discussions, the link between Arabesk and the South was present in negative terms, although one could argue that this negativity concealed a more ambiguous attitude. Arabesk is associated with pleasures (particularly of alcohol and sex) that sit uncomfortably with both Turkist republicanism and Sunni Islam. If northerners can blame occasions of moral laxity on southerners, then these moments can be woven into their daily lives without too much disruption of their world view. In the Hatay, however, Arabesk is celebrated. This celebration is not unambiguous. It might easily be missed, if one were to concentrate only on what people were saying. The strength of northern metropolitan condemnatory discourse is such that, in the unusual context of discussions with a foreign researcher such as myself pressing his informants for clear and unambiguous statements, people would often contradict themselves. Ahmet, for example, an Arab in İskenderun in his late teens with whom I frequently discussed music, acknowledged these condemnations by commenting that Arabesk was moral rot suitable only for the feeble-minded, and stated his preference (*tercih*) for more recent popular genres, in particular Turkish Pop (*Türk Popu*). He went on to mention that he had collected every single cassette produced by the prolific Arabesk singer Müslüm Gürses.

It is this verbal evasiveness, often accompanied by irony and humour, that makes it difficult to perceive the significance of Arabesk in the social life of the Hatay. Arabesk itself is almost impossible to ignore. Posters of İbrahim Tatlises, Müslüm Gürses and Bülent Ersoy cover the walls of workplaces and down-market restaurants. In midsummer, the sound of Arabesk pulses through the cities of Antakya, İskenderun and the *gazino* clubs in the mountain resorts, in particular Belen, Sarımazı and Soğukoluk.[5] A large number of local bands play for weddings throughout the summer, and well-known hits are almost immediately recycled. This local performance industry nurtures musicians and singers, a number of whom find opportunities to further their careers in Adana and Mersin (the main port cities on the Anatolian Mediterranean coast) and, from there, in Istanbul. Famous Arabesk singers from the Hatay include Gökhan Güney and Küçük Ceylan, thereby strengthening the connection that people make between this region and Arabesk. The sound of Arabesk provides a constant counterpoint to the patterns of everyday life in the Hatay. It is a permanent feature in the bars and brothels for which both Iskenderun and Antakya are famous. The local radio station, *Güney FM* ('South FM'), operating from Payas following the deregulation of the radio airwaves by Tansu Çiller in 1992, broadcasts non-stop Arabesk on a string of request programmes.

While interest in Arabesk was not restricted by age group, gender or ethnicity, it seemed to have a particularly unshakeable role to play in the life of Turkish young men in the region, self-styled 'tough guys' (*kabadayı,* pl. *kabadayıları*) who were, characteristically, whiling away a few years of low-paid apprenticeships amongst the *esnaf* (the artisan classes) before military service and marriage. Much of my time was spent in their company, for reasons connected with the time and energy that the Hatay's *kabadayıları* had to spare, and their good-humoured curiosity about me. My observations on the local significance of Arabesk are heavily based on discussions with them concerning the role it played in their lives.[6] This was deeply shaped and conditioned by their experiences of border life. I will outline these experiences under the headings of relations between Arabs and Turks within the region, and perceptions of power and powerlessness.

Arabs and Turks in the Hatay

The 'Arabness' that is widely imputed to this area, as a result of its proximity to two Turkish–Arab borders, and the Arab minority population that exist within them raise a question mark over experiences of Turkishness in the Hatay, and anxiety over local Arabs. Among the young *kabadayıları* of Antakya, much banter, in front of me at least, was taken up by stories of fights with the local Arabs (dismissively referred to as *fellah*, 'peasants') over access to particular leisure spots such as cafés and billiard saloons, and dismissive and racist comments concerning filth (*pislik*) and untrustworthiness (*yaramazlık*). Cuma, a young *kabadayı* from Antakya who made shoes for his father's small business, spent an afternoon telling me about himself as we climbed to a shrine on the steep hillside above the city. He had no time for Arabs at all, although his selfhood and masculinity were clearly bound up with the stories of fights with Arabs with which he regaled me.

This kind of antipathy has a collective and institutional basis, finding its way into party politics. Memories of the violence in the area in the late 1970s are maintained by both Arabs and Turks. This violence was heavily bound up with the atmosphere of Cold War confrontation between Turkey and Syria, when chauvinist attitudes were cultivated through political parties on both sides.[7] Rightist political parties (such as the nationalist *Milli Hareket Partisi* and Islamist *Refâh Partisi*, which currently flourish in the industrial coastal strip) continue to assert that Hatay Arabs are still staunchly pro-Syrian socialists, and that Syrian flags can be seen flying from houses in the mainly Arab areas of Samandağ and Arsuz. However, these statements are clearly related to the particular political agendas of Turkish supremacism and Sunni Islam, for which the Hatay's Arabs (who mainly belong to the heterodox Nusairi or Alevi sect, and tend to return left-of-centre candidates at national and local elections) constitute a useful target. This is somewhat ironic. Generally, Syrian expansionist claims on the area are regarded with great unease by Arabs in the Hatay, particularly among young men who have no desire to spend four years in the Syrian army in the service of what they consider to be a totalitarian and irredeemably 'backward' (*geri*) state. Neither Arabs nor Turks, it should be pointed out, travelled with any regularity over the border unless they were involved in the transit business, and their views of Syria were consequently entirely formed from hearsay.[8] While Arabs, in my presence, made quite a point of saying that relations with Turks were better than they were in the 1970s, antipathy towards Turks continues to be cultivated around a number of issues. For example, it is often claimed by Alevi and Sunni Arabs in the Hatay that after 1939 the area was swamped with 'second-class' Turks from the most underprivileged parts of Anatolia, people who were entirely out of place in a region with Antakya's distinguished past. Alevi Arabs who, in the early 1990s, threw their political weight behind the left-of-centre *Sosyal Halkçı Partisi*'s vision of an ethnically plural, secular and Western-oriented state, claim that the then dominant coalition (led by Tansu Çiller's rightist *Doğru Yol Partisi*) was encouraging a climate of organised oppression against religious minorities such as the Alevis in the Hatay and elsewhere.

Turks and Arabs maintain a distance between themselves in these kinds of ways for a variety of reasons. Partly this is to do with the separate niches occupied by different ethnic groups in the Hatay, which must be briefly explained. The current distribution of groups, as Aswad has pointed out (1971), is directly related to the efforts of the Ottoman and modern Turkish state in settling nomads and moving Anatolian communities into the area in the ongoing processes of militarising a sensitive border region. In the pre-modern period, before the Tanzimat reforms of the mid-nineteenth century, Turkish and Kurdish tribes used the central Amik plain on their migrations, dominating settled Sunni Arab villagers. The town and villages on both sides of the mountains, which form a central spine running through the province, nurtured Turkish, Arab and Armenian communities, who provided agricultural produce and the raw materials for a lively textile trade linking Antakya with Aleppo and Anatolia. Garrisons, caravanserais and roads were built to facilitate this trade. As part of this process, Ottoman sultans settled Turkoman tribes in the area and cultivated their loyalty to counterbalance the control exercised by other tribal groups over these routes. The most notable of these groups are today known as the Bayır-Buçak Turks, living in the Şenköy and Yayladağ area in the south of the province, who were settled here in the eighteenth century, and a number of whom now, ironically, live on the Syrian side of the border.[9] Armenians fled into the area following massacres in southern Anatolia at the end of World War I, when the Hatay was part of the French Syrian mandate, and fled again, to Aleppo, when the area was annexed by Turkey in 1939. Large towns which were predominantly Armenian, such as Kırıkhan, Soğukoluk and Belen, were resettled by Turks, and another influx of Turks and Kurds to the north-western part of the province and around the port of İskenderun took place with the arrival of heavy industry in the early 1970s. The Nusairi Arabs of the Hatay now occupy almost exclusively the mountainous land and coast around Samandağ and Arsuz. While industry, the bureaucracy and the *esnaf* classes in İskenderun and Antakya are predominantly Sunni Turkish (although including today a large number of incoming Kurds), together with the Amik plain and the large towns on either side of it, the exceptionally well-watered mountain land in the south-west of the province (with the exception of the Bayır-Buçak villages) is in the hands of Alevi Arabs.[10]

The positions occupied by these groups have altered substantially as a result of more recent events. Agriculture has flourished in the Hatay over the past ten years. The *laissez-faire* policies pursued by the Özal government throughout the 1980s was extremely beneficial to the small market-gardening businesses, whose main markets – Istanbul, Ankara and western Europe – were largely unaffected by wider political events. Migrant remittances from Germany are also particularly significant, and have undergone no major changes over the past decade. However, heavy industry, and the web of small businesses connected to it (transport, customs agents and so forth) were devastated by Özal's dismantling of the State Economic Enterprises, and by the fact that their markets in the Middle East were simultaneously disrupted by the Iran–Iraq war and the occupation of Kuwait. In effect, this has meant prosperity for the Alevi Arabs of the Hatay and decline for the Sunni Turks.

This fact has had a direct and somewhat painful impact on the lives of Turks in the Hatay. Young Sunni Turks grow up in small towns and squatter areas (*gecekondu*) of the city separate from Arabs, who are concentrated in outlying districts, and initially meet with little in their daily lives which challenge the nationalist notion of a Turkey for the Turks. Intermarriage is extremely rare, although this has as much to do with an antipathy between orthodox and heterodox groups of Muslims as with ethnic antipathy. Arabs learn Turkish because they are obliged to do so by the schooling system, but Turks learn Arabic only in order to understand the basics of the Koran, and this, of course, bears little relation to the spoken Arabic dialect of the Hatay. A barrier of cultivated ignorance and endogamy therefore keeps Turks and Arabs apart. Today, however, people such as Cuma have to adjust to the omnipresent signs of Alevi wealth and influence in the city, and his day-to-day work and leisure involves constant accommodation to a subaltern population which has recently found its feet. Comments by Cuma and his mates, tinged (to my ears) with a certain bitterness and resignation, about one of '*bizim fellah*' ('our peasants') driving around in a brand new Mercedes, or of the Alevi *dedes* constituting a '*mafya*' in the city, were highly resonant.

In a context where Turkish nationalism demands an antipathy to Arabs, but where the practicalities of daily life demand accommodation, compromise and some degree of mutual understanding, symbols, histories and narratives which are concerned with relations and conti-nuities between Arabs and Turks are likely to be highly significant. Arabesk undoubtedly fulfilled this role in Cuma's life. As his passion for Arabesk took up more and more of his chatter that day, it also became clear to me that he was extremely adept at dealing both civilly and sociably with Arabs. For Cuma, Arabs were simultaneously objects of desire as well as repulsion. By the end of the evening, after a few beers, conversation oscillated between the two subjects of Arabesk (a recent Bülent Ersoy cassette was playing on the establishment's ghetto-blaster) and a Palestinian prostitute called Filiz in one of the city brothels (nicknamed the *fakülte*), with whom he was clearly obsessed, and visited with great regularity. These two imaginary theatres, the world of Arabesk and the world of the *fakülte*, constituted a glamorous and exotic other world which stretched beyond the boundaries of Turkey and the Hatay. It was a world of refinement, sophistication, luxury and mature worldly pleasures (*keyf*). There was nothing 'low-brow' about Arabesk for Cuma. On the contrary, he specifically excluded many singers others would consider to be mainstream Arabesk singers (such as İbrahim Tatlises) from the Arabesk he loved, considering them uncouth louts (*kırro*), mere 'folk' (*halk*) singers. He included singers such as Bülent Ersoy and Zeki Müren, who also sing the urban art music genre (*sanat müziği*), a genre which explicitly involves images of luxury, refinement and delicacy.

The actors in Cuma's imaginary theatre were clearly and distinctly gendered. The two singers with whom he most identified are, respectively, a transsexual transvestite and one of Turkey's earliest and most famous media gays. His affections and desires were firmly focused on the Palestinian prostitute, Filiz. The prominence of these characters in the way he presented himself to others clearly gendered him as a pleasure-seeking and receiving male subject, and also feminised the 'non-male' objects of that pleasure. This gendering provided him with the means of persuading himself and others that it was he who had a grip on these pleasures, and not the other way around. Arabesk and the *fakülte* were thus crucial components of his self-perception as a young *kabadayı*. This gendering was also clearly racialised. For Cuma, significantly, Antakya's *kabadayıları* were all Turks. Arabs could not attain this paradigmatic state of youthful, aggressive masculinity. However, the imagery of Arabesk allows for ambiguity. Bülent Ersoy, for example, has retained her male name. Arabesk was important to Cuma, penetrating his daily routines, pleasures and banter with friends, precisely because of this ambiguity, mediating a certain realisation of the frailty of his position, and his understanding of the fact that sociable relations between Arabs and Turks were, at a practical level, necessary.

Power and powerlessness

The economic well-being of the area is entirely dependent upon the political relations existing between Turkey and its neighbouring Arab states, namely Syria and Iraq. The Hatay is a vital conduit for the export of Turkish manufactured goods and raw materials to these countries, and for Iraqi oil to the Western world. As Robins points out (1991: 27), economic links with the Arab world were not cultivated in Kemalist Turkey for ideological reasons. The first 'liberal' elected regime, that of Adnan Menderes between 1950–60, was tied to its Cold War creditors (particularly through the Marshall Plan) and unable to develop these other links. It was only after the 1960 coup that economic relations with Iraq, in particular, were advanced. By 1986, when Turkish relations with neighbouring Middle Eastern countries were at their peak, the formal trade figures show that Turkey imported $7,303 million from OECD countries and $2,041 million from Middle Eastern countries, and exported $4,292 million to OECD countries and $2,578 million to the Middle East. These figures (OECD Economic Surveys 1987) include the reckoning that trade from Iran and Iraq was down by 45 per cent. as a result of the war between them (OECD Economic Surveys 1987: 21). They indicate an increasing priority being given at a national level to trade within the Middle East. The export facilities at the port of İskenderun in the Hatay are, however, almost entirely directed to the Middle East. The economic report of the İskenderun Chamber of Commerce in 1990 reckoned that 405 million kilograms had been exported from the city's docks to Islamic Conference countries, and a mere 69 million to the EC, and 88 million to OECD countries (ITSO 1987–90 Yılları Ekonomic Raporu ve Adres Rehberi 1990: 95).

The relative prosperity of the area's business élites, and those who are reliant upon them, is entirely dependent upon decisions made in Ankara, Damascus, Baghdad and Washington. These decisions are made in relation to NATO strategies in a 'troubled neighbourhood' and the sensitive movement of oil and water between Middle Eastern states. The Hatay province has to a certain extent been able to reap some benefits from its precarious position in superpower politics. When relations between the Baath parties of Syria and Iraq broke down, and the Syrian oil pipeline was closed in 1982, the Turkish petroleum industry benefited from the construction of the two new pipelines (in addition to the 1977 Botaş line) in 1984 and 1987, running from northern Iraq across southern Turkey to Yumurtalık in the Gulf of İskenderun, and from the transportation of Iraqi oil by road across the country. By the same token, and with perhaps more devastating consequences, it is vulnerable to the slightest of tremors in this diplomatic and economic house of cards. The Iran–Iraq war generated demand for Turkish raw materials and manufactured goods, but this demand was liable to disruption. The Gulf War in 1990, in which, at the highest military and diplomatic levels Turkey was split between perceived obligations to Europe and Iraq, was an unmitigated disaster for the business élites of the Hatay and those who depended upon them, since the bulk of the Hatay's transit and internal productive capacity was geared not to the Syrian but to the Iraqi export market. The port facilities at İskenderun ground to a halt in 1990, the oil pipeline running across the north of the province to Yumurtalık was closed, and the Russian-built iron and steel works at Payas (the largest in Turkey) were unable to export their produce to their main market.[11] The extent of dependence upon the Iraqi market can be seen from the fact that, in 1990, membership of the İskenderun Ticaret ve Sanayı Odası (Chamber of Commerce and Industry) was down from 3,585 members to 2,714, (ITSO 1987–90 Yılları Ekonomik Raporu ve Adres Rehberi 1990: 25), and the port registered a 90 per cent decrease in activity (ITSO 1987–90 Yılları Ekonomik Raporu ve Adres Rehberi 1990: 39).

The flow of commodities and capital through the region, then, is directed at Iraq, not Syria. Since this is a significant aspect of the Hatay's border culture, it is worth explaining in a little detail. Turkish–Syrian relations are marked by a long history of tension. The annexation of the Hatay by Turkey in 1939 still rankles in Syrian nationalist memory. The Cold War divided Turkey as a NATO ally and Syria, as a Soviet satellite, imbuing the Hatay border with an extra military significance. Today, at the end of the Cold War, Turkish–Syrian diplomatic relations are still cool, being poised between Turkish claims that Syria supports and trains Kurdish separatists in the Bekaa valley, and Syrian claims that the Turkish state has illegally assumed control of the Euphrates water vital for agriculture and for the generation of its electricity (see Robins 1991). While these factors in themselves might have hindered the development of Turkish–Syrian cross-border trade (at a formal level), they pale into insignificance in relation to the closeness of diplomatic ties between Turkey and Iraq. Both states shared strategic roles against the Soviet bloc in the early years of the Cold War, particularly under the umbrella of the Baghdad pact of 1959. Both continue to perceive a shared problem with Kurdish insurgency, and numerous treaties have enabled Turkish forces to cross the Iraqi border and mount attacks on Kurdish rebel bases deep in Iraqi Kurdistan. The Baath parties of Syria and Iraq diverged in the late 1970s, following which the borders between the two countries were closed in 1982.

The extremely close ties between Iraq and Turkey, therefore, have been a significant factor in the relatively low level of formal trade between Turkey and Syria. The fact that the border is heavily militarised along its entire length also prohibits an informal cross-border trade (or, perhaps, conceals it within the ranks of the bureaucracy and military who control the border zone and official crossing points). Even though drug smuggling by boat is reckoned to be widespread, smuggling seems to consist of more homely items. Syrian cigarette papers are much in demand for the tobacco grown around Yayladağ, since the Turkish state's efforts to break all forms of self-sufficiency and bind people to the internal market resulted in a ban on smoking 'roll-your-own' cigarettes and the virtual unavailability of paper with which to do so. All manner of Russian goods, such as tents (for summer seaside trips), could be found in Kilis, just to the north of the Hatay, although the opening of the Georgian–Turkish border, and the large number of 'Russian' traders to be found throughout the Middle East, mean that the same goods can now be bought legally and cheaply from Russians and other former Soviet citizens selling on the streets in Iskenderun. For these reasons, the Hatay's economic fortunes are much more closely bound to Iraq than Syria. Robins's calculations from IMF statistics over the 1980s show that Turkey has exported $6,335.5 million to Iraq and only $548.3 million to Syria, and imported $9,101 million from Iraq and only $97.1 million over the same period from Syria (1991: 102). The major proportion of this trade passes through the Hatay.

The Gulf War brought home to many in the Hatay the fragility of this area in international networks of trade and military obligation, and their powerlessness to control events that could ruin their lives. Nobody was unaffected by it, and few were incapable of diagnosing the problem. For many of the young men with whom this chapter is concerned, this most directly affected the availability of highly desirable work mending or driving vehicles, and also the well-paid work in the state-run heavy industry on the coast. Under these circumstances, fulfilling the demands of *kabadayı* machismo becomes highly problematic. How does one project an image of power, when the realities of one's powerlessness are all too obvious?

This again is where one might usefully perceive the significance of Arabesk. Arabesk is explicitly concerned with the operations of power, and the experiences of powerlessness and manipulation at the hands of others. The films that accompany and promote Arabesk cassettes tell stories that might be described as rags to riches to rags again, of southern migrants making good in Istanbul, but finding themselves caught in a trap created by their 'traditional' morality, and ruined by their dependence on unscrupulous employers and 'modern' women. It is not difficult to see the significance of such stories to young men who are struggling for some control over the social process by which sexual and gendered roles are conferred in Turkey today, and who are also serving apprenticeships, working hard at the beck and call of others for very little financial or social reward, in an environment which is characterised at a higher level by massive reversals of fortune. For reasons that will be discussed below, the experience of masculinity and the figure of the *kabadayı* is crucially tied up with notions of prestige, command and coercion. The struggles that they have to be young *kabadayları*, and their simultaneous recognition that there are in fact very few domains over which they actually do have much power, finds a powerful focus in Arabesk.

Local perceptions of Arabesk are sharpened by the fact that this is a profoundly stratified society, and one which revolves around a highly visible culture of coercion and command. The social structure of the Hatay is extremely visible, and the *kabadayı* lives, and is conscious of living, in a world whose social ranking revolves crucially around appearances. What makes the *kabadayı* is an appearance and a style: a certain effortless smartness of turnout, carefully cut hair and cleanly-shaven chin, the tilt of an expensive cigarette in the mouth, crucial minutiae of stance, swagger and accent. What is said and done is not as important as the way in which it is said or done. The imperative of adopting this coercive style sits uneasily with the limitations of the domains over which they experience any direct personal control. In a similar manner to the young men of *agha* families in Gilsenan's (1990) discussions of honour ideologies in north Lebanon (and for largely similar reasons), the young Sunni Turks of the Hatay are exquisitely aware of the transitory and illusory nature of such tokens of power and prestige, and the ease with which they can be exposed as lacking in substance.

The nature of stratification in the Hatay must be explained in a little detail. The steady integration of the Hatay into north-west European trade networks during the nineteenth century have been crucial in determining the nature of stratification and power in the area, producing simultaneously inequalities in the access to power and means of production among the local population, and a dependence on external markets which has lead to a chronic (but by no means untypical) political insecurity and volatility. This situation attained its present shape in the period of reforms and reorganisation known as the Tanzimat (conventionally dated from 1832), which was necessitated both by Ottoman self-perceptions of collapse in the face of their traditional Christian foes, but also by the more powerful demands established by the penetration of north-western European capital in the Middle East. The Ottomans were concerned with the abuses of tax-farming on the part of rural lords (*derebeys*) operating entirely outside of their control in Anatolia, and, in 1859, saw land-reforms as a means of controlling their power. These same reforms, however, also constituted the necessary preconditions for a wholesale transformation to capitalist agriculture in certain regions, and laid the foundations for a rural regime which was entirely dependent upon foreign capital, and subject to the vagaries of its demands. Integration within international markets took place largely through the medium of cotton production. Keyder notes the intensive capitalisation of cotton production in the Çukurova region of Turkey immediately before World War I (Keyder 1987: 56–7). Certain regions of the Hatay, particularly the Amik plain, became heavily dependent upon cotton production during this period, but were also involved in the production of other commodities, in particular silk and gall-nuts.

As Aswad (1971) and others (see also van Briunessen 1992) have shown for this region, far from decreasing the power of rural elites, the land reforms of the Tanzimat era strengthened them. In the Hatay region prior to the Tanzimat, as Aswad's detailed study of land-holding in the Amik plain has shown, the Turkoman Reyhanlı tribal confederacy – one of many in the eighteenth and early nineteenth centuries to enjoy great power throughout this region (van Bruinessen 1992: 149) – dominated settled Arab villagers, operating through the intermediary role of short-range herders such as the Al-Shiukh who constituted the subject of Aswad's 1971 study. Their position of power was deeply entrenched by the Tanzimat reforms. The existence of small plots of land enabled them to buy out smaller producers, and even when small landowners were able to hold on to their land, they were dependent upon these elites for loans of equipment, seed and animals. This kind of dependency became enshrined in the institution of sharecropping agreements which were particularly unfavourable to the land-poor party. The mechanisation of the cotton industry, following Menderes' reforms in the 1950s, resulted in the development of a specific sharecropping agreement called *icar* (Aswad 1971: 36) whereby tenants were responsible for providing equipment and material, but kept the profits of the crop in return for a fixed sum. They were thereby required to shoulder almost the entire burden of risk in the system, and were still dependent upon an emerging class of bailiffs who possessed and rented out tractors. While the lack of a fully-fledged latifundist system of big estates and landless waged labourers failed to emerge in Turkey, as it did under similar circumstances in Latin America and Poland, for reasons which are hotly disputed by Turkish rural sociologists (see Keyder and Tabak 1991, Aydın 1989), the Tanzimat did eventually generate a substantial landless and land-poor rural proletariat whose only realistic option by the 1950s was to migrate to the emerging shanty towns on the fringes of southern Turkey's industrial cities.

It is also an area which since Ottoman times has had a rich culture of social dissent and rural banditry. The heavy fortification of the Belen Pass in the eighteenth century (Marcus 1989: 30) indicates the efforts to which the Ottomans were obliged to go to counter the banditry which disrupted the flow of commodities between Aleppo and Antakya. Tekin remarks on the activities of a number of mountain bandits during the establishment of the Sanjak of Alexandretta and its annexation in 1939, some of whom, such as Kara Hasan Paşa, ended up on the 'right' side of Turkish historiography, for the role they are now considered to have played in resisting the French in 1919 (Tekin 1993: 104). Others did not: Tekin briefly mentions the so-called *partizan* who scoured the countryside in the panicky movement of Arab and Armenian populations over the border in 1939, most of whom he describes as *kır bekçileri* (watchmen appointed by villages to look after the communal flock of sheep in mountain pastures) (Tekin 1993: 187). Such defiant figures of charismatic authority were evidently capable of recruiting and manipulating followers and must have possessed an unrivalled knowledge of the mountainous countryside. While their role during this period would repay close investigation, it is clear that such figures are both products of and contributors to a concept of masculinity which thoroughly informs the *kabadayı* ethos. The *kabadayıları* strongly subscribe to traditional and pastoral images of masculine toughness and command, in particular through a collective fascination with the figure of the horseman and the wrestler.

However, the *kabadayı* of today has little to fight for, and few people that he can boss or coerce in any sense at all. The image of the wrestler is one shot through with a recognition that things are not necessarily what they seem (Stokes 1996). It is in this gap, between perceptions of appearance and reality, that the key symbols of Arabesk have a vital role to play. It is through Arabesk that young men are simultaneously able to negotiate the demands of honourable masculinity on the one hand, and on the other, the lack of means by which, and arenas in which, these ideals can be exercised. The model of masculinity for many young men in the Hatay is İbrahim Tatlıses (although, as I have mentioned, not all share this opinion). Tatlıses is well known in the metropolitan north of Turkey, and for many epitomises the provincial thug of oafish and quintessentially 'southern' bad manners. His films, however, tell tales of failure and manipulation in the big city, solitude, drink and grief. The İbrahim Tatlıses phenomenon encapsulates and expresses a contradiction between the ideals of the honour ethic and the powerlessness, fracture and alienation of the modern subject. The films and the music thereby provide crucial means for many in Turkey to cope with, or at least come to some dignifying comprehension of, a situation of vulnerability and dependence upon outside forces. The meticulous pursuit of the honour ethic and a highly visible dependence upon outside forces converge in the lives of the *kabadaylan* of the Hatay; the experience of Arabesk derives its power and intensity precisely from this convergence.

Conclusion

Arabesk on the Turkish–Syrian border demarcates cultural practices which, taken as a whole, constitute a significant and powerful resource which enables people at least to reconcile themselves to some of the problems of border life, problems over which they can experience little personal or collective control. In many ways these problems can only get worse. European integration has peripheralised neighbouring states and tightened the grip of European markets upon supplies of raw materials, products and labour from these states. A region such as the Hatay, which is highly dependent upon migrant remittances and European markets, becomes doubly peripheralised: first in relation to the Turkish state, and second in relation to European markets. As the Gulf War showed, the political dependence of Turkey upon NATO means that the area is still economically tied to the Middle East, but prone to decision-making which is forced to privilege Turkish NATO commitments. Finally, in the unlikely event of Turkey being admitted as a full member of the EU over the next decade, the burden of controlling the movement of people and commodities across the borders of the Community will fall squarely on Turkish shoulders. Other states in this position have sometimes been able to reap certain benefits from this position in terms of EU revenues allocated specifically for this purpose (on Spain, see, for example, Escribano (1992)), but there are also human costs. In the Hatay, these would include a widening gulf between Arabs and Turks and an increased sense of isolation of Hatay Arabs from Arabs across the border. One can only speculate about such things, but, at a local level, wider political events are unlikely to improve on a situation shaped by a chronic dependency on outside powers. As a popular cultural form, Arabesk deals with matters of manipulation, betrayal, alienation and exclusion, in short, all conditions associated with dependence upon others who do not necessarily have one's interests close to their own hearts. I have tried to demonstrate in this chapter some of the ways in which Arabesk might be seen as a means of allegorical representation, simultaneously articulating and explaining some of the ruptures of border life in the Hatay.

Arabesk is popular beyond border areas in Turkey. However, the extent to which outsiders and insiders alike in the Hatay see themselves and their relations with others through Arabesk suggests a distinctly local configuration of the 'Arabesk complex', whose significance, I have argued, can only be understood in terms of the problems that the Turkish–Syrian border introduces into the daily life of Arabs and Turks in this region. This chapter has concentrated on a Turkish and male viewpoint which might be considered doubly dominant. While this perspective has been shaped mainly by the fact that I do not speak Arabic, and by the fact that I have been perceived generally as an unattached young man, it does, however, provide some specific insights. First, it shows that not all masculinities are equally dominant and powerful. Secondly, the lives of majorities in border regions shed as much light on the cultural problems that borders often create as do the lives of minorities. Thirdly, it provides a precise focus for the issue of people who identify with nationalist ideologies but are obliged to 'use' these ideologies in situations with which nationalism does not cope. In the case of the young Sunni *kabadayları* of the Hatay, it is possible to argue that Arabesk has a vital role to play in bridging the gap between nationalism and its all too visible limits.

Finally, I have argued in this chapter that cultural forms such as Arabesk might be seen in terms of how they shape trajectories and movements, rather than bounded and static essences. This notion of 'mobile' or 'travelling' culture is not one with which anthropologists have always been happy (Clifford 1992), but it is clearly important in the study of border cultures, which are, in many instances, very much absorbed by the question of the ways in which movement (imaginary and otherwise) is constrained and permitted. It is also important if we are to understand how interpretations of popular cultural texts are produced in specific situations. In a medium such as popular music, rich in allusion and simultaneity of meaning, it is perhaps not too fanciful to suggest that popular music constitutes its own heterotopic space, and that, within this space, we are able to imagine ourselves in motion, in mutating and plural relations with others, and act accordingly. In the analysis presented here, Arabesk is seen both as a popular cultural text, and as a mode of discourse which constitutes a way of simultaneously imagining and questioning one's relationships with others. There are certainly other representations of Arabesk, interpretations and conclusions which undoubtedly have a less benign role to play in the production of racist and sexist ideologies. Yet even within these interpretations, as I have tried to illustrate in relation to the aspiring *kabadayları* of the Hatay, there is much within Arabesk as a popular cultural genre which suggests to those who appropriate it the limitations of these modes of thinking. In a region such as the Hatay, this kind of resource is vital. Within the Turkish state as a whole, the continued production of Arabesk maintains a critical way of thinking about difference and hierarchy, and, by extension, national borders and ethnic difference. This in turn entails the possibility of covert or overt resistance to the phenomenal resources of those whose interests are best served either by keeping borders in their places or by moving them. Growing disquiet at the prolongation of military operations against the Kurds in the south-east of Turkey and excursions across the border into Iraqi Kurdistan by Turkish armed forces (where Turkish governments have maintained a long-standing border dispute with an eye on the oil riches of this region) indicate that this scenario is not entirely fanciful. The growing identification of İbrahim Tatlıses with Kurdish concerns has accompanied the intensification of the war in the south-east.[12] The fact that protest has always been veiled in Arabesk (in contrast to other genres, such as Özgün, which is closely modelled on Euro-American protest rock) has perhaps fooled cultural legislators and intellectual commentators in Turkey, who have seen Arabesk as fundamentally 'lacking teeth',[13] and have taken steps to co-opt Arabesk musicians and their fans. The stars are immersed in the business machinery of the music industry, and many have successfully pursued their interests by accepting these overtures on the part of the state and intellectual classes. The same is not necessarily true of their fans, for whom the co-option of Arabesk has always been partial, if not explicitly rejected. The impulse to question those who enforce the observance of borders and boundaries comes from many sources, but Arabesk has undoubtedly played a role.

Notes

1. This chapter uses current Turkish place names. The term 'Hatay' was coined from a Hittite word by Mustafa Kemal Atatürk on 2 November 1936 (Tekin 1993: 166), and causes offence to Syrian nationalists, who prefer to think of the area as the province of Alexandretta. I use Turkish place-names because they are familiar to me and the people who live there now, in the hope that I can still maintain some critical distance between my use of the terms and the political events that produced them. I also refer to Antioch by its current Turkish name of Antakya, and Alexandretta as İskenderun.

2. At the same time, as Kandiyoti (1991) points out, it should not be forgotten that quite new notions of patriarchy emerged in the late Ottoman and early Republican periods, which paraded a concern with women's issues as a crucial aspect of a general discourse of modernity. Atatürk's relations with women and his adoption of daughters rather than sons were highly

significant aspects of what has sometimes been called 'state feminism' in Turkey. It is worth pointing out in this context that notions of masculinity and patriarchy are not static and uniform (see also Kandiyoti 1994), and that Delaney's notion of traditional rural patriarchy needs perhaps to be seen in more mobile terms.

3. Subdivision of an Ottoman province.

4. For a study of Arabesk in Istanbul in the 1980s, see Stokes (1992). This study, along with the comments in this chapter, draw on my own fieldwork and also on two detailed Turkish language studies, Güngör (1990) and Özbek (1991).

5. These towns were developed for tourism by the French. Tekin remarks that electricity was bought into these towns in 1931 to cultivate colonial tourism (1993: 141). Soğukoluk gained notoriety in the late 1970s when the national press discovered its brothel, whose size and attractions turned it into a national institution. The generals closed it down following the 1980 coup, and had the name of the town changed. These towns are still given over to more innocent leisure pursuits in the summer months, while a major sex industry continues to thrive in İskenderun and Antakya.

6. These discussions were, I suspected, an unusual experience for them. When not simply tagging along, or answering their questions about my own life, my main conversational role was to encourage explicit verbal statements regarding experiences which were not conventionally verbalised. One of the interpretative difficulties of my position lies in connecting these awkward though often humorous commentaries with the unverbalised, everyday, commonsense categories of the *kabadayları*. There are, of course, other interpretations of the role of Arabesk amongst different groups constituted by ethnicity, age or gender.

7. Pipes (1990: 140) notes the establishment of a Baath party office in the Hatay in the late 1970s.

8. An exception are those Arabs who have cross-border marriages. Extended families were split up in 1939, perhaps not anticipating the formidable political barriers that were to be erected between them in later years. The maintenance of father's brother's daughter marriage strategies can some-times entail sending daughters over the border. In the one case with which I became familiar, a machine worker in a technical college in Payas had not seen his sister, who was married to his patrilateral parallel cousin, an electrician in Aleppo, for several years, even though the journey would only have taken a few hours. Both brother and sister regretted this, but put it down to the inordinate expense and trouble of dealing with border authorities.

9. Tekin suggests that the Bayır-Buçak villages were included on the Syrian side of the border in 1939 to compensate the Armenians by excluding the established Armenian Protestant town of Kesseb from the area to be annexed by Turkey (Tekin 1993: 248).

10. Numbers are still hard to estimate because Turkish censuses do not divide the population by ethnic group, and in the mandate period, and in the years immediately after, Turkish commentators, including Atatürk himself, argued that Alevi Arabs were 'Hittite Turks' to establish their claims on the

area (Aswad 1971: 11). Sanjian's figures published in 1956, cited by Aswad, indicate a total Turkish-speaking population of 85,242, constituting 32 per cent of the province's population, and a total Arabic-speaking population of 102,538, constituting 46.8 per cent of the population, of which approximately 75 per cent were Alevi and 25 per cent Sunni. The rest consisted mainly of Armenians, Arabic-speaking Greek orthodox Christians, Kurds, Jews and Circassians. The industrialisation of the Dörtyol–İskenderun strip would have greatly increased the proportion of Turks and Kurds in the area in the 1970s.

11. The factory, with over 15,000 workers, is the largest single employer in the province (ITSO 1987–90 Yılları Ekonomic Raporu ve Adres Rehberi 1990: 37). Iron and steel constitute the bulk of Turkish exports to both Syria and Iraq.

12. İbrahim Tatlıses now describes himself openly as Kurdish, and has had frequent brushes with the authorities over his performances of Kurdish songs and his offer to act as an intermediary between the government and the Kurdish separatist organisation, the PKK.

13. Murat Belge, a well-known commentator on Turkish popular culture, remarked at the end of Hugo de Burgh's Channel Four documentary *Arabesk!* (1990) that 'one day, perhaps, we shall have an Arabesk with teeth'.

References

Appadurai, A. 1993. 'Minor subjects', unpublished paper given at the annual meeting of the American Anthropological Association, Washington.

Aswad, B. C. 1971. *Property control and social strategies: settlers on a Middle Eastern plain*. Ann Arbor, Anthropological Papers, Museum of Anthropology, University of Michigan No. 44.

Aydın, Z. 1989. 'Household production and capitalism: a case study of South Eastern Turkey', in K. and P. Glavanis (eds.), *The rural Middle East: peasant lives and modes of production*. London and New Jersey: Zed Books, pp. 163–82.

van Bruinessen, M. 1992. *Agha, Sheigh and State: the social and political structures of Kurdistan*. London and New Jersey: Zed Books.

Burgh, Hugo de 1990. *Arabesk*. London: Channel Four Television.

Clifford, J. 1992. 'Traveling cultures', in L. Grossberg, C. Nelson and P. Treichler (eds.), *Cultural studies*. London and New York: Routledge, pp. 96–116.

Delaney, C. 1991. *The seed and the soil: gender and cosmology in a Turkish village*. Berkeley: University of California Press.

Escribano, M. 1992. 'Guarding Europe's gate: letter from Spain', *MERIP* 22 (5): 30–1.

Gilpin, R. 1981. *War and change in world politics*. Cambridge: Cambridge University Press.

Gilsenan, M. 1990. 'Word of honour', in R. Grillo (ed.), *Social anthropology and the politics of language*. London: Routledge.

Güngör, N. 1990. *Arabesk: Sosyokültürel Açıdan Arabesk Müziği*. Ankara: Bilgi.

Hall, S. 1992. 'The question of cultural identities', in S. Hall, D. Held and

T. McGrew (eds.), *Modernity and its futures: understanding modern societies.* Cambridge: Polity.

Harvey, D. 1989. *The condition of postmodernity.* Oxford: Blackwell.

ITSO 1987–90. Yılları Ekonomik Raporu ve Adres Rehberi, 1990. İskenderun Ticaret ve Sanayı Odası, İskenderun.

Kandiyoti D. 1991. 'Introduction', in D. Kandiyoti (ed.), *Women, Islam and the state.* Philadelphia: Temple University Press, pp. 1–21.

——— 1994. 'The paradoxes of masculinity: some thoughts on segregated societies', in A. Cornwall and N. Lindisfarne (eds.), *Dislocating masculinity: comparative ethnographies.* London: Routledge.

Keyder, Ç. 1987. *State and class in Turkey: a study in capitalist development.* London and New York: Verso.

Keyder, Ç and F. Tabak, 1991. *Landholding and commercial agriculture in the Middle East.* Albany: State University of New York Press.

Kinross, Lord 1964. *Atatürk: the rebirth of a nation.* London: Weidenfeld and Nicolson.

Lavie, S. 1990. *The poetics of military occupation: allegories of Bedouin identity.* Berkeley: University of California Press.

Marcus, A. 1989. *The Middle East on the eve of modernity: Aleppo in the eighteenth century.* New York: Columbia University Press.

OECD Economic Surveys 1987. *Turkey.* Paris: OECD Publications.

Özbek, M. 1991. *Popüler Kültür ve Orhan Gencebay Arabeski.* Istanbul: İletişim.

Pipes, D. 1990. *Greater Syria: the history of an ambition.* Oxford: Oxford University Press.

Robins, P. 1991. *Turkey and the Middle East.* London: Pinter.

Stokes, M. 1992. *The Arabesk debate: music and musicians in modern Turkey.* Oxford and New York: Clarendon.

——— 1994. '"Local Arabesk" and the Turkish–Syrian border', in H. Donnan and T. M. Wilson (eds.), *Border approaches: anthropological perspectives on frontiers.* Lanham, MD: University Press of America.

——— 1996. '"Strong as a Turk": power, performance and representation in Turkish wrestling', in J. MacClancy (ed.), *Sport, identity and ethnicity.* Oxford: Berg.

Tekin, M. 1993. *Hatay Tarihi.* Antakya, Hatay Kültür, Turizm ve Sanat Vakfı ile Antakya Gazeteciler Cemiyeti.

Author index

Abu-Lughod, Lila, 159
Adas, M., 218, 222
Agulhon, M., 32, 33
Al-Haj, Majid, 146
Allen, Bruce, 188
Alliès, P., 36, 49
Alonso, A. M., 7
Alvarez, R. R., 3, 5, 6, 25
Anderson, Benedict, 32, 47, 119, 216, 217–18, 218, 219, 222, 227, 232
Anzaldua, G., 17, 142
Appadurai, A., 263, 264
Armstrong, A., 207
Armstrong, L., 33
Aronoff, M., 5
Artola, M., 42
Ash, Timothy Garton, 188
Assier-Andrieu, L., 38, 39, 52
Aswad, B. C., 274, 281
Aydin, Z., 281

Banks, D. J., 223
Bar-Gal, Y., 146
Barbalet, J. M., 193, 196
Bard, Rachel, 66, 69
Barth, F., 4, 52, 142
Beaune, C., 33
Beer, William R., 78
Bellér-Hann, I., 13, 15, 23, 216, 252, 263, 268
Bendix, R., 31
Berenson, D., 32
Bezucha, R., 32
Bilbao, Jon, 75, 77
Bisky, Lothar, 187
Blackburn, R., 191
Bleiberg, Germán, 66
Bloch, M., 39
Bohannan, P., 4
Boissevain, J., 5
Bonney, R., 219, 220
Borneman, J., 5, 13, 18, 19, 23, 24, 164, 174, 181, 182, 183, 184

Bourdieu, Pierre, 118, 151
Boyarin, Daniel, 142
Boyarin, Jonathan, 142
Bratt Paulston, Christina, 74, 75
Braudel, F., 11, 38, 99
Brette, A., 36
Briunessen, M. van, 281
Brousse, E., 54
Bruhnes, J., 37
Brunet, M., 43
Bryer, Anthony, 240, 259
Burawoy, Michael, 125

Capdeferro, Marcelo, 66, 68
Carsten, Janet, 8, 11, 12, 20, 221, 226, 227, 229, 230, 267, 269
Cheater, A. P., 18, 19, 22, 196, 204, 207
Chinchaladze, N., 243
Clark, Robert P., 73, 82
Clifford, James, 142, 284
Cohen, A., 4, 192, 209
Cohen, A. P., 33
Cohen, Robin, 125
Cole, J. W., 4
Collier, G. A., 3, 5
Comaroff, Jean, 159
Comaroff, John L., 129, 159
Corrigan, Philip, 118, 125, 134
Costa i Costa, J., 51
Costa, Joaquin., 268
Cowan, C. D., 221

Davis, N. Z., 43
Defourneaux, M., 48
Delaney, C., 268
Descheemaeker, Jacques, 70
Deutch, K., 31
Del Valle, Teresa, 83
Dion, R., 37
Donnan, H., 4, 88
Douglass, M., 207
Douglass, W. A., 5, 13, 14, 15, 21, 23, 24, 75, 77, 85, 96,

Subject index

Abkhazia, 243
Aceh, 221, 222
Acquitaine, 81
Adana, 272
Adzharia, 243, 244
AEK, 83
Africa, 8, 96, 102, 103, 105, 109
  North, 23
  West, 8
agricultural revolution, 42
AIDS, 257
Aja, 54
Albania, 169
Aleppo, 274, 282
Alevis, 273, 274–5
Alexandretta, 269
  Sanjak of, 269, 282
Algeciras, 101, 104–6,
Algeria, 100, 102, 105
Allah, 254
Almeria, 107
Almirall, Valentí, 72
Alphonse X, King, 66
Alps, 55, 85
Anatolia, 238, 240, 241, 243, 245, 268,
  274, 280
  and rural culture, 268
Andalusia, 101–2, 109, 111
  and Arab heritage, 109
Andorra, 37, 78, 86
Anglo-Siamese Treaty (1909), 221
Angostrina, 40, 44, 48, 50
Ankara, 243, 253, 254, 265, 275, 277
Ankara Accord (1921), 269
Ankara Agreement (1923), 265
Antakya, 272, 273, 274, 282
anthropology, 117–18, 119, 131, 133, 136,
  142
  of borders, 3–6
  cultural, 7, 11
  epistemology of, 136
  ethnic, 11
  historical, 5

indigenous, 133–4
of liminality, 129
political, 2, 4, 5, 25
of Self and Other, 131–2, 136
social, 7, 117
Apollonius, 240
Araba, 66, 69, 74, 75, 80, 81, 89
Arabesk, 19–20, 217, 264, 265–7, 270–2,
  275–6, 279–80, 283–5
Aragón, 66, 69
  invasion of, 68
  and municipal charters, 66–7
Arana y Goiri, Sabino de, 73, 79, 80
Aravó river, 44
archaeology, 7,
Ardesen, 257
Arhavi, 245, 257
Aristotle, 249
Arizona, 126
Arsuz, 273, 274
Artvin, 238, 240–2, 243–4, 246, 248, 251,
  257
  people of, 244–5
Asia
  Central, 268
  Southeast, 12, 215, 216, 222
  Centrist Archipelago, 224–5
  political ideology and power, 216,
    217–18, 232
  traditional state in, 217–21
Atatürk, 15, 19, 243; see also Kemal
Atlantic Ocean, 101, 103
Australia, 198
authority, 2
  male, 185
autonomy, 37
Azerbaijan, 251

Baghdad, 277
  pact of (1959), 278
Baku, 248
Balearic Islands, 80
Barcelona, 73, 79, 96, 103, 104, 107

293

Moroccan, 107
in Turkey, 250–1
in Zimbabwe, 202–3
see also gender
workers, North African, 22
working class, 170
World War I, 241, 274
World War II, 78, 85, 131, 242, 265

Yayladağ, 274
Yılmaz, Mesut, 247

Yom Ha'atsmaut, 152
Yom Hazikaron, 152
youths and conflict, 43–4
Yugoslavia, 187
Yumurtalık, 277, 278

Zambia, 200, 203
Zimbabwe, 12, 19, 22, 23
and gender, 191–209
and mobility, 193–4
see also Rhodesia, Southern